D1231784

HARRY CARR'S WORLD OF FREEMASONRY

HARRY CARR

*To all my
Friends and Colleagues
in Masonic research
over so many years,
I Greet You Well*

Harry Carr's
World of Freemasonry

The Collected Papers and Talks of Harry Carr

Ian Allan Group

LONDON
LEWIS MASONIC

A NOTE FROM THE PUBLISHER

For many years Harry Carr had given and received much pleasure from writing and delivering his masonic lectures to all parts of the English speaking world. During the production of this book his health declined and it is our great sadness to report that he died on 20 October 1983. He will be sadly missed by his many friends worldwide but his spirit and enthusiasm for freemasonry will continue to give pleasure to brethren for many years to come through his lectures and writings which have been published either singly or in volume form.

© 1983 Harry Carr
First Published in the
United Kingdom in 1984

Published by
Lewis Masonic
Terminal House
Shepperton, Middlesex
who are members of the
Ian Allan Group
of Companies

Printed and bound in Great Britain by
The Garden City Press Limited,
Letchworth, Hertfordshire SG6 1JS.

ISBN 0 85318 134 9

Previous title from the same author
The Freemason at Work

Carr, Harry, *1900-1983*
    Harry Carr's World of Freemasonry
    1. Freemasons
    I. Title
    366'.1   HS395

CONTENTS

List of Illustrations xi
List of Abbreviations xii
Foreword xiii
Introduction xv

1 **Six Hundred Years of Craft Ritual** 1
Synopsis. Beginnings of Mason Trade organisation, 1356. Gilds and Lodges. Only one degree, c1390. First hint of two degrees. Earliest ritual for two degrees, 'Entered Apprentice' and 'Master or Fellow-craft', 1696. Later texts; watching the ritual grow. Hints of three degrees. Prichard's *Masonry Dissected*, 1730, the first ritual of three degrees. Further evidence from France on ritual and floor-work, 1744. Floor-drawings, 1745. Passwords, 1745. The polishers and interpreters of the ritual. A note for Brethren in the U.S.A.

2 **Pillars & Globes; Columns & Candlesticks** 27
Synopsis. The first two Pillars in Craft tradition. Solomon's Pillars in the ritual. Chapiters, Globes & Bowls. Maps; 'Masonry Universal'. The Pillars as archives. Three Lights; Three Pillars; Three Candlesticks. The growth of Masonic symbolism.

3 **The Transition from Operative to Speculative Masonry.**
(The Prestonian Lecture for 1957) 44
Synopsis. Beginnings of Mason Craft organisation in England. The Lodge. The MS Constitutions or Old Charges. The Constitutions in use. The rise and power of the Operative Lodges. Operative Lodges in England. Lodges in course of transition; primarily operative Lodges. Non-operative Lodges and 'Accepted Masons'. The stages in the transition. The reasons for the transition; the transition in Edinburgh. The transition in England. The social or convivial phase. The advent of 'Speculative Masonry'.

4 **Lodge Mother Kilwinning No 0** 72
Synopsis. Kilwinning and the Schaw Statutes, 1599. The oldest minute, 1642. The second meeting, 1643. An operative Lodge in action. Bills and Bonds: the

Lodge as Money-lender. The transition at Kilwinning; admission of non-operatives. Poor support from local nobility. Kilwinning, the Mother Lodge, constitutes eleven masons as a Lodge at Canongate (in Edinburgh territory). At the foundation of the Grand Lodge of Scotland, in 1736, the Lodge of Edinburgh, is given No 1 on the Roll. Kilwinning secedes. Constitutes many Lodges in Scotland and several overseas. Building the new Lodge. Hard times, 1780–1806. The re-union, 1807. The Number 0. After the re-union, 1807–42. Problems with Article 5.

5 Samuel Prichard's *Masonry Dissected*, 1730 104
Synopsis. Bibliographical notes. Prichard's Masonic background. The Old Charges in Prichard's day. Three clues to his status in Grand Lodge. Accepted Masonry. 'The Author's Vindication of Himself'. Masonic Catechisms and Exposures. The 'Haughfoot "fragment" '. Stages in the evaluation of the Catechisms and Exposures. Masonry Dissected; the text. The first Hiramic legend; sources? Evolution of the three-degree system. Masonry Dissected: its influence on the ritual in England and France.

6 Freemasonry in the USA 145
Synopsis. Fifty Grand Lodges. The Background. Masonry for the family. Women's, Girls' & Boys' Orders, all 'Bodies Identified with Masonry'. Masonic Badges; for business? Large memberships but poor attendances. Emergent and Work meetings. The Scottish Rite. The Shrine. Craft Ritual. Rituals & Monitors. Visiting a Lodge in USA.

7 More Light on the Royal Arch 163
Synopsis. The reasons for the Royal Arch. Early development. Place of origin. The RA under two Grand Lodges. Sources and ritual of the RA. The 'Ineffable Name'. The 'Trible Voice'; the secret shared by three. The 'Vault' legend. The union of the Grand Lodges, and ritual uniformity. Innovations.

8 The Letter G 180
Synopsis. The 'Seven Liberal Arts or Sciences'. The G in early English ritual documents. The 'Blazing Star'. The letter G in the 'Middle Chamber'. The letter G, before or after 1730? Symbolism of the 'Blazing Star'. Evidence from the French exposures. Position of the G in relation to the degrees. The English exposures of the 1760s and later. The 'Pocket Companions'. The expounders and embellishers. The G and the 'Blazing

Star' as tangible symbols. Illustrations in exposures and other Masonic sources. Survey and conclusions. The G in modern practice; Britain and other countries.

9 Kipling and the Craft 222
Synopsis. Part I. Parents and family background. Childhood. School. Lahore and Simla, 1882–87. Early years in the Craft. Literary success. Resignation from Lodge. Marriage and fame. Torquay and Rottingdean. The South African war: Kipling the Imperialist. Kipling, the Politician. The World War. Finale. Part II. Freemasonry and Masonic allusions in Kipling's work.

10 Women and Freemasonry 280
Synopsis. Dr Anderson's 'No Women'. Mme Carton. 'Mollie, the chambermaid'. Mrs Bell. The Hon Elizabeth St Leger. Mme de Xaintrailles. The Chevalier d'Eon. Women and Freemasonry in England today. In the USA. Constant service to the Craft.

11 The Evolution and Ritual of the Third Degree 288
Synopsis. The Old Charges; a single admission ceremony, c1390. Two degrees, 1598–99. Earliest ritual of two degrees in Scottish texts, 1696–c1714. EA degree based on two pillars. Second degree for 'Master or Fellow-craft' contains the FPOF and a whispered word (in four versions, all debased). The *Graham MS*, 1726. Noah's three sons raise him on the FPOF Bazalliell, with two princely pupils and a 'trible Voice'; his epitaph. All these are possible early versions of the Hiramic legend. Prichard's *Masonry Dissected*, 1730. A greatly expanded ritual, all in Q & A. *The Master's Degree* (given here in full). Prichard's *M.D.* in many editions helps to standardise English ritual throughout the next 30 years. The French exposures, 1737 onwards. *Le Catéchisme . . .* 1744. Splendid third degree in narrative, with earliest floorwork, based on *M.D.*, but with useful French improvements (text given in full). The 'former Word of a Master'. The floordrawing. *L'Ordre . . . Trahi.* Passwords. Survey. The origins and meaning of the Word(s). Origins of the Hiramic legend. Origin of the Points of Fellowship, a major problem. Fourteen versions up to 1730, twelve without a hint of where they came from, why they were used, or what they meant. A solution in the *Schaw Statutes*, 1598.

12 Two Short-lived Lodges 321
Synopsis. The first Grand Lodge, troubled by exposures in the 1730s, authorises changes in the ritual.

Several regular, and some unattached Irish lodges, reject the changes. In 1751, these unattached bodies, mainly Irish, form a rival Grand Lodge, 'The Most Ancient and Honble. Society of Free and Accepted Masons', soon to become known as the 'Antients', with ten Lodges on its Roll. Under Laurence Dermott, their Grand Secretary, they prosper. Towards the end of the eighteenth century former animosities diminish. Proposals for a union of the rivals fail in 1797 and in 1801–02. In April 1809, the 'Moderns' resolve to resume their former ritual, a major step towards a union. In October 1809 the 'Special Lodge of Promulgation' (Moderns) is constituted. Charles Bonnor, SW of Antiquity No 1, is among the 23 new members elected at the first meeting. At second Meeting, 1 December 1809, they are exhorted to give 'Special attention . . . to the ascertaining what were the Ancient Landmarks which they were required to restore'. Bonnor, now Secretary of Promulgation, demonstrates 'the Ancient manner' of opening, closing, and conferring the secrets in all three degrees; discussion continues until 12.30 am. Meetings weekly, covering all aspects of the ceremonies, including Installation, much neglected by the Moderns. Many of their Masters and PM's, including actual members of Promulgation, had never been regularly Installed. A spate of Installations. The Lodge, warranted only for fourteen months (until 31 December 1810) extensions are requested; but a one-year extension is refused and the Lodge is ordered to cease work on 31 March 1811. Meanwhile, after a Committee had reported on 'practicability', the Antients' Grand Lodge resolves favourably that 'a Masonic Union' would be 'expedient and advantageous to both' Grand Lodges. Leaders of both bodies meet privately, and their Committees hold their first meeting on 31 July 1810. The union of the Grand Lodges takes place on 27 December 1813. On 10 January 1814 Grand Lodge, by circular, invites Provincial Lodges to send Deputations to attend L of Reconciliation, and learn the 'acknowledged forms'. But the L of R is sadly unprepared for the instruction it is to give. Demonstrations begin in August 1814. Twelve meetings in two months, covering all three degrees, with openings and closings. Opposition arises from Antients' Lodges in London complaining of too many alterations. Meanwhile, most London Lodges have received the necessary instruction. Members of

Reconciliation travel the country, demonstrating and explaining the changes, On 26 February 1816, a special meeting of the L of R to deal with Installation. Finally, after alteration on two points in the third degree, the work of the L of R is ended. 'Promulgation' 1809–11, paved the way towards the Union; 'Reconciliation', 1813–16, instructed the united Craft in the new forms. Two short-lived Lodges.

13 The Relationship Between the Craft and the Royal Arch 325
Synopsis. They found a 'formula', but many questions arise. Evidence from the two-degree system, 1696–c1714. Other ritual documents, c1710–30. Earliest conferment of the third degree. Subsequent documents: the *Graham MS*, 1726. *Masonry Dissected*, 1730. Early evidence of the RA in practice, 1743–53. Evidence from the French exposures: *Le Catéchisme . . .* 1744; *Le Parfait Maçon*, 1744; *Le Sceau Rompu*, 1745; *L'Ordre . . .Trahi*, 1745; *La Désolation . . .* 1747; *Le Maçon Démasqué*, 1751. The later English texts; *Three Distinct Knocks*, 1760; J & B, 1762. Accretions and changes. The Ineffable Name. The Secret shared by three. The Questions and the Answers.

14 The Obligation and Its Place in the Ritual 367
Synopsis. The *Regius MS*, c1390; 'all shall swear the same oath of the masons . . .' *Grand Lodge No 1 MS*, 1583, gives the posture for the Ob. *Harleian MS*, c1670; the oath refers to 'several words and signs' plural, proving more than one degree. Three Scottish texts, 1696–c1714, of the two-degree system, give the oath for the EA, 'repeated anew' by the 'Master-Mason or fellow-craft'. Penalties mentioned in the texts, but *not in the Ob's. Sloane MS*, c1700; 'without Equivocation or mentall Resarvation'. Later versions, c1710 to 1727. *A Masons Confession*, c1727, *The Wilkinson MS*, c1727, *Mystery of Freemasonry*, 1730, *Masonry Dissected*, 1730, all contain a single Ob. for the EA, with triple penalties. *Three Distinct Knocks*, 1760, and later versions during that era, contain separate Obligations for each degree, each with its own penalty.

15 Evolution of the Installation Ceremony and Ritual 384
Synopsis. No trace of an Installation ceremony until after formation of Grand Lodge, 1717. The first version is embodied in the Duke of Wharton's 'Manner of constituting a New Lodge' in the first *Book of Constitutions*, 1723. The Grand Master is assured that

the 'Candidate-Master is well skill'd in the *noble Science*'. The *Charges* of a *Master* are read to him, and he submits '*as Masters have done in all Ages*'. The Master is Installed 'by certain significant Ceremonies' (not described) and receives the *Constitutions*, *Lodge Book* and *Instruments* of his Office. No mention of any Obligation, signs, grip or words. *Three Distinct Knocks*, 1760, Antients, deals only with esoteric items. The new Master swears he will not reveal the 'Word and Gripe' except to a Master or PM. He promises to 'fill the Chair every Lodge-night, . . . and will keep good Orders'. Still kneeling, he is invested with Master's Jewel, raised with Master's grip and saluted with Master's Clap. The Modern's working, when used, was probably very similar. Preston's *Illustrations*, 1775, is virtually Wharton's procedure plus the full text of the 'Charges of a Master' and details of Investiture of Officers, with Addresses, brief versions of our present usage. The Lodge of Antiquity (then No 1) practises the Inner Working in 'an adjacent room', returning to the Temple for the actual Installation etc. Installation widely neglected by Moderns until the Lodge of Promulgation 1809–11 prepares for the union of the rival Grand Lodges. *The Turk MS*, 1816; elaborate procedure. Much diversity of practice; the United Grand Lodge creates a special 'Lodge or Board of Installed Masters' to give instruction in the 'Ceremonies of Installation as the same have already been approved'. Minutes of the 'Lodge or Board, February to April, 1827. Problems with the 'Extended Working of (Opening and Closing) the Board of Installed Masters' and the Grand Lodge ruling in 1926.

Appendix Facsimile pages of Samuel Prichard's *Masonry Dissected* 410

ILLUSTRATIONS

1 Pillars with bowls from the collection of lodge equipment known as the 'Bath Furniture' presented to the Royal Cumberland Lodge No 41 in 1805. 34

2 Advertisements for Samuel Prichard's *Masonry Dissected*, 1730 106-7

3 From the *Dialogue between Simon and Philip*, c1740 showing 'the form of the old Lodges' with G in a diamond. 186

4 From the *Dialogue between Simon and Philip*, c1740 showing 'the form of the new lodges under Desaguliers' with the G in a circle. 186

5/6 Two EA/FC 'plans' depicting the letter G. From *L'Orde des Franc-Maçons Trahi*, 1745. 195

7 Frontispiece to *Mahhabone*, 1766. 200

8 The letter G depicted in two illustrations from Hutchinson's *Spirit of Masonry*, 1775. 203

9 A 'Floor cloth' dated 1764 of the Lurgen Lodge, GL of Ireland. 207

10 Pierced silver jewels of the eighteenth century. 209

11 Frontispiece to Cole's *Constitutions*, 1728–29. 211

12 A modern German Tracing Board. 213

LIST OF ABBREVIATIONS USED IN THIS BOOK

AQC — *Ars Quatuor Coronatorum* (Transactions of the Quatuor Coronati Lodge, No 2076, London.

BofC — *Book of Constitutions.*

CC MS — *Chetwoode-Crawley MS*, c1700.

Edinburgh Group — The *Edinburgh Register House MS* and its sister texts, the *Chetwoode-Crawley* and the *Keven MS.*

EFE — *The Early French Exposures* published by QC Lodge.

EMC — *The Early Masonic Catechisms* by Knoop, Jones and Hamer.

ERH MS — *The Edinburgh Register House MS*, 1696.

J & B — *Jachin and Boaz*, 1762.

QCA — *Quatuor Coronatorum Antigrapha* (Masonic reprints of the QC Lodge).

TDK — *Three Distinct Knocks*, 1760.

Trahi — *L'Ordre des Francs-Maçons Trahi*, 1745.

FOREWORD
By RW Bro Sir Lionel Brett, P Dist GM, Nigeria

IT WAS a great compliment to be invited by the late Brother Harry Carr to contribute a Foreword to what will be the last collection of his works to be chosen and prepared for the press by himself.

In his Introduction Brother Carr spoke of a lifetime in which many busy years had been devoted to Masonic education, and this book will be a notable contribution to that cause. He had a scholar's grasp of the subjects he dealt with, and a talent for presenting them in a way that would appeal to the ordinary reader or listener. He enjoyed lecturing and knew how to communicate his enjoyment, to others.

The papers in this book are longer than the articles in Brother Carr's well-known book *The Freemason at Work*, and each paper deserves and requires undivided attention, whether it is studied in private or, as expressly authorised in the Introduction, read aloud in Lodges or other assemblies of Freemasons. A Brother interested in extending his Masonic knowledge will find no more agreeable way of doing so than by reading or listening to these papers, and I wholeheartedly commend the book to Freemasons all over the world.

November 1983   LIONEL BRETT

INTRODUCTION

After a lifetime in which many busy years have been devoted to Masonic education, it is very satisfying to see these 'Selected Lectures and Papers' in print, as a collection. The present volume is by no means complete, but it does contain the 'speaking' versions of my most popular talks, that have won standing ovations in four Continents, from New Zealand to British Columbia, and from Jerusalem to the Bahamas.

Several other papers are included here, which are perhaps more suitable for leisurely reading at one's own fireside. These have also been used as the basis of Lectures to Research Lodges etc, and they are included here because I believe they have added something of value to our store of the materials of Masonic history and practice.

All the papers have been carefully revised and it is my fervent hope that they will be used by Brethren who enjoy their Masonry, as Lectures to their own Lodges, or Lodges of Instruction. Permission is granted here and now for Brethren to read any of the papers to Lodges, Royal Arch Chapters, Lodges of Instruction, Research Lodges and Study Groups. (Special permission must be obtained from the publishers for reproduction or reprinting.)

Several papers of some importance have been omitted. Those published here were selected so as to provide a collection that would display the variety of subjects that have proved of high interest to the Brethren when they are not conferring Degrees.

It is necessary to emphasise that the ritual matters discussed in several of the papers in this volume, represent the practices claimed, in surviving documents, to have been in use in their day, from 1696 to the 1760s. We do not discuss, nor have we taken any account of, the massive changes that appeared in English usage towards the end of the eighteenth century, and of the revisions adopted at the union of the Grand Lodges from 1813 to 1827, when our present-day practice was more-or-less standardised for England.

Finally, my sincere thanks to W Bro T. O. Haunch, Dep G Supt Wks, the recently-retired Librarian and Curator of Grand Lodge, and to his successor, Bro J. M. Hamill, BA, for their invaluable help during many years. Also my thanks go to W Bro Michael Fenton for his immense help in checking these proofs.

1

SIX HUNDRED YEARS OF CRAFT RITUAL

BRETHREN, MANY of you will know that I travel vast distances in the course of my lecture duties and the further I go the more astonished I am to see how many Brethren believe, quite genuinely, that our masonic ritual came down straight from heaven, directly into the hands of King Solomon. They are all quite certain that it was in English, of course, because that is the only language they speak up there. They are equally sure that it was all engraved on two tablets of stone, so that, heaven forbid, not one single word should ever be altered; and most of them believe that King Solomon, in his own lodge, practised the same ritual as they do in theirs.

But, it was not like that at all, and tonight I am going to try to sketch for you the history of our ritual from its very beginnings up to the point when it was virtually standardised, in 1813; but you must remember, while I am talking about English ritual I am also giving you the history of your own ritual as well. One thing is going to be unusual about tonight's talk. Tonight you are not going to get any fairy-tales at all. Every word I utter will be based on documents which can be proved: and on the few rare occasions when, in spite of having the documents, we still have not got complete and perfect proof, I shall say loud and clear 'We think . . .' or 'We believe . . .'. Then you will know that we are, so-to-speak, on uncertain ground; but I will give you the best that we know. And since a talk of this kind must have a proper starting point, let me begin by saying that Freemasonry did not begin in Egypt, or Palestine, or Greece, or Rome.

BEGINNINGS OF MASON TRADE ORGANISATION

It all started in London, England, in the year 1356, a very important date, and it started as the result of a good old-fashioned

1

demarcation dispute. Now, you all know what a demarcation dispute is. When the boys in a trade union cannot make up their minds who is going to knock the nails and who will screw the screws, that is a demarcation dispute. And that is how it started, in 1356, when there was a great row going on in London between the mason hewers, the men who cut the stone, and the mason layers and setters, the men who actually built the walls. The exact details of the quarrel are not known, but, as a result of this row, 12 skilled master masons, with some famous men among them, came before the mayor and aldermen at Guildhall in London, and, with official permission, drew up a simple code of trade regulations.

The opening words of that document, which still survives, say that these men had come together because their trade had never been regulated in such form as other trades were. So here, in this document, we have an official guarantee that this was the very first attempt at some sort of trade organisation for the masons and, as we go through the document, the very first rule that they drew up gives a clue to the demarcation dispute that I was talking about. They ruled, 'That every man of the trade may work at any work touching the trade if he be perfectly skilled and knowing in the same.' Brethren, that was the wisdom of Solomon! If you knew the job, you could do the job, and nobody could stop you! If we only had that much common sense nowadays in England, how much better off we should be.

The organisation that was set up at that time became, within 20 years, the London Masons Company, the first trade guild of the masons and one of the direct ancestors of our Freemasonry of today. This was the real beginning. Now the London Masons Company *was not a lodge; it was a trade guild* and I ought to spend a lot of time trying to explain how lodges began, a difficult problem because we have no records of the actual foundation of the early operative lodges.

Briefly, the guilds were town organisations, greatly favoured by the towns because they helped in the management of municipal affairs. In London, for example, from 1376 onwards, each of the trades elected two representatives who became members of the Common Council, all together forming the city government. But the mason trade did not lend itself to town organisation at all. Most of their main work was outside the towns – the castles, the abbeys, the monasteries, the defence works, the really big jobs of masonry were always far from the towns. And we *believe* that it was in those places, where there was no other kind of trade organisation, that the masons, who were engaged on those jobs for years on end, formed themselves into lodges, in imitation of the guilds, so that they had some form of self-government on the job, while they were far away from all other forms of trade control.

The first actual information about lodges comes to us from a collection of documents which we know as the 'Old Charges' or the Manuscript Constitutions' of masonry, a marvellous collection. They begin with the *Regius Manuscript* c1390; the next, the *Cooke Manuscript* is dated c1410 and we have 130 versions of these documents running right through to the eighteenth century.

The oldest version, the *Regius Manuscript*, is in rhyming verse and differs, in several respects, from the other texts, but, in their general shape and contents they are all very much alike. They begin with an Opening Prayer, Christian and Trinitarian, and then they go on with a history of the craft, starting in Bible times and in Bible lands, and tracing the rise of the craft and its spread right across Europe until it reached France and was then brought across the channel and finally established in England. Unbelievably bad history; any professor of history would drop dead if he were challenged to prove it; but the masons believed it. This was their guarantee of respectability as an ancient craft.

Then, after the history we find the regulations, the actual Charges, for masters, fellows and apprentices, including several rules of a purely moral character, and that is all. Occasionally, the name of one of the characters changes, or the wording of a regulation will be altered slightly, but all follow the same general pattern.

Apart from these three main sections, prayer, history and Charges, in most of them we find a few words which indicate the beginnings of masonic ceremony. I must add that we cannot find all the information in one single document; but when we study them as a collection, it is possible to reconstruct the outline of the admission ceremony of those days, the earliest ceremony of admission into the craft.

We know that the ceremony, such as it was, began with an opening prayer and then there was a 'reading' of the history. (Many later documents refer to this 'reading'.) In those days, 99 masons in 100 could not read, and we believe, therefore, that they selected particular sections of the history which they memorised and recited from memory. To read the whole text, even if they could read, would have taken much too long. So the second part of the ceremony was the 'reading'.

Then, we find an instruction, which appears regularly in practically every document, usually in Latin, and it says: 'Then one of the elders holds out a book [sometimes "the book", sometimes the "Bible", and sometimes the "Holy Bible"] and he or they that are to be admitted shall place their hand thereon, and the following Charges shall be read.' In that position the regulations were read out to the candidate and he took the oath, a simple oath of fidelity to the king, to the master and to the craft, that he would obey the regulations and never bring the craft to shame. This was a direct lift from the guild oath, which was probably the only form that they knew; no frills, no penalties, a simple oath of fidelity to the king, the employer (the master) and to the trade.

From this point onwards, the oath becomes the heart and marrow, the crucial centre of every masonic ceremony. The *Regius*, which is the first of the versions to survive, emphasises this and it is worth quoting here. After the reading of the Charges in the *Regius Manuscript*, we get these words:

'And all the points hereinbefore
To all of them he must be sworn,
And all shall swear the same oath
Of the masons, be they willing, be they loth'

Whether they liked it or not, there was only one key that would open the door into the craft and that was the mason's oath. The importance, which the *Regius* attaches to it, we find repeated over and over again, not in the same words, but the emphasis is still there. The oath or obligation is the key to the admission ceremony.

So there I have described for you the earliest ceremony and now I can justify the title of my paper, *Six Hundred Years of Craft Ritual*. We have 1356 as the date of the beginnings of mason trade organisation, and around 1390 the earliest evidence which indicates a ceremony of admission. Split the difference. Somewhere between those two dates is when it all started. That is almost exactly 600 years of provable history and we can prove every stage of our development from then onwards.

Masonry, the art of building, began many thousands of years before this, but, for the antecedents of our own Freemasonry, we can only go back to the direct line of history that can be proved, and that is 1356, when it really began in Britain.

And now there is one other point that must be mentioned before I go any further. I have been speaking of a time when there was only one degree. The documents do not say that there is only one degree, they simply indicate only one ceremony, never more than one. But I believe it cannot have been for the apprentice, or entered apprentice; it must have been for the fellow of craft, the man who was fully trained. The Old Charges do not say this, but there is ample outside evidence from which we draw this conclusion. We have many law-suits and legal decisions that show that in the 1400s an apprentice was the chattel of his master. An apprentice was a piece of equipment, that belonged to his master. He could be bought and sold in much the same way that the master would buy and sell a horse or a cow and, under such conditions, it is impossible that an apprentice had any status in the lodge. That came much later. So, if we can think ourselves back into the time when there was only one degree it must have been for the fully-trained mason, the fellow of craft.

Almost 150 years were to pass before the authorities and parliament began to realise that maybe an apprentice was actually a human being as well. In the early 1500s we have in England a whole collection of labour statutes, labour laws, which begin to recognise the status of apprentices, and around that time we begin to find evidence of more than one degree.

From 1598 onwards we have minutes of two Scottish Lodges that were practising two degrees. I will come to that later. Before that date there is no evidence on degrees, except perhaps in one English document, the *Harleian MS, No 2054*, dated *c*1650, but believed to be a copy of a text of the late 1500s, now lost.

FIRST HINT OF TWO DEGREES

The *Harleian MS* is a perfectly normal version of the Old Charges, but bound up with it is a note in the same handwriting containing a new version of the mason's oath, of particular importance because it shows a major change from all earlier forms of the oath. Here it is:

There is seu^{r}all words & signes of a free Mason to be revailed to y^u wch y^u will answ: before God at the Great & terrible day of Judgm^t y^u keep secret

& not to revaile the same in the heares of any pson but to the M^{rs} & fellows of the said Society of free Masons so helpe me God xc.

Brethren, I know that I recited it too fast, but now I am going to read the first line again:

There is several words and signs of a free mason to be revealed to you . . .' *'Several words and signs . . .' plural*, more than one degree. And here in a document that should have been dated 1550, we have the first hint of the expansion of the ceremonies into more than one degree. A few years later we have actual minutes that prove two degrees in practice. But notice, Brethren, that the ceremonies must also have been taking something of their modern shape.

They probably began with a prayer, a recital of part of the 'history', the hand-on-book posture for the reading of the Charges, followed by an obligation and then the entrusting with secret words and signs, whatever they were. We do not know what they were, but we know that in both degrees the ceremonies were beginning to take the shape of our modern ceremonies. We have to wait quite a long while before we find the contents, the actual details, of those ceremonies, but we do find them at the end of the 1600s and that is my next theme. Remember, Brethren, we are still with only two degrees and I am going to deal now with the documents which actually describe those two ceremonies, as they first appeared on paper.

EARLIEST RITUAL FOR TWO DEGREES

The earliest evidence we have, is a document dated 1696, beautifully handwritten, and known as the *Edinburgh Register House Manuscript*, because it was found in the Public Record Office of Edinburgh. I deal first with that part of the text which describes the actual ceremonies. It is headed 'THE FORME OF GIVING THE MASON WORD' which is one way of saying it is the manner of initiating a mason. It begins with the ceremony which made an apprentice into an 'entered-apprentice (usually about three years after the beginning of his indentures), followed by the ceremony for the admission of the 'master mason or fellow craft', the title of the second degree. The details are fascinating but I can only describe them very briefly, and wherever I can, I will use the original words, so that you can get the feel of the thing.

We are told that the candidate 'was put to his knees' and 'after a

great many ceremonies to frighten him' (rough stuff, horse-play if
you like; apparently they tried to scare the wits out of him) 'after a
great many ceremonies to frighten him', he was made to take up the
book and in that position he took the oath, and here is the earliest
version of the mason's oath *described as part of a whole ceremony.*

> By god himself and you shall answer to god when you shall stand nakd
> before him, at the great day, you shall not reveal any pairt of what you
> shall hear or see at this time whither by word nor write nor put it in wryte
> at any time nor draw it with the point of a sword, or any other instrument
> upon the snow or sand, nor shall you speak of it but with an entered
> mason, so help you god.

Brethren, if you were listening very carefully, you have just heard the
earliest version of the words 'Indite, carve, mark, engrave or
otherwise them delineate'. The very first version is the one I have just
read, 'not write nor put it in wryte, nor draw it with a point of a
sword or any other instrument upon the snow or sand.' Notice,
Brethren, there was no penalty in the obligation, just a plain
obligation of secrecy.

After he had finished the obligation the youngster was taken out of
the lodge by the last previous candidate, the last person who had
been initiated before him. Outside the door of the lodge he was
taught the sign, postures and words of entry (we do not know what
they are until he comes back). He came back, took off his hat and
made 'a ridiculous bow' and then he gave the words of entry, which
included a greeting to the master and the brethren. It finished up with
the words 'under no less pain than cutting of my throat' and there is a
sort of footnote which says 'for you must make that sign when you say
that'. This is the earliest appearance in any document of an entered
apprentice's sign.

Now Brethren, forget all about your beautifully furnished lodges; I
am speaking of operative masonry, when the lodge was either a little
room at the back of a pub, or above a pub, or else a shed attached to
a big building job; and if there were a dozen masons there, that would
have been a good attendance. So, after the boy had given the sign, he
was brought up to the Master for the 'entrusting'. Here is the Master;
here, nearby, is the candidate; here is the 'instructor', and he, the
instructor, whispers the word into the ear of his neighbour, who
whispers the word to the next man and so on, all round the lodge,
until it comes to the Master, and the Master gives the word to the

candidate. In this case, there is a kind of biblical footnote, which shows, beyond all doubt, that the word was not one word but two. B and J, two pillar names, for the entered apprentice. This is very important later, when we begin to study the evolution of three degrees. In the two-degree system there were two pillars for the entered apprentice.

That was really the whole of the floorwork, but it was followed by a set of simple questions and answers headed 'SOME QUESTIONES THAT MASONS USE TO PUT TO THOSE WHO HAVE YE WORD BEFORE THEY WILL ACKNOWLEDGE THEM'. It included a few questions for testing a stranger outside the lodge, and this text gives us the first and oldest version of the masonic catechism. Here are some of the fifteen questions. 'Are you a mason? How shall I know it? Where were you entered? What makes a true and perfect lodge? Where was the first lodge? Are there any lights in your lodge? Are there any jewels in your lodge?' the first faint beginnings of masonic symbolism. It is amazing how little there was at the beginning. There, Brethren, 15 questions and answers, which must have been answered for the candidate; he had not had time to learn the answers. And that was the whole of the entered apprentice ceremony.

Now remember, Brethren, we are speaking about operative masonry, in the days, when masons earned their living with hammer and chisel. Under those conditions the second degree was taken about seven years after the date of initiation when the candidate came back to be made 'master or fellow craft'. Inside the lodge those two grades were equal, both fully trained masons. Outside the lodge, one was an employer, the other an employee. If he was the son of a Freeman Burgess of the city, he could take his Freedom and set up as a master immediately. Otherwise, he had to pay for the privilege, and until then, the fellow craft remained an employee. But inside the lodge they both had the same second degree.

So, after the end of his indentures of apprenticeship, and serving another year or two for 'meat and fee', (ie board plus a wage) he came along then for the second degree. He was 'put to his knees and took the oath anew'. It was the same oath that he had taken as an apprentice, omitting only three words. Then he was taken out of the lodge by the youngest master, and there he was taught the signs, posture and words of entry (we still do not know what they were). He came back and he gave what is called the 'master sign', but it is not described, so I cannot tell you about it. Then he was brought up for the entrusting. And now, the youngest master, the chap who had taken him outside, whispered the word to his neighbour, each in turn passing it all round the lodge, until it came to the Master, and the Master, *on the five points of fellowship* – second degree, Brethren – gave the word to the candidate. The five points in those days – foot to foot, knee to knee, heart to heart, hand to hand, ear to ear, that is how it was at its first appearance. No Hiramic legend and no frills; only the FPOF and a word. But in this document the word is not mentioned. It appears very soon afterwards and I will deal with that later.

There were only two test questions for a fellowcraft degree, and that was the lot. Two degrees, beautifully described, not only in this document but in two other sister texts, the *Chetwode Crawley MS*, dated about 1700 and the *Kevan MS*, quite recently discovered, dated about 1714. Three marvellous documents, all from the south of Scotland, all telling exactly the same story – wonderful materials, if we dare to trust them. But, I am sorry to tell you Brethren that we, as scientists in masonry, dare not trust them, because they were written in violation of an oath. To put it at its simplest, the more they tell us the less they are to be trusted, unless, by some fluke or by some miracle, we can prove, as we must do, that these documents were actually used in a lodge; otherwise they are worthless. In this case, by a very happy fluke, we have got the proof and it makes a lovely story. That is what you are going to get now.

Remember, Brethren, our three documents are from 1696 to 1714. Right in the middle of this period, in the year 1702, a little group of Scottish gentlemen decided that they wanted to have a lodge in their own backyard so to speak. These were gentlemen who lived in the south of Scotland around Galashiels, some 30 miles S.E. of Edinburgh. They were all notable landowners in that area – Sir John Pringle of Hoppringle, Sir James Pringle, his brother, Sir James Scott of Gala (Galashiels), their brother-in-law, plus another five neighbours came together and decided to form their own Lodge, in the village of Haughfoot near Galashiels. They chose a man who had a marvellous handwriting to be their scribe, and asked him to buy a minute book. He did. A lovely little leather-bound book (octavo size), and he paid 'fourteen shillings' Scots for it. I will not go into the difficulties of coinage now but today it would be about the equivalent of twenty-five cents. Being a Scotsman, he took very careful note of the amount and entered it in his minute book, to be repaid out of the first money due to the society. Then, in readiness for the first meeting of the lodge, he started off at what would have been page one with some notes, we do not know the details. But he went on and copied out the whole of one of these Scottish rituals, complete from beginning to end.

When he finished, he had filled ten pages, and his last twenty-nine words of ritual were the first five lines at the top of page eleven. Now, this was a Scotsman, and I told you he had paid 'fourteen shillings' for that book and the idea of leaving three-quarters of a page empty offended against his native Scottish thrift. So, to save wasting it, underneath the twenty-nine words, he put in a heading 'The Same Day' and went straight on with the minutes of the first meeting of the Lodge. I hope you can imagine all this, Brethren, because I wrote the history of 'The Lodge of Haughfoot', the first wholly non-operative Lodge in Scotland, thirty-four years older than the Grand Lodge of Scotland. The minutes were beautifully kept for sixty-one years and eventually, in 1763, the Lodge was swallowed up by some of the larger surrounding lodges. The minute book went to the great Lodge of Selkirk and it came down from Selkirk to London for me to write the history.

We do not know when it happened but, sometime during those sixty-one years, somebody, perhaps one of the later secretaries of the lodge, must have opened that minute book and caught sight of the opening pages and he must have had a fit! Ritual in a minute book! Out! And the first ten pages have disappeared; they are completely lost. That butcher would have taken page eleven as well but even he did not have the heart to destroy the minutes of the very first meeting of this wonderful lodge. So it was the minutes of the first meeting that saved those twenty-nine golden words at the top of page eleven, and the twenty-nine words are virtually identical with the corresponding portions of the *Edinburgh Register House MS* and its two sister texts. Those precious words are a guarantee that the other documents are to be trusted, and this gives us a marvellous starting point for the study of the ritual. Not only do we have the documents which describe the ceremonies; we also have a kind of yardstick, by which we can judge the quality of each new document as it arrives, and at this point they do begin to arrive.

Now Brethren, let me warn you that up to now we have been speaking of Scottish documents. Heaven bless the Scots! They took care of every scrap of paper, and if it were not for them we would have practically no history. Our earliest and finest material is nearly all Scottish. But, when the English documents begin to appear, they seem to fit. They not only harmonise, they often fill in the gaps in the Scottish texts. From here on, I will name the country of origin of those documents that are not English.

Within the next few years, we find a number of valuable ritual documents, including some of the highest importance. The first of these is the *Sloane MS*, dated *c*1700, an English text, in the British Library today. It gives various 'gripes' which had not appeared in any document before. It gives a new form of the Mason's oath which contains the words 'without Equivocation or mentall Resarvation'. That appears for the very first time in the *Sloane MS*, and Brethren, from this point onwards, every ritual detail I give you, will be a first-timer. I shall not repeat the individual details as they reappear in the later texts, nor can I say precisely when a particular practice actually began. I shall simply say that this or that item appears for the first time, giving you the name and date of the document by which it can be proved.

If you are with me on this, you will realise – and I beg you to think of it in this way – that you are watching a little plant, a seedling of Freemasonry, and every word I utter will be a new shoot, a new leaf, a new flower, a new branch. You will be watching the ritual grow; and if you see it that way, Brethren, I shall know I am not wasting my time, because that is the only way to see it.

Now, back to the *Sloane MS* which does not attempt to describe a whole ceremony. It has a fantastic collection of 'gripes' and other strange modes of recognition. It has a catechism of some twenty-two Questions and Answers, many of them similar to those in the Scottish texts, and there is a note which seems to confirm two pillars for the EA.

A later paragraph speaks of a salutation (?) for the Master, a curious 'hug' posture, with 'the masters grip by their right hands and the top of their Left hand fingers thurst close on ye small of each others Backbone . . .'. Here, *the word is given as* 'Maha – Byn', half in one ear and half in the other, to be used as a test word.

That was its first appearance in any of our documents, and if you were testing somebody, you would say 'Maha' and the other would have to say 'Byn'; and if he did not say 'Byn' you would have no business with him. (Demonstrate).

I shall talk about several other versions as they crop up later on, but I must emphasise that here is an English document filling the gaps in the three Scottish texts, and this sort of thing happens over and over again.

Now we have another Scottish document, the *Dumfries No 4 MS*, dated *c*1710. It contains a mass of new material, but I can only mention a few of the items. One of its questions runs: 'How were you brought in?' 'Shamfully, w^t a rope about my neck'. This is the earliest cable-tow; and a later answer says the rope 'is to hang me if I should betray my trust'. *Dumfries* also mentions that the candidate receives the 'Royal Secret' kneeling 'upon my left knee'.

Among many interesting Questions and Answers, it lists some of the unusual penalties of those days. 'My heart taken out alive, my head cut off, my body buried within ye sea-mark.' 'Within ye sea-mark' is the earliest version of the 'cable's length from the shore'. Brethren, there is so much more, even at this early date, but I have to be brief and I shall give you all the important items as we move forward into the next stage.

Meanwhile, this was the situation at the time when the first Grand Lodge was founded in 1717. We only had two degrees in England, one for the entered apprentice and the second was for the 'master or fellow craft'. Dr Anderson, who compiled the first English *Book of Constitutions* in 1723, actually described the English second degree as '*Masters* and *Fellow-Craft*'. The Scottish term had already invaded England.

The next big stage in the history of the ritual, is the evolution of the third degree. Actually, we know a great deal about the third degree, but there are some dreadful gaps. We do not know when it started or why it started, and we cannot be sure who started it! In the light of a lifetime of study, I am going to tell you what we know, and we will try to fill the gaps.

It would have been easy, of course, if one could stretch out a hand in a very good library and pull out a large minute-book and say 'Well, there is the earliest third degree that ever happened;' but it does not work out that way. The minute-books come much later.

HINTS OF THREE DEGREES

The earliest hints of the third degree appear in documents like those that I have been talking about – mainly documents that have been written out as *aide-mémoires* for the men who owned them. But we have to use exposures as well, exposures printed for profit, or spite; and we get some useful hints of the third degree long before it actually appears in practice. And so, we start with one of the best, a lovely little text, a single sheet of paper known as the *Trinity College, Dublin, Manuscript*, dated 1711, found among the papers of a famous Irish doctor and scientist, Sir Thomas Molyneux. This document is headed with a kind of Triple Tau, and underneath it the words 'Under no less a penalty'. This is followed by a set of eleven Q. and A. and we know straight away that something is wrong! We already have three perfect sets of fifteen questions, so eleven questions must be either bad memory or bad copying – something is wrong! The questions are perfectly normal, only not enough of them. Then after the eleven questions we would expect the writer to give a description of the whole or part of the ceremony but, instead of that, he gives a kind of catalogue of the Freemason's words and signs.

He gives this sign (EA demonstrated) for the EA with the word B. He gives 'knuckles, & sinues' as the sign for the 'fellow-craftsman', with the word 'Jachquin'. The 'Master's sign is the back bone' and for him (ie the MM) the writer gives the world's worst description of the FPOF. (It seems clear that neither the author of this piece nor the writer of the *Sloane MS*, had ever heard of the Points of Fellowship, or knew how to describe them.) Here, as I demonstrate, are the exact words, no more and no less:

> Squeese the Master by ye back bone, put your knee between his, & say Matchpin.

That, Brethren, is our second version of the word of the third degree. We started with 'Mahabyn', and now 'Matchpin', horribly debased. Let me say now, loud and clear, nobody knows what the correct word was. It was probably Hebrew originally, but all the early versions are debased. We might work backwards, translating from the English, but we cannot be certain that our English words are correct. So, here in the *Trinity College, Dublin, MS*, we have, for the very first time, a document which has separate secrets for three separate degrees; the enterprentice, the fellowcraftsman and the master. It is not proof of three degrees in practice, but it does show that somebody was playing with this idea in 1711.

The next piece of evidence on this theme comes from the first printed exposure, printed and published for entertainment or for spite, in a London newspaper, *The Flying Post*. The text is known as a 'Mason's Examination'. By this time, 1723, the catechism was much longer and the text contained several pieces of rhyme, all interesting, but only one of particular importance to my present purpose and here it is:

> '*An enter'd Mason I have been,*
> *Boaz and Jachin I have seen;*
> *A Fellow I was sworn most rare,*
> *And Know the Astler, Diamond, and Square:*
> *I know the Master's Part full well,*
> *As honest Maughbin will you tell.*'

Notice, Brethren, there are still two pillars for the EA, and once again somebody is dividing the Masonic secrets into three parts for three different categories of Masons. The idea of three degrees is in the air. We are still looking for minutes but they have not come yet.

Next, we have another priceless document, dated 1726, the *Graham MS*, a fascinating text which begins with a catechism of some thirty Questions and Answers, followed by a collection of legends, mainly about biblical characters, each story with a kind of Masonic twist in its tail. One legend tells how three sons went to their father's grave.

> to try if they could find anything about him for to Lead them to the vertuable secret which this famieous preacher had . . .

They opened the grave

> finding nothing save the dead body all most consumed away takeing a greip at a ffinger it came away so from Joynt to Joynt so to the wrest so to the Elbow so they Reared up the dead body and suported it setting ffoot to ffoot knee to knee Breast to breast Cheeck to cheeck and hand to back and cryed out help o ffather . . . so one said here is yet marow in this bone and the second said but a dry bone and the third said it stinketh so they agreed for to give it a name as is known to free masonry to this day . . .

This is the earliest story of a raising in a Masonic context, apparently a fragment of the Hiramic legend, but the old gentleman in the grave was Father Noah, not Hiram Abif.

Another legend concerns 'Bazalliell', the wonderful craftsman who built the mobile Temple and the Ark of the Covenant for the Israelites during their wandering in the wilderness. The story goes that near to death, Bazalliell asked for a tombstone to be erected over his grave, with an inscription 'according to his diserveing' and that was done as follows:

Here Lys the flowr of masonry superiour of many other companion to a king and to two princes a brother
Here Lys the heart all secrets could conceall
Here lys the tongue that never did reveal

The last two lines could not have been more apt if they had been specially written for Hiram Abif; they are virtually a summary of the Hiramic legend.

In the catechism, one answer speaks of those that

. . . have obtained a trible Voice by being entered passed and raised and Conformed by 3 severall Lodges . . .

'Entered, passed and raised' is clear enough. 'Three several lodges' means three separate degrees, three separate ceremonies. There is no doubt at all that this is a reference to three degrees being practised. But we still want minutes and we have not got them. And I am very sorry to tell you, that the earliest minutes we have recording a third degree, fascinating and interesting as they are, refer to a ceremony that never happened in a lodge at all; it took place in the confines of a London Musical Society. It is a lovely story and that is what you are going to get now.

In December 1724 there was a nice little lodge meeting at the Queen's Head Tavern, in Hollis Street, in the Strand, about three hundred yards from our present Freemasons' Hall. Nice people; the best of London's musical, architectural and cultural society were members of this lodge. On the particular night in which I am interested, His Grace, the Duke of Richmond was Master of the lodge. I should add that His Grace, the Duke of Richmond was also Grand Master at that time, and you might call him 'nice people'. It is true that he was the descendant of a royal illegitimate, but nowadays even royal illegitimates are counted as nice people. A couple of months later, seven of the members of this lodge and one brother they had borrowed from another lodge decided that they wanted to found a musical and architectural society.

They gave themselves a Latin title a mile long – *Philo Musicae et Architecturae Societas Apollini* – which I translate, 'The Apollonian Society for the Lovers of Music and Architecture' and they drew up a rule book which is beautiful beyond words. Every word of it written by hand. It looks as though the most magnificent printer had printed and decorated it.

Now these people were very keen on their Masonry and for their musical society they drew up an unusual code of rules. For example, one rule was that every one of the founders was to have his own coat-of-arms emblazoned in full colour in the opening pages of the minute book. How many lodges do you know, where every founder has his own coat-of-arms? This gives you an idea of the kind of boys they were. They loved their Masonry and they made another rule, that anybody could come along to their architectural lectures or to their musical evenings – the finest conductors were members of the society – anybody could come, but if he was not a Mason, he had to be made a Mason before they would let him in; and because they were so keen about the Masonic status of their members, they kept Masonic biographical notes of each member as he joined. It is from these notes that we are able to see what actually happened. I could talk about them all night, but for our present purposes, we need only follow the career of one of their members, Charles Cotton.

In the records of the Musical Society we read that on 22 December 1724 'Charles Cotton Esqr. was made a Mason by the said Grand Master' [ie His Grace The Duke of Richmond] in the Lodge at the Queen's Head. It could not be more regular than that. Then, on 18 February 1725 '. . . before We Founded This Society A Lodge was held . . . In Order to Pass Charles Cotton Esqr. . . . .' and because it was on the day the society was founded, we cannot be sure whether Cotton was passed FC in the Lodge or in the Musical Society. Three months later, on 12 May 1725 'Brother Charles Cotton Esqr. Broth^r. Papillion Ball Were regularly passed Masters'.

Now we have the date of Cotton's initiation, his passing and his raising; there is no doubt that he received three degrees. But 'regularly passed Masters' – No! It could not have been more irregular! This was a Musical Society – not a lodge! But I told you they were nice people, and they had some very distinguished visitors. First, the Senior Grand Warden came to see them. Then the Junior Grand Warden. And then, they got a nasty letter from the Grand Secretary and, in 1727, the society disappeared. Nothing now remains except their minute book in the British Library. If you ever go to London and go to Freemasons' Hall you will see a marvellous facsimile of that book. It is worth a journey to London just to see it. And that is the record of the earliest third degree. I wish we could produce a more respectable first-timer, but that was the earliest.

I must tell you, Brethren, that Gould, the great Masonic historian believed, all his life, that this was the earliest third degree of which there was any record at all. But just before he died he wrote a brilliant article in the *Transactions of the Quatuor Coronati Lodge*, and he changed his mind. He said, 'No, the minutes are open to wide interpretation, and we ought not to accept this as a record of the third degree.' Frankly, I do not believe that he proved his case, and on this point I dare to quarrel with Gould. Watch me carefully, Brethren, because I stand a chance of being struck down at this moment. Nobody argues with Gould! But I dispute this because, within ten months of this date, we have incontrovertible evidence of the third degree in practice. As you might expect, bless them, it comes from Scotland.

Lodge Dumbarton Kilwinning, now No 18 on the register of the Grand Lodge of Scotland, was founded in January 1726. At the foundation meeting there was the Master, with seven master masons, six fellowcrafts and three entered apprentices; some of them were operative masons, some non-operative. Two months later, in March 1726, we have this minute:

> Gabriel Porterfield who appeared in the January meeting as a Fellow Craft was unanimously admitted and received a Master of the Fraternity and renewed his oath and gave in his entry money.

Now, notice Brethren, here was a Scotsman, who started in January as a fellowcraft, a founding fellowcraft of a new Lodge. Then he came along in March, and he renewed his oath, which means he took another ceremony; and he gave in his entry money, which means he paid for it. Brethren, if a Scotsman paid for it you bet your life he got it! There is no doubt about that. And there is the earliest 100 per cent gilt-edged record of a third degree.

Two years later, in December 1728, another new Lodge, Greenock Kilwinning, at its very first meeting, prescribed separate fees for entering, passing, and raising.

PRICHARD'S *MASONRY DISSECTED*

From then on we have ample evidence of the three degrees in practice and then in 1730 we have the earliest printed exposure which claimed to describe all three degrees, *Masonry Dissected*, published by Samuel Prichard in October 1730. It was the most valuable ritual work that had appeared until that time, all in the form of question and answer (apart from a brief introduction) and it had enormous influence in the stabilisation of our English ritual.

Its 'Enter'd Prentice's Degree' – by this time ninety-two questions – gave two pillar words to the EA, and the first of them was 'lettered'. Prichard managed to squeeze a lot of floor-work into his EA questions and answers. Here is one question for the candidate: 'How did he make you a mason?' Listen to his answer:

> With my bare-bended Knee and Body within the Square, the Compass extended to my naked Left Breast, my naked Right Hand on the Holy Bible: there I took the Obligation (or Oath) of a Mason.

All that information in one answer! And the next question was, 'Can you repeat that obligation?' with the answer, 'I'll do my endeavor', and Prichard followed this with a magnificent obligation which contained three sets of penalties (throat cut, heart torn out, body severed and ashes burned and scattered). This is how they appeared in 1730. Documents of 1760 show them separated, and later developments do not concern us here.

Prichard's 'Fellow-Craft's Degree' was very short, only 33 questions and answers. It gave J alone to the FC (not lettered) but now the second degree had a lot of new material relating to the pillars, the middle chamber, the winding stairs, and a long recitation on the letter G, which began with the meaning 'Geometry' and ended denoting 'The Grand Architect and Contriver of the Universe'.

Prichard's 'Master's Degree or Master's Part' was made up of thirty questions with some very long answers, containing the earliest version of the Hiramic legend, literally the whole story as it ran in those days. It included the murder by 'three Ruffians', the searchers, 'Fifteen Loving Brothers' who agreed among themselves 'that if they did not find the Word in him or about him, the first Word should be the Master's Word'. Later, the discovery, 'the Slip', the raising on the FPOF, and another new version of the MM word*, which is said to mean 'The Builder is smitten'.

There is no reason to believe that Prichard invented the Hiramic legend. As we read his story in conjunction with those collected by Thomas Graham in 1726 (quoted above), there can be little doubt that Prichard's version arose out of several streams of legend, probably an early result of speculative influence in those days.

But the third degree was not a new invention. It arose from a division of the original first degree into two parts, so that the original second degree with its FPOF and a word moved up into third place, both the second and third acquiring additional materials during the period of change. That was sometime between 1711 and 1725, but whether it started in England, Scotland, or Ireland is a mystery; we simply do not know.

Back now to Samuel Prichard and his *Masonry Dissected*. The book created a sensation; it sold three editions and one pirated edition in eleven days. It swept all other exposures off the market. For the next thirty years Prichard was being reprinted over and over again and nothing else could stand a chance; there was nothing fit to touch it. We lose something by this, because we have no records of any ritual developments in England during the next 30 years – a great 30-year gap. Only one new item appeared in all that time, the 'Charge to the Initiate', a miniature of our modern version, in beautiful eighteenth-century English. It was published in 1735, but we do not know who wrote it. For fresh information on the growth of the ritual, we have to go across the Channel, into France.

FURTHER EVIDENCE FROM FRANCE

The English planted Freemasonry in France in 1725, and it became an elegant pastime for the nobility and gentry. The Duke of So-and-So would hold a lodge in his house, where he was Master for ever and ever, and any time he invited a few friends round, they would open a lodge, and he would make a few more Masons. That was how it began, and it took about ten or twelve years before Masonry began to seep down, through to the lower levels. By that time lodges were beginning to meet in restaurants and taverns but around 1736, things were becoming difficult in France and it was feared that the lodges were being used for plots and conspiracies against government.

At Paris, in particular, precautions were taken. An edict was issued by René Herault, Lieutenant-General of Police, that tavern-keepers and restaurant-keepers were not to give accommodation to Masonic lodges at all, under penalty of being closed up for six months and a fine of 3,000 livres. We have two records, both in 1736–37, of well-known restaurants that were closed down by the Police for that reason. It did not work, and the reason was very simple. Masonry had started in private houses. The moment that the officials put the screw on the meetings in taverns and restaurants, it went back into private houses again; it went underground so-to-speak, and the Police were left helpless.

Eventually, Herault decided that he could do much more damage to the Craft if he could make it a laughing-stock. If he could make it look ridiculous, he was sure he could put them out of business for all time, and he decided to try. He got in touch with one of his girl-friends, a certain Madame Carton. Now, Brethren, I know what I am going to tell you sounds like our English *News of the World*, but I am giving you recorded history, and quite important history at that. So he got in touch with Madame Carton, who is always described as a dancer at the Paris opera. The plain fact is that she followed a much older profession. The best description that gives an idea of her status and her qualities, is that she slept in the best beds in Europe. She had a very special clientèle. Now this was no youngster; she was fifty-five years old at that time and she had a daughter who was also in the same interesting line of business. And I have to be very careful what I say, because it was believed that one of our own Grand Masters was entangled with either or both of them. All this was in the newspapers of those days.

Anyway, Herault got in touch with Madame Carton and asked her to obtain a copy of the Masonic ritual from one of her clients. He intended to publish it, and by making the Masons look ridiculous he was going to put them out of business. Well! She did, and he did. In other words, she got her copy of the ritual and passed it on to him. It was first published in France in 1737, under the title *Réception d'un Frey-Maçon*. Within a month it was translated in three London newspapers, but it failed to diminish the French zeal for Freemasonry and had no effect in England. I summarise briefly.

The text, in narrative form, described only a single two-pillar ceremony, dealing mainly with the floor-work and only fragments of ritual. The Candidate was deprived of metals, right knee bare, left shoe worn 'as a slipper' and locked in a room alone in total darkness, to put him in the right frame of mind for the ceremony. His eyes were bandaged and his sponsor knocked three times on the Lodge door. After several questions, he was introduced and admitted in the care of a Warden (*Surveillant*). Still blindfolded, he was led three times round the floor-drawing in the centre of the Lodge, and there were 'resin flares'. It was customary in the French lodges in those days to have a pan of live coals just inside the door of the lodge and at the moment the candidate was brought in, they would sprinkle powdered resin on the live coal, to make an enormous flare, which would frighten the wits out of the candidate, even if he was blindfolded. (In many cases they did not blindfold them until they came to the obligation.) Then, amid a circle of swords, we get the posture for the obligation with three lots of penalties, and details of Aprons and Gloves. This is followed by the signs, tokens and words relating to two pillars. The ceremony contained several features unknown in English practice, and some parts of the story appear to be told in the wrong sequence, so that as we read it, we suddenly realise that the gentleman who was dictating it had his mind on much more worldly matters. So Brethren, this was the earliest exposure from France, not very good, but it was the first of a really wonderful stream of documents. As before, I shall only discuss the important ones.

My next, is *Le Secret des Francs-Maçons* (The Secret of the Freemasons) 1742, published by the Abbé Perau, who was Prior at the Sorbonne, the University of Paris. A beautiful first degree, all in narrative form, and every word in favour of the Craft. His words for the EA and FC were in reverse order (and this became common practice in Europe) but he said practically nothing about the second degree. He described the Masonic drinking and toasting at great length, with a marvellous description of 'Masonic Fire'. He mentioned that the Master's degree was 'a great ceremonial lamentation over the death of Hiram' but he knew nothing about the third degree and said that Master Masons got only a new sign and that was all.

Our next work is *Le Catéchisme des Francs-Maçons* (The Free-masons' Catechism) published in 1744, by Louis Travenol, a famous French journalist. He dedicates his book 'To the Fair Sex', which he adores, saying that he is deliberately publishing this exposure for their benefit, because the Masons have excluded them, and his tone is mildly anti-Masonic. He continues with a note 'To the Reader', criticising several items in Perau's work, but agreeing that *Le Secret* is generally correct. For that reason (and Perau was hopelessly ignorant of the third degree) he confines his exposure to the MM degree. But that is followed by a catechism which is a composite for all three degrees, undivided, though it is easy to see which questions belong to the Master Mason.

Le Catéchisme also contains two excellent engravings of the Tracing Boards, or Floor-drawings, one called 'Plan of the Lodge for the Apprentice-Fellow' combined , and the other for 'The Master's Lodge'.

Travenol begins his third degree with 'The History of Adoniram, Architect of the Temple of Solomon'. The French texts usually say Adoniram instead of Hiram, and the story is a splendid version of the Hiramic Legend. In the best French versions, the Master's word (Jehova) was not lost; *the nine Masters who were sent by Solomon to search for him, decided to adopt a substitute word out of fear that the three assassins had compelled Adoniram to divulge it.*

This is followed by a separate chapter which describes the layout of a Master's Lodge, including the 'Floor-drawing', and the earliest ceremony of opening a Master's Lodge. That contains a curious 'Master's sign' that begins with a hand at the side of the forehead (demonstrate) and ends with the thumb in the pit of the stomach. And now, Brethren, we get a magnificent description of the floorwork of the third degree, the whole ceremony, so beautifully described and in such fine detail, that any Preceptor could reconstruct it from beginning to end – and every word of this whole chapter is new material that had never appeared before.*

Of course there are many items that differ from the practices we know, but now you can see why I am excited about these French documents. They give marvellous details, at a time when we have no corresponding material in England. But before I leave *Le Catéchisme*, I must say a few words about its picture of the third degree Tracing Board or Floor-drawing which contains, as its central

---

* This section is reproduced in full on pp 306.

theme, a coffin design, surrounded by tear drops, the tears which our ancient brethren shed over the death of our Master Adoniram.

On the coffin is a sprig of acacia and the word '*JEHOVA*', '*ancien mot du Maitre,* (*the former word* of a Master), but in the French degree it was not lost. It was the Ineffable Name, never to be uttered, and here, for the first time, the word *Jehova* is on the coffin. The diagram, in dots, shows how three zig-zag steps over the coffin are to be made by the candidate in advancing from West to East, and many other interesting details too numerous to mention.

The catechism, which is the last main item in the book, is based (like all the early French catechisms) directly on Prichard's *Masonry Dissected*, but it contains a number of symbolic expansions and explanations, the result of speculative influence.

And so we come to the last of the French exposures that I must deal with today *L'Ordre des Francs-Maçons Trahi* (The Order of Freemasons Betrayed) published in 1745 by an anonymous writer, a thief! There was no law of copyright in those days and this man knew a good thing when he saw it. He took the best material he could find, collected it into one book, and added a few notes of his own. So, he stole Perau's book, 102 pages, the lot, and printed it as his own first degree. He said very little about the second degree (the second degree was always a bit of an orphan). He stole Travenol's lovely third degree and added a few notes including a few lines saying that before the Candidate's admission, the most junior MM in the Lodge lies down on the coffin, his face covered with a blood-stained cloth, so that the Candidate will see him raised by the Master before he advances for his own part in the ceremony.

Of his own material, there is not very much; chapters on the Masonic Cipher, on the Signs, Grips and Words, and on Masonic customs. He also included two improved designs of the Floor-drawings and two charming engravings illustrating the first and third degrees in progress. His catechism followed Travenol's version very closely but he did add four questions and answers (seemingly a minor contribution) but they are of high importance in our study of the ritual:

Q. When a Mason finds himself in danger, what must he say and do to call the brethren to his aid?
A. He must put his joined hands to his forehead, the fingers interlaced, and say 'Help, ye Children (or Sons) of the Widow'.

Brethren, I do not know if the 'interlaced fingers' were used in the USA or Canada; I will only say that they were well known in several European jurisdictions, and the 'Sons of the Widow' appear in most versions of the Hiramic legend.

Three more new questions ran:

Q. What is the Password of an Apprentice?   Ans: T . . . .
Q. That of a Fellow?   Ans: S . . . .
Q. And that of a Master?   Ans: G . . . .

This was the first appearance of Passwords in print, but the author added an explanatory note:

> These three Passwords are scarcely used except in France and at Frankfurt on Main. They are in the nature of Watchwords, introduced as a surer safeguard (when dealing) with brethren whom they do not know.

Passwords had never been heard of before this date, 1745, and they appear for the first time, in France. You will have noticed, Brethren, that some of them appear to be in the wrong order, and, because of the 30-year gap, we do not know whether they were being used in England at that time or if they were a French invention. On this puzzle we have a curious piece of indirect evidence, and I must digress for a moment.

In the year 1730, the Grand Lodge of England was greatly troubled by the exposures that were being published, especially Prichard's *Masonry Dissected*, which was officially condemned in Grand Lodge. Later, as a precautionary measure, certain words in the first two degrees were interchanged, a move which gave grounds in due course for the rise of a rival Grand Lodge. *Le Secret*, 1742, *Le Catéchisme*, 1744 and the *Trahi*, 1745, all give those words in the new order, and in 1745, when the Passwords made their first appearance in France, they also appear in reverse order. Knowing how regularly France had adopted – and improved – on English ritual practices, there seems to be a strong probability that Passwords were already in use in England (perhaps in reverse order), but there is not a single English document to support that theory.

So Brethren, by 1745 most of the principal elements in the Craft degrees were already in existence, and when the new stream of English rituals began to appear in the 1760s the best of that material had been embodied in our English practice. But it was still very crude and a great deal of polishing needed to be done.

The polishing began in 1769 by three writers – Wellins Calcutt and William Hutchinson, in 1769, and William Preston in 1772, but Preston towered over the others. He was the great expounder of Freemasonry and its symbolism, a born teacher, constantly writing and improving on his work. Around 1800, the ritual and the Lectures (which were the original catechisms, now expanded and explained in beautiful detail) were all at their shining best. And then with typical English carelessness, we spoiled it.

You know, Brethren, that from 1751 up to 1813, we had two rival Grand Lodges in England (the original, founded in 1717, and the rival Grand Lodge, known as the 'Antients', founded in 1751) and they hated each other with truly Masonic zeal. Their differences were mainly in minor matters of ritual and in their views on Installation and the Royal Arch. The bitterness continued until 1809 when the first steps were taken towards a reconciliation and a much-desired union of the rivals.

In 1809, the original Grand Lodge, the 'Moderns', ordered the necessary revisions, and the Lodge of Promulgation was formed to vet the ritual and bring it to a form that would be satisfactory to both sides. That had to be done, or we would still have had two Grand Lodges to this day! They did an excellent job, and many changes were made in ritual and procedural matters; but a great deal of material was discarded, and it might be fair to say that they threw away the baby with the bath-water. The Beehive, the Hour-glass, the Scythe, the Pot of Incense etc, which were in our Tracing Boards in the early nineteenth century have disappeared. We have to be thankful indeed for the splendid material they left behind.

A NOTE FOR BRETHREN IN THE USA

I must add a note here for Brethren in the USA. You will realise that until the changes which I have just described, I have been talking about your ritual as well as ours in England. After the War of Independence the States rapidly began to set up their own Grand Lodges, but your ritual, mainly of English origin – whether Antients or Moderns – was still basically English. Your big changes began in and around 1796, when Thomas Smith Webb, of Albany, NY, teamed up with an English Mason, John Hanmer, who was well versed in Preston's Lecture system.

In 1797 Webb published his *Freemason's Monitor or Illustrations of*

Masonry, largely based on Preston's *Illustrations*. Webb's *Monitor*, adapted from our ritual when, as I said, it was at its shining best, became so popular, that the American Grand Lodges, mainly in the Eastern states at that time, did everything they could to preserve it in its original form; eventually by the appointment of Grand Lecturers, whose duty it was (and is) to ensure that the officially adopted forms remain unchanged.

I cannot go into details now, but from the Rituals and Monitors I have studied and the Ceremonies and Demonstrations I have seen, there is no doubt that your ritual is much fuller than ours, giving the candidate much more explanation, interpretation, and symbolism, than we normally give in England.

In effect, because of the changes we made in our work between 1809 and 1813, it is fair to say that in many respects your ritual is older than ours and better than ours.

2

PILLARS AND GLOBES, COLUMNS AND CANDLESTICKS

IN THE QC Lodge summons, dated 22 December 1961, there was a brief note relating to the Wardens' Columns which attracted considerable attention and comment. As author of the note, and Secretary of the Lodge, I had to answer a number of letters on that subject and on several other topics closely allied to it. During the course of this work it became obvious that there is much confusion on the subject of Pillars, Globes, Columns and Candlesticks, on the dates and stages of their introduction into Craft usage, and most of all, perhaps, on the curious way in which some of these items (which originally had places in the ritual, or furnishings, in their own right) are now made to serve a dual purpose, thereby adding to the confusion as to their origins.

There are, apparently, two main reasons for these difficulties. First, we have grown so accustomed to seeing our present-day Lodges all more or less uniformly furnished that we accept the furnishings and their symbolism without question. Secondly, the Lectures on the Tracing Boards are given rarely nowadays so that Brethren are unfamiliar with the subject, or with the problems that are involved.

This essay was compiled, therefore, not with the intention of answering all the questions that arise, if indeed that were possible, but in order to separate the various threads which are now so badly entangled.

As these various items appear in our modern procedure, there is an extraordinary mixture of ritual-references with odd items of furniture, some of which had a purely practical origin, while others were purely symbolical. I have tried to deal with each of these features separately, showing, as far as possible, their first introduction into the Craft, and tracing the various stages through which they passed into our present usage.

27

THE PILLARS
Extract from the Lecture on the Second Tracing Board:

> . . . the two great pillars which were placed in the porchway entrance on
> the south side . . . they were formed hollow, the better to serve as archives
> to Freemasonry, for therein were deposited the constitutional Rolls . . .
> These pillars were adorned with two chapters . . . [and] . . . with two
> spheres on which were delineated maps of the celestial and terrestrial
> globes, pointing out 'Masonry universal'.

THE FIRST TWO PILLARS IN CRAFT TRADITION
The two earliest pillars in the literature of the Craft are those
described in the legendary history which forms part of the *Cooke MS*
*c*1410, and many later versions of the Old Charges. The story goes
that they were made by the four children of Lamech, in readiness for
the feared destruction of the world by fire or flood. One of the pillars
was made of marble, the other of *lacerus* (ie *lateres* or burnt brick)
because the first 'would not burn' and the other 'would not drown'.
They were intended as a means of preserving 'all the sciences that
they had found', which they had carved or engraved on the two
pillars.

This legend dates back to the early apocryphal writings, and in the
course of centuries a number of variations arose in which the story of
the indestructible pillars remained fairly constant, although their
erection was attributed to different heroes. Thus, Josephus ascribed
them to Seth, while another apocryphal version says they were built
by Enoch.*

For some reason, not readily explained, the early MS *Constitutions*
favour the children of Lamech as the principals in this ancient legend,
which was embodied in the texts to show how all the then-known
sciences were preserved for mankind by this early piece of practical
mason work.

The Old Charges were designed primarily to display the antiquity
and high importance of the Craft, and it is highly significant that
Solomon's two pillars *do not appear* in the early versions. David and
Solomon are named among a long list of biblical and historical
characters who '. . . loved masons well . . .', and gave or confirmed

---

* For an excellent survey of pre-Christian and other early versions and variations of this legend, see
Knoop, Jones and Hamer, *The Two Earliest Masonic MSS*, pp 39–44 and 162–63.

'their charges', but Solomon's Temple receives only a casual mention, and the pillars are not mentioned at all. It seems fairly certain, therefore, that in the fourteenth and fifteenth centuries Solomon's two pillars had no special significance for the mason craft.

SOLOMON'S PILLARS IN THE RITUAL

The first appearance of Solomon's pillars in the Craft ritual is in the *Edinburgh Register House MS*, 1696, in a catechism associated with the 'Mason Word' ceremonies.

The earliest-known reference to the 'Mason Word' appears in 1637, in a diary-entry made by the Earl of Rothes, and although no kind of ceremony is described in that record, it is reasonable to assume that the 'Mason Word' ceremonies were already known and practised at that date. The *Edinburgh Register House MS* is the oldest surviving document which describes the actual *procedure* of the ceremonies. The text is in two parts. One section, headed 'The Forme of Giveing the Mason Word', describes the rather rough and ready procedure for the admission of an entered apprentice, including ceremonies to frighten the candidate, an oath, a form of 'greeting', and certain verbal and physical modes of recognition. There is also a separate and similar procedure for the 'master mason or fellow craft'. (Only two degrees were known at that time.)

The second part of this text is a catechism of some seventeen questions and answers, fifteen for the EA and a further two for the master or FC. It is probable that these questions, with the obligation, entrusting and greeting, represent the whole of the 'spoken-work' of the ceremonies at that time.

The questions are of two kinds:

(a) Test questions for the purpose of recognition.
(b) Informative questions for the purpose of instruction and explanation.

Among these we find the first faint hints of the beginning of Masonic symbolism.

A question in the catechism of 1696, and in six of the texts that followed soon after, runs:

Q. Where was the first lodge?
A. In the porch of Solomon's Temple.

Now, the *Edinburgh Register House MS* is a complete text; no part of it has been lost or obliterated during the 290 years or so since it was written, in 1696. In fact, there are several related texts belonging to the next twenty years, which amply demonstrate its completeness. It is therefore noteworthy that in this whole group of texts the two earlier pillars, built by the children of Lamech, have virtually disappeared. Barely a hint of them remains in any of the *ritual documents* from 1696 onwards.

The *Dumfries No 4 MS c*1710, is a version of the Old Charges which has been greatly enlarged by a collection of ritual questions and answers, with many items of religious interpretation. In its first part, it has the expected reference to the four children of Lamech and their two pillars, but towards the end of the catechism the pillars are mentioned again:

> Q.   Where [was] the noble art or science found when it was lost?
> A.   It was found in two pillars of stone the one would not sink the other would not burn.

This is followed by a long passage of religious interpretation saying that Solomon named his own two pillars in reference to 'ye two churches of ye Jews & gentiles . . .' That need not concern us here, but Solomon's pillars are not normally mentioned in the Old Charges, and the appearance of both sets of pillars in the two parts of the *Dumfries MS*, suggests that when the ceremonies were shaped to contain Solomon's J and B, *the earlier 'indestructible' pair were abandoned.*

There is, in fact, no evidence that they had ever formed any part of the *admission ceremonies*, but we know very little about the ceremonies in their earliest forms. It seems fairly certain, however, that Solomon's pillars had achieved a really important place in the Craft ritual in the early 1600s.

Soon after their first mention in the early ritual-texts these two pillars became a regular part of the 'furnishings' of the lodge, and it is possible to trace them from their earliest introduction up to their present place in the lodge-room, as follows:

> (1) Their first appearance as part of a question in the catechism, with much additional evidence that they then had some esoteric significance. The early catechisms are particularly interesting in this respect, because they indicate that both of

Solomon's Pillar-names belonged at one time to the EA ceremony.

(2) They were drawn on the floor of the lodge in chalk and charcoal, forming part of the earliest versions of our modern 'Tracing Boards'. In December, 1733, the minutes of the Old King's Arms Lodge, No 28, record the first step towards the purchase of a 'Floor Cloth'. (*AQC*, vol lxii, p 236.) 'Drawings' on the floor of the lodge are recorded in the minutes of the Old Dundee Lodge, No 18, from 1748 onwards. The *Herault Letter* of 1737 describes the 'Drawing', and the later French exposures, from 1744 onwards, contain excellent engravings showing both pillars (marked J and B) on the combined EA and FC floor-drawing.

(3) Between *c*1760 and 1765 several English exposures of the period indicate that the Wardens each had a column representing one of the Pillars, as part of his personal equipment in the lodge. The following extract is typical:

'The senior and junior Warden have each of them a Column in their Hand, about Twenty Inches long, which represents the two Columns of the Porch at *Solomon*'s Temple, Boaz and Jachin.

The Senior is Boaz, or Strength.

The Junior is Jachin, or to establish.'

(From *Three Distinct Knocks*, 1760)

(4) Finally, the two pillars appear as handsome pieces of furniture, perhaps four to eight feet high, standing usually at the western end of the lodge room. The earliest descriptions of the lay-out of the lodge in the 1700s show both Wardens in the west, facing the Master. The two pillars were generally placed near them, forming a kind of portal, so that the candidates passed between them on their admission, a custom which exists in many lodges to this day.

This was perhaps the last development of all, though some of the wealthier lodges may have possessed such pillars at a comparatively early date. When we consider how many lodge rooms (especially in the provinces) still use pairs of large pillars, it is surprising that the eighteenth- and nineteenth-century inventories make no mention of them. Probably this was because they were part of the equipment of

Masonic Halls, so that they belonged to the landlords and not to the various lodges that used the rooms.

So we trace the two pillars from their first appearance as part of a question in the ritual through various stages of development until they became a prominent feature of lodge furniture.

But modern practices are not uniform in regard to the pillars; in London, for example, there are very few lodges which have the tall pillars, but they are always depicted on the second T.B., and they appear in miniature on the Wardens' pedestals.

CHAPITERS, GLOBES AND BOWLS

The biblical descriptions of Solomon's pillars give rise to many problems, especially as regards their dimensions and ornamentation. For us, the chapiters, bowls or globes which surmounted them are of particular interest, because of ritual developments and expansions during the eighteenth century.

In this particular problem a great deal depends on the interpretation of the original Hebrew text. The chapiters appear in *I Kings*, VII, 16: '. . . and he made two chapiters . . .'

The word is Ko-thor-oth = chapiters, capitals or crowns. Later, in verse 41, without mention of any further works, the text speaks of '. . . the two pillars *and the two bowls of the chapiters* . . .' The Hebrew reads Gooloth Ha-ko-thor-oth, and the word Gooloth is a problem. Goolah (singular) means a ball or globe; also, a bowl or vessel, and various forms of the same root are used quite loosely to describe something round or spherical.

Our regular contacts with modern lodge Tracing-Boards and furnishings have accustomed us to the idea that Solomon's two pillars were surmounted by chapiters or capitals, with a globe resting on each, but that is not proven. The early translators and illustrators of the Bible were by no means unanimous on this point, and the various terms they used to describe the chapiters, etc, show that they were not at all certain as to the appearance of the pillars. To take one example, the Geneva Bible, of 1560, a very handsome and popular illustrated Bible, which provided the interpretation for some of the proper names and seems to have been much used by the men who framed the Masonic ritual.

At *I Kings*, VII, v. 16, '. . . and he made two chapiters . . .', there is a marginal note, 'Or pommels', ie globular features. At this stage the Geneva Bible clearly indicates that the chapiters were globes or spheres, and not the crown-shaped heads to the pillars that we would understand them to be.

Among the illustrations to this chapter in the Geneva Bible there are several interesting engravings of the Temple and its equipment, including a sketch of a pillar, surmounted by a shallow capital, with an ornamental globe poised on top. A marginal note to this illustration speaks of 'The height of the *chapiter or round bal* vpon the pillar of five cubites hight . . .' (My italics.) So the chapiter was a round ball.

At II *Chron.*, IV, v. 12, the same Bible gives a new interpretation, '. . . two pillars, *and the bowles, and the chapiters* on the top of the two pillars . . .' Here it is evident that the 'bowles' and the chapiters were two separate features.

Whether we incline to bowls or globes, there is yet another interpretation which would exclude both. The accounts in both *Kings* and *Chronicles* refer to the pomegranate decoration which was attached to the 'bowles' or bellies *of* the chapiters (I *Kings*, VII, v. 41, 42, and II *Chron.*, IV, v. 12, 13), and from these passages it is a perfectly proper inference that the chapiters were themselves 'bowl-shaped', and that there were neither bowls nor globes above them.

Although the globes were finally adopted in Masonic furniture and decoration as head-pieces to Solomon's Pillars, they came in very slowly, and during a large part of the eighteenth century there was no uniformity of practice on this point. The *Trahi*, one of the early French exposures, contains several engravings purporting to be 'Plans' of a *Loge de Reception*; in effect they are Tracing Boards for the 1st and 2nd combined, and another for the 3rd degree. The Apprentice Plan contains illustrations of the two pillars, marked J and B, both conventional Corinthian pillars, with *flat tops*. There is also, among a huge collection of symbols, a sketch which is described in the Index as a 'sphere', a kind of lattice-work globe (actually an armillary sphere) used in astronomy to demonstrate the courses of the stars and planets.

The Lodge of Probity, No 61, Halifax (founded in 1738), was in serious decline in 1829, and an inventory of its possessions was taken at that time. One item reads: 'Box with Globes and Stands'.

The Phoenix Lodge, No 94, Sunderland (founded in 1755), has a

Pillars with bowls from the collection of lodge equipment known as the 'Bath Furniture' presented to the Royal Cumberland Lodge No 41 in 1805.

pair of eighteenth-century globes, each mounted on three legs, standing left and right of the Master's pedestal. All Souls' Lodge, No 170 (founded in 1767), had until 1888 a handsome pair of globes, each mounted on a tripod base, clearly of eighteenth-century style, similarly placed left and right of the WM. The Lodge of Peace and Unity, No 314, Preston (founded in 1797), in a recent sketch of its lodge-room, shows a pair of globes on low, three-legged stands, placed on the floor of the lodge, left and right, a yard or two in front of the SW.

Among the unique collection of lodge equipment known as the 'Bath Furniture' is a pair of globes, 'celestial and terrestrial', on low four-legged stands, and the minutes show that they were presented to the Royal Cumberland Lodge in 1805. It is interesting to observe that the equipment also includes a handsome pair of brass pillars, each about 5ft 9in in height, standing as usual in the west, and each of them surmounted with a large brass bowl. These date from the late eighteenth century.

In this case especially, as in all the cases cited above, there is no evidence of globes on top of the BJ pillars; the globes formed a part of the lodge equipment entirely in their own right.

The frontispiece to Noorthouck's *Constitutions* of 1784 is a symbolical drawing in which the architectural portion represents the interior of the then Free Mason's Hall. At the foot of the picture, in the foreground, is a long table bearing several Masonic tools and symbols, with two globes on tripod stands, and the description of the picture refers to '. . . the Globes and other Masonic Furniture and Implements of the Lodge'.

All this suggests that the globes were beginning to play some part in the lodge, or in the ritual, *although they were not yet associated with the pillars.* But even after the globes or bowls had begun to appear *on* the pillars, there was still considerable doubt as to what was correct. This is particularly noticeable in early Tracing Boards and decorated aprons, some showing 'bowls', and others 'globes'. (See illustrations, pp 140–41 in *AQC*, vol lxxiv, for pillars with bowls, and ibid, p 52, where the pillars are surmounted by profuse foliage, growing presumably from bowls.)

To summarise:

(1) In the period of our earliest ritual documents, 1696 to 1730, there is no evidence that the globes formed any part of the

catechism or ritual, and it is reasonably certain that they were unknown as 'designs' or as furnishings in the lodges.

(2) Around 1745 it is probable that the sphere or globe had been introduced as one of the symbols in the 'floor drawings' or Tracing Boards. There is no evidence to show that it appeared in the catechism. There are several highly-detailed catechisms belonging to this period, 1744 and later, but globes are not mentioned in any of them. The appearance of the sphere in the 1745 exposure is the only evidence suggesting that it played some part in the more or less impromptu explanations of lodge symbolism which probably came into practice about this time, or shortly afterwards.

(3) In the 1760s and 1770s, Solomon's Pillars *with globes* appear frequently in illustrations of lodge equipment and on aprons, but there is no uniformity of practice. In some lodges (as we have seen and shall see below) the globes were already a recognised part of the lodge furniture; elsewhere they surmounted the pillars, and were probably being 'explained' in 'lectures'. In other places the globes were virtually unknown.

MAPS: MASONRY UNIVERSAL

The tradition that the globes on Solomon's Pillars were covered with celestial and terrestrial maps is certainly post-biblical, and appears to be a piece of eighteenth-century embroidery to the ritual. We may wonder how this interest in earthly and heavenly maps arose, and there seems to be no sure answer. The early catechisms, c1700 to 1730, all indicate a growing interest in the subject, eg:

Q. How high is your lodge?
A. . . . it reaches to heaven.*
    . . . the material heavens and the starry firmament.†

Q. How deep?‡
A. . . . to the Centre of the Earth.‡

There are also the more frequent questions relating to the Sun, Moon and Master Mason, with subsequent variations and expansions.

---

* *Sloane MS*, c1700; Knoop, Jones and Hamer, *The Early Masonic Catechisms*, [*E.M.C.*], 2nd edn., 1963, p 48.
† *Dumfries No 4 MS*, c1710, ibid., p 62.
‡ Prichard's *Masonry Dissected*, 1730, ibid., p 162.

These questions may well be the first pointers towards the subsequent interest in maps, and the armillary sphere of 1745, noted above, carries the subject a stage further.

The Lodge Summons of the Old Dundee Lodge, dated *c*1750, showed three pillars, two of them surmounted by globes depicting *maps of the world and the firmament*. A certificate issued by the Lodge of Antiquity in 1777 displayed, *inter alia*, a similar pair of maps. The 1768 edition of *J. and B.* has an engraved frontispiece showing the furniture and symbols of the lodge, including two pillars surmounted by globes – one with rather vague map markings, and the other clearly marked with stars.

The various sets of geographical globes in pairs, described above (not 'pillar-globes'), all indicate a deep Masonic interest in the celestial and terrestrial globes during the eighteenth century.

Preston, in his *Illustrations of Masonry*, 1775 edition, in the section dealing with the Seven Liberal Arts and Sciences, dwelt at some length on the globes and on the importance of astronomy and, of course, on the spiritual and moral lessons to be learned from them.

All this seems to imply that the maps were beginning to appear at this time, *in the verbal portions of the ritual*. The introduction of maps, 'celestial and terrestrial', led to a further development which eventually gave the Craft a phrase that has become a kind of hall-mark of Freemasonry everywhere. The first hint of that expression appeared in *l'Orde des Francs-Maçons Trahi*, 1745, which added a new question to those passages in the catechism:

Q. And its depth?
A. From the Surface of the Earth to the Centre.
Q. Why do you answer thus?
A. To indicate, that Free-Masons are spread all over the Earth, and all together they form nevertheless only one Lodge.

In 1760, *Three Distinct Knocks* (Antient's ritual) altered the final answer very effectively:

Q. Why is your Lodge said to be from the Surface to the Centre of the Earth?
A. Because that Masonry is Universal.

In 1762, *J. & B.* (Moderns' ritual) gave the same answer, word for word. That is how we acquired the catchphrase 'Masonry Universal'.

THE PILLARS AS ARCHIVES

The biblical accounts of the casting of the pillars make no mention of their being cast hollow, although this may be inferred from the fact that, if they had been solid, their removal from Zeradatha and their final erection at Jerusalem would have been a quite exceptional feat of engineering. *Jeremiah*, lii, v. 21, states that they were formed hollow, the metal being cast to a thickness of 'four-fingers', but there is no suggestion that this was done so that the pillars might serve as 'armoires', or containers of any kind, or that Solomon used them for 'storing the constitutional Rolls'.

Here again is a curious piece of eighteenth-century 'Masonic embroidery', and it seems possible that this was an attempt to link the pillars of Solomon with the two earlier pillars upon which 'all the sciences' had been preserved. The earliest Masonic note I have been able to find on the subject is extremely vague. In 1769, Wellins Calcott wrote in his *Candid Disquisition*, p 66:

> . . . neither are the reasons why they were made hollow known to any but those who are acquainted with the arcana of the society . . .

This was undoubtedly intended to suggest that the hollow pillars were designed to serve some peculiarly Masonic purpose, but Calcott says nothing more on the subject, and I have been unable to trace any such reason for hollow pillars in eighteenth-century Masonic ritual.

THREE LIGHTS: THREE PILLARS: THREE CANDLESTICKS

Seventeen Masonic documents have survived, dated from 1696 to 1730, and they provide the foundation for our study of the evolution of the ritual. The earliest of them is the *Edinburgh Register House MS* (*ERH*), dated 1696, with a valuable description of the two-degree system of those days. The last of that series is Samuel Prichard's *Masonry Dissected* (*MD*), which contains the oldest ritual of the three degrees, and the earliest version of the Hiramic legend. In all these early texts the ritual was mainly in the form of catechism, and we get some idea of its development during those thirty-five years when we compare these two documents. The first contains fifteen questions and answers for the EA, and two for the 'master or fellow-craft'. *Masonry Dissected* has 155 Q and A in all, ie ninety-two for the EA; thirty-three for the FC; thirty for the MM.

THREE LIGHTS

Twelve of the oldest rituals contain a question on the 'lights of the lodge':

Are there any lights in your lodge
yes three . . .

[*ERH*, 1696]

The lights soon acquire a symbolic character, but originally they were probably candles or windows, with particular positions allocated to them, eg 'NE, SW, and eastern passage', or 'SE, S, and SW', etc, until we reach *MD* in 1730, which says the lights are three windows in the E, S and W and their purpose is 'To light the Men to, at, and from their work'. *MD* distinguishes between symbolical lights and 'fix'd lights', explaining that the latter are 'large Candles placed on high Candlesticks'.

Symbolically, several texts say that the lights represent the Master, Warden and fellow-craft. Four versions say 'Father, Son and Holy Ghost. Three others say twelve lights, 'Father, Son, Holy Ghost, Sun, Moon, Master-Mason, Square, Rule, Plum, Line, Mell, Chizzel'. All these are of the period *c*1724–26.

MD says 'Sun, Moon and Master-Mason' and after the question 'Why so?' he answers 'Sun to rule the Day, Moon the Night, and Master-Mason his Lodge'. So we trace the lights from their first appearance in our ritual up to the point where they acquire their modern symbolism.

THREE PILLARS

Extracts from the modern Lecture on the First Tracing Board:

Our Lodges are supported by three great pillars. They are called Wisdom, Strength and Beauty. Wisdom to contrive, Strength to support, and Beauty to adorn . . . but as we have no noble orders in architecture known by the names of Wisdom, Strength and Beauty, we refer them to the three most celebrated, which are, the Ionic, Doric and Corinthian.

The problems relating to the furnishings of the lodge do not end with Solomon's two pillars. As early as 1710 an entirely different set of *three* pillars makes its appearance in the catechisms and exposures. They appear for the first time in the *Dumfries No 4 MS*, which is dated about 1710:

Q. How many pillars is in your lodge?
A. Three.

Q. What are these?
A. Ye square the compass & ye Bible.

The three pillars do not appear again in the eleven versions of the catechisms between 1710 and 1730, but the question arises, with a new answer, in Prichard's *Masonry Dissected*:

Q. What supports a Lodge?
A. Three great Pillars.

Q. What are they called?
A. Wisdom, Strength and Beauty.

Q. Why so?
A. Wisdom to contrive, Strength to support, and Beauty to adorn.

Almost identical questions appeared in the *Wilkinson MS c*1727, and in a whole series of English and European exposures throughout the eighteenth century, invariably with the same answer, 'Three. Wisdom to contrive, Strength to support, and Beauty to adorn'. But the descriptions of actual lodge furnishings in the early 1700s do not mention any *sets of three*, and it seems evident that these questions belong to a period long before there was any idea of turning them into actual pieces of furniture in the lodge-room.

Early lodge inventories are too scarce to enable us to draw definite conclusions from *the absence of references* to any particular items of lodge furnishings or equipment. While it is fairly certain, therefore, that the early operative lodges were only sparsely furnished, it is evident, from surviving eighteenth-century records, that in the 1750s there were already a number of lodges reasonably well equipped. A set of three pillars was mentioned in the records of the Nelson Lodge in 1757, and the Lodge of Relief, Bury, purchased a set of three pillars, for WM, SW and JW, in 1761. To this day, the ancient Lodge of Edinburgh (Mary's Chapel), No 1, now nearly 400 years old, uses a set of three pillars, each about three feet tall. The Master's pillar stands on the Altar, almost in the centre of the Lodge; the other two stand on the floor at the right of the SW and JW respectively. (The three principal officers, there, do not have pedestals.)

Masonry Dissected remained the principal stabilising influence on English ritual until 1760, when a whole new series of English exposures began to appear, all displaying substantial expansion in the floor-work of the ceremonies, and in their speculative interpretation. *Three Distinct Knocks* appeared in 1760, and *J. & B.* in 1762, claiming to expose respectively the rituals of the rival Grand Lodges, 'Antients' and 'Moderns'. Both of them now included several new questions and answers on the 'Three great Pillars' agreeing that 'they represent . . . The Master in the East . . . The Senior Warden in the West . . . [and] The Junior Warden in the South', with identical full explanations of their individual duties in those positions.

It seems likely that these questions were originally intended only to mark the geographical positions of the pillars, but in that period of speculative development the explanations were almost inevitable.

THREE CANDLESTICKS

Apart from Prichard's note in the 1730s on 'large Candles placed on high Candlesticks', the first evidence of *a combination of these two sets of equipment* (that I have been able to trace) is in the records of the Lodge of Felicity, No 58, founded in 1737, when the Lodge ordered 'Three Candlesticks to be made according to the following orders Vizt. 1 Dorrick, 1 Ionick, 1 Corrinthian and of Mahogany . . .'. In the Lodge inventory for Insurance in 1812 they had multiplied and were listed as 'Six Large Candlesticks. Mahogany with brass mountings and nossils, carv'd of the three orders'. In 1739, the Old Dundee Lodge ordered a similar set, still in use today.

The connection is perhaps not immediately obvious, but these were the architectural styles associated with the attributes of the three pillars belonging to the Master and Wardens, 'Wisdom, Strength and Beauty'. The Masonic symbolism of the three pillars had been explained by Prichard in 1730, and it is almost certain that these two Lodges were putting his words into practical shape when they had their candlesticks made up in those three styles.

These two early examples may serve as a pointer to what was happening, but it was not yet general practice, and early evidence of their combined use is scarce. But we can trace the sets of three pillars from their first appearance in the ritual as a purely symbolical question, in which they support the Lodge, and are called 'Wisdom, Strength and Beauty'. Later, they represent the three principal Officers, in the East, South, and West. From the time when they were being explained in this fashion, *c*1730 to 1760, it is fairly safe to assume that they were beginning to appear in the 'Drawings', Floor-Cloths or Tracing Boards. We know, of course, that they appeared regularly in the later versions, but the general pattern of their evolution seems to indicate that they were almost certainly included in many of the early designs that have not survived.

In the 1750s, and the 1760s, we have definite evidence (meagre indeed), that sets of three pillars were already in use as *furniture* in several lodges, and this adds strong support to the view that they had formerly appeared in the Tracing Boards. When, towards the end of the eighteenth century, the lodge rooms and Masonic Halls were being furnished for frequent or continuous use, the three pillars became a regular part of the furnishings, occasionally in their own right, but more often as the ornamental bases for the three 'lesser lights', thus combining the two separate features into the one so frequently seen today.

THE GROWTH OF MASONIC SYMBOLISM

The growth in the number of symbols, as illustrated in the French exposures of the 1740s, and in the English versions of the 1760s, deserves some comment. In the Grand Lodge Museum there is a collection of painted metal templates, belonging apparently to several different sets. There are pillars with globes, a set of two small pillars without globes, and a separate set of three pillars. There is also a set of templates of 'Chapiters and Globes', ie, headpieces only, clearly designed for adding the globes on to normal flat-topped pillars. All these, with many other symbols, were used in drawing the 'designs' on the floor of the lodge. As early as 1737, when the 'floor-drawing' showed only 'steps' and two pillars, it was a part of the Master's duty to explain the 'designs' to the candidate, immediately after he had taken the obligation.* There appears to have been no set ritual for this purpose, and the explanations were doubtless given impromptu. From 1742 onwards there is substantial evidence that the number of symbols had vastly increased,† and this would seem to indicate a real expansion in the 'explanations',

---

* The *Herault Letter*, 1737. See translation in Leics. L. of Research Reprints, No xiv.
† *Le Catéchisme des Francs-maçons*, 1742, and *L'Ordre des Francs-maçons Trahi*, 1745, and in the Frontispiece of a whole stream of English exposures that began to make their appearance from 1762 onwards. All three texts are reproduced in English translation in *The Early French Exposures*, published by the Quatuor Coronati Lodge, No 2076.

implying some sort of dissertation akin to the later 'Lectures on the Tracing Boards'.

Many of these old symbols, which appear frequently on the later eighteenth-century Tracing Boards and in contemporary engravings, etc, have now disappeared from our modern workings, among them the Trowel, Beehive, the Hour-glass, etc, and it is interesting to notice that in the USA, where much of our late eighteenth-century ritual has been preserved, these symbols, with many others, appear regularly on the Tracing Boards.

In this brief essay, I have confined myself only to a few symbolised items of our present-day furnishings whose origins are liable to be clouded because of standardisation, but there is a whole world of interest to be found in the remaining symbology of the Craft.

3

THE TRANSITION FROM OPERATIVE TO SPECULATIVE MASONRY

The Prestonian Lecture for 1957

'. . . WE ARE not operative, but free and accepted or speculative masons . . .' The implication of these words often passes un-noticed by those who hear them. In fact, they summarise· practically the whole history of the craft, and they are a direct link between the present and the past.

The story of the craft in Britain may be carried back safely to the middle of the fourteenth century, but the Freemasonry of today bears no resemblance to the craft organisation of the 1300s. During those 600 years, under the play of industrial, social and economic influences, the craft has suffered enormous changes, and it is the sum total of those changes which makes up the story of the transition from operative to speculative masonry.

To tell the story in detail is a well-nigh impossible task. The masons in medieval England found their main employment at castles, abbeys, monasteries and defence works, far from the large towns, usually under circumstances which were not conducive to any kind of municipal or guild controls. The Fabric Rolls and building accounts which survive, yield much information on wages and working conditions, etc, but virtually no evidence of a stable organisation. Much of the early history of the craft is based upon brief scraps of evidence, valuable in themselves, but apparently unconnected with each other, like random pieces of a jig-saw puzzle, and vital records, which would have made the story clear, have now disappeared. As an example, the earliest surviving *records* of the London Masons'

Company are dated 1620; yet there is definite proof that the Company was in existence in 1472, and a strong probability that the date may be carried back 100 years earlier still.

For these reasons the development of craft organisation, and the story of the 'Transition' in England, cannot be told as a continuous narrative, but rather as a series of glimpses of the craft in its different stages of growth and change. Happily, the story falls into two parts. In Scotland, where a number of early lodge records have miraculously survived, we are able to trace the changes more clearly and, despite important differences in the development of the craft in the two countries, the Scottish records help to throw valuable light on English practice.

THE BEGINNINGS OF MASON CRAFT ORGANISATION IN ENGLAND

In 1356, following a *demarcation dispute* between the mason hewers and the 'setters or layers', twelve skilled masters, representing both branches of the craft, came before the Mayor and Aldermen at Guildhall in London and, with the sanction of the municipal authorities, drew up a simple code of trade regulations.

The preamble to this early code states that '. . . their trade has not been regulated in due manner by the government of folks of their trade, in such form as other trades are'. Here is a clear statement that this was the first attempt to set up a proper governing body for the mason trade, and the first rule in the new code provides the clue to the demarcation dispute. They ordered:

1. . . . that every man of the trade may work at any work touching the trade, if he be perfectly skilled and knowing in the same.

Only seven further rules were made at this time:

2. Sworn masters were to be chosen as overseers, to ensure that no mason undertook work unless he was fully qualified to complete it.
3. No mason was to take contract work 'in gross' unless he could provide four or six men of the trade as sureties, they being responsible for the completion of the work if the original contractor failed.
4. Apprentices and journeymen were to work only in the presence of their masters, until they had been perfectly instructed in their calling.
5. Apprentices were not to be taken for less than seven years.
8. Enticement of apprentices was forbidden, under penalty of a fine for each offence.

Although the text contains no elaborate machinery for government of the craft, such as we find in later codes, the appointment of sworn masters with special duties as overseers shows that this was not going to be an outside committee of management, but an organisation for direct control of the masons and their work. The full extent of this development is not clear at this stage but twenty years later, in 1376, the Guildhall records show that the masons were now one of the 47 'sufficient misteries' (ie recognised guilds) of the City of London, when they were called upon to elect four men of the trade to serve on the Common Council, sworn to give counsel for the common weal, and 'preserving for each mistery its reasonable customs'.*

No comparable mason regulations or records have been traced in Britain before the late fifteenth century, and we are therefore justified in dating the *beginning of mason trade organisation* in England at some time between 1356 and 1376.

In 1389, there is record of a bequest of 12d to the 'Fraternity of Masons, London', and in a will dated 1418, a London mason made provision for a legacy of 6/8d '. . . to the fraternity of my art . . .' and bequeathed '. . . the livery cloak of my old and free mistery . . .' to a colleague. These two items are of interest as evidence of continuity, and there can be little doubt that the 'Hole Crafte and felawship of Masons', which was given a Grant of Arms in 1472, was directly descended from the craft guild whose beginnings we have traced back to *c*1356.

In 1481 a new code of ordinances was published. The Fellowship had been a livery company since 1418 at least, and the new code included regulations for the livery, annual assemblies, election of wardens with powers of search for false work, restrictions against outsiders or 'foreigners', payment of quarterages, and the maintenance of a 'Common Box'; in fact, all the machinery of management for an established craft guild.

Apprentices were 'presented' and booked in the Company's records at the beginning of their terms of service; in some trades, apprentices were 'sworn', and that may have been customary among masons. Access to the freedom was a matter of right to those who had completed their terms, and time-served men were presented before

---

* E. Conder Jr *The Hole Craft and Fellowship of Masons*, 1894, pp 63–5.

the 'Wardens' of the Company and by them 'enabled', ie examined and certified as craftsmen sufficiently skilled to set up as masters. New freemen took an oath of loyalty to the trade, the town and the Crown, but there is no evidence at this time of any kind of secrets, or degrees, or lodge, in connection with the London Masons' Company.

At Norwich there is evidence of some kind of craft organisation amongst masons during the fifteenth century, but elsewhere in the provinces there are no mason guild ordinances until the sixteenth century and even these are so rare as to suggest that the conditions of their employment prevented the masons from setting up the normal type of guild organisation which exercised its powers under municipal sanction.

The guilds were greatly favoured by municipal authorities because they facilitated the management of the towns in matters of wages, prices, taxation and defence. But the really important building works, the castles, abbeys, monasteries and defence works, were usually far from the towns, and masons travelled, often long distances, to find work. When they found it, they would stay on the job for long periods until their work was finished, and they travelled again. This necessary mobility made the guilds unsuitable for the masons, and it explains the dearth of evidence on mason guilds. Instead, they formed themselves into lodges, more or less temporary bodies, governing themselves by long-established craft customs.

THE LODGE

In its primary masonic sense, the word 'lodge' appears in documents of the thirteenth century and later, to describe the workshop or hut, common to all sizeable building works, in which the masons worked, stored their tools, ate their meals and rested.

At places where building works were continuously in progress the lodge acquired a more permanent character. At York Minster, in 1370, an elaborate code of ordinances was drawn up by the Chapter regulating times of work and refreshment in the 'lodge', etc, and new men were sworn to obey the regulations, and not to depart from the work without leave. Probably it was this continuity of employment in one place which gave rise to an extended meaning of 'the lodge' so that it began to imply a group of masons permanently attached to a particular undertaking. Thus, at Canterbury in 1429, we find reference in the Prior's accounts to the 'masons of the lodge,'

(*Lathami de la Loygge*) with lists of their names; but no regulations for this particular body have survived.

Generally, it would appear that these and similar groups of 'attached' masons, which are known to have existed in the middle ages, were wholly under the control of the authorities whom they served. There is no evidence that they exercised any trade controls; they were governed, not governing bodies. The question whether such groups of 'attached' masons might have tended to form themselves into lodges (in our modern sense) is discussed more fully later.

The word 'lodge' appears in a third, and more advanced sense, in Scotland in the sixteenth century, where it is used to describe the working masons of a particular town or district, *organised to regulate the affairs of their trade, and having jurisdiction usually within town or city limits*, but occasionally over a wider area. In their earliest form these lodges, best described as *operative* lodges, were intended primarily for purposes of trade control, and for the protection of the masters and craftsmen who came under their jurisdiction; and, in these functions, the aims of the operative lodge were broadly similar to those of the trade companies, such as the London Masons' Company, described above.*

There was one peculiarity, however, which later distinguished the lodges from the craft guilds or companies. The members of the lodge shared a secret mode of recognition, which was communicated to them in the course of some sort of brief admission ceremony, under an oath of secrecy. In Scotland this system of recognition was generally known as 'the Mason Word', and there is good reason to believe that it consisted of something more than a mere verbal means of identification.

The 'Mason Word' as an operative institution probably came into use in the mid-sixteenth century; and there are a number of references to it in documents from 1637 onwards, sufficient to show that its existence was widely known in Scotland (where several operative lodges can be traced to the sixteenth century). In England, apart from the Old Charges, there is no comparable evidence of any similar organisation amongst operative masons until the early eighteenth century.

* D. Knoop & G. P. Jones, *The Scottish Mason and The Mason Word*. (Manchester University Press, 1939) pp 60–63.

Throughout the remainder of this essay, unless there is some special qualifying note in the text, the word 'lodge' is to be defined as an association of masons (operative or otherwise) who are bound together for their common good, *and who share a secret mode of recognition to which they are sworn on admission.*

THE MS CONSTITUTIONS OR OLD CHARGES*

Our next evidence of development in mason lodge organisation in England, is derived from the *MS Constitutions*, a collection of some 130 texts beginning *c*1390, and running right through to the eighteenth century. Many of them are closely related to each other, and it is possible to group them into some eight distinct 'families', with a number of unclassified versions. Their general pattern, however, is the same all through, and broadly speaking they each consist of three parts:

(i) A opening prayer.

(ii) A fabricated history of the mason craft, in which various biblical and historical characters are all supposed to have had a great love for masons and for the 'science' of masonry. Many of these characters gave the masons 'charges', and the history purports to show how the 'science' was handed down until it was finally established in England. It is probable that this 'history' was compiled in order to provide a kind of traditional background for longstanding craft customs that were embodied in the texts.

(iii) A code of regulations for masters, fellows (ie qualified craftsmen), and apprentices. The texts usually contain *vague* arrangements for large-scale 'assemblies' of masons, implying a widespread territorial organisation; but there is no evidence at all to show whether any such assemblies took place.

Some of the texts contain substantial additions and variations which need not concern us for the present. The two earliest versions are the *Regius MS, c*1390 and the *Cooke MS, c*1410, and the latter contains textual evidence which suggests that its regulations may have been copied from an 'original' text of the 1350s.

* D. Knoop, G. P. Jones & D. Hamer, *The Two Earliest Masonic MSS.* (Manchester University Press, 1938) for transcripts and a valuable study of the oldest versions. For an excellent study of the historical sections, see *The Genesis of Freemasonry*, by Knoop & Jones, 1947, pp 62–85. This chapter is largely based on the above, and on the numerous transcripts of the *MS Constitutions* published in the *Transactions* of the Quatuor Coronati Lodge, No 2076, London.

The actual Charges or regulations form a lengthy and interesting collection. The 'Charges General' related mainly to personal conduct. The 'Charges Singular' were chiefly concerned with trade matters. The following are a few selected items, to give some idea of their contents:

Charges General. Masons were to be true to God and Holy Church, to the King, to their 'Lord' (ie their employer) or Master, to be respectful and true to each other and to respect their womenfolk.

Charges Singular. No Master or fellow should take any work unless he was able and skilful enough to complete it. Masters should take work at reasonable pay, paying their fellows according to trade custom. No apprentice was to be taken for less than seven years, and only if the Master had enough work for two or three fellows at least. Masters were to pay fellows no more than they deserved, so that they were not cheated by false workmen. The Warden was to be a true mediator between Master and fellow. Itinerant masons coming in search of work were to be 'cherished' and given work for two weeks at least; but if there was no work for them, they were to be 'refreshed' with money to the next lodge.

The regulations are addressed to masters and fellows. Where they relate to apprentices, they are usually identical with the kind of conditions that were customarily embodied in apprentices' indentures. Despite these similarities, however, it is important to stress that the regulations in the *MS Constitutions* are *not* guild ordinances, because they lack certain provisions which were an essential feature of all such codes, ie.

(a) Arrangements for election of administrative officers and overseers with powers of 'search'.

(b) Arrangements for annual assembly (and other meetings at specified dates).

(c) Sanction of the municipal authorities, which gave craft ordinances the force of law.

One other feature distinguishes the *MS Constitutions* or 'Ancient Charges' from the normal codes of medieval craft ordinances, ie the inclusion of a number of items in the regulations which were not trade matters at all, but designed to preserve and elevate the moral character of the craftsmen. It is this extraordinary combination of 'history', trade and moral regulations which makes these early MSS unique among contemporary craft documents.

THE MS CONSTITUTIONS IN USE

We have already noted that the texts lack certain distinguishing features which would characterise normal codes of ordinances. In addition to this negative evidence, there are passages in the texts which indicate that the documents were not, originally, designed for use by established bodies of masons permanently located in towns or cities. The infrequent references to 'the lodge' are almost certainly intended to mean 'workshop'; the instruction to the steward that all craftsmen were to be served willingly, and to be charged equally for their food; the instruction to the warden to mediate between masters and fellows; all these points suggest that the documents were primarily intended for those semi-permanent groups of masons who were brought together for a time in the course of their work, and who were, for that very reason, out of reach of established trade organisations in the towns.

At the building of Eton College, c1400–60, and many other great undertakings in the thirteenth to sixteenth centuries where records survive, it is evident that large numbers of masons were in continuous employment for several years on end, and the *MS Constitutions* may well have been designed for use by such groups. It is equally possible that the documents were used by masons attached to ecclesiastical undertakings such as those at York and Canterbury (mentioned above) where, despite proximity to the towns, the masons came wholly under the control of the Church authorities.

It is impossible now to say whether any of these semi-permanent groups of masons did in fact form themselves into lodges. The existence of such lodges in England at any time before the seventeenth century is a matter of pure speculation, for there is no evidence by which we could *prove* that they existed. Yet we may envisage the probability that, in places where there was no kind of trade guild or fellowship, lodges would arise to serve the masons as places of meeting and recreation, where they could discuss trade matters, air their grievances, and settle their disputes. It would be under such conditions that we might expect to see the rise of the English operative lodges.

The texts make provision for an oath of obedience to be taken by new men 'that were never charged before'. This suggests some kind of 'admission ceremony' for newcomers. It would have been a very brief affair consisting of a recital of the opening prayer, with which all versions of the *MS Constitutions* begin, followed by the oath, and a reading of the appropriate 'charges' or regulations, ie a procedure roughly similar to that for admission into a craft company or fellowship.

In some of the later texts, however (and in other contemporary documents) we find a posture for the obligation and evidence of some kind of secret 'words and signes' to which the newcomers were sworn, implying that the *MS Constitutions* were indeed used in 'operative lodges'.

THE RISE AND POWER OF THE OPERATIVE LODGES

Our best evidence on the rise and powers of the operative lodges comes from Scotland where a fine collection of documents relating to the mason trade has survived. The first of these is the 'Seal of Cause',* granted by the Edinburgh authorities in 1475, when the masons and wrights combined to form the Masons and Wrights Incorporation, a single guild for both trades. That document prescribed the rules by which the trades were to be governed, but there were powers to make additional rules, subject to official approval. Each of the trades was to choose two of 'the best and worthiest of their craft' who were sworn 'to search and see' that the craftsmen's work was 'lawfully and truly' done. Apprentices, at the end of their terms of training, were to be examined by the 'four men' to ensure that they were qualified to become fellow craft. If found worthy, they paid the requisite fee and could enjoy their new status. The 'Seal of Cause' does not mention a lodge and there is no evidence of a lodge in Edinburgh at this period.

The Lodge of Edinburgh probably came into being in *c*1500, but its earliest surviving minutes begin in 1599, when it was certainly the head Lodge of Scotland. There we find that the guild's duty of passing EAs as fellow crafts had been taken over by the Lodge.† A magnificent set of town and guild records has survived, and from

---

* J. R. Dashwood & Harry Carr, *Minutes of the Lodge of Edinburgh (Mary's Chapel) No 1.* (QC Lodge, 1962) pp 8–11.
† Ibid, p 46 *et passim*.

these together with Lodge minutes, it is possible to trace the careers of hundreds of masons in the four main stages of their working lives.* Apprentices, at the beginning of their indentures, had to be 'booked' in the town's *Register of Apprentices*. About three years later, they were admitted into the Lodge as 'entered apprentices'. At the end of their terms, if found qualified, they were passed fellow craft in the Lodge. They were now fully-trained craftsmen, and in the smaller places, where there were no controls beyond those imposed by the Lodge, their status was in all respects equal to that of Master, and the titles of 'Master or fellow craft' were often used jointly and synonymously.

In the larger towns or burghs, the FC had to pass the fourth stage of Freeman-Burgess, before he could set up as Master. That was open to all qualified 'indwellers of Edinburgh' on undertaking the duties of 'watch and ward', provision of a weapon for defence, and payment of the requisite fees. Broadly, the Incorporation controlled the mason trade in their duties to the town and to the public at large, eg price-fixing, wage scales and the 'search for false work', while the Lodge controlled the day-to-day internal business of the craft.

In addition to the splendid run of Lodge minutes at Edinburgh, Kilwinning and other Scottish Lodges, there are two codes of regulations, the *Schaw Statutes* of 1598 and 1599, promulgated by William Schaw, Warden-general of the Mason Craft and Master of Works to the Crown of Scotland. The first was addressed to the Masters of the Lodge of Edinburgh 'and all the maister maissounis within this realme'; the second, to the Lodge of Kilwinning, then described as 'secund ludge' of Scotland. From all these sources we can see how the operative lodges exercised their powers.†

They dealt with the admission of entered-apprentices and passing fellow crafts. To restrict the supply of cheap labour, they controlled the number of apprentices that could be taken, no more than three in a Master's life-time without special permission. Runaway apprentices were not to be employed and the enticement of apprentices was a crime. No mason was to take work under a man of another trade (eg under a carpenter) who had undertaken work that belonged to the mason trade. No Master was to take over another Master's work after

* Harry Carr, *The Mason and the Burgh, AQC.* 67, pp 38–42.
† D. Murray Lyon, *History of the Lodge of Edinburgh (Mary's Chapel) No 1*, Tercent. edn. 1903, pp 9–14.

a price had been agreed with the owner, under penalty of £40. All disputes were to be reported to the Warden or Deacon (=WM) within twenty-four hours, under penalty of £10. All faults or defective works were to be reported, under penalty of £10 against the 'concealers'.

Two cases from the minutes of the Lodge of Edinburgh may serve to show how the Lodge dealt with offenders. In 1600, Alex[r.] Schiell, 'servand' to Adam Walker, was accused by his master and several members, of

> . . . the taking of certain works from the ground to the completing thereof . . . over the free masters heads as he confessed by having taken a deposit thereupon . . . [Quoted in modern English].

As a 'servand' Schiell may have been a 'stranger' working as journeyman for Walker, or at best he would have been a time-served entered-apprentice who had not yet passed FC. In the latter status, he was only entitled to take one job of work up to £10 in value, and no more without permission of the 'masters or Warden where they dwell', under penalty of £20.

Schiell had undertaken a complete contract 'over the free masters heads', ie work which belonged only to masters. When charged, he gave a saucy answer, boasting that he had taken a money deposit on the work, and that he would rather quit Edinburgh than submit to their laws. It is virtually certain that he had finished the work. But, as a 'servand' he was in no position to pay a substantial fine, and the Lodge ordered that no master in Edinburgh was to give him employment, under penalty of £40 (approximately three months wages of a skilled craftsman). That was the end of Schiell.*

At the other end of the scale, on 27 December 1679, in the presence of the Deacon, Warden and Brethren of the Lodge, John Fulton, master mason, and Freeman Burgess of Edinburgh, was charged with 'seducing (=enticing) two entered-apprentices belonging to our Lodge . . .'. The Lodge ordered

> . . . that he shall receive no benefit from this place nor no converse with any brother and likewise, his servants (= employees) to be discharged from serving him in his employment . . . until he give the deacon and the masters satisfaction.

---

* Dashwood & Carr, *Mins of the L of Edr, pp 52–3.*

They literally closed him down! Nothing more was heard of Fulton until 12 April 1680. He attended that meeting and on his 'humble petition' in which he acknowledged 'his former fault . . . promised to behave as a brother and never to commit such a fault again in all time coming', he was reinstated. But still he paid a fine of £40, equal to about eight weeks' wages of a Master Mason.*

There were restrictions against the employment of 'strangers'; if labour was scarce and a Master had to employ a 'stranger', he paid a stiff fine for every day the outsider worked for him. There were severe penalties for working with 'cowans', who had never been apprenticed to the trade. At Kilwinning in 1647 the penalty for this offence was £40 Scots, but it varied from time to time, according to the supply of labour. In 1705, the Lodge ordered that.

> . . . if there be one mason to be found within fifteen miles he is not to employ a cowan under penalty of forty shillings Scots (ie only £2)†

One more item may be selected from the many that deserve mention. All Masters were ordered to take special care about the security of their scaffolding and 'walkways', so that their men could work in the utmost safety. That was the Master's personal responsibility. If any man suffered hurt or damage as a result of his Master's carelessness, that Master could never take work again as a Master as long as he lived.‡ Breaches of the regulations were usually punished by fines, which were often doubled if they were not paid at the next meeting; but the lodge had much wider powers. For a serious offence by an employee, the lodge could order that nobody was to give him work. If a Master offended, the lodge could put him out of business by ordering that nobody was to work for him.

It must be remembered that every operative lodge was *the lodge in charge of all the masons within its own territory* and under the system of strict controls they were powerful and they flourished.

OPERATIVE LODGES IN ENGLAND

In England, the Lodge at Alnwick (Northumberland) is the earliest operative lodge whose records survive. They begin with a curious code of operative and 'moral' regulations drawn up in 1701, followed

---

* *Ibid, pp 182—3.*
† Harry Carr, *Lodge Mother Kilwinning No 0,* (QC Lodge 1961); pp 39–43.
‡ D. Murray Lyon, op. cit p 11.

by the minutes up to 1757. There is nothing in the text to indicate whether the lodge was newly erected in 1701, or if it had been in existence before that time. So far as can be ascertained, all the men who were admitted during the period of its earliest records were operative masons.*

Although they styled themselves 'The Company and Fellowship of Free Masons', they met as a lodge, made operative regulations, 'admitted masons', and made them 'free'. Apprentices were 'given their charge' at the time of their entry, and as we know that the lodge possessed a copy of the *MS Constitutions*, we may assume that some part of their ceremonial was based upon a reading of the Charges. The minutes, however, yield no evidence on the subject of ceremonies.

The records of early operative lodges in England are so scarce that it would have been difficult to say whether the Alnwick Lodge is to be considered typical. Fortunately, the minutes survive of another operative lodge, at Swalwell† in Durham, and their general contents are sufficiently similar to those of Alnwick to confirm that these lodges are indeed representative of their time.

In so far as we can compare them with the Scottish operative lodges, they performed a few limited functions of a similar nature, but if they had ever had the range of powers enjoyed by operative lodges north of the Border, they had certainly lost or relinquished them by the early 1700s, when their minutes begin.

At the time of their earliest surviving records, both Alnwick and Swalwell apparently had one rare characteristic in common, ie they were purely operative lodges; so far as can be ascertained, there is no evidence to show that either of them had any non-operative members at this stage.

I have been at some pains to establish the probable nature of the earliest English operative lodges, because a starting point – even a hypothetical one – is essential, if we are to assess the extent of the changes which were involved in the transition from operative to speculative masonry.

---

* W. H. Rylands, 'The Alnwick Lodge Minutes', *AQC*, 14, pp 4–26.
† W. Waples, 'The Swalwell Lodge', *AQC*, 62, pp 89–90. The oldest minute is dated 1725, but there is little doubt that the Lodge was in existence before that date.

LODGES IN COURSE OF TRANSITION

Primarily Operative Lodges

The earliest evidence as to lodges in the transition stage appears in Scotland, where lodges which were purely operative in character began to admit non-operatives, that is to say men who had no connection with the trade at all, as members. They were usually drawn from the local gentry, and occasionally distinguished visitors to the district were also admitted. Generally their status in the lodges was that of honoured guests, and there is no reason to believe that their coming had any immediate effect on the functions or the character of the lodges.

At first, admissions of non-operatives were very rare. At a meeting of the Lodge of Edinburgh (Mary's Chapel) in 1600, John Boswell of Auchinleck attended with William Schaw, Warden General and Master of Works to the Crown of Scotland, but that was not a normal Lodge meeting. It was called for the trial of Johne Broune, 'wairden of ye ludge' who had committed a serious but unspecified offence. They must both have been there in an official capacity; they were not members of the Lodge. (The penalty should have been £40, but moved by 'certain considerations', it was reduced to £10.)

There are no records of non-operative *admissions* into the lodge until 3 July 1634, when Lord Alexander and his brother Sir Anthony Alexander, sons of the Earl of Stirling, with Sir Alexander Strachan, Bart, were separately admitted fellow crafts, presumably receiving the elements of the EA and FC degrees in a single session.*

Later, the minute-book gives us all the information we need to enable us to compare the steady admission of working masons with the infrequent records of non-operative entrants.

Despite its non-operative members, the lodge continued to exercise its functions as an operative lodge right up to the 1700s, making trade regulations for apprentices, journeymen and masters, collecting quarterages and punishing offenders.

At Aitchison's Haven, where lodge minutes begin in 1598, there are records of non-operative admissions in 1672, 1677 and 1693. At Kilwinning (minutes from 1642) there are several records of admissions of nobility and gentry from 1672 onwards.† At Aberdeen,

---

* Dashwood & Carr, *Mins. of the L. of Edr.*, pp 99–102.
† There are occasional minutes recording non-operatives who received both EA and FC in a single session (eg Carr, *Kilwinning*, pp 86, 89) but they are comparatively rare.

where the earliest surviving lodge records are dated 1670, a list of members shows that there were 10 operative master-masons or fellowcrafts on the roll, against 39 non-operatives, drawn from the nobility and gentry, professional men, merchants, and tradesmen.

Like Mary's Chapel all these lodges were still conducting themselves as operative lodges, though there can be little doubt that the Lodge of Aberdeen was already substantially affected by its overwhelming non-operative membership; indeed it made special regulations in 1670 for its gentlemen members. The character of the lodge was beginning to change.

Such lodges as these, during the transition stage, may well be described as 'primarily-operative lodges'.

NON-OPERATIVE LODGES AND ACCEPTED MASONS

In England another stage in the Transition appears during the seventeenth century when we find the first evidence relating to lodges which had nothing to do with the trade at all – purely non-operative lodges.

Perhaps the most interesting of these was the lodge which arose in connection with the London Masons' Company. The Company's early records are lost, but an old account-book survives with entries from 1620. At that time it was a trade-controlling body, governed by a Master and Warden, with a Court of Assistants. Apprentices to the trade, having completed their terms, took up their freedom, paid various fees amounting to 23/10d in all, and came 'on the Yeomanry'; in due course they paid a further £9 and were advanced to 'the Livery'; and the general body of the Company's membership was made up of these two grades.

The first hint of a *lodge* in connection with this trade organisation appears in the *Company's* accounts for 1621:

> Att the making Masons, viz. John Hince, John Browne, Rowland Everett, Evan Lloyde, James ffrench, John Clarke, Thomas Rose. Rd. of them as apereth by the Quartge booke . . . £9. 6s. 8d.

ie an entry for money received from these men, showing an average of 26s. 8d. from each.

At first glance it might appear that they were paying some part of their Company-fees, but the accounts (for 1620) show that three of them were already on the Livery, and another had been on the

Yeomanry for seven years at least. Those men had been masons by trade for years, and it is clear that this business of 'making Masons' was something quite separate from normal trade routine.*

Membership of this separate body was open to the Yeomanry and the Livery, but it was purely optional, and there were working masons of both grades in the Company who were never 'made masons' in this special sense. On the other hand, the records reveal that a *number of men were 'made masons' who were not members of the Company at all, and who in fact were not connected with the mason trade in any way!*

It was perhaps for these entrants from outside the trade that the word 'accepted' came to be used. It appears first in some special sense in 1631 when the accounts show that 6/6 was paid '. . . in goeing abroad and att a meeteing att the hall about ye Masons yt were to bee accepted'. In 1650 an entry shows two men paying the balance of their 'fines . . . for coming on the Liuerie and admission uppon Acceptance of Masonry'; the Acception then cost 20/-; and later, *two strangers* who had no connection with the Company paid 40/- each for 'coming on the accepcon'. It should be stressed that when they joined the Acception these two had been 'made masons' but they still had nothing to do with the Masons' Company, and for that reason they paid twice the normal fee.†

Dr Plot described the business of becoming an Accepted Mason in his *Natural History of Staffordshire* which was written in 1686. After stating that one of the customs of the county was that of admitting men into the Society of Free-Masons, a custom spread more-or-less all over the Nation, he adds that *'persons of the most eminent quality . . . did not disdain to be of this Fellowship'*. Plot's description of the admission ceremony and the purpose of the Society is very brief.

> . . . they proceed to the admission of them, which chiefly consists in the communication of certain secret signs, whereby they are known to one another all over the Nation, by which means they have maintenance whither ever they travel: for if any man appear though altogether unknown that can shew any of these signes to a Fellow of the Society, whom they

---

* Conder, op. cit pp 146, 155, 170.
† Under precise definition the title 'Accepted Masons' is used for men admitted into the 'Acception', or into wholly non-operative lodges. The term 'non-operative masons' is reserved for those unconnected with the mason trade, who were admitted into operative lodges.

otherwise call an accepted mason, he is obliged presently to come to him . . . if he want work he is bound to find him some; or if he cannot doe that, to give him mony, or otherwise support him till work can be had; which is one of their Articles.

Plot has more to say about the Free-Masons, but the extracts above, with other scraps of contemporary information help to show what the 'Accepcon' was doing. It was a Society for 'making Masons', an adjunct of the London Masons' Company. It made 'accepted Masons' out of men who were already masons by trade and members of the Company; it also made 'accepted masons' out of men who had no connection with either the trade or the Company.

Financially, the 'Accepcon' was in the Company's pocket, and its whole income from admission-fees went into the Company's coffers; but from first to last it had no connection with trade affairs. The accounts suggest that its meetings were infrequent, but we cannot be sure of this. The Company's accounts are void of all reference to entertainment expenses for the 'Accepcon' which implies that such charges were defrayed by a whip-round or 'club'. In that case it is possible that meetings were held at frequent or regular intervals, and only admissions were rare.

How long the 'Accepcon' had been in existence before 1620 is a matter of pure speculation. As late as 1677 a minute in the Court Books of the Company ordered the disposal of £6, '. . . which was left of the last accepted masons money . . .' and Ashmole visited the Lodge in 1682, showing that the 'Accepcon' had a continuous and lengthy (if erratic) existence, and may well have served as a pattern for similar organisations elsewhere.*

A point of major importance, which seems to have escaped notice, is that the Company and the 'Accepcon' jointly were exercising practically the same functions as those 'primarily operative lodges' (described *ante*) of which we have several contemporary examples in Scotland. It seems highly probable that the London organisation in two parts and the Scottish Lodge in its 'merged' form represent two alternative lines of development.

Early evidence relating to other non-operative lodges is very scarce. One of the best known cases was the meeting held on 16

---

* Meekren, 'Grand Lodge', *AQC*, 69, was inclined to treat the 'Accepcon' as a series of *ad hoc* or occasional lodges, but this view does not seem to give due weight to the records.

October 1646, at Warrington, at which Elias Ashmole and another gentleman *were made Free-Masons*. The lodge on this occasion consisted of only seven men who were apparently all non-operatives. Apart from the brief reference to this meeting in Ashmole's diary, all contemporary records of this lodge have disappeared. The fact that Ashmole described one of the gentlemen as 'warden', suggests that this was an established lodge, having a continuous existence; but we must envisage the possibility that it was an 'occasional' lodge, ie an assembly of five or six masons, met by inherent right, for the purpose of admitting new masons, and then disbanding without further trace.*

Among the collected papers of the third Randle Holme there is a page of notes giving evidence of the existence of a non-operative lodge at Chester, *c*1672–75. It had some 26 members at least (including Holme himself) mainly belonging to the building trades, but there were other tradesmen, and merchants and gentlemen as well. Little is known of the Lodge at that time, but the fact that all the members appear to have been Chester men, with Holme's known interest in the Fellowship of the Masons, suggests that this was a 'continuous' non-operative lodge whose records are now lost.

There are records of a non-operative lodge at York, with details of admissions from 1712. The gentry were strongly represented in its membership, but Francis Drake in a speech to the Lodge in 1726, addressed himself to the 'working masons', men of other trades, and the gentry, a mixed membership similar to that at Chester.

Unfortunately, we know nothing about the *beginnings* of all these Lodges; we cannot be sure whether they were operative or non-operative in origin, or how far they had changed *before* they make their first appearance in our old records. In Scotland, in 1702, a new Lodge was founded at Haughfoot (near Galashiels) and it occupies a unique place in the history of the Transition for it was the first wholly non-operative Lodge, non-operative at its foundation, and throughout its existence.

THE STAGES IN THE TRANSITION

In the preceeding pages I have sketched very briefly the evolution

---

* In Scotland, 'out-entries' (ie the admission of EA's or FC's away from the lodge) were not uncommon, and quite legal, provided there was a quorum of five or six members (usually including an officer of the lodge) and the 'entries' were reported at the next meeting of the lodge, when the requisite fees had to be paid. Carr, *Kilwinning*, pp 121–27.

of mason trade and lodge organisation up to the stage at which the lodges were beginning to lose their strictly operative purpose. Conditions were not uniform everywhere, and the lines of development varied considerably in different places but, so far as we can follow the stages generally, their sequence seems to have been as follows:

(1) The formation of mason guilds or companies, scarce in England.

(2) The evolution of operative lodges in places where there were no official trade organisations. These would have been contemporaneous with (1).

(3) Operative lodges taking over the internal management of the craft and working side by side with the Incorporations, which controlled the *external functions* of the trade in relation to wages, prices, and the protection of the customer and the public at large from 'false work' and faulty materials.

(4) The admission of non-operatives into operative lodges.

(5) The transition from wholly operative to non-operative status, by an actual change in the character and composition of the lodge. There were two contributory causes: (a) diminishing powers of trade control; (b) the admission of non-operatives.

(6) The rise of wholly non-operative lodges, having secret 'words and signes', but being mainly associations for social, and convivial purposes.

(7) In the eighteenth century, the rise of the 'speculative' influence in the lodges, and the gradual evolution of 'speculative' freemasonry.

In Scotland, perhaps because of the close connection between the crafts organisations and the municipal authorities, the minute-books of several old lodges have survived, and it is possible to trace the various stages in the transition, as recorded by the participants. Perhaps the best example for our purpose is the Lodge of Edinburgh, Mary's Chapel, whose minutes run virtually unbroken from 1599 to the present day.

THE REASONS FOR THE TRANSITION
The Transition in Edinburgh

The attendance records of the three gentlemen who were admitted (honorary) members of the Lodge of Edinburgh, and of the very few non-operatives who were admitted in the later 1600s, indicate that their interest in the Lodge was of brief duration; they were present at a few meetings and then disappeared. This implies that they probably played no part in any structural changes in the character of the lodge, although we know that the admission-ceremonies were modified for their benefit.

At no time during the seventeenth century was the non-operative membership high enough to 'swamp' the lodge, and there is absolutely no evidence to suggest that they were trying to make any changes. On the contrary, there is good evidence that the changes were largely due to economic causes.

The first evidence of decline appears c1650 when the town records reveal that a large proportion of the apprentices who were being entered in the lodge had never been 'Booked' in the *Register of Apprentices*. This is even more noticeable in the period 1671–90 when there was an enormous increase in the number of apprentices 'entered', without any corresponding rise in 'Bookings'. Municipal regulations required all Apprentices to be 'Booked' as an essential preliminary to their ultimate freedom, and the frequent breaches of this rule indicate that craftsmen were able to find ample employment outside the jurisdiction of the town.

During the same period 1676–90 the Lodge records show a marked reluctance on the part of its 'entered-apprentices' to take on their full responsibilities as craftsmen, by passing as Fellow-Crafts. In 1677, following a series of disastrous fires, the Edinburgh Town Council ordered that all ruined buildings should be rebuilt in stone. As a result, there was plenty of work available, and apprentices who had finished their terms of service were able to make a living as journeymen, without having to bear the financial burdens of becoming 'Fellowcraft or Master'. In effect, the Lodge was losing men who should have been its 'full members', and who were its main source of income.

In 1681, The Lodge ordained that any master who employed EAs who remained 'unpassed' for more than two years after they had completed their terms of service, was to pay a fine of 20/- per day, a very stiff penalty. This, and similar edicts in the succeeding years, helped to check the decline.*

* Dashwood & Carr, *Edinburgh*, pp 192–3.

But the whole idea of *compulsory passing* was out of keeping with the basis of craft organisation, which had centred on the principle of trained apprentices *earning their promotion* to the rank of FC by proving their qualifications in an essay, or test of practical skill. If entered apprentices were *compelled* to pass FC within two years of their discharge, there could be no question of a real qualifying test. From about this time, the 1680s, we may date the gradual change in the character of the Lodge, from a 'closed-shop' association of skilled craftsmen to a trade association of 'members', ie, a society in which actual numbers and Lodge income were to become more important than technical skill.

There were many other difficulties with which the Lodge had to contend. From 1673 onwards, the minutes show that the Edinburgh masons were greatly troubled by the intrusion of itinerant labour from outside the city. Severe penalties were ordained against masters who employed these 'inhibited men' but with little avail.*

In 1677 a new Lodge was founded in the Canongate, which was a separate burgh adjoining the eastern part of the city of Edinburgh. The Canongate had had its own Incorporation of Wrights, Coopers, and Masons, since 1585, and the new Lodge† was outside the jurisdiction of the Lodge of Edinburgh. A rival Lodge on their doorstep!

In 1688 yet another Lodge was founded, this time by masons seceding from Mary's Chapel.‡ Despite protests and the threat of penalties, only one of the seceders ever returned to Mary's Chapel, and the new Lodge continued to flourish. The enormity of this blow can only be judged when we remember that up to this time every operative lodge was *the* lodge of its own district, and had full control over all the masons in its own area. No operative lodge could function properly if it had a rival in its own territory, and the very existence of these rivals was proof that Mary's Chapel was losing the strong local trade control which it had formerly exercised.

In 1682, the Lodge of Edinburgh ordained that a fee of 12/- per annum was to be paid by all journeymen-masons who did not belong to the Lodge, the income to be used for benevolent purposes, and, from 1688 onwards the minutes reveal an ever-increasing interest in

---

* Ibid, pp 172–3, 198–9.
† Now Lodge Canongate Kilwinning No 2 (SC).
‡ Now Lodge Canongate and Leith, Leith and Canongate, No 5 (SC).

financial matters, with much time devoted to the lending of idle money, collection of debts and inspection of accounts. The Lodge was acquiring some of the characteristics of a benefit society.

In 1708 the Lodge ran into difficulties with its own journeymen, who complained that they had not got a proper oversight of the Lodge accounts and funds. It was a prolonged dispute which ended in the Law Courts in 1715, when the journeymen won the right to maintain a Lodge that they had set up in Edinburgh,* and to confer the 'Mason Word'. This was yet another blow to the power and status of the mother Lodge, but the final stage in the Transition was still to come.

In December 1726, one of the members, James Mack, reported that a number of 'creditable tradesmen' in the city were anxious to join the Lodge, and were each of them willing to give 'a guinea in gold for the use of the poor'. The proposed candidates were all men from other trades, and although the golden guineas were very tempting, the diehard operatives in the Lodge rejected the proposal.

A month later, Mack returned to the attack at a meeting of seven masters (mainly friends of his) which he had apparently called without permission of the Master of the Lodge. The question of the proposed admissions was re-opened, and there was a thundering row. The Master and Warden 'walked out', and the remaining five proceeded to elect new officers, choosing Mack as 'preses' or Master. The Lodge then admitted the Deacon of the Wrights as a joining FC; three 'entered-apprentices' from other lodges, all non-operative, were admitted and passed FC; and seven burgesses, none of them masons, were received 'entered apprentices and fellow crafts'.† In February 1727 another eight non-operatives were admitted, and the operative character of the Lodge was completely lost. The extent of the change may be judged from the fact that in 1736, when the Lodge compiled its first code of Bye-laws, not a single regulation was made which concerned the mason trade. The 'Transition' was complete!

In the few Scottish lodges where adequate records survive,‡ the changes followed much the same pattern as at Mary's Chapel, and

---

* Now the Lodge of Journeymen, No 8 (SC).
† These men of other trades who received both degrees in one evening, were treated much better than the masons themselves, who waited approx. seven years between the grades of 'Entered Apprentice' and 'Fellow Craft'. Dashwood & Carr, *Edinburgh*, pp 278–282.
‡ eg Lodge Mother Kilwinning No 0 and the Lodge of Aberdeen No 1ter.

generally it is clear that the main reasons for the changes were purely economic. The rapid growth of the towns, and the ability of craftsmen to find employment readily outside the jurisdiction of Lodge and Incorporation, led to a decline in the trade-controlling powers of the lodges, so that they began to pay more attention to social and charitable works than to their old functions of trade control. The unrestricted admission of non-operatives was an additional factor in helping to develop the social and convivial aspects of the lodges which, when their trade functions had faded altogether, were ready for those 'speculative' influences which began, very gradually, to come in.

THE TRANSITION IN ENGLAND

In England, however, the reasons for the changes are not so easily explained, chiefly because of the absence of early lodge records.

We premise that here, as in Scotland, the purest or most perfect type of operative lodge combined two functions, ie, trade control, and the communication of 'secrets'. Thus we may treat the Lodges at Alnwick and Mary's Chapel as virtually identical organisations, and the London Masons' Company *in conjunction with the 'Accepcon'* as a similar type of organisation at a different stage of development.

There is no evidence that the Acception had been a part of the London Masons' Company in the earlier stages of the Company's history. On the contrary, the manner in which Acception items appear in the Company's account-book suggests that it was a sort of side-line probably intended at first for members of the Company alone.

Next we observe that the 'Accepcon' was beginning to admit non-operatives though their fees still went into the Company's box. Unlike the arrangements in the Scottish lodges, the situation here was such that when economic pressures began to play a part, it was the Trade Company that was affected, while the Acception probably remained untouched.

As regards English masons, the strongest economic forces came into play after the Great Fire of London in 1666, when it became necessary to encourage alien and 'foreign' builders from outside London to come into the city. In four days 13,000 houses, 400 streets and 89 churches had been destroyed by the fire. All sorts of privileges were offered to newcomers. The old restrictions against 'intruders' and the customary requirements in regard to apprenticeship and 'freedom' were all discarded. All incoming labourers in the building trades were to have the same rights as full freemen of the Crafts for seven years, (and more if necessary), until the city was rebuilt. By this Act of 1667, Parliament practically deprived the Company of its chief trade-controlling powers.*

From about this time we may date the multiplication of lodges in London, for there can be little doubt that the immigrants brought their own particular customs and practices. It may be from this period that we can date the curious mixture of Scottish and English practices which appear to have been embodied in early versions of the masonic ritual.

It may be noted that whatever lodges there were in London at that time (including the 'Accepcon') were practically void of any real connection with trade affairs. Just as the rapid growth of Edinburgh had brought about a diminution in the trade-controlling powers of Mary's Chapel, so in London the urgent need for builders had deprived the Masons' Company of its influence; and the lodges, ephemeral at first, and having no anchorage in the way of trade functions, tended to become mere social and convivial clubs of masons, of mixed membership,† still practising the procedure of 'making masons', but with little or no interest in the trade. Unfortunately, no records survive of these early lodges save those relating to the four (at least) which were in existence in London when the first Grand Lodge was founded in 1717.

THE SOCIAL OR CONVIVIAL PHASE

Feasting and drinking was no novelty in masonic life, and the term 'convivial masonry' (for lack of a better description) does not imply a decadent period in craft history. In the days of the earliest social and religious guilds, and later in the trade guilds and livery companies, ale-drinkings, dinners and feasts were an important adjunct to the regular business of each meeting.

At Edinburgh in the late fifteenth century there are many records of new burgesses paying for their freedom with 'spices and wine', a banquet, and in England the records of the trade companies in all the larger cities show that the provision of a breakfast, dinner or banquet

---

* Conder, op cit pp 183–6 and 192.
† ie, operative and non-operative.

was one of the recognised expenses of the freedom. In Scotland generally there are numerous regulations as to the banquets to be provided by masons when they became fellows-of-craft, and occasionally by apprentices at their 'entry', and it is probable that similar practices were customary amongst English masons.

The Scottish lodge minutes show that with the gradual diminution of their authority and power in trade matters, the lodges began to acquire the characteristics of social and benevolent clubs, collecting funds for their 'poor', lending money at interest, and meeting annually (if not more frequently) for their feasts. Despite the lack of records, there can be no doubt that English operative masonry followed a somewhat similar pattern in the course of the Transition.

It is impossible to date this phase of convivial masonry with any degree of accuracy. We must first of all discard our present-day notion of all lodges under the control of a Grand Lodge, all working under the same regulations, and all practising the same rites. Up to the early eighteenth century each lodge was virtually a law unto itself; generally it made its own regulations, and it was subject only to the changing conditions of the trade in its own locality.

For these reasons the symptoms of decline and change did not make their appearance simultaneously. In England the evolution of 'convivial masonry' probably began in the mid-seventeenth century, and the Acception in the 1620s may be a good example of this type of Lodge without any operative *'raison d'être.'*

In Scotland, where the lodges generally were still exercising operative controls in the late seventeenth century, the convivial phase seems to have begun in the early 1700s, but the whole business was a very gradual one. The lodges, slowly bereft of their original purpose and functions, and having no specific aims, continued as social clubs throughout a period of decline, until the Speculative renaissance gave them a new sense of direction.

THE ADVENT OF SPECULATIVE MASONRY

In the course of this essay, some care has been taken to avoid the use of the adjective 'speculative' in relation either to lodges or their members. In our present-day sense of the word as applied to the Craft, it means 'a peculiar system of morality, veiled in allegory, and illustrated by symbols'. If this definition be adopted, it is highly improbable that the word could be used in relation to any of the seventeenth century lodges, either in England or Scotland.

The advent of 'Speculative' Masonry is a problem directly connected with the subject of early Masonic ritual. The origins or sources of the ritual are unknown. We assume that at some early date, perhaps before the fourteenth century, the masons as a craft possessed a body of customs, craft-lore and, at a later stage, 'secrets', from which the earliest elementary masonic ceremonies ultimately evolved. There is little doubt that they were known in Scotland before 1600, and in England before 1620.

Our earliest evidence as to the actual contents of the craft ritual is drawn from a series of masonic *aide-memoires* compiled *c*1696–*c*1714, all having a distinctly Scottish flavour. Despite their dubious origin it has been shown that these texts do represent the ceremonies as practised at that time, and perhaps even a century earlier.* They depict a rite of two degrees, 'entered apprentice', and 'master or fellow craft', each containing an obligation, entrusting with 'secrets' and a series of questions and answers.† The texts contain nothing that might be described as *speculative* masonry, and on these documents alone there would be no grounds to infer that they are the same ceremonies as were practised in England generally, or in the London Acception.

Nevertheless, it seems likely that both English and Scottish ritual drew their inspiration from the same sources. There is a whole series of later texts *c*1700–30, including several of non-Scottish origin, and it is possible to trace in them a nucleus of ritual that seems to have been common to both countries. This nucleus of 'catechism and esoteric matter' was probably the basis of the masonic ceremonies throughout the stages of operative, non-operative and accepted masonry.‡

Since we cannot set a precise date to the period of so-called 'convivial' masonry, which preceded the speculative reformation, the next question arises, 'when and how did the reformation begin'? In Scotland, the trade functions of the lodges helped to prevent any rapid changes, and it is possible that there were no real speculative developments until the 1730s. In all Scottish lodges where early minutes survive, this reluctance to change is a marked characteristic.

* Carr, *600 Years of Craft Ritual*, AQC, 81 pp 158–9.
† *EMC*, pp 31–43.
‡ Ibid, pp 71–5 for the first *printed* exposure, 1723. All the texts collected in this work are interesting, and Prichard's *Masonry Dissected*, ibid, pp 157–70, shows useful evidence of early speculative expansion.

The same is true of Alnwick, where the Lodge functioned as an operative lodge until 1748, when it was virtually re-constituted as a speculative body.

In England, it seems likely that the changes began in the Acception, which was (so far as is known) the only Lodge completely void of any trade functions, and it was perhaps the first lodge in England to admit non-operative masons. If it did in fact practise a ceremony related to the 'nucleus', we know that the questions and answers, very simple in themselves, were such as would lend themselves readily to Speculative expansion.

In this connection, we have to consider the kind of men who were beginning to take an interest in the society. As early as 1646, when Ashmole was made a Freemason in a Lodge composed mainly of gentlemen-masons, the craft in England was already attracting men of quality and learning; indeed all the seventeenth century commentators on the craft confirm this, either directly or by implication.

The reasons for this widespread interest are not known, but if the gentry were seeking anything more than mere companionship and conviviality they must have been sadly disappointed. The 'words and signes', which had formed an additional bond for men who were already united in service to an ancient craft, must have been almost meaningless when they were divorced from their operative roots and purposes.

We can only speculate as to whether these seventeenth century accepted (or non-operative) masons were in any way responsible for the changes which subsequently arose in the ritual practices, and in the aims of the craft. At the end of the century however, and in the first two decades of the eighteenth century, there was another revival of interest in the craft, which resulted in the formation of the first Grand Lodge. Its original and expressed objects were very modest, ie, to constitute an organisation under a Grand Master, to revive (?) or hold Quarterly Communications and an annual feast. The new body apparently neither claimed nor hoped for any wider jurisdiction than the few lodges in London and Westminster. But within a few years the Grand Lodge had gained adherents far and wide and the men who had been in the forefront of the movement had the requisite machinery to hand for propagating the ideas and ideals which were at the root of the Speculative transformation.

The earliest evidence from which we can infer some kind of

modification of the ceremonies appears in Scotland in the 1600s,* and it was a change which could never have come naturally in a purely operative lodge. We have no textual evidence of subsequent changes until the eighteenth century. In these later texts, side by side with the evidence of re-arrangement, we also find a certain amount of Speculative expansion, innovation and embellishment, which gives some sort of hint of what was taking place.

Undoubtedly, the formation of the Grand Lodge in 1717 was a decisive step towards the Speculative revival, but it was a slow process. The convivial phase did not disappear instantly; indeed smoking and drinking inside the lodge were quite customary throughout the eighteenth century.

But a new meaning and purpose was given to the ceremonies as the Craft gradually emerged from its aimless phase. From about 1730, largely as a result of the publication of 'Exposures', there is evidence of a certain amount of standardisation of the ritual, but it was not until the 1760s and 1770s that the Craft began to acquire that unique combination of symbolism with the teaching of religious and moral principles, which have helped to make it a real 'centre of union between good men and true'.

---

*Non-operatives were admitted in a kind of 'combined' ceremony, to the status of FC, whereas masons waited some seven years between EA and FC.

4

LODGE MOTHER KILWINNING, No 0

This essay, reproduced by courtesy of the Leicester Lodge of Research, No 2429, from its Transactions for 1960–61, is a précis of the full-length history, *Mother Lodge Kilwinning, No 0*, 1642–1842, by the same author, which was published by the Quatuor Coronati Lodge, No 2076. It is now out of print.

KILWINNING AND THE *SCHAW STATUTES*, 1599

KILWINNING, IN Ayrshire, on the right bank of the Garnock, about 24 miles SW of Glasgow, is today a town of some 7,000 inhabitants. In 1755 its population was 2,541, and in the 1600s, the period with which we are mainly concerned, it can have been little more than a village. It took its name after St Winnin who lived there in the eighth century, and the great glory of this little place was the Abbey of Kilwinning, founded probably between 1140 and 1190. When it was completed it must have been one of the noblest structures on the west coast of Scotland.

The abbey and monastery, however, did not play any great part in Scottish history, and its chief interest for us in our present study lies in the ancient tradition that it was the birthplace of Freemasonry in Scotland and that the Lodge, supposed to have been founded by the monastery builders, was the Mother Lodge of the Craft in the west of Scotland. Unfortunately, no documentary evidence has survived to support this theory.

The earliest surviving document which relates to *the mason trade at Kilwinning* – is the code of regulations known as the *Schaw Statutes* of 1599. They were promulgated by William Schaw, Master of Works to the Crown under James VI and Warden General of the Mason Craft. They show that at this date, 1599, the mason lodge at Kilwinning was of such standing as to be described by him as the '. . . heid and second ludge of Scotland . . .', and that it was then vested with substantial trade-controlling powers over a wide area.

It granted Charters to some 34 new lodges, and claimed allegiance

72

from them; it enjoyed a nationwide respect amounting almost to reverence, and it was, masonically, a law unto itself for more than two centuries.

William Schaw issued two main codes of regulations. The first, dated 28 December 1598, consisted of '. . . statutis and ordinanceis to be obseruit be all the maister maissounis within this realme . . .' [of Scotland]. It was directed to the mason craft throughout Scotland; its regulations were deemed to apply to all masons in that kingdom, and no single lodge is specifically mentioned in this code.

The second code of regulations was dated 28 December 1599, and that document was clearly addressed to the Lodge of Kilwinning alone. It contained regulations and provisions which may have held good in mason communities all over Scotland; it defined the relationship of the Lodge of Kilwinning to other masonic bodies, but essentially it was intended for Kilwinning.

It is not merely the oldest document relating to the Lodge, but is of special importance in regard to its authenticity and impartiality, because the regulations which it contains were not drawn up by the Lodge itself but were promulgated for the Lodge under the authority of an officer of the Scottish crown.

Broadly the regulations fall into three distinct groups:

(a) Regulations which define the status of the Lodge in relation to the whole craft in Scotland.

(b) Regulations which define the status and powers of the Lodge in relation to other Lodges within its own territory.

Briefly, Kilwinning was given powers over all the Lodges in an area of roughly 1,000 square miles, with the right to have her representatives present at the elections of all Deacons and Wardens, to convene them when needed, and to make whatever regulations were required to preserve good order in the Craft.

It should be noted, however, that no contemporary records have survived of any of these lodges which were 'subject to' Kilwinning, and it is extremely doubtful whether any such widespread organisation really existed. The earlier Kilwinning minutes show that the Lodge regularly appointed its own quartermasters in places far distant from Kilwinning, but there is no hint (*in the early records*) of any lodges subject to the Mother Lodge.

(c) Regulations for the proper management and 'guid ordor' of the Lodge

They included provisions for the admission of Apprentices and Fellows of Craft, fees of entry, the imposition of 'essays', annual examinations with power to fine any who failed their test. Kilwinning was to hold an Annual Court 'to take trial of offences' with powers to expel the disobedient and punish offenders.

It is not easy to appraise the accuracy of this code of 1599 in regard to some of its provisions (eg banquets, examinations, etc) because the Lodge Minutes afford no evidence on those practices. The main importance of this text lies in the confirmation which it gives of the existence of the Lodge in 1599 as a headquarters of mason trade-control on the west coast of Scotland, exercising its powers by sanction of the highest authority, while the frequent references to ancient acts and statutes, apparently so well known that they did not need to be repeated, suggest a high degree of organisation within the craft at Kilwinning, though it must be admitted that no evidence of such organisation prior to 1599 has survived.

That a mason Lodge existed here before 1599 is certain beyond reasonable doubt; but it is likely that we shall never know when the Lodge came into being, or whether it had any kind of continuity of existence before 1599.

Reg. 3 places Edinburgh as the 'first and principall ludge in Scotland', with Kilwinning second, and Stirling third.

There is no suggestion here that Kilwinning or Stirling were in any way subservient to Edinburgh, and it is evident that the regulation deals here with three 'head' lodges, each supreme in its own territory. Thus, although Kilwinning is frequently described as the 'second Ludge of Scotland', the first regulation puts the situation more accurately with the phrase '. . . the heid and second Ludge of Scotland . . .'.

THE OLDEST MINUTES, 1642
Re-organisation or Revival?

The oldest surviving minutes of the Lodge are dated 20 December 1642, and there is no indication of its activities during the 43 years which had elapsed since the *Schaw Statutes* were published in 1599. From 1642 onwards, with few exceptions, the minutes were kept regularly, and despite the religious and other troubles which afflicted the country the old Lodge books provide practically an unbroken record of one of the oldest and most famous lodges in the world.

The first minute poses a problem, because it only needs a glance at the subsequent minutes to see that this assembly in 1642 was not an ordinary lodge meeting. The minute runs:

xx December 1642
In the Ludge of Kilwinning convenit of the maissoun craft the persons following and Inrollit thame selffis in the said Ludge and submittit thame selffis thairunto and to the actis and statutis thairof . . .

followed by the names of 26 apprentices and fellows-of-craft, all with their marks attached. No other business was recorded. These men convened, enrolled themselves in the lodge, and promised to submit to its rules and regulations – and that was all they did.

If we were not sure that the Lodge had been in existence since 1599, we might well believe that this was the foundation of a new lodge, but it was not. The only interpretation of the minute is that this meeting was called either to revive a dormant lodge, or to reorganise it after a period of internal trouble. There is valuable evidence on this question in the minutes of 1644 when John Smithe, who was present as a fellow-craft in 1642, paid the balance of his fees for admission as a fellow-craft, which had taken place *some time before* 1642.

Several other arguments might be added, but John Smithe's payment in 1644 makes it certain that the 1642 meeting was a reorganisation.

THE SECOND MEETING

The next recorded meeting was held on 20 December 1643, and 20 December became the regular date for the Annual Meetings.

The Court of the Ludge . . . holdin in the vpper chamber of the Duelling hous of hew smithe . . .

From 1643 onwards and for many years afterwards the Kilwinning meetings were held in Hew Smithe's upper chamber. Incidentally, his name does not appear in any of the early rolls of those present at meetings, and it is highly probable that he was not a mason. In that case his house was probably chosen for its size, its accessibility 'at the Cross of Kilwinning' and perhaps for the quality of the liquid refreshment which was doubtless available in his, as in many other Scottish 'dwelling-houses' at that time.

The unusual nature of the business transacted by the brethren at this meeting, tends to confirm that the Lodge was being reorganised. There was a restatement of the old powers for excluding the disobedient and procedure for the admission of 'fellow-crafts or masters'. They fixed a new scale of quarterage, imposed fees-of-honour to be paid by the principal officers, and made arrangements for an annual meeting in July at Kilbarchan, a village about 15 miles north of Kilwinning, in addition to the regular meeting on 20 December.

The Kilbarchan meeting was designed to provide for the masons living in Kilwinning's northern territory, and fines for absence were fixed at 20/- or 40/-, according to distance, apprentices paying only half those sums. As 40/- represented more than one-third of a skilled mason's weekly wage, the penalties for non-attendance were quite severe!

All sums quoted in this paper are reproduced from the original minutes in Scots money. To arrive at the Sterling equivalents divide by twelve, ie £1 Scots equals 1/8d Sterling. One Merk Scots, ie 13/4 Scots, equals 1/1½d Sterling at that time.

The best rough guide however is to compare these sums with the mason's wages. In summer (ie at the period of highest earnings), a skilled mason in Scotland received £5 6s 8d Scots per week, ie 8/11d Sterling.

In addition to all this, there was the ordinary annual business, ie the election of Deacon and Warden (corresponding roughly to our Master and Treasurer), the appointment of Quartermasters as representatives of the Lodge in its outlying districts (whose main duty was the collection of Quarterage) and the appointment of a local lawyer to serve as Clerk.

It was indeed an enormous day's work, the only meeting of its kind in the whole history of the lodge, and after this date the minutes take on a more normal character, recording the routine proceedings of an Operative Lodge.

AN OPERATIVE LODGE IN ACTION

We may imagine the Lodge meetings held in the first-floor room of a house in a little Scottish village in the depths of winter. Attendances were small, ten or fifteen men, including apprentices, and several of them had travelled many miles, on dreadful roads, in order to be present.

The early minutes describe the lodge as:

The Court of the Mason Trade of the Lodge of Kilwinning . . .

The Court was 'lawfully affirmed' and proceedings began with a Roll-call and fines for absentees. The lists of names of those present and absent during the 1640s indicate a total membership of about 40, ie about 25 'fellows of craft or masters', and 15 apprentices. Fines were collected and recorded. Men owing money for previous absence would pay up on the spot, or furnish guarantors for payment in future.

There would be the usual entry of apprentices, and admission of fellows-of-craft. A typical minute of this kind on 19 December 1646.

> The qlk day the wardane deacone & remanint brethrein of the Maissoun tred within the forsaid ludge presentis ressauit and acceptit Hew Miller maissoun in Paisley, William Craufurd in Braidstaine, John Miller in Air, Robert Cauldwell fellow brethrein to ye said tred quha hes sworne to ye standart of ye said ludge *ad vitam*. As also hes ressauit ye persones following enter prenteiss to ye said craft Robert Corruithe, John Cauldwell. Allane Cauldwell Jon Craufurd & Andro Hart.

and there is no hint of ceremony except that the fellow-craft swore the oath *ad vitam*.

Then there would be the election of Officers, a democratic affair with a 'leet' of two or three candidates for each office, and quite often all the votes for each candidate were carefully recorded. After this the Lodge would settle down to its business as a 'Court' dealing with offenders. The early minutes afford many examples.

> xx December 1645
> Item they have ordainit that no man sal tak in wark Patrik Greir Robert Cauldwell & John Corruithe nor geve them ony service till they have satisfiet ye craft for thair saids unlaues [= fines] and dissobedienc nayther sall ony wark to thame till they have satisfiet as said is Vnder ye paine of ten merkis of Vnlaw for ilk contravener.

In this case three men had incurred the Lodge's displeasure. According to the minutes of 1644 their crime was a modest one; they had been absent from an appointed meeting, and they were duly fined. Normal procedure in such cases was to pay, or to promise payment, but these three men must have put up an argument, with disastrous results, and we see the full power of the Lodge in action. *No man was to employ the culprits or render them any service, and no man was to work for them until they had made amends.* The Lodge could decide whether a mason would work or not and it could deprive him of his livelihood.

> A year later (19 December 1646)
> . . . Heu Mure in Kilmarnok wes decernit to pay to the box ten merkis money of vnlaw for wirking with cowanes contrair to ye actis & ordinances of the said ludge . . .

The Lodge was being generous. 'Ten merks' was only £6 13s 4d, and Mure had already been threatened with a fine of £40.

The first official ban against cowans is one of the regulations in the Schaw Statutes of 1598, here given in modern spelling:

> Item: that no master or fellow of craft receive any cowans to work in his society or company, nor send any of his servants to work with cowans, under the penalty of twenty pounds for each offence under this rule.

The word 'cowan' is defined as 'One who builds dry stone walls (ie without mortar); a dry-stone-diker; applied derogatorily to one who does the work of a mason, but has not been regularly apprenticed or bred to the trade.' – (OED). From our point of view, a better definition is to be found in the minutes of Mother Kilwinning for 1705, probably the most-quoted minute in the whole body of masonic literature:

> the same day by consent of the meetting his aggried that no meason shall imploy no cowan which is to say without the word to work if ther be one masson to be found within ffifftin mylls he is not to imploy one cowan under the paine of fortie Shilling Scots. (– 20*th December*, 1705, *folio* 103).

In order to clarify this regulation it is transcribed here in modern spelling with the addition of three words and modern punctuation:

> The same day by consent of the meeting [it] is agreed that no mason shall employ a cowan, which is to say [one] without the [mason] word, to work. If there be one mason to be found within fifteen miles, he is not to employ a cowan, under the penalty of forty shillings Scots.

'Without the word', ie the 'Mason Word', which was conferred upon entered apprentices upon their first admission into the Lodge. By inference therefore a cowan was an untrained worker in stone, who had not been apprenticed, and who was not connected with a mason Lodge.

It is often difficult to understand how this Scottish prejudice against cowans arose, especially as there must have been innumerable unskilled jobs for which these men would have been well suited. Perhaps the main reason is revealed in that phrase in the Kilwinning minute giving a 15 mile limit, ie the employment of cowans was forbidden because it was bad for the trade as a whole, and it was only to be tolerated in extreme cases when no qualified employees were available within a fifteen mile radius, a great distance in those days.

At Kilwinning, where the authority of the Lodge extended over a wide area, cowans were a fairly constant source of trouble, and the Lodge regulations prohibiting their employment were frequently enforced.

Apart from the records relating to cowans, the Kilwinning minutes are curiously silent as to the actual details of the offences which were judged and punished during the seventeenth and eighteenth centuries. The names of the offenders and the penalties were recorded, usually a substantial fine and disbarment from all employment until it was paid.

As the story of the Lodge unfolds itself in the pages of the minute-book there is ample evidence of the difficulties which it encountered in the administration of the craft over a vast area, and it is strange to see how the larger towns, Ayr, Irvine, Renfrew, Paisley, Kilmarnock, etc, all accepted the masonic domination of the Mother Lodge in this little Ayrshire village. From c1687 onwards the custom of appointing Quartermasters was abandoned, but the territories which had formerly been under Kilwinning's direction were ever ready to acknowledge their allegiance, and most of the early Charters issued by the Mother Lodge were granted in those districts which had originally been under her own care.

BILLS AND BONDS. THE LODGE AS MONEY-LENDER

The study of our old Lodge records often reveals curious and unexpected facets of Masonic history, and at Kilwinning, most surprising of all perhaps, is the revelation that (apart from admission fees) the most steady and continuous source of income was derived, quite simply, from money-lending!

The earliest minutes afford little or no evidence on the subject and most of the entrants apparently paid cash for their admission fees.

In December 1655, John Hammiltoun upon his admission as FC gave 'bond' for £8, and Wm Cowane who was also made FC, 'promised to pay 40/- Scots . . . at the next meeting'. From this time onwards it became a fairly regular practice to pay admission fees by bill, bond, or promissory-note. These documents were duly deposited in the Lodge 'Box', and debtors were called upon to pay interest at the December meeting. The sums involved were not large, even when (as often happened) they included accumulated fines for absence.

The system probably started by the Lodge giving credit terms for admission fees, but it soon developed into a regular business of money-lending.

A minute of 1653 leaves no doubt on the subject of loans. '. . . Jon Cowane has paid this last year interest of twenty-five merks he is owing to the box of *borrowed money* and is to pay the sum (ie the principal), and a year's interest at the next Court, 1654.'

It is almost possible to trace the stages by which the system developed. At first, the granting of credit facilities for the payment of admission fees. Then, when funds permitted, the lending of sums ranging from ten to eighty merks (£6 to £50 Scots) to members of the Lodge, perhaps for the purchase of materials and equipment when they needed it for a particular job.

The loans were not only for Masters. Entered Apprentices were also eligible, and they were even able to negotiate the loans before they entered the Lodge, eg in 1674:

> . . . John Smith at the Kirk of Stewartoune was admitted and entered prentise and has paid to the box and his booking money, and is hereby discharged thereof, except his bond of twentie merks which is not hereby discharged . . .

The minute is quite explicit. Smith paid all his admission fee and booking money but he still owed the Lodge 20 merks for a loan which must have been granted to him on the day of his admission, if not earlier. When funds became plentiful the Lodge began to lend money to non-members, and very soon the Lodge began to have troubles with debt-collection. All sorts of precautions were taken to ensure that the monies were safe.

12 January 1728:
. . . it is enacted that when any money is to be lent out of the box, that the borrower shall give an Cautioner which is not entered in with the Lodge, and if the Cautioner [ie a guarantor] shall enter with the Lodge the borrower shall be obliged at the first term to give a new Cautioner that is not entered.

These were not all simple transactions, in which the borrower took his loan, gave his bill and paid his interest annually. There are all sorts of complicated minutes which indicate that the bonds were passed round among the members of the Lodge for purposes of negotiation.

The Loan and Bill transactions continued to be recorded in the minutes for about 140 years, punctuated by regular instructions to various officers and members to take legal proceedings for collection – and the practice did not end until the 1770s.

THE TRANSITION AT KILWINNING

The Kilwinning version of the Schaw Statutes, 1599, prescribed that the Lodge was to obtain the services of a notary to act as 'clark & scryb' or secretary, and the minutes of 1643 show that the instruction was observed.

The early minutes of the Lodge of Mary's Chapel, Edinburgh, were also signed by a notary, serving in the same capacity.

It is inconceivable that these gentlemen could have discharged their duties unless they were actually present in the Lodge-room during the meetings, and they were, in fact, non-operative members, who received some payment for their services from admission fees and from the preparation of apprentices' indentures, discharges, and other legal documents.

It was not until the early 1670s, however, that the Lodge at Kilwinning began to admit non-operatives as ordinary members, and the minutes of the years from 1672 to 1678 may be said to mark the first stage in the transition of the Lodge from a purely operative or trade-controlling body, towards the kind of speculative Lodge that exists today.

In 1672, the minutes read:

Eodem die Lord John Kennedie Earle off Cassells wes chosen to be Deacon. [Note. Deacon then was equivalent to WM today.]

The Earl of Cassillis, a local landowner, was not present. He was not a member of the Lodge, and had never previously visited there; indeed it is extremely doubtful if he was ever made a Mason. There is no hint in the preceding minutes of any reason why he should have been selected for this office, and he never visited the Lodge after his election.

Immediately after this extraordinary entry, William Cowan, an operative mason, was chosen as 'Deput-Deacon'. This was the first-ever appointment of a Deput-Deacon, and it seems to imply that the Lodge did not expect the noble Lord to attend very regularly, and was merely seeking his patronage. It is probable that he was formally invited to take the Office *after* his election, and that he rejected the invitation, for if he had accepted, he would doubtless have been re-elected year after year, whether he attended or not.

At the next meeting, in December, 1673, several gentlemen were admitted as fellows of craft, among them Sir Alexander Cunynghame of Corshill. That night the list of names for the election of Deacon contained six names, three men of gentle birth and three operatives. Cassillis – still absent – got only 1 vote. Cunynghame received 9 votes and was elected, choosing an operative mason as Deput-Deacon – and two operatives were elected as Wardens.

About four weeks later, Sir Alex^r Cunynghame presided at a special meeting of the Lodge, and

> The said day Alex^r Earle of Eglintoune and Lawrence Wallace brother to the Laird of Sewaltoune were admitted prentises and fellows of Croft within the Lodge of Kilwinning and payed . . .

In 1674 the Earl of Eglington was elected Deacon. He never attended, and during the next few years the principal offices were always taken by the gentry, with operatives acting as their Deputies. But the gentlemen were seldom present and in 1679 the Lodge discarded its noble patrons, and reverted to the practice of choosing Officers from its own ranks as it had always done before.

We can only speculate on the reasons which prompted the Lodge to open its doors to non-operatives generally and to the nobility and gentry in particular. It seems likely that there were two main reasons, patronage, and income. Doubtless it was hoped that the Lodge would gain in prestige and power if it was administered under the supervision and patronage of the local lairds and landowners.

Whatever the reasons which prompted the step, Kilwinning did open its doors to non-masons, but nothing much came of this first attempt. On the face of it, the whole affair seems to have petered out, but in the years that followed the number of non-operative entrants grew steadily. The Lodge remained primarily operative in character, and continued for many years under operative management; but attendances began to fall off, and the Lodge went through a bad time.

The 25 years or so from 1689 to 1714 may be counted as the era of the 'Lodge in decline', yet there is nothing in the minutes to explain what had happened. A small team of four or five members rotated through the various offices of Deacon, Warden and Clerk, and somehow they managed to hold the Lodge together until 1716 when the first signs of revival appear.

In 1716 there began a practice of holding a meeting in July regularly every year, and attendances started to improve. Doubtless the summer weather was helpful, and the July meetings were well supported. From 1716 onwards there were new men joining the Lodge at each meeting, the minutes become more detailed, and it is noticeable that there was a new spirit abroad.

At the meeting on 20 December 1733, three non-operatives were admitted, ie: Mr Charles Hamilton, Collector of Excise. Patrick ffullerton Esqre. Mr Alex^{r} Baillie, Merchant in Glasgow.

This record marks the beginning of the last phase in Kilwinning's transition from operative to speculative masonry. From this time onwards a huge number of new men began to join the Lodge, many of them men of gentle birth, with local landowners, lawyers, surgeons, ship-masters, Excise Officers, and sailors. There were indeed mason craftsmen and other artisans among the new intrants, but the management of the Lodge was now in the hands of the gentry.

At the end of 1734 we note the change in the title of the principal officer from 'Deacon' to 'Master'; not a major change perhaps, but good evidence of some new influence in the Lodge, and of a readiness to move with the times.

Probably the most important single item in the history of the Lodge during this exciting period was the arrangement (by invitation, no doubt), which brought Patrick Montgomery, the Laird of Bourtreehill, to the Chair of the Mother Lodge, on 27 March 1735. The circumstances were curious.

David Muir was elected Deacon in December 1734, and he signed the minutes as Master in January and February 1735, and also in July and December 1735. But there were three meetings in March 1735, when Patrick Montgomerie presided as Master, and signed the minutes in that capacity. At that stage he was not yet a member of the Lodge and it was not until the third of the March meetings that he paid half-a-guinea 'for Entering himself a Member . . .'.

In December 1735, Muir, as Master, nominated Montgomery to be his successor, regardless of many worthy members who might have claimed the office. Montgomery had only been a member for nine months, but when the Lodge was assured that he was willing to accept office, and that it was legal to elect him in his absence, Montgomery was unanimously chosen.

The whole tenor of the minutes testifies to the eagerness with which he was welcomed into the principal office, at first as a guest, and he was elected at the earliest opportunity, almost certainly because he had some wider knowledge of the most advanced ritual and Lodge-practice of that time.

It was during his tenure of the Chair in March that we find the first reference in the Kilwinning minutes to the third degree.

In December 1735, the Lodge for the first time styled itself as the 'Lodge of the ffree and accepted Masons of Kilwinning'. Montgomery in January 1736 presented '. . . a sett of Jewels, viz, the Compass Square Plummet & Level . . .' the first jewels mentioned in the Minute book. In June the Lodge, under his presidency, drew up its first double-scale of fees, non-masons paying double the rate for 'working masons'. In that same minute we find the first reference to 'Livery' (probably Aprons and Gloves). Montgomery was the first Master of the Lodge to be honoured with the designation 'The Right Worshipful'. In January 1736, on his first attendance at the Lodge after his election, he appointed James Marshall, an Irvine lawyer, to serve the Lodge as *Secretary* in addition to Alex^r Cunningham who had been continued as Clerk. This was the first appointment of a Secretary, and in December 1736, when Montgomery was continued in the Chair, he was the first Master of Kilwinning to appoint Stewards. Altogether, the change in the Lodge during the course of these two years was really phenomenal.

Mother Kilwinning still had a substantial operative membership, but by now it was no longer exercising any trade controls. Operative masons and artisans continued to be admitted into the Lodge at specially reduced fees, but they were joining for social rather than industrial reasons, and the concession in fees represented Kilwinning's last link with the mason trade.

The advent of the trigradal system implies that there were substantial changes in ritual practice and indicates the adoption of certain elements of ceremonial procedure which were of a Speculative nature. The period roughly from 1730 to 1760 may be counted as the time when Speculative ideas were gradually embodied into the ritual, and when the ceremonial practices began to take shape in their modern form.

The Kilwinning minutes, with their customary reticence on all ritual matters, furnish no detailed evidence of the changes, but the minutes of 1735 and 1736 show that the Lodge had passed through all the earliest stages of the transition, and was ready for the beginning of a new era.

KILWINNING, THE MOTHER LODGE

In December 1677, eleven masons from the Canongate, at Edinburgh, travelled right across the country to Kilwinning and were constituted as a Lodge in their own right with Kilwinning as their Mother and creator.

The circumstances were quite extraordinary. The Canongate was a separate burgh, adjoining the royal burgh of Edinburgh at its eastern end. It had had its own Incorporation of Wrights, Coopers and Masons since 1585, but it had no Lodge.

Under the tight system of trade-control exercised by the Lodge of Edinburgh, Mary's Chapel, these men must have known that they could expect no encouragement from Edinburgh and so they came to Kilwinning.

There is no indication in the Kilwinning minutes as to how the matter was broached, or how long it had been under discussion before it came to fruition on 20 December 1677, but the minutes suggest that Kilwinning must have given deep thought to this action, which might well have been considered as a manifest invasion of the territory of the Lodge of Edinburgh.

Until this time lodges had arisen naturally wherever groups of masons were settled in one place for lengthy periods, and every lodge was its own master, a sovereign lodge. There can be no question as to whether Kilwinning had the right to create a new lodge, because every Lodge had that right if it so desired; the only doubt was as to the infringement of Mary's Chapel's territory. Kilwinning overcame this difficulty by resorting to a polite fiction, erecting the new society in terms which indicate that it was merely a branch of the Mother Lodge.

Thus the minute contains a note which refers to the Canongate Brethren as '. . . ane part of our number being willing to be booked & inrolid . . .'. The implication of the first five words of this extract is that these men were actually members of the lodge of Kilwinning (who were anxious to open a branch in the Canongate). Despite the phrase 'ane part of our number' it is very doubtful whether any of these men had ever been entered or passed at Kilwinning. Yet it seems certain that they were (with one possible exception) all masons by trade, probably unattached to any particular Lodge, and wishing to erect their new Lodge in an orderly manner, they made their approach to Kilwinning as the traditional birthplace of all masonry in Scotland.

This Lodge, now Canongate-Kilwinning No 2, was the first offspring of the Mother Lodge and it is undoubtedly the first Lodge that was ever created by another Lodge.

More than 50 years later, in 1729, another petition was delivered at Kilwinning, from a 'Company of Masons at Tarpichen', a village roughly midway between Glasgow and Edinburgh. The Lodge at Torpichen had certainly been in existence some time before it made this approach to the Mother Lodge, and the main object of the petition was:

> . . . that ye may grant us a power of contstitutione and acting in our society under you in all things, to the recovering and maintaining of good order and suppressing immoralities and licenciousness . . .

(One wonders how far the Mother Lodge could assist in this last matter!)

It is curious to notice that the petitioners acknowledged themselves as holding all their rights and privileges from Kilwinning even though Torpichen was well outside Kilwinning territory, but the whole tone of the petition indicates the reverence in which the Mother Lodge was held, and the benefits which Torpichen hoped to derive from its adopted Mother.

During the following years, a great number of Charters were

granted to new Lodges, and soon it became fashionable for Lodges to incorporate the word Kilwinning into their titles without any justification or permission at all. That did no serious harm to anyone, and it was all a great compliment to an ancient and honourable Lodge, but it led to a great deal of confusion.

It is now quite impossible to say definitely how many Lodges owed their existence to Kilwinning. There is indisputable evidence for at least 34, including two in Virginia, USA (when that country was still a British Colony), one in Antigua, West Indies, and one in Ireland.

Although Kilwinning was generally recognised as the 'Mother Lodge' before the formation of the Grand Lodge of Scotland in November 1736, she did not adopt that title, either in Lodge minutes or in general correspondence, until 1747. Her last Daughter-lodge was erected in 1803, with the Number 79. It may well be that the Mother Lodge was responsible for 79 Lodges in all, but – unfortunately – we shall never be able to prove it.

THE GRAND LODGE OF SCOTLAND AND THE SECESSION 1735–44

In 1735, with its management firmly held in non-operative hands, the Mother Lodge entered into a period of growth and prosperity. It was drawing its members from all grades of society, masons, wrights and artisans, Excise officers and seamen, lawyers, ministers of religion, lairds and landed gentry. In 1741, the Earl of Kilmarnock served as Master for one year, and he was followed by Alexander, Earl of Eglinton, who thus revived a family link with the lodge which has continued for more than two centuries.

Entrance fees in 1736 were fixed for working masons, at 5/- Sterling for entered-apprentices, 2/6d for fellows-of-craft (with extras for their 'liverys'). Non-operatives had to pay double those sums, and qualified men of both grades were entitled to be raised to the degree of master-mason, *gratis*.

These preferential admission-fees for working masons were virtually the last link between the Lodge and the craft from which it had arisen. There is no justification yet for describing it as a 'speculative' lodge in our present sense of the word; its membership was substantially non-operative, and at this period we begin to get an insight into the expanding benevolent work of the Lodge, as well as its newly-developing social and convivial character.

Since the 1680s the Lodge had distributed small sums to members in distress, and to widows of former members. Now the gifts in charity were expanded to include 'travelling masons', and soon it became the practice to allocate small but regular payments to 'the poor' in Irvine and Stevenston as well as Kilwinning.

In 1735 the Lodge recorded the purchase of a stone punch-bowl and ladle, and a few months later the minutes acknowledge the receipt from the daughter-lodge, Canongate-Kilwinning, the gift of 'a Sett of Songs,' ie a song-book, evidently a valued and useful gift. In 1754, there is an expense item of 34/- for five dozen 'Mason Glasses' (previously they had used glasses belonging to the 'house' in which they met).

The changes of character and functions described here, were common to all the older Scottish Lodges. The newer creations, having no traditional link with the mason trade, developed quite natually in the modern non-operative pattern.

In 1736, after a year of preliminary manoeuvres and negotiations, the Grand Lodge of Scotland was founded. Thirty-three Lodges from all parts of Scotland were represented at the foundation meeting, Kilwinning among them. The Mother Lodge had participated whole-heartedly in the preliminaries and although she had made a number of valid and useful proposals for the management of the Grand Lodge to be, they were at first shelved, and subsequently vetoed. Kilwinning did not protest against this or any other ruling of the Grand Lodge, but remained a loyal adherent of the new organisation.

One of the early difficulties which the new Grand Lodge encountered was the task of trying to determine the seniority of its adherent lodges and it took the wholly logical step of inviting the Lodges to establish their positions on the Roll by documentary proof, with the reasonable proviso that the Roll would be adjusted to make proper place for those which might subsequently prove their right to a higher status.

Under this ruling, Mary's Chapel, Edinburgh, with minutes from 1599 was enrolled as No 1, although it must have been common knowledge within the Craft that Kilwinning – despite the absence of records – could claim a history as old, if not older than this. For many lodges with quite genuine claims, real documentary proof would have been impossible. On such evidence alone, the Lodge of Aitchison's

Haven would have taken precedence over the Mother Lodge and Edinburgh too, for it had minutes from 1598 (although they were probably not available at that time).

In 1744, following a letter from Canongate-Kilwinning, the Mother Lodge replied, complaining that she had been placed second on the Roll to Mary's Chapel No 1, but the Grand Lodge indicated that nothing could or would be done in the absence of documentary proof.

The Mother Lodge, secure in her acknowledged antiquity, did not dispute the Grand Lodge decision and did not attempt to lessen the status of any other Lodge, or to improve her own. Quietly she withdrew from her association with the Grand Lodge and resumed her ancient status, exercising rights which she had in fact never surrendered, granting Charters, offering fraternal welcome to visiting Masons regardless of their allegiance to the Grand Lodge or any other Lodge, and in every way conducting herself as though the Grand Lodge had never existed.

For its part, the Grand Lodge also treated the whole matter very calmly, and in 1750 Alexander, Earl of Eglinton, was chosen Grand Master Mason of Scotland *while still RWM of the Mother Lodge*, which suggests that there was no bad feeling on either side. In subsequent years, the Grand Lodge began to view the matter in a different spirit, instructing Lodges which owed allegiance to her to have no Masonic intercourse either with Kilwinning or any of her Daughter Lodges.

There is no doubt that some bad feeling was engendered in this way, but perhaps it was all for the best, since it may have helped considerably to pave the way towards the reunion which took place in 1807.

BUILDING THE NEW LODGE 1744–80

It is quite clear that Kilwinning's secession from the Grand Lodge organisation entailed no loss of prestige for the Mother Lodge; indeed, it is possible that her status was enhanced by her action. In the 60 years of her separation from the Grand Lodge there are minutes showing that she Chartered at least 29 new lodges, and there may have been many more.

Membership was growing steadily by ordinary admissions within the Lodge, and these numbers were greatly increased by frequent admissions under the pernicious system of 'out-entry'.

There is in fact, ample evidence, in the seventeenth and eighteenth centuries, of the practice, fully recognised and accepted by a number of Lodges, of allowing their members to admit masons away from the Lodge, ie as 'out-entries'. The essential characteristic of 'out-entry' meetings was that they might be held at any time or place away from the Lodge, without the specific permission of the Lodge or its officers; and so long as the admissions complied with the Lodge regulations (and quite often when they did not) the Lodges were willing to ratify the admissions.

Although the Kilwinning records afford little evidence on the subject, there is good reason to believe that 'out-entries' had taken place since 1648. The Lodge enacted a rule in 1686 forbidding the practice but it continued at intervals until 1728 when, under new regulations, the practice was made legal again. From 1735 onwards there was a real spate of 'out-entries', most of them properly recorded and ratified. In the 1750s, Irvine and Stevenston gradually became reception centres for prospective members of the Mother Lodge. Irvine recorded 11 intrants in 1755; 12 in 1762 and five in 1764; and Stevenston brought in nine new members in 1764. The last Kilwinning out-entry was recorded in 1792.

The Lodge was now growing at a tremendous pace. Attendances at the annual meetings ranged from the sixties to over a hundred occasionally, and inevitably the question arose as to the Lodge finding or building a new 'House' for its meetings. The project had first been mooted in 1747 and had been shelved. Now, in 1770, the matter had become really urgent, and a Committee was appointed '. . . for purchasing ground to build . . .' and to collect outstanding monies for the purpose.

Despite the urgency nothing definite was done until 1778, when the Earl of Eglinton brought the matter to a head by offering the Lodge a 500 years' lease of the Eglinton 'Court House' or girnal, at a really nominal rent of 2/6d per annum. The reaction of the Lodge was instantaneous:

> The Brethren . . . in Consideration of the Family of Eglintoune being often Friendly in protecting and countenancing the Ancient Mother Lodge and that the present Earl . . . in particular has been long a Member of this Lodge and often shewn his attachment to it . . . and that he lately presented the Lodge with a Stedding for Building a New Lodge . . . for a trifling Quit-rent . . . Therefore in hopes of his further Continuance and in

gratitude for his past favours, they . . . do unanimously Elect Archibald Earl of Eglintoune to be Most Worshipful Grand Master of the Mother Lodge for Life . . .

This was the first use of the title 'Most Worshipful' for the Master of the Mother Lodge, and the style 'Most Worshipful Grand Master' remained in general use at Kilwinning for the next 60 years.

The Foundation stone for the new Hall was laid in 1779 and the re-building was completed a year later, but the cost of the undertaking brought the Lodge to the edge of bankruptcy; it had used up all its funds and was hopelessly in debt.

The minutes in the succeeding years pathetically bemoan the low state of the funds which prevented the Lodge from bestowing Charity as it was wont to do, but a continuous – if modest – income was derived from hiring out the premises regularly for dances and other entertainments.

Ten years later in 1790 the Lodge still owed £52, plus interest, to the builder; he did not live to see the debt paid.

The Lodge funds under careful management were eventually brought into better shape, but an amusing finale to this chapter appeared in the minutes for 1841, when it was suddenly discovered that the Lodge had never paid one penny of its ground rent (2/6d pa) since the lease was first granted more than sixty years before.

The building that had been erected after so much effort served as the Lodge Hall for 113 years, until July 1893, when it was demolished.

A few months later a new Temple was completed and furnished at a cost of some £2,000, and the present Lodge building was consecrated on 30 September 1893.

HARD TIMES 1780–1806

Following an era of great prosperity, the Mother Lodge passed through a very bad period in the twenty years or so from c1780 to c1800. Charity payments were reduced, money-lending facilities ceased altogether, and attendances shrank disastrously (at several of the Annual Meetings in the 1780s the records show attendances ranging from six to eleven men in all, including the officers!).

By this time, the Grand Lodge of Scotland, now firmly established, had ordered its adherent lodges to refrain from all Masonic intercourse with Kilwinning and her Daughters, and an incident in

1791 was doubtless typical of the kind of difficulties that ensued.

In December 1791, a few weeks after their constitution as a Daughter Lodge of Mother Kilwinning, the Lodge of Paisley St Andrew Kilwinning, anxious to establish fraternal relations with other Lodges in their neighbourhood, sent a deputation to visit the Lodge Paisley St James. The latter, owning allegiance to the Grand Lodge of Scotland, took the lamentable course of refusing to receive the deputation. It was a gratuitous insult, aggravated by a great deal of unpleasant publicity

If there were any similar incidents elsewhere, they were less widely advertised; this was the only case that was actually recorded in the Kilwinning minutes, and it was never mentioned again.

The Lodge gradually began to recover from its difficulties. Towards the end of the 1700s, admissions began to increase, attendances improved, and there were frequent visits from members of other lodges. More important still – as evidence of Mother Kilwinning's status at this period – there were a number of joining members, and numerous records of the election of 'honorary members'.

In 1767, the Lodge had imposed a new triple-scale of admission fees; every apprentice who was a 'Real working mason with Stone and Lime' paid 7/6d Sterling: a 'Wright or Square Man' paid 10/-; a 'Gentleman' paid 21/-, and these rates remained in force until 1807. The accounts (which were kept meticulously at this period) afford evidence that the Lodge was beginning to prosper again.

In 1796 it paid the last £10 owing on the building plus six years' interest! In 1797 the Lodge spent over £4 Sterling on Candelabra and Lamps. Increases in the payments of Charity, and minor extravagances such as the provision of Toddy for the Tyler and Stewards all go to indicate that the bad times were finished.

THE RE-UNION, 1807

The re-union of the Mother Lodge with the Grand Lodge of Scotland was a major event in her history, and the story of the negotiations which led to it (and of some of the results that followed) provides a good finale to this study of Kilwinning's oldest records.

When the Mother Lodge decided in 1744 to withdraw from her association with the Grand Lodge, she went her own way – and flourished. From 1744 to 1807 there was no official contact between

Kilwinning and the Grand Lodge, but a number of brethren from Lodges under the Grand Lodge joined Kilwinning without hindrance.

At the turn of the century she had begun to recover from her financial distress, there were many influential men amongst her officers and members, and attendances were growing steadily.

It was at this stage that well-wishers appeared on both sides, eager to heal the breach, and the first unofficial moves were made, in private letters and discussions, in 1806. The whole tenor of the subsequent negotiations shows that the Grand Lodge had much to gain from an amicable solution to the difficulties which had caused the separation, and the official proceedings began in 1807 with a most tactful letter from the Grand Lodge, addressed to the Secretary of the Mother Lodge:

R.W. Sir,

It has been the Subject of much great regret that the misunderstanding so long subsisting between the Grand Lodge of Scotland and the Kilwinning Lodge Should not ere now have been Accomodated, It does not from Our Records, Appear very clearly, what were the reasons which induced your Lodge to leave the Bosom and protection of the Grand Lodge. But whatever was the Cause it must now be Obvious that it will tend greatly to the Interest, Honour and Respectability of the Craft in general, were Masonry in Scotland to be practised only in the Bosom of, and under the protection of the Grand Lodge, whereby she as the only head of the Masonic Body in Scotland, would feel herself responsible, for the Regularity and good Conduct, of every Lodge, enjoying the privilage of Meeting as a Masonic Body under her Charters . . .

The letter ended with a note that the Grand Lodge had appointed a Committee of prominent officers, with powers to meet a Kilwinning Committee in order to settle outstanding difficulties and arrange a mutually satisfactory settlement.

The Mother Lodge gave 'deliberate consideration' to the Grand Lodge letter and appointed a Committee with similar powers.

There followed a meeting of the Kilwinning Committee at Irvine on 25 May 1807, at which a number of points were drawn up to serve as a basis for discussion when the two Committees should meet.

At first glance the minutes of that meeting seem to suggest that Kilwinning was preparing to impose stiff conditions as a preliminary to any talk of re-union, but the situation of the Mother Lodge was, of course, vastly different from any of the other Lodges which had joined the Grand Lodge. It was inevitable that the re-union would involve the surrender of some of her ancient privileges, and she had also the duty of protecting the interests of her Daughter Lodges.

The two Committees met at Glasgow in October 1807, and in a single session they drew up a code of five articles which they jointly recommended:

1st That the Mother Lodge Kilwinning shall Renounce all right of Granting Charters, and come in along with all the Lodges holding under her, to the bosom of the Grand Lodge.

2dly That all the Lodges holding of the Mother Kilwinning shall be Obliged to Obtain from the Grand Lodge Confirmations of their respective Charters, for which a ffee of three Guineas only shall be exigible.

3dly That the Mother Kilwinning Lodge shall be placed at the head of the Roll of the Grand Lodge under the denomination of Mother Kilwinning; and her Daughter Lodges shall in the meantime be placed, at the end of the Said Roll, and as they shall apply for Confirmations, but under this Express declaration, that so soon as the Roll shall be arranged and Corrected which is in present Contemplation, the Lodges holding of Mother Kilwinning shall be entitled to be Ranked According to the dates of their Original Charters, and of those granted by the Grand Lodge.

4thly That Mother Kilwinning and her Daughter Lodges, shall have the same Interest in, and Management of the funds of the Grand Lodge as the Other Lodges now holding of her; The Mother Lodge Kilwinning Contributing – annually to the said funds a sum not less than two shillings and sixpence for each Intrant, and her Daughter Lodges Contributing in the same manner as the present Lodges holding of the Grand Lodge.

5thly That the Master of the Mother Kilwinning Lodge, for the time, shall be *ipso facto* Provincial Grand Master for the Ayrshire District – And lastly while both Committees are satisfied that the preceding arrangements will be highly conductive to the honour and Interest of Scottish Masonry, and tho vested with the fullest powers, to make a final adjustment the Committees do only respectfully recomend its adoption to their respective Constituents.
Signed (10 Signatures).

The Lodge considered the points agreed by the two Committees, unanimously ratified and approved them, and after the Committee had been thanked for its efforts '. . . the healths of the Committee were drunk Standing with all the honours of Masonry', and it was resolved that the Grand Lodge delegates be elected members of the Mother Lodge.

The Grand Lodge also met on 2 November, with 64 Lodges represented, and the conditions of the settlement were approved by all present with only one dissenting voice from the SW of Mary's Chapel '. . . on the ground of that Lodge being deprived of her place on the Roll . . .' Despite the protest, Grand Lodge accepted the proposals and ratified them, and the schism of more than 60 years was ended.

Both Mother Kilwinning and the Grand Lodge had just cause to be pleased with the settlement, and so far as the Mother Lodge was concerned, the matter was happily ended. But the Grand Lodge had not yet reconciled the Lodge of Mary's Chapel, Edinburgh, to the change that was involved in placing Mother Kilwinning at the head of the Roll, especially as the Mother Lodge had produced no really satisfactory documentary evidence of her right to that position.

There were many Kilwinning legends and traditions current in the Scottish Craft at that time that might have been cited at the Glasgow meeting in 1807. Historically, they were all equally ill-founded, and incapable of proof. But the Grand Lodge representatives were not historians. They had no means at their disposal for verifying the claims, and having been appointed specifically 'to Settle all disputes', they were not disposed to cavil at the claims which were made by the Kilwinning men.

There can be no doubt that, with or without proof, the Kilwinning brethren genuinely believed that theirs was the oldest masonic foundation in Scotland, and for all that we know, they may have been right in their claim. But a new situation had arisen in the 64 years that had elapsed since Mother Kilwinning had withdrawn from the Grand Lodge. In 1736–43 the Grand Lodge was primarily concerned with the seniority of its adherent Lodges; in 1807 its main object was to effect the re-union, and it had much to gain from persuading Kilwinning to return as an adherent. During those 64 years, the Mother Lodge had pursued its own independent course, virtually as a Grand Lodge in her own right. She had been for more than 200 years the focal centre of Masonry in the West of Scotland, and had erected or Chartered a huge number of Daughter Lodges which owed her allegiance.

Several of these Lodges had already joined in with the Grand Lodge, but if Mother Kilwinning and all her remaining Daughters could be brought under her banner the result would bring a useful accession of funds as well as a vast improvement in her status as '. . . the only head of the Masonic Body in Scotland'.

Kilwinning was therefore in a strong position to bargain for whatever rights and privileges she was about to relinquish. In the event, so long as her premier position on the Roll was assured, she asked for only one concession, the clause which made the Master of the Mother Lodge, *ipso facto* Provincial Grand Master for Ayrshire. It was a natural request, designed to enhance the status of the Mother Lodge within the Province, and to ensure that none of her junior lodges could acquire precedence over Kilwinning.

The readiness with which the Grand Lodge agreed to this unusual privilege may be taken as a measure of her eagerness to bring about the re-union as speedily and smoothly as possible. It was largely a matter of expediency, and the main body of the Craft supported the Grand Lodge in its action. Mary's Chapel alone argued that the procedure was unfair to them.

The dispute was not finally settled until 1815 when in response to a petition from Mary's Chapel, '. . . it seemed to be the general sense of the Grand Lodge, that, after the solemn agreement entered into with Mother Kilwinning in 1807, and ratified, approved of, and acted upon by all parties ever since that period, that such petition and remonstrance by Mary's Chapel Lodge could not now be received and entertained, and ought, therefore, to be dismissed as incompetent and inadmissible; upon which the Right Worshipful Brother Robertson, Master of Mary's Chapel Lodge, agreed to withdraw the same, and the petition was accordingly withdrawn'.

THE NUMBER "0"

Much curiosity is aroused nowadays by the unique No 0 which the Mother Lodge bears on the register of the Grand Lodge of Scotland. The terms of the re-union did not specify it; indeed it seems evident that the original intention was that Kilwinning was to have no number at all. The proposals which formed the basis of discussion at the Irvine meeting on 25 May, contained the following:

1st That the Lodge of Kilwinning shall be placed at the head of the Roll of

Lodges in Scotland *without any number* but by the Title of the Mother Lodge Kilwinning or by the said Title and Number One if the Grand Lodge rather prefer the latter.

The clause in its ratified form, simply did not mention the number at all:

3rdly That the Mother Kilwinning Lodge shall be placed at the head of the Roll of the Grand Lodge under the denomination of Mother Kilwinning; . . .

Neither the Mother Lodge nor the Grand Lodge made use of the No 0 (or any other number) during the negotiations which led to the re-union. The No 0 does not appear in any of the Kilwinning minutes during 1807 to 1842 (ie the whole of the third minute-book) nor is it found in any of the contemporary minutes of the Grand Lodge.

For the purpose of this record, an attempt was made to ascertain when, and in what circumstances the number was allocated to the Mother Lodge, and the question was posed to Bro Dr A. F. Buchan, the Grand Secretary. After a careful search he reported that there is no minute recording that the number was ever allocated officially.

The Mother Lodge was not numbered in the minutes relating to the re-union, and when the first edition of the *Constitutions and Laws of the Grand Lodge* was published, in 1836, Kilwinning was listed at the head of the Roll, *without a number*. In the second edition, 1848, the No 0 made its first appearance in print, and so far as can be ascertained, that was the first time the number was used officially.

Bro G. S. Draffen, Past Depute Grand Master, who assisted in this enquiry is of the opinion that it:

'. . . was a purely administrative action on the part of the clerical staff in the Grand Lodge. Obviously when making a list of Lodges by number only, it was highly inconvenient to have a Lodge with no number at all . . . They appear to have started the list with the number '0', and gradually that has become accepted, even to the extent of brethren who are members of that Lodge using that number when they sign the Visitor's Book when they go to another Lodge.
It is not impossible that this practice of designating Lodge Mother Kilwinning as number '0' did in fact arise from the difficulty that its members found themselves in when visiting other Lodges and having to fill in the number of their Lodge which, of course, they could not do.
To sum up, Grand Lodge, as far as I can trace, has never *officially* adopted

the number '0' . . . It appears to have arisen from an administrative practice necessitated by purely practical reasons.

Until May 1983 the No 0 does not appear on Lodge stationery and summonses, although it was and is readily accepted by the Lodge. The Mother Lodge is known locally and throughout the world as No 0 (but Americans use the No Zero) and the Lodge aprons bear the letters MKO on their flaps.

Nevertheless, many of the old Depute Masters preferred the ancient designation, 'The Mother Lodge of Scotland'.

AFTER THE RE-UNION, 1807–42

The third Minute Book of the Mother Lodge runs from 1806 to 1842, so that the records contained in the first three books cover almost exactly a period of 200 years, 1642 to 1842.

An immediate result of the re-union was that Ayrshire became a Masonic Province of the Grand Lodge, with Kilwinning as its chief Lodge, and the RW Master of Kilwinning as its Prov Grand Master. In the Commission or Document which conferred that right the Grand Lodge carelessly inserted a proviso 'so long as such Masters are approved of by Grand Lodge'. Kilwinning immediately protested that she alone had the right to choose and approve her Masters, and that such Masters were to be *ipso facto* Prov GM; and the offending words were removed.

One curious result of this close link between the Mother Lodge and the Provincial Grand Lodge, was the frequent appearance in the *Lodge* minutes, of items of business which would belong properly to the Minute book of the Provincial Grand Lodge. At the Anniversary meeting in 1816 the Lodge minutes record that the Prov GM was calling a meeting of the Provincial Grand Lodge for March 1817, for 'propogating the good of Masonry . . .' and to ensure that the Lodges in the district '. . . Conforme themselves to the Laws and Regulations of the Grand Lodge . . .'.

In due course a full report of the Meeting appeared *in the Lodge minutes*, and it must have been quite an occasion! There was an attendance of over 200 Brethren and proceedings began with a procession to the Church, a Sermon, then back to the Lodge; a loyal Address to the Prince Regent; '. . . a substantial and plentiful dinner . . . (and the Meeting) . . . broke up at a late hour'.

Early in 1825 the rapid growth in the number of new Lodges on the Roll prompted the Grand Lodge to make a fresh classification of the Lodges under the various Provinces; and because of the large number of Lodges in Ayrshire, many of them at a great distance from Kilwinning, it was proposed that the Province should be divided, Masonically, into two parts; West Ayrshire, with 15 Lodges including Mother Kilwinning; East Ayrshire with 13 Lodges; and four Lodges were to be struck off the Roll.

In pursuance of this plan, *which had apparently been settled without consulting the Mother Lodge or its Master*, the Grand Lodge wrote to Mother Kilwinning on 20 April 1825, outlining the plan in some detail, and announcing that the division had already been made!

'. . . The Grand Lodge of Scotland . . . being highly sensible that it will tend to the good of Masonry, as well as to the comfort and conveniency of the Brethren, to divide the county into two districts or provinces, which they have accordingly done as follows . . .

There followed a list of Lodges for the proposed West Province under Alex^r Hamilton of Grange the then Prov GM and another list of lodges for the East Province under an un-named Prov GM with headquarters at Maybole, and the Grand Lodge invited the Prov GM of Ayrshire to name the Brother who was to share the province with him.

The Prov GM and the Mother Lodge, counting this arrangement to be an infringement of their ancient rights, protested by letter to the Grand Lodge, and the matter should have ended at this point because Grand Lodge accepted the protest and abandoned the plan to divide the Ayrshire Province. But she was still busy with the re-arrangement of other Provinces and, in 1826/27 a piece of mismanagement on her part nearly led to serious trouble.

In 1826, without consulting the Mother Lodge, the Grand Lodge decided to transfer two Lodges (Beith St John, and Largs St John) to the jurisdiction of the Renfrew Province, and the RWM of Beith St John reported the matter to the Mother Lodge at the anniversary meeting, in December 1826. A letter was despatched in January 1827, to Bro James Maconochie, the Proxy Master (an advocate, member of St Luke's Lodge) at Edinburgh, directing him to protest against this transfer and to have the matter put right.

No reply was received to this note, and in June 1827, a sharp letter was sent to him, again seeking his intervention. A note in similar terms was sent directly to the Grand Lodge:

> '. . . As I am anxious, as becomes my duty, to preserve the jurisdiction of the Provincial Grand Lodge in the same way as I received it, I insist that the lodges transferred into the two new provinces of Renfrew shall immediately be restored; and if not, I shall call a chapter of the lodge to take their advice.

Upon receipt of the second letter from the Mother Lodge, Maconochie replied that he had, upon receipt of the first letter, laid the complaint before the Grand Secretary with a request that the two Lodges should be 'restored'. The Grand Secretary later told Maconochie that 'this had been done', and he had undertaken to advise the GM of Mother Kilwinning that this was so. Maconochie had accepted the word of the Grand Secretary, and had therefore not troubled to report back to the Mother Lodge.

The arrival of the June letter showed Maconochie that the Grand Secretary had forgotten or failed to keep his promise, and Maconochie saw him again. This time the Grand Secretary replied *by letter addressed to Maconochie*:

> Dear Sir, I have read the letter from the RW Master of Mother Kilwinning to you, and I do assure you that when I received your communication *I have made such arrangements as that no alteration has taken* place, or will happen.
>
> *Signed*, Alex^r Lawrie, *Gr Secy*

Maconochie dutifully reported all this to the Mother Lodge, with protestations of his continued interest and loyalty, and the matter was finally settled, but with no great show of courtesy on the part of the Grand Secretary.

In September 1834, the Kilwinning minutes report a letter from the Grand Secretary requesting the Lodge to '. . . Make a show of our books and pay arrears said to be due . . .'.

In 1835, the Grand Lodge decided to raise the Registration fees for Intrants to 5/6d and Kilwinning sent a protest saying that in terms of the 'Agreement' the fee was fixed at 2/6d. Here, the Mother Lodge was definitely in the wrong, because the fee had been fixed at '. . . a sum *not less than* . . .' 2/6d for each intrant. Two years later the point was still in dispute.

At first glance it would seem as though the Mother Lodge during the years following the re-union, was constantly at odds with the Grand Lodge, but of course it was not so. The incidents which are described here in close sequence, actually occurred in a period of 35 years. For the Grand Lodge it was a period of rapid growth, quite apart from the accession in one year of so many of Kilwinning's Daughters, and the problems of re-organisation, procedure and management must have presented all sorts of difficulties.

For the Mother Lodge, having surrendered some of her ancient rights, and jealously guarding the concessions she had won at the re-union, it was inevitable that the settling-down period was full of anxiety, and in these circumstances each little difference with the Grand Lodge was magnified, sometimes out of all proportion to its importance.

The original Five Articles of the Settlement in 1807 were clearly inadequate to cover all the problems that were to arise, and as each difficulty was settled in its turn, precedents were laid and the Mother Lodge settled peacefully into her position at the head of the Roll of Lodges under the Grand Lodge of Scotland.

MODERN TIMES

The privileges enjoyed by the Mother Lodge have nevertheless given rise to difficulties, even within her own Province of Ayrshire, and this brief sketch would be seriously out of date without some reference to the most recent problems.

In Scotland, unlike our English practice, the appointment of Provincial and District Grand Masters rests with the Grand Lodge itself, and not with the Grand Master. Those Commissions (or Patents of Office) are invariably for five years, and they are renewable. In practice, when a vacancy occurs at the expiration of this term, or on death or retirement of the holder, the Grand Secretary will write to the Provincial or District Grand Lodge, inviting nominations. This procedure applies to all the Scottish Provinces and Districts, but not to Ayrshire, where the Master of No 0 is *ex officio* Provincial Grand Master of Ayrshire.

It has long been the custom of Mother Kilwinning to keep watch for a Brother of status suitable to serve as Master of No 0 and *ex officio* Prov GM of Ayrshire. When they find a Brother with the requisite qualifications he is invited to become a joining member of the Lodge, and is elected Master in due course.

Some years ago, an Ayrshire Brother, feeling that the system is very undemocratic, was proposed and elected as a joining member of No 0. He was a persuasive and forceful character, sufficiently well known and respected by the Ayrshire Lodges to get himself 'nominated' by them as a prospective Prov Grand Master.

All very well, but when the time came for the election of Master of No 0, he was not elected. The Lodge had ignored the 'nomination', in effect depriving more than forty Lodges in the Province of the rights they would enjoy in every other Scottish Province. They simply have no say at all in the appointment of their Prov GM, and they are not at all happy about that.

Broadly, the Kilwinning problems today arise out of the social, industrial and economic changes that have taken place in that area during the past 175 years. In 1807, Kilwinning was *the Lodge* of its own territory, with the local nobility and gentry among its members. Today, the membership consists mainly of small shopkeepers and miners.

But their zeal for the preservation of their ancient privileges as the senior-ranking Province has led them, occasionally, to claim rights over other Provinces, rights which belong only to that Province, or to the Grand Lodge itself.

Recently, without any desire to alter the basic terms of the re-union of 1807, the Grand Lodge moved to amend Clause 5 of that agreement in a manner that would avoid or satisfy some of the modern problems that were totally unforeseen in 1807.

Unfortunately, in a series of meetings with the Grand Committee, those proposals had been resisted and rejected by the Kilwinning Committee to the point where Kilwinning had taken legal proceedings against the Grand Lodge, to maintain and uphold their supposed rights and privileges.

The mills of justice grind slowly, and those proceedings were still *sub judice*, so that it would be improper to comment. One can only hope and pray that there will be a speedy settlement to the legal action, and that a truly Masonic goodwill and tolerance may prevail.

LATEST DEVELOPMENTS

While these pages were being prepared for press, news arrived of the settlement of the difficulties arising out of the 1807 Agreement. Both parties have now agreed the following.

(*Proceedings of the Grand Lodge of Scotland*, 5 May 1983)

That the existing Clause V of the Agreement between the Grand Lodge of Scotland and the Lodge Mother Kilwinning, No 0, dated 14 October 1807 be deleted and the following inserted:

That there be erected and constituted the Provincial Grand Lodge of Kilwinning and any future Lodge erected within the Parish of Kilwinning.

That Mother Kilwinning at its Annual Meeting in November will nominate a suitable Brother for the Office of Provincial Grand Master for submission to Grand Lodge as in the case of all Provincial and District Grand Masters.

That Mother Kilwinning for all time coming shall have the honour to nominate annually a suitable Brother for the Office of Grand bible-bearer whom Grand Lodge shall elect.

That the numbering of any new Lodge within the Parish of Kilwinning shall be prefaced with "0", such as "01" and "02", etc.

That dispensation be granted to all Past Depute Masters of Lodge Mother Kilwinning to receive the Chair Degree. Page 58 of Proceedings.

5

SAMUEL PRICHARD'S
MASONRY DISSECTED, 1730

THIS ESSAY WAS compiled as an Introduction to the facsimile edition of *Masonry Dissected*, 1730, published by the Masonic Book Club of Illinois, USA, in 1977, which produces rare and important masonic books in limited editions available only to members.

Prichard's text is not included here (see p 410), but it is readily accessible in full, in the *Early Masonic Catechisms*, 2nd edn, 1963.

BIBLIOGRAPHICAL NOTES
In compiling the notes under this heading, I am much indebted to three specialist studies: (i) *The Early Masonic Catechisms*, by Knoop, Jones and Hamer, second edition, pp 157/8: (ii) 'Prichard's *Masonry Dissected*', by Comdr S. N. Smith, *AQC*, 51 pp 138/9: (iii) John T. Thorp in *Leicester Lodge of Research Masonic Reprints*, Vol XII (1929) pp 10/11.

Masonry Dissected
The first edition of this 32pp 8vo pamphlet (approx 7⅝″ × 4½″) was advertised for sale in a London newspaper, the *Daily Journal*, on Tuesday 2 October 1730:

> This day is published . . . MASONRY DISSECTED . . . by Samuel Prichard . . . Printed for J. Wilford . . . (Price 6d)

The second edition was advertised the very next day, 21 October, and again on the 23rd, two days later: the third edition was advertised on Saturday, 31 October 1730, and these two editions were also printed for Wilford. (See advertisements reproduced.)

Meanwhile the pamphlet had been reprinted in *Read's Weekly Journal or British Gazetteer*, on Saturday 24 October 1730. This was apparently a pirated version in which the whole thirty-one printed pages of the original were crammed into two pages of the newspaper, each approximately 15″ × 10″.

Another pirated edition, dated MD.CC.XXX. printed by Thomas Nichols, 'without Temple Bar' (London) had also probably made its appearance by the end of October 1730.

Prichard's text was reprinted, in two parts, in separate issues of the *Northampton Mercury*, the first section, up to the end of the Enter'd 'Prentice's Degree, in October 1730, and the remainder, from the Fellow-Craft's Degree to the end, on 2 November 1730.

Thus, there were three separate editions by Prichard, and a pirated edition (Nichols), plus a newspaper version (Read's) all printed in London, and a two-part newspaper version, printed in the Midlands, all within fourteen days!

Thorp, writing in 1929, listed another fourteen editions before 1760 and nine more before the end of the eighteenth century. Bro Knoop and his collaborators, writing in 1943, mentioned 'thirty numbered editions . . . printed in England, and eight . . . in Scotland'.

In spite of this seeming profusion of copies, all the earlier editions are scarce and the four versions dated 1730 are extremely rare. There is a copy of the first edition in the Library of the United Grand Lodge of England and one in the Library of the Grand Lodge of Massachusetts. Another first edition (formerly in the Wallace Heaton collection) is now owned by the present writer. There is a copy of the second edition in the Leicester Masonic Library (reprinted by J. T. Thorp in 1929). The third edition is the earliest in the British Museum collection. That version was the first to contain 'A List of Regular Lodges according to their Seniority and Constitution' and it was reproduced by Bro Douglas Knoop and his colleagues in *The Early Masonic Catechisms*, 1943. The excellent collection in the Library of the Grand Lodge of Massachusetts also includes a copy of the Nichols pirated print.

SAMUEL PRICHARD
HIS MASONIC BACKGROUND

Among the many characters who made their mark in Masonic history during the early decades of the first Grand Lodge, Samuel Prichard

The *Daily Journal*, Tuesday, 20 October 1730

This Day is Publiſhed,

(Dedicated to the Right Worſhipful and Honourable Fraternity of Free and Accepted Maſons, and the Author's Affidavit before Sir Richard Hopkins prefix'd)

MASONRY DISSECTED: Being a Univerful and Genuine Defcription of all its Branches, from the Original to this Prefent Time; as it deliver'd in the Conftituted Regular Lodges both in City and Country, according to the feveral Degrees of Admiffion. Giving an Impartial Account of their Regular Proceeding in Initiating their New-Members in the whole Three Degrees of Mafonry, viz. I. Enter'd Apprentice. II. Fellow Craft. III. Mafter. To which is added, The Author's Vindication of himfelf. By SAMUEL PRITCHARD, late Member of a Conftituted Lodge.

Printed for J. WILFORD, at the Three Flower-de-Luces behind the Chapter-Houfe, near St. Paul's. Price 6 d.

The first advertisement.

The *Daily Journal*, Wednesday, 21 October 1730

This Day is Publiſhed,

(Dedicated to the Right Worſhipful and Honourable Fraternity of Free and Accepted Maſons, and the Author's Affidavit before Sir Richard Hopkins prefix'd)

The SECOND EDITION, of

MASONRY DISSECTED: Being a Univerfal and Genuine Defcription of all its Branches, from the Original to this Prefent Time; as it deliver'd in the Conftituted Regular Lodges both in City and Country, according to the feveral Degrees of Admiffion. Giving an Impartial Account of their Regular Proceeding in Initiating their New-Members in the whole Three Degrees of Mafonry, viz. I. Enter'd Apprentice. II. Fellow Craft. III. Mafter. To which is added, The Author's Vindication of himfelf. By SAMUEL PRITCHARD, late Member of a Conftituted Lodge.

Printed for J. WILFORD, at the Three Flower-de-Luces behind the Chapter-Houfe, near St. Paul's. Price 6 d.

The second advertisement. "The Second Edition of"
has been inserted after line 4.

The *Daily Journal*, Friday, 23 October 1730

This Day is Publiſhed,
(Dedicated to the Right Worſhipful and Honour-
able Fraternity of Free and Accepted Maſons,
The SECOND EDITION, of
MASONRY DISSECTED: Being a Uni-
verſal and Genuine Deſcription of all its Branches, from the
Original to this Preſent Time; as it deliver'd in the Conſti-
tuted Regular Lodges both in City and Country, according
to the ſeveral Degrees of Admiſſion. Giving an Impartial
Account of their Regular Proceeding in Initiating their
New-Members in the whole Three Degrees of Maſonry, viz.
I. Enter'd Apprentice. II. Fellow Craft. III. Maſter. To
which is added, The Author's Vindication of himſelf. By
SAMUEL PRITCHARD, late Member of a Conſtituted Lodge.
    Printed for J. WILFORD, at the Three Flower-de-Luces
behind the Chapter-Houſe, near St. Paul's. Price 6 d.
    N. B. There is prefixed to this Account, a True Copy of
the Affidavit made before Sir RICHARD HOPKINS, of its
Truth and Genuineneſs in every Particular, without which
all other Accounts are ſpurious, and groſs Impoſitions on
the Publick.

The third advertisement. Original lines 4 and 5 are
omitted and a footnote is added.

The *Daily Journal*, Saturday, 31 October 1730

This Day is Publiſhed,
(With a Liſt of the Regular Lodges, according
to their Seniority and Conſtitution)
The THIRD EDITION, of
MASONRY DISSECTED: Being a Uni-
verſal and Genuine Deſcription of all its Branches, from the
Original to this Preſent Time; as it is deliver'd in the Conſti-
tuted Regular Lodges both in City and Country, according
to the ſeveral Degrees of Admiſſion. Giving an Impartial
Account of their Regular Proceeding in Initiating their
New-Members in the whole Three Degrees of Maſonry, viz.
I. Enter'd Apprentice. II. Fellow Craft. III. Maſter. To
which is added, The Author's Vindication of himſelf. By
SAMUEL PRITCHARD, late Member of a Conſtituted Lodge.
    Printed for J. WILFORD, at the Three Flower-de-Luces
behind the Chapter-Houſe, near St. Paul's. Price 6 d.
    N. B. There is prefixed to this Account, a True Copy of
the Affidavit made before Sir RICHARD HOPKINS, of its
Truth and Genuineneſs in every Particular, without which
all other Accounts are ſpurious, and groſs Impoſitions on
the Publick.

The fourth advertisement. 'Third' instead of 'Second' and the
word 'is', previously omitted, is now added in line 6.

must surely rank as one of the most extraordinary. As a person, nothing is known about him, his family, social status, trade, or profession; he remains a complete mystery.

In October 1730 he published *Masonry Dissected*, a very successful pamphlet which claimed to be 'A Universal and Genuine Description of [Masonry in] all its Branches'. At the next Quarterly Communication of Grand Lodge on 15 December 1730 he was roundly condemned as 'an Impostor':

> The Deputy Grand Master took notice of a Pamphlet lately published by one Pritchard [*sic*] who pretends to have been made a regular Mason: In Violation of the Obligation of a Mason wch he swears he has broke in order to do hurt to Masonry and expressing himself with the utmost Indignation against both him (stiling him an Impostor) and of his Book as a foolish thing not to be regarded. But in order to prevent the Lodges being imposed upon by false Brethren or Impostors: Proposed . . . that no Person whatsoever should be admitted into Lodges unless some Member of the Lodge then present would vouch for such visiting Brothers being a regular Mason, and the Member's Name to be entered against the Visitor's Name in the Lodge Book, which Proposal was unanimously agreed to (*QCA IX, pp 135*/6).

This was the only occasion on which Prichard's name appeared in the Grand Lodge Minutes. His Lodge was not mentioned and, so far as official records go, it is not even certain that he had ever been admitted into the Craft.

The only information to be found about him is that which can be deduced from his book as a whole, but especially from the eight preliminary pages, and from '*The Author's Vindication of himself . . .*', which formed its final chapter. The sources from which these details can be gathered are of two kinds:

(a) Direct statements, made by Prichard, about himself and his reasons for compiling the book.

(b) Inferences that may properly be drawn from the knowledge of the Craft that he displayed in his introductory pages and in the text of his exposure.

There is reason to believe that the information thus obtained may furnish useful light on Prichard as a Mason and on his capacity as a writer on Masonry, all the more valuable, perhaps, because of the total absence of other sources. In the following notes the page numbers shown in [   ] refer to un-numbered pages in the first edition of *Masonry Dissected*.

LATE MEMBER OF A CONSTITUTED LODGE: [p I]. Prichard's claim that he was '*late Member of a CONSTITUTED LODGE*' implies that he was a Mason who had resigned or been excluded. This was probably true. Quite apart from his ritual text (which does not necessarily prove that he had been a Mason) there is evidence to show that he had a very good knowledge of Masonry and its background, and there is no reason to doubt his claim.

There is indeed a record of a 'Mr Sam[1]. Pritchard' in the minutes of the Lodge held at the Swan and Rummer Tavern, in Finch Lane, London, showing that he was a visitor to that Lodge on 25 September 1728, and the record also mentions his Lodge. It runs:

'Mr Sam[1]. Pritchard [of] Harry ye
8th head of 7 Dyalls'   (Hughan, *AQC* 10, p 134).

The names Prichard and Pritchard are interchangeable, and this entry may have been made by the Secretary of the Lodge, who included the 't'. Grand Lodge also used the spelling 'Pritchard' in the minutes of 15 December 1730, above, and it appeared so in the advertisements, but not in Prichard's book.

Little is known about the Lodge at 'King Henry ye VIII Head' except that it was a 'Regular Constituted Lodge', and was so recorded in the Grand Lodge List for 25 November 1725* when it had seventeen members whose names are also recorded (but Prichard's name was not among them). The Lodge sent representatives, Master and Wardens, to the Quarterly Communications in June 1728 and in December 1730†, after which it seems to have disappeared.

If we could be sure that the visitor to the Swan and Rummer on 25 September 1728 was *our* Samuel Prichard, the record would be doubly interesting, partly because we know that the Lodge had a number of distinguished visitors, but chiefly because it was one of the earliest English Lodges recorded as working the third degree. Needless to say, Prichard's chief claim to Masonic fame or notoriety was his publication of *Masonry Dissected*, the first exposure of the ritual of three degrees.

* *Minutes of the Grand Lodge . . . 1723–1739*, QCA, X, p 43.
† ibid. pp 86, 133.

The word '*CONSTITUTED*', on Prichard's title-page, had a special significance at that time. The first *Book of Constitutions*, 1723, contained a chapter describing 'the Manner of constituting a New Lodge' and on 25 November 1723 the Grand Lodge had ruled:

> That no new Lodge in or near London without it be regularly Constituted be Countenanced by the Grand Lodge, nor the Ma^r or Wardens admitted at the Grand Lodge.*

Prichard's use of the word 'Constituted' was intended to emphasise the regularity of his former Lodge, but it may well indicate a better than average knowledge of what was going on in the Grand Lodge.

THE OATH: [p II]. A greatly inferior exposure, *The Mystery of Free-Masonry*, had been on sale in London under various titles, since August 1730. Prichard's work was infinitely better and he probably decided to use the Oath as a plain piece of salesmanship, guaranteeing the quality of his own publication. It was sworn, before a magistrate, Sir Richard Hopkins, an Alderman of the Lime Street Ward of the City of London, on 13 October 1730.

It seems that pirated versions, under the same title, had begun to appear immediately after Prichard's first edition came out on 20 October, and he altered the 23 October advertisement for his second edition, by inserting a note which referred to the Oath (or Affidavit):

> NB There is prefixed to this Account, a True Copy of the Affidavit made before Sir Richard Hopkins, of its Truth and Genuineness in every Particular, without which all other accounts are spurious and gross Impositions on the Publick . . .

THE DEDICATION: (pp III, IV]. This was addressed to the Fraternity itself, in polite and respectful terms, but when read in conjunction with the 'Author's Vindication of himself' at the end of the work, the dedication appears to be tinged with irony.

Masonry Dissected: pp 5–8. In this section, Prichard compared 'the original Institution of Masonry' with the 'Accepted Masonry' of his own day. He began with a very brief précis of the story of the Craft, as told (with many variations) in practically every version of the *Old Charges* or *MS. Constitutions*. He mentioned 'the Liberal Arts and

---

* ibid. p 54.

Sciences; but more especially . . . *Geometry*' and traced the trans-
mission of 'the Art and Mystery of Masonry' from 'the Building of the
Tower of Babel', through Euclid, who

> communicated it to *Hiram*, the Master-Mason concern'd in the Building of
> *Solomon's* Temple in *Jerusalem*, where was an excellent and curious
> Mason that was the chief under their Grand-Master *Hiram*, whose Name
> was *Mannon Grecus*, who taught the Art of Masonry to one *Carolos
> Marcil in France*, who was afterwards elected King of France, . . .

Omitting many details, but still following the *Old Charges* in outline,
Prichard noted that the Craft was brought from France and became
established in England, where 'Masons were made in the Manner
following':

> *Tunc unus ex Senioribus teneat Librum, ut illi vel ille ponant vel ponat
> Manus supra Librum; tum Praecepta debeant legi, ie* Whilst one of the
> Seniors holdeth the Book, that he or they put their Hands upon the Book,
> whilst the Master ought to read the Laws or Charges.

It is obvious that Prichard was well acquainted with one or more
versions of the *Old Charges*, although he did not name specific texts;
but he did leave several clues, and the search is rewarding, because it
produces valuable evidence of his status as a student of Freemasonry.

THE OLD CHARGES IN PRICHARD'S DAY

Some 130 versions of the *Old Charges* have survived to this day,
ranging in date from c1390 right through to the mid-eighteenth
century. Several of them are copies of earlier versions, but all of them
– even the *early copies* – are rare and valuable manuscripts. Modern
students are fortunate, because most of them have been reproduced
in print during the past hundred years or more, so that their contents
are readily accessible nowadays.

In Prichard's day, however, the majority of them would have been
stored in private libraries, or in antiquarian collections, out of reach
of the public, and their existence in most cases was unknown. There
was, nevertheless, a great interest among Masonic leaders in these
old documents which purported to recount the history of the Craft
since' Bible times, together with the Charges or Regulations by which
the masons were governed. In the 'historical' section of Anderson's
Book of Constitutions, 1738, (p 110) he recorded, for 24 June 1718:

George Payne Esq: *Grand Master* . . . desired any Brethren to bring to the Grand Lodge any old *Writings* and *Records* concerning *Masons* and *Masonry* in order to shew the Usages of antient Times: And this Year several old Copies of the *Gothic Constitutions* were produced and collated.

On 24 June 1720, at the beginning of Payne's second term as Grand Master, Anderson noted that:

This Year, at some *private* Lodges, several very valuable *Manuscripts* (for they had nothing yet in Print) concerning the Fraternity, their Lodges, Regulations, Charges, Secrets, and Usages . . . were too hastily burnt by some scrupulous Brothers, that those Papers might not fall into strange Hands. (ibid. p 111)

At the Grand Festival in June 1721, Payne exhibited the *Cooke MS*, *c*1410 (now acknowledged as the second oldest version of the *Old Charges*).

Anderson had said, correctly, that 'they had nothing yet in Print' (in 1720), but this was partially remedied in the next few years. In 1722, a version of the *Old Constitutions* was 'Printed, and Sold by J. Roberts, in *Warwick Lane*' [London].

In 1724, and again in 1725, another pamphlet was 'Printed for Sam. Briscoe, at the Bell-Savage, on *Ludgate-Hill*', and came on sale there and at three other places in London. It is now known as the *Briscoe Pamphlet*, and contains a varied collection of Masonic odds-and-ends including a version of the *Old Charges*.

In 1728–29 Benjamin Cole published another version, in book form; it was printed from engraved plates in three different states and the first 'edition' may have appeared a year or two before 1728. These three versions are *the only texts known to have been in print* at the time when Prichard was preparing to publish his exposure. In addition there were a number of copies of several versions, most of them made by William Reid, who was Grand Secretary from 1727–34. He was responsible for three texts, now known as the *Fisher MS*, *c*1726; *Songhurst MS*, *c*1726; and the *Spencer MS*, 1726, all three being virtually identical. Two years later, he produced another version, the *Woodford MS*, 1728, which was a copy of the *Cooke MS* of *c*1410.

One more text must be added to this list, because it is of special interest, ie the *Bolt-Coleraine MS*, dated 1728, which will be discussed more fully, below.

This completes the list of all the print and manuscript versions of the *Old Charges* that could have been readily accessible to Prichard in the years before he published his *Masonry Dissected*. He may, indeed, have had access to other versions, but that is extremely doubtful because – had they been available – there would almost certainly have been some record of their being copied, as was the case with the *Cooke MS* and *Songhurst, Spencer, Fisher and Bolt-Coleraine MSS*.

THE THREE CLUES

We may return now to the three clues which Prichard left; they consist of the two names, '*Mannon Grecus*' and '*Carolos Marcil*', with the Latin instruction '*Tunc unus ex Senioribus . . .*' Among the 130 surviving versions of the *Old Charges*, there are many which lack all three items. Some contain one or both names in a fantastic variety of spellings*, but they omit the Latin instruction; others contain that instruction in English. Only a small proportion contain all three items, ie two names with the Latin text, but their spellings differ widely from Prichard's clues. The following extracts, all earlier than 1730, may serve as illustrations, from versions that contain all three 'clues'.

Prichard's words, for comparison →	MANNON GRECUS	CAROLOS MARCIL	Latin text (see p. 111 above)
Thorp MS, 1629. *AQC*, Vol 11, pp 209/210	NAYMUS GREEUS	CHARLES MARTILL	Spellings differ
Beaumont MS, 1690 *Yorkshire Old Charges*, pp 76/8 By Poole & Worts	MAMON GRECUS	CARALUS MARCHILL	Spellings differ
Bain MS, 1670-1680 *AQC*, Vol 20, pp 260, 263.	[BLANK] GROECUS	CHARLES MARTELL	Spellings differ

* The first name, 'Mannon Grecus' appears in versions ranging from 'Naymus Grecus' to 'minus Greenatus, alias Green'. The second name 'Carolos Marcil' appears in versions ranging from 'Carolus Martyll' to 'Charles Marshall'.

Drinkwater MS,			
*No 1. c.*1710	Mannon Graecum	Carolus Martyll	Words
Trans.Manchester			differ
Assn. for Mas.			
Research, Vol XV			

It is doubtful if Prichard had access to any of these texts, but even if he had, it is clear that none of them could have been his source for those names, or for the Latin instruction.

The manuscript and printed versions of the *Old Charges* that are *known to have been accessible to Prichard before 1730* are equally unhelpful except in one case. As regards the three clues, for which we are searching, they exhibit wide variations of detail, eg the *Spencer, Songhurst,* and *Fisher MSS,* and the *Cole* engraved versions have neither the two names nor the Latin instruction. The *Cooke MS* of *c*1410 (and the *Woodford MS,* which was a copy made in 1728) have only one of the names, given as 'Carolus Secundus', but they lack the Latin passage. The *Briscoe* print of 1724 gives both names 'Nainus Groecus' and 'Charles Martil', but again the Latin instruction is omitted. The *Roberts* print, of 1722, has both names, with the Latin instruction, but none of the three items matches Prichard's clues, ie

Roberts, 1722.   Memongrecus: Carolus Martel
Masonry Dissected, 1730.   Mannon Grecus: Carolos Marcil

and for the Latin passage:

Roberts, 1722	*Prichard, 1730*
Tunc Unus ex Senioribus veniat librum illi qui Injurandum reddat & ponat Manum in Libro vel supra librum dum Articulus & Precepta sibi legentur.	*Tunc unus ex Senioribus teneat Librum, ut illi vel ille ponant vel ponat Manus supra Librum; tum Praecepta debeant legi.*

After much searching, there is only one version of the 'Old Charges' that contains all three of Prichard's clues and that can be proved to have been in circulation at the time when Prichard was preparing his material. It is the *Bolt-Coleraine MS,* dated 1728, and is believed to have been copied by one, William Askew, from an original now lost. This text of 1728 was in a small book of forty-three pages, with an inscription which suggests that it was commissioned by Lord Coleraine, or prepared for presentation to him, at the time when he was Grand Master in 1727/8. The inscription runs:

> The Constitutions of the Right Honble
> and Worshipfull Fraternity of Free
> and Accepted Masons
>
> A.M.   5728
> A.D.   1728
>
> The Rt. Honble Henry Lord Colerane
> Baron of Colerane in the Kingdom of Ireland
>
> Grand Master
> *Odi Profanum*

(The Latin is from Horace, *Odes* III, 1. I. and means 'I hate the uninitiate crowd . . .'). The book was in the possession of the Bristol Masonic Society until 1941, when it was destroyed by enemy action. Fortunately a transcript survived and that was reproduced in full in Gould's *History of Freemasonry* (Poole's edition, 1951, Vol I pp 25-29).

As to Prichard's *name* clues, those in *Bolt-Coleraine* are almost, but not quite identical:

Prichard, 1730	Mannon Grecus	Carolos Marcil
Bolt-Coleraine, 1728	Mannon Grecus	Carolus Marcill

As to the Latin instruction, in all except the spelling of one word, the two versions are word-for-word identical:

Prichard's *Masonry Dissected* 1730	*The Bolt-Coleraine MS., 1728* (From the Bristol Transcript)
Tunc unus ex Senioribus teneat Librum, ut illi vel ille ponant vel ponat Manus supra Librum: tum Praecepta debeant legi.	Tunc Unus Ex Senioribus teneat Librum ut illi vel illem ponant vel ponat manus supra Librum Tum praecepta debeant Legi.

Because of the destruction of the 1728 copy of the *Bolt-Coleraine MS*, in 1941, Bro Poole was unable to vouch for the accuracy of the Bristol transcript, which was the basis of his reproduction in 1951, and this may perhaps explain the minute differences that appear in the two versions under discussion. But there is another explanation that may be far more satisfying.

All the manuscript versions of the *Old Charges* that can be proved to have been accessible to Prichard in 1730 were in some way connected with the Grand Lodge itself, or with Lord Coleraine, Grand Master in 1727–28. The *Spencer MS* 1726, the *Songhurst* and *Fisher MSS*, *c*1726, were all copied by William Reid, who was Grand Secretary from 1727–33. The *Woodford MS* (a copy of the *Cooke MS*, of *c*1410), was copied by him in 1728, and it contains an inscription headed 'Ld Coleraine – Gr^d Master'. The *Bolt-Coleraine MS* was also copied in 1728, by order of Lord Coleraine, or for his ultimate use.

At this period, two years before Prichard's *Masonry Dissected* was condemned by the Grand Lodge, Prichard obviously had access to the *1728 copy* of the *Old Charges* which eventually became known as the *Bolt-Coleraine MS*; but in that case, *it is more probable that he had access to the original text* from which that copy was made, and that his three clues were extracted from that version which is now lost. All this suggests that Prichard was in touch with William Reid, the Grand Secretary, and perhaps with Lord Coleraine as well.

Immediately following the Latin instruction, Prichard printed a very adequate English translation (*which was not in the Bolt-Coleraine MS*) and this shows that he had, at the very least, a useful working knowledge of Latin.

The results of this somewhat involved examination of the sources of Prichard's clues show him to have been a man of some education, a student of the early documents of the Craft, with access to one or more texts of the *Old Charges* which were in the custody of the Grand Lodge, or of some of its senior officers; and this implies that in the years preceding the publication of *Masonry Dissected*, he had been a respectable member of a regular Lodge.

We shall see, moreover, when we examine the text of Prichard's three degrees, that he must have had a useful working knowledge of the ritual and usages of that time. Anderson recorded the destruction, in 1720, of 'several very valuable Manuscripts . . . concerning the Fraternity, their Lodges, . . . Secrets and Usages' and we have no means of knowing if Prichard had had access to those or to similar documents. But when we observe how vastly superior his work was to any of the early documents that have survived, and how much of his work can be directly linked with the earlier texts, it is obvious that he was much more than an average student of the Craft, its ritual and procedures.

ACCEPTED MASONRY: (pp 6–7)

Prichard continued his introductory remarks with a note on the Accepted Masonry of his own day:

> . . . Accepted Masonry (as it now is) has not been heard of till within these few Years; no Constituted Lodges or Quarterly Communications were heard of till 1691, when Lords and Dukes, Lawyers and Shopkeepers, and other inferior Tradesmen, Porters not excepted, were admitted into this Mystery or no Mystery;

It would have been difficult for Prichard to give a precise date for the rise of 'Accepted Masonry', but there are records of the 'Accepcon' in the London Masons Company from 1621 onwards, and Plot, in his *Natural History of Staffordshire*, had written in 1686 that 'persons of the most eminent quality . . . did not disdain to be of this *Fellowship*', and that he had found it 'spread more or less all over the Nation'.

Prichard's date, 1691, for the beginning of Quarterly Communications, would be beyond proof nowadays; there is no evidence to support the existence of any such established organisation in 1691.

Prichard's division of the classes of men who were joining the Craft, reflected the social distinctions of his own era:

> the first sort [Lords and Dukes] being introduc'd at a very great Expence, the second sort [Lawyers and Shopkeepers] at a moderate Rate, and the latter [inferior Tradesmen, Porters not excepted] for the Expence of six or seven Shillings, for which they receive that Badge of Honour, which (as they term it) is more ancient and more honourable than is the Star and Garter, which Antiquity is accounted, according to the Rules of Masonry, as delivered by their Tradition, ever since *Adam*, which I shall leave the candid Reader to determine.

This appears to be the earliest comparison of the Apron with the 'Star and Garter', in words which have survived some 250 years as part of the Masonic ritual in English Lodges all over the world. This note on the Apron as a Badge of Honour is particularly interesting because there is no mention of the Apron in the text of Prichard's exposure, showing – on his own admission – that his text is incomplete.

The reference to 'their Tradition, ever since *Adam*' is a gentle jibe at the opening words of the historical section of Anderson's first *Book of Constitutions*, 1723:

> *Adam*, our first Parent, . . . must have had the Liberal Sciences, particularly *Geometry*, written on his Heart; . . .

Prichard's introductory chapter continued with brief references to some of the mock-Masonic societies of the 1730s, and the final paragraph consisted of a complaint that a Brother, having to withdraw from the Craft because of the 'Quarterly Expenses' would be

> denied the Privilege (as a Visiting Brother) of knowing the Mystery for which he has already paid, which is a manifest Contradiction according to the Institution of Masonry itself . . .

The tone of this passage seems to suggest that Prichard was perhaps writing about himself as a sufferer under this rule. He cited another example of 'loss of visiting privileges' in the '*Vindication*', which formed the final chapter of his book.

THE AUTHOR'S VINDICATION OF HIMSELF . . . pp 30, 31;

The contents of this brief section are not at all in keeping with its pompous but promising title, *The Author's Vindication of himself from the prejudiced Part of Mankind*'. By way of vindication, the only reason he could find, to justify him in the breach of his Masonic oath, was that the Obligation had already been published:

> . . . the grand Article, *viz.*, the *Obligation*, has several Times been printed in the publick Papers, but is entirely genuine in the *Daily Journal* of *Saturday, Aug. 22.* 1730. which agrees in its Veracity with that deliver'd in this Pamphlet; and consequently when the Obligation of Secrecy is abrogated, the aforesaid Secret becomes of no Effect, and must be quite extinct;

It had indeed been published under the title '*The Mystery of Freemasonry*', in the *Daily Journal* of 15 August, 1730 (and in several broadsides under various titles); but even if all these had been correct in every particular, their appearance in print could not have released or absolved him of his own oath. (Incidentally, the text in the *Daily*

Journal was vastly inferior to Prichard's version.)

At this point, and with total irrelevance to his supposed vindication of himself, Prichard entered on a new theme, telling the story of some Masons* who

> made a Visitation from the first and oldest constituted Lodge (. . . in *London*) to a noted Lodge in this City, and was denied Admittance, because their old Lodge was removed to another House, which, ... requires another Constitution, at no less Expence than two Guineas, with an elegant Entertainment, under the Denomination of being put to charitable Uses. . . .

He expressed serious doubts as to whether these costs would really be applied to the charitable uses for which such funds were intended, believing that they would 'be expended towards the forming another System of Masonry, the old Fabrick being so ruinous, . . .' There is no record of this incident in the Grand Lodge Minutes; and there was no rule in the 1723 *Book of Constitutions* that would have justified a fee for a new Constitution in this case, unless the Brethren who were 'denied Admittance' had actually withdrawn or separated themselves from their original Lodge, in which case Reg. VIII would have applied.

The story, if it were true, might well have influenced Prichard's views on the Masonry of his day and, doubtless, he recounted it as an additional excuse for his defection. His comments on the 'ruinous' condition of the 'Fabrick' of Masonry seem to reflect the resistance to change which must have been generated fairly widely during that era of major changes in the government of the Craft, while the young Grand Lodge was beginning to acquire control over old and new Lodges in London and the Provinces.

In the *Records of the Lodge of Antiquity No 2* (Original No 1) pp 35/6, our late Bro W. H. Rylands identified the 'first and oldest constituted Lodge . . . in London' as a reference to Original No 1 and examining Prichard's tirade, he came to the conclusion that

> the whole attack is directed not against Masonry in general, but against the new Fashions which threatened the "old Fabrick".

The final paragraph of Prichard's '*Vindication*' claimed that he was

---

* He described them as 'Operative Masons (but according to the polite Way of Expression, Accepted Masons)'.

induced to publish his exposure 'at the Request of several Masons' and he expressed the hope that it would

> give entire Satisfaction, and have its desired Effect in preventing so many credulous Persons being drawn into so pernicious a Society.

Whether he was actually persuaded, *by Masons*, to undertake the publication is open to doubt and need not be taken seriously. The sting in the *Vindication* is contained in his opening and closing words:

> Of all the Impositions that have appear'd amongst Mankind, none are so ridiculous as the Mystery of Masonry . . . . so pernicious a Society.

These are the only passages in the whole book that are tinged with real animosity. They suggest that the exposure was not published merely as a protest against changes or innovations. Something had embittered him against the Craft and that is the final detail in the portrait of Prichard that we have tried to reconstruct from the evidence that he left for us. He had been a member of a regular Lodge, had read Anderson's *Book of Constitutions* and was a student of the history of the Craft. He was probably well known to senior officers of the Grand Lodge and certainly had free access to documents in which they were deeply interested. Soon after the *Bolt-Coleraine MS* had been copied, in 1728, an incident had occurred – trivial or serious, we do not know – but it turned him against the Craft, and he betrayed his Obligation.

MASONIC CATECHISMS AND EXPOSURES*

Until the late 1600s the only evidence we have on Masonic ritual consists of several versions of the masons' Obligation (in the *Old Charges*) with occasional notes describing how it was administered (as in the Latin instruction quoted on p 111, above). The earliest versions are simple oaths of fidelity to the King, the trade, and the Master, without any reference to esoteric matters, or penalties. Some of the later versions contain references to secrets, but without details.

---

* For students of the evolution of Masonic ritual, the following works are particularly recommended: 'Masonic Ritual and Secrets before 1717' by the Rev Herbert Poole, *AQC*, 37, pp 4–43; *The Early Masonic Catechisms*, by Knoop, Jones and Hamer, which contains transcripts of all the texts up to c1740, with a valuable introduction (2nd edn, publ. by the QC Lodge); 'An Examination of the Early Masonic Catechisms', by H. Carr, in *AQC*, Vols 83, 84 and 85, in which the contents of the earlier texts are compared with *Masonry Dissected*; *The Genesis of Freemasonry*, pp 204–293, by Douglas Knoop and G. P. Jones. A less detailed sketch, covering developments up to c1813, *600 Years of Craft Ritual*, by H. Carr, may also prove useful.

The Harleian MS, No 2054, c1650, contains a form of the Masons' obligation which speaks of 'sev^{r}all [ie several] words & signs of a free Mason', plural, implying secret modes of recognition for more than one degree, and indicating that the ceremonies were beginning to take on their modern shape, ie an obligation and 'entrusting'; but the text gives no other details. From 1598 onwards, there are Scottish Lodge minutes which prove the existence of two degrees, the first for the Entered Apprentice, and the second for the 'Master or Fellow-craft', but they give no information as to the contents of those ceremonies.

Today, there are altogether seventeen Masonic documents that comprise the whole of the surviving evidence on the ritual up to 1730. Seven of these were printed in newspapers, or as broadsides or pamphlets, and all seven were published from motives of curiosity, profit, or spite; hence their general classification as 'Exposures'.

The remaining ten documents are manuscripts, mainly in the form of Question and Answer, occasionally with the addition of notes on various Masonic matters. At least three of these texts (discovered respectively in 1904, 1930 and 1954) were undoubtedly copied out carefully by hand in order to serve as *aides-mémoires* to the ceremonies and they are particularly valuable on that account. All these hand-written texts were obviously prepared for personal use and they are usually described under the more respectable heading of 'Catechisms'.

The senior Grand Lodges (England, Ireland and Scotland) have never issued any official Rituals or Monitors, so that there are no authoritative documents that would provide a proper starting-point for studies on the evolution and development of early Masonic ritual. It is this total absence of officially authorised material that has invested the Catechisms and Exposures with a degree of importance far beyond the interest they would otherwise have merited. Because all such documents – whether hand-written or printed – were compiled in violation of the Mason's oath, they were collectively deemed to be of dubious origin and therefore suspect; and no matter how interesting their contents might be, they were considered unworthy of serious study. In effect, *the more they revealed, the less they were to be trusted, unless it could be proved that the rituals and procedures which they described were linked in some way with the actual Lodge practice of their time.* That kind of proof was not easy to come by, but it did come – in stages – during a period of some thirty years. The story may seem irrelevant here, but it is not possible to make a fair assessment of Prichard's work without knowing how the cloud of mistrust that rested on all such documents was finally removed. It begins with a fragment of ritual, dated 1702, on the opening page of an old Scottish minute book.

THE 'HAUGHFOOT FRAGMENT'

In 1702, a little group of gentlemen, all Masons, decided to found a Lodge in the village of Haughfoot, some twenty miles S.E. of Edinburgh. Two of them, Sir John Hoppringle of that Ilk and his younger brother, Sir James Pringle, were notable landowners in that district. Another founder, Andrew Thomson, probably a lawyer, was due to become their 'Boxmaster' and he served in that office, ie as Treasurer, combining it with the duties of Secretary. He was ordered to buy a minute-book, for which he was reimbursed in due course 'ffourteen shillings Scotts'.

The minute book survives to this day as one of the treasures of the ancient Lodge of Selkirk, now No 32, S.C. Its contents begin, in the middle of a sentence, at the top of page 11, the preceding ten pages having been lost or destroyed. As far as we can reconstruct the story, it seems that Thomson began his records with details of the preliminaries before the foundation of the Lodge, and then continued with what must have been a complete copy, or a précis, of the two-degree ritual of that time. When this was finished, he had filled the first ten pages, and the last five lines of ritual were at the top of page 11, leaving three-quarters of the page blank. But his native Scottish thrift would not allow him to waste that page and, immediately after the end of his ritual text, he added a heading:

'The same day'

and continued with the minutes of the meeting held on 22 December 1702, apparently the first 'working' meeting at which six 'Intrants . . . were duely and orderly admitted apprentice and ffellow Craft'.

The minutes were beautifully kept throughout the next sixty-one years, but the Lodge disappeared in 1763, probably being swallowed up by some of its more powerful neighbours. At some stage in its history – we do not know when – the minute-book must have fallen into the hands of a zealous busy-body, who was so horrified at finding the ritual copied out into its opening pages that he tore out the first ten. He was constrained to leave the last fragment of ritual on page 11 intact, doubtless because that page contained the earliest minutes of the lodge. Hence, the 'Haughfoot fragment', just twenty-nine words of ritual-procedure, preserved since 1702 in the minute-book of a small but very respectable Lodge. They begin in the middle of a sentence:

> of Entrie as the apprentice did Leaving our (The Common Judge.)
> Then they whisper the word as befor – and the master mason grips his hand after the ordinary way.

The 'fragment' with its uninformative references to a whispered word, and a grip given by the 'master mason' did not attract serious attention from scholars because the main body of the text was missing and the surviving words, the 'fragment', could not be matched to any other known text. It was left, so-to-speak, in mid-air, simply because there were no means of ascertaining its real significance.

STAGES IN THE EVALUATION OF THE CATECHISMS AND EXPOSURES

The first hesitant step towards a proper evaluation of the Catechisms and Exposures was taken in 1904, when Bro W. J. Hughan, a notable scholar and founder of the QC Lodge, compiled a brief note (in *AQC* Vol 17, pp 91/2) on a newly-discovered manuscript that he had just acquired for the Grand Lodge of Ireland. It is now known as The *Chetwode Crawley MS, c*1700, and is reproduced in *EMC*, 2nd edn, pp 35-38. The text is headed

THE GRAND SECRET,OR THE FORME OF GIVING THE
MASON-WORD

and it describes, in narrative form, the ritual and procedure of the two admission ceremonies of its day. Its contents are of high importance in our present study and they may be summarised briefly, as follows:

> FOR THE ENTERED-APPRENTICE. The candidate was put 'upon his knees: And after a great many Ceremonies, to frighten him', he took up the Bible and repeated the Oath. He was then 'removed out of the Company with

the youngest Mason;' There, he endured further horseplay. Then, still outside the Lodge, he was taught 'the manner of making Guard, which is the Sign, Word & Postures of his Entry'.

He returned to the Lodge, made the [E.A.] Sign, recited the 'Words of Entry' and made the Sign again. Then, the 'word' was passed by 'the youngest mason' in a whisper to his neighbour who passed it on similarly, and so on all round the Lodge, until it came to the Master, who whispered it to the candidate. (There is a note indicating that the E.A. had *two* Pillar-words). After this there was a Catechism of sixteen Questions and Answers, and that was all.

FOR THE 'MASTER-MASON OR FELLOW-CRAFT. All Apprentices were removed '. . . non Suffered to stay, but only Mason Masters' and there was no horseplay. The candidate had the same 'Oath administered . . . anew'. He was taken out by 'the youngest Master to learn the words & Signs of ffellowship'. Returning, he gave 'the Master-Sign' [not described] and 'the Same words *of Entry as the prentice did, only leaving out the Common Judge*', i.e. those three words, which *were* in the E.A. greeting. Then '*the Masons whisper the word . . . as formerly*', i.e., the 'word' was passed by the youngest Master in a 'rotational whisper', until it reached the Master. The candidate placed himself in a posture, for what was subsequently described as 'ffive . . . Points of ffellow-ship', and he gave a whispered greeting to the Brethren. '*Then the Master Mason gives him the word & grips his hand*, and afterwards, all the Masons, which is all to be done to make a perfect Mason'. Associated with this ceremony was a Catechism of only four test Questions and Answers, and that was all for the 'Master-Mason or ffellow-Craft'.

In his notes on '*The Chetwode Crawley MS*, Bro Hughan, after having compared it with all the early Exposures and Catechisms that were known in his day, observed that 'the Common Gudge' [*sic*] had been cited as part of the equipment of 'a just and perfect Lodge' in two printed Exposures, *A Mason's Examination*, 1723, and *The Mystery of Free-Masonry*, 1730. To his credit, he was the first to notice the close similarity between the 'Haughfoot fragment' and the comparable section of the *Chetwode-Crawley MS* (ie the words shown in italics in the above summary) but for reasons unknown, probably excessive caution, he dated the newly-found text as 'about the year 1730, or slightly earlier'. Nevertheless, he accorded it a substantial degree of respectability when he wrote that the distinctive features in *Chetwode-Crawley* suggest to my mind that it represents a more or less accurate account of the Ceremonies of the period, written by a brother, who took this plan to assist his memory, and who himself had been Admitted as an "Apprentice and Master Mason, or ffellow-Craft" accordingly.

This was a bold admission in 1904, but it was clear that Bro Hughan's caution, in dating the text c1730, had misled him as to the true significance of the obvious relationship between the 'Haughfoot fragment' and the *Chetwode Crawley MS.*

In 1924, Bro Herbert Poole, in his 'Masonic Ritual and Secrets before 1717' (*AQC*, 37 p 7) discussed the same question and concluded that

> . . . the latter [i.e. the *Chetwode-Crawley MS*] though it may have been *copied* as late as 1730, must be regarded as a faithful description of a ceremony which was worked at the very beginning of the eighteenth century.

This was proper recognition at last, not merely of the *CCMS* for itself, but of the authentication which it gained from the 'fragment' of ritual in the minute book of the Haughfoot Lodge.

Bro Poole's conclusions were completely justified in 1930 on the discovery of a sister text to the *CCMS*, now known as the *Edinburgh Register House MS*, (because it was found in the Public Record Office of Edinburgh). It bore an endorsement 'Some Questiones Anent the mason word 1696' and that date 1696, after strict examination, is accepted by the experts. The two texts differ in many respects, eg in spelling, phrasing, and in the 'catechism-narrative' sequence of the Edinburgh text, which is the reverse of that in the *CCMS*. In spite of these minor differences, there is no doubt that they are descended from a common original, and they certainly describe the same two ceremonies.

In 1954, a third version was discovered, now known as the *Kevan MS*, c1714, and this – because of the omission of several words and phrases – is clearly a defective text. Yet, there is no doubt that all three describe the same general procedure. Their differences, indeed, are helpful, because it is obvious that *they were not copied from each other*, implying – *so long as they can be authenticated* – that they represent lodge working over a fairly wide area in the south of Scotland. The authentication comes from the 'Haughfoot fragment' which is clearly a précis of the corresponding passages in all three texts.

One major benefit that arises from these documents, as soon as they are recognised as respectable versions of the ritual of their day, is that *they provide, collectively, a firm basis for further studies and for testing the validity of some of the later texts*; but it must be emphasised that the three sister-texts, now often described as the 'Edinburgh group', represent only Scottish practice.

The English Masonic ceremonies, so far as may be judged from surviving evidence, were largely based on the *Old Charges* or *MS Constitutions*. In their early form they consisted of an invocation or opening prayer; a reading of some part of the 'history' of the Craft; a recital of the 'Charges' or regulations; an obligation of fidelity, taken 'upon the book' (as indicated in several versions of the 'Latin instruction' quoted on p 111 above). Originally that was all; but in the seventeenth century, when we find versions of the *Old Charges* that contain references to 'secrets', and to several 'words & signs' etc, it is obvious that the ceremonies had been expanded to include some form of 'entrusting'. At this stage, the English ceremonies were already beginning to resemble the Scottish forms.

It would not be practicable, here, to make a prolonged study of how the practices of the two countries became merged. Gradually, the ritualistic influence of the *Old Charges* or *MS Constitutions* declined; but there is no doubt that

> . . . both types of operative ceremony, the one depicted in the *MS Constitutions*, and the one depicted in the *MS Catechisms*, have undoubtedly contributed to the development of present-day working, and justify us in saying that the existing working has not a single, but a twofold origin.*

It is only necessary to stress that so far as the Catechisms and Exposures are concerned, the best of the English texts (when they begin to appear from c1700 onwards) are in harmony with their Scottish counterparts. Generally, they complement each other, and often, a document, in one group, furnishes details that are lacking in the other. In this way, the sixteen texts that preceded Prichard's work supply a valuable body of evidence to show the sources of much of the material in *Masonry Dissected*.

---

* *The Genesis of Freemasonry*, by Knoop and Jones, M'ter. Univ. Press, 1947 p 217.

MASONRY DISSECTED – THE TEXT OF THE EXPOSURE

There is a peculiar fascination attaching to the study of the text of Prichard's exposure, not only because it was the first publication that claimed to describe a system of three degrees, but also because of the variety of the problems that are involved. The work, as a whole, was unlike any of the earlier documents of its kind, both in its general structure and in the manner in which its parts are presented. Much of Prichard's material was already in existence, but some very important sections had never appeared in manuscript or in print; yet, there is good reason to believe that he did not invent those novelties, but had simply collected and arranged them.

In their Introduction to the *Early Masonic Catechisms* (pp 11–13 and 18–19) the authors, discussing the early documents up to c1740, were able to find textual affinities that might have formed a basis for classifying them in four separate groups, with Prichard's *Masonry Dissected* as the first of a fifth grouping; but this left them with six highly individualistic texts which did not bear 'a close affinity to any other known document' and they were forced to conclude that 'there is not sufficient material available to formulate a satisfactory classification'. There is nevertheless, good reason to believe that these groups represent *separate streams* of ritual.

Masonry Dissected, no matter how well it deserved to be placed at the head of a separate group, might well have been included with the six that could not be classified. It was not only the longest and most comprehensive document of its kind, but it also contained items that were more-or-less closely connected with most of the earlier texts. This suggests that it did not necessarily represent the working of a particular lodge, but may have been a composite of several different workings, a distinct possibility, since there was no official control of the ritual or procedures.

Generally, Prichard produced his text for each of the three degrees in the form of a catechism, or a 'Question and Answer Lecture', which took place, presumably, *after* a candidate had passed that particular degree, ie the catechism was not a ceremony in itself, but an exercise in the explanation and interpretation of the ritual and procedure relevant to a particular degree.

There were certainly some omissions. Prichard made no mention of a 'Prayer', or of any kind of 'Charge to a newly admitted Brother': it may be that these were not customary in Prichard's Lodges. But his ritual text also omitted all reference to the Apron, though he mentioned the 'Badge of Honour' and actually quoted some of the words which accompanied the investiture. These are minor blemishes, however, and they do not seriously detract from the interest or the value of the work as a whole.

The Questions in Prichard's catechism fall readily into three groups:

1. Test questions which were doubtless used prior to the admission of an unknown visitor to a lodge, but which were also designed for test purposes, outside, or away from, the lodge.

2. Questions relating to the actual ceremonies and depicting the preparation of the candidates, and floorwork or procedure inside the lodge.

3. Questions relating to Lodges and Masonry generally, eg the 'Form of the Lodge', its jewels, lights, furniture, the composition of a Lodge, the situation and duties of its officers, principles, modes of recognition etc, etc. This group also included much new material of an explanatory or mildly symbolical nature.

The new explanatory material marked an important stage in the expansion of the catechisms. *The Edinburgh Register House MS*, 1696, contained brief narrative descriptions of the EA and FC ceremonies, but it had only fifteen Questions and Answers for the EA, and two for the 'Master or Fellow-craft'. From c1700 onwards, most of the documents of this class, both in manuscript and print, showed the introduction of material that had not appeared in the earlier texts. They may have represented separate streams of ritual, or the practice of particular localities; but by 1730, we find much of this material – from several sources – in *Masonry Dissected*. Prichard had ninety-two Q & A for the EA, thirty-two for the FC, and thirty for the '*Master's* Degree'. A typical example of this expansion is a question in the *Sloane MS, 3329, c*1700:

Q. wch is the mast^{ers} place in the Lodge

It appeared in various forms in most of the texts that followed, and by the time it was printed in *Masonry Dissected*, it had grown into eight questions, beginning 'Where stands your Master?', with answers covering all the officers down to the 'Junior Enter'd 'Prentice', their situations, jewels and duties.

It would not be practicable here to undertake an examination of Prichard's sources for all his material.* The authenticity or trustworthiness of his work can best be checked by comparison with earlier documents of the same class. Virtually the whole of his *Enter'd 'Prentice's* Degree can be traced back (as in the *Sloane* example just quoted) to texts from 1696 onwards and the same applies to substantial parts of his FC and MM degrees. But when we find major items in Prichard's text for which there are no precedents, we can only test their reliability by seeing how much of that material was accepted and used in the best of the publications that appeared in the following decades. (These aspects of Prichard's work are discussed in the Notes that follow the Facsimile. Not published here.) For the present we are concerned with one section of his work that distinguished *Masonry Dissected* from all its predecessors, ie the Hiramic Legend.

THE FIRST HIRAMIC LEGEND – SOURCES

From Q 133 to the end of the catechism, the text gives us the earliest known version of the 'Hiramic Legend' and (apart from one interesting procedural note to Q 149) it is all in the form of question and answer. Our study, at this stage, is only concerned with Prichard's sources.

The story of Hiram's part in the building of Solomon's Temple is told twice in the Old Testament (1 *Kings* VII and 2 *Chron* II) Masonic sources for the Legend are almost non-existent. The *Old Charges*, in their historical section, trace the 'science' of building through a collection of early biblical characters in which Solomon and his Temple are barely mentioned, and Hiram appears usually under a pseudonym, Aynon, Aymon, etc, in numerous variations. But there is no mention of Hiram's death in the biblical accounts, nor in the commentaries, nor in any of the *Old Charges*. Indeed, nowhere in all of these early sources is there any trace of the various incidents which made up the story, now generally known as the Hiramic Legend, and it seems certain that Prichard's version – the earliest that has come down to us – was a comparatively late introduction into Craft working.

---

* A detailed study of this aspect of Prichard's material will be found in *AQC*, 83, pp 337–357; *AQC*, 84, pp 293–307 and *AQC*, 85, pp 331–348.

If we examine his text to ascertain its principal elements, the story divides into four main sections:

1. The Master-mason of KST who refused to divulge the MM Word, and was slain in consequence, ie 'faithful unto death'.
2. The assassins hide the body and bury it.
3. Solomon orders the search and *the searchers agree amongst themselves* that 'if *they* do not find the Word in him or about him, the first Word should be the Master's Word'.
4. The discovery of the corpse. The 'raising' on the FPOF and the 'Funeral'.

In all these items there is only one 'constant' that had appeared in practically all the earlier Masonic catechisms and exposures, ie the 'Points of Fellowship'. Sixteen of these texts have survived that preceded the publication of *Masonry Dissected*, many of them differing widely from each other. Yet, in spite of their differences, fourteen of them, from 1696 onwards, contain descriptions of the 'Points of Fellowship' and some five or six of them furnish their own sadly-debased versions of the word that is supposed to have accompanied those Points.

There can be no doubt whatever that this part of the 'Hiramic Legend' was very strongly established in Craft usage long before Prichard's work appeared, yet in all these there is no hint of a *Hiramic* Legend, except in one late version, *The Wilkinson MS*, c1727, which contains a curious answer to one of its questions, without mention of the 'Points of Fellowship':

Q. What is the form of your Lodge
A. An Oblong Square
Q. Why so
A. The Manner of our Great Master Hiram's grave

This tiny fragment of evidence proves nothing of any importance, but it does at least imply that 'Hiram's grave' was of some interest to the Craft at that time.

So, we are left, in the period 1696 to 1730, with the 'Points of Fellowship' and a Word, parts of the skeleton of a legend, and it is very difficult to believe that this is all there was. Throughout the middle ages and well into the eighteenth century, hundreds of years before the invention of radio and television, stories and legends, music and songs were the main social recreation of the people. Indeed, the *Old Charges* themselves, with their numerous legends concerning the supposed founders of the Craft, and others 'who loved masons well and gave them their charges', suggest very strongly that there must have been a store of craftlore, *not necessarily in the ritual*, with which the masons entertained themselves off duty. As to the 'Points of Fellowship', even at the stage when the ritual contained no hint of a legend, it is impossible to believe that any group of masons could have recited the words, or demonstrated the postures that they described, without some kind of story or legend in explanation of their origin, or meaning.

In our search for sources, there is one document of supreme importance, the *Graham MS*, 1726, which must be cited frequently in connection with other aspects of Prichard's work. That text is unique in many respects. It is headed:

> THE WHOLE INSTITUTIONS OF FREE MASONRY
> OPENED AND PROVED BY THE BEST OF TRADITION
> AND STILL SOME REFERANCE TO SCRIPTURE

Its compiler was probably a churchman, or at least a deeply religious Christian, and he exercised his powers of interpretation on the catechism and on many aspects of the ritual that have rarely been handled in that way. After he had finished with the catechism, which consisted largely of elected questions that lent themselves to his purpose, he completed his manuscript with a collection of legends, each of them with a kind of Masonic twist in its tail. The characters were mainly biblical and one of the legends concerns three brothers who went to their father's grave

> . . . for to try if they could find anything about him ffor to Lead them to the vertuable secret which this famieous preacher had . . . Now these 3 men had allready agreed that if they did not ffind the very thing it self that the first thing that they found was to be to them as a secret they not Douting but did most ffirmly be Lieve that God was able and would . . . cause what they did find for to prove as vertuable to them as if they had received the secret at ffirst from God himself . . . so came to the Grave finding nothing save the dead body all most consumed away takeing a greip at a ffinger it came away so from Joynt to Joynt so to the wrest [wrist] so to the Elbow so they R Reared up the dead body and suported it setting

ffoot to ffoot knee to knee Breast to breast Cheeck to cheeck and hand to back and cryed out help o ffather . . . so one said here is yet marow in this bone . . .

(*E.M.C.* pp. 92/3)

It is hardly necessary to comment on the resemblances between this extract and the relevant portions of Prichard's 'Master's Part', but it is noteworthy that here too, the searchers *agreed in advance* 'that if they did not ffind the very thing it self the first thing that they found was to be to them as a secret'. The details of decay, which led to what Prichard called 'the Slip', are very similar in both texts, though the 'greips' in the *Graham MS* do not agree with those in Prichard's '*NB* note' to Q 149.

The major difference between the two versions is in the principal characters. In Prichard, the victim was Hiram, the builder; in the 1726 version it was Father Noah and it was his three sons, Shem, Ham and Japhet, who 'Reared him up' by the 'Points of Fellowship'.

We have already had occasion to refer to separate 'streams' of ritual; the *Graham MS*, with its Noah Legend, provides us with a 'separate stream' of legend, and we need not be surprised to find that the earliest story of a raising *within a Masonic context*, concerned Noah instead of Hiram. The *Graham MS* may have emanated from Yorkshire, and if we were fortunate enough to find similar documents from Kent or Cornwall we might expect to find the same legend, with still different characters.

The *Graham MS* contains another collection of legends, one of which seems (to the present writer at least) to have considerable bearing on our search. It concerns another architect in the Old Testament who achieved great fame by his works. At last, being near to death,

. . . he disired to be buried in the valey of Jehosephate and have cutte over him according to his diserveing [i.e. an appropriate epitaph on his tombstone] which was performed . . . . . and this was cutte as follows—
Here Lys the flowr of masonry
Superior of many other
Companion to a King and
to two princes a brother
Here Lys the heart all secrets could conceall
Here lys the tongue that never did reveal—

now after his death the inhabitance there about did think that the secrets of masonry had been totally Lost . . . . (*EMC* pp 93/4)

Had this been an epitaph for HA it could not have been more apt, especially 'the tongue that never did reveal'; but the hero, in this case, was Bezaleel, architect of the Tabernacle and designer of the Temple equipment and furnishings. The relationship of this legend to the 'faithful unto death' theme in Prichard's Hiramic legend is neither so clear nor so close as in the Noah legend; yet its very existence is sufficient to show that such legends were current in craft-lore, ready to be adapted and embodied in the ritual by those who were interested in expanding it for Speculative use.

There is good reason to believe that the compiler of the *Graham MS* was not the inventor of the legends. In his catechism he only provided *the religious interpretation of traditional materials*, and that was almost certainly the case in his Noah legend. The date of his manuscript, 1726, is no real guide to the age of the Noah and Bezaleel stories. If Hiram the builder had been the principal character in those stories, we would be unable to date them much earlier than Prichard's Hiramic legend, which may be assumed to represent practice in the London area. The fact that the *Graham* legends deal with different characters and exhibit other textual differences as well, shows that they represent 'separate streams' of legend, and that implies a greater antiquity and a more widespread usage.

One more document, a newspaper advertisement dated 1726, may be cited here as evidence that many times in Prichard's work, including several phrases relevant to the Hiramic Legend, were well known to Masons some years before *Masonry Dissected* was published. It was found in a collection of newspaper-cuttings in the Grand Lodge Library. The name of the journal is unknown, but internal evidence in the text confirms the date, 1726. The advertisement is headed 'Antediluvian Masonry'.

The whole piece is a jibe against Dr John Theophilus Desaguliers, who was Grand Master in 1719, for innovations he is supposed to have introduced into the Craft, and it was apparently written by someone well informed on contemporary ritual and practice. The following brief extracts are selected only because of their relevance in the study of Prichard's Hiramic Legend:

> . . . There will likewise be a Lecture giving a particular Description of the Temple of Solomon . . . with the whole History of the Widow's Son killed by the Blow of a Beetle, afterwards found three Foot East, three Foot West, and three Foot perpendicular, and the necessity there is for a Master to well understand the Rule of Three.

Later, there are references, *inter alia*, to

> . . . oblong-Squares, cassia, and mossy Graves . . .

and the piece is signed

> By Order of the Fraternity
> Lewis Gilbin, M.B.N.

> (*AQC*, 23, pp 325-6)

Returning now to the emergence of the Hiramic Legend, we have proof of the existence of the two-degree system from 1598 onwards. In 1696, we have proof of the 'Points of Fellowship' together with the 'Word' *as the core of the second degree in that system*, and there is reasonable probability that they may have been there in 1598 if not earlier. Jointly, those 'Points' with the 'Word' were the prime elements among the materials which subsequently became the legend of the third degree. Until *Masonry Dissected* was published in 1730, one or both of those elements had appeared in most of the earlier ritual documents, English as well as Scottish, always without explanation. Yet, the curious details of the 'Points' and the nature of the 'Word' that accompanied them, compel us to accept that there must have been a legend of some sort, within the Craft-lore of those days, that would explain their origin and meaning. Indeed, to those who witnessed them, the actual movements in the 'Points' must have been – in themselves – a useful reminder of the legend from which they were derived.

The absence of documentary proof, makes it impossible to determine when the legend or its elements first came into Craft usage. But when we consider the 1590s as a possible date for the 'Points' and 'Word', the variety of detail in the Noah and Bezaleel legends in the *Graham MS*, 1726, with the scarcely veiled hints in the 'Antediluvian' advertisement of that year, and 'the Manner of our Great Master Hiram's grave' in the *Wilkinson MS*, of c1727, it is obvious that *the source materials of the legend were much earlier than 1696*, though we have no proof of them *in the ritual* until the 1720s.

THE EVOLUTION OF THE THREE-DEGREE SYSTEM

The evolution of the trigradal system is one of the major unsolved problems of Masonic research. We know a great deal about the third degree, but we do not know why it came into practice, when or where it began, or who was responsible for its evolution. No less important is the question 'How did it take root and spread as it did, at a time when there was no governing body that organised the contents and dissemination of the ritual, and no prescribed working of any kind?'

The reason for our ignorance on these matters is the absence of records of the third degree or the trigradal system in the *Books of Constitutions* and Grand Lodge minutes of that period. In the 1723 *B of C*, at a time when there were only two degrees in practice, Regulation XIII had prescribed that

> Apprentices must be admitted Masters and Fellow-Craft only here, unless by a Dispensation.

'Only here', ie in the Grand Lodge. This was an attempt, on the part of the Grand Lodge, to arrogate to itself the right to confer the senior degree. Dr Anderson, the compiler-editor of the regulations, was a Scotsman and he used the joint title 'Master and Fellow-craft' in exactly the same way as it had been used in the 'Edinburgh-group' of catechisms (and in early Scottish Lodge minutes from 1598 onwards) to describe the second degree in the two-degree system.

The reasons for this Regulation may have originated in a desire for close control and good management of the Lodges, but the rule was an infringement of their inherent rights, which must have been deeply resented and which proved wholly unworkable. On 27 November 1725, this part of the Regulation was repealed:

> A Motion being made that Such part of the 13th Article of the Gen[ll] Regulations relating to the Making of Ma[rs] only at a Quarterly Communication, may be repealed, And that the Ma[rs] of Each Lodge with the Consent of his Wardens, And the Majority of the Brethren being Ma[rs] may make Ma[rs] at their Discretion
>
> Agreed Nem. Con. (*QCA*, X, p 64).

At face value this minute might be taken to mean that the Grand Lodge was giving permission for Lodges to confer the third degree, but it is equally likely that this was simply intended to give back to the Lodges their ancient right to confer the second degree of 'Master and Fellow-Craft'.

There is some reason to believe that Reg. XIII and the resentment it aroused was the reason for the splitting of the first degree into two parts, thus creating an 'artificial' second degree (which was already known in its essentials to all Entered Apprentices) and thereby making the original second degree into the third. This certainly describes what was happening, but it is impossible to say definitely whether the Grand Lodge minute of 27 November 1725 referred to the second degree of the two-degree system, or the third in the newly-evolving trigradal system. The only official evidence on the subject appears in Charge IV in the 1723 *Book of Constitutions*, relating to the qualifications of Wardens, and in the altered version of the same Charge in the second edition in 1738:

> In 1723: No Brother can be a *WARDEN* until he has pass'd the part of a *Fellow-Craft*; . . .
> In 1738: The *Wardens* are chosen from among the *Master-Masons*, ...

Grand Lodge had obviously recognised the status of Master-Masons, but there is certainly *no trace of the third degree being promulgated by the Grand Lodge, or that any of its leading members were engaged in framing this new arrangement.* As a result, we are compelled to seek even the faintest hints wherever they are to be found.

The earliest evidence suggesting the evolution of a three-degree system is in the *Trinity College, Dublin, MS, 1711*. It begins as a very short catechism of only eleven Q and A, followed by a paragraph in narrative form, which lists a collection of signs, words, etc. In the course of this section, various modes of recognition are allocated to the Enterprentice, fellow craftsman, and Master (ie MM) the latter having the world's worst description of the Points of Fellowship, with a word that is quite unbelievably debased. This text, despite its numerous defects, lists the three separate grades with distinguishing modes of recognition belonging to each, the first hint that someone was experimenting with the idea of a system of three degrees. (*EMC*, p 70).

The 'Mason's Examination', 1723, was the first exposure to be printed in a London newspaper *The Flying Post or Post-Master*, 11–13 April 1723. Its catechism had been substantially expanded and it contained no hint of trigradal practice; but the text contains a rhymed verse which appears to allocate certain distinguishing characteristics to three grades, 'enter'd Mason, Fellow, and Master-

Mason'. The details do not agree with those in the *Trinity College, Dublin, MS*, and some of them are puzzling, but they are, nevertheless, a possible hint of a system of three degrees. (ibid. pp 71–2)

However interesting such hints may be, they cannot be accepted as *proof* of the trigradal system in practice. For that *proof* we must have actual Lodge minutes recording the conferment of the third degree, minutes which were scarce in 1720–40, and very few have survived to this day. We do have a minute describing the conferment of the third degree in May 1725 in London and that is the earliest surviving record. That ceremony took place in a Musical Society, *not in a Lodge*, and it was Masonically highly irregular. But the story is interesting, and well documented.

In December 1724, there was a London Lodge which met at the Queen's Head Tavern, Hollis Street, in the Strand, only a few hundred yards from the present Grand Lodge building. It is recorded in the Grand Lodge Minute book, in the 'List of Regular Constituted Lodges . . ' dated 27 November 1725, with a list of fourteen of its members, though there were probably several more whose names are not listed. The membership was small and select, and there were among them several cultured gentlemen who were keenly interested in music and architecture. Around the end of 1724, seven of the members with one Brother from another Lodge decided to 'fix and establish a Mutual Society of True Lovers of Music and Architecture', which was duly founded on 18 February 1725, under the title '*Philo Musicae et Architecturae Societas Apollini*'.

They drew up a book of 'Constitutions and Orders' (a masterpiece of the art of calligraphy, now in the British Library) which displayed on its title-page the armorial bearings of the Founders, good evidence of their social status! These men enjoyed their Masonry and among their Rules was one which prescribed:

> 'That no person shall be admitted as a
> Visitor unless he be a Free Mason'

and that rule applied, of course, to the members of the Society.

The preamble to their 'Constitutions' listed the names of their Founders, with details of when and where they were made Masons. They also kept similar records for the Masons who joined their Society. Among these details there is a note that 'some time before'

1 February 1725 four of the Founders of the Musical Society 'were regularly Pass'd Masters in the before mentioned Lodge of Hollis Street'.

This may well refer to a third degree but, because we have no record of the two earlier degrees being conferred on these Brethren, we must accept the possibility that this note may be a reference only to the second degree in the two-degree system.

For indisputable evidence of the three degrees being conferred on one candidate, there are two entries in the same preamble followed by an item in the minutes of the Musical Society, and they are summarised here:

> *Preamble:* 22 December 1724. At a meeting attended by the Grand Master, His Grace the Duke of Richmond, who acted as Master on that evening, 'Charles Cotton Esqr was made a Mason by the said Grand Master'.

> *Preamble:* 18 February 1725. 'And before We Founded This Society A Lodge was held Consisting of Masters Sufficient for that Purpose In Order to Pass Charles Cotton Esqr Mr Papillon Ball and Mr Thomas Marshall Fellow Crafts. . . .' [Note: 'A lodge was held' and *because that happened on the day the Society was founded*, it is not certain whether the Lodge was a regular meeting of the Hollis Street Lodge, or only a meeting of members of the Musical Society. But this was certainly the second degree for Bros Cotton and Ball, the latter having been initiated in the Lodge on 1 February 1725.]

> *Philo-Musicae* Minutes: 12 May 1725. 'Our Beloved
> Brothers & Directors of this Right
> Worshipfull Societye whose Names are here.
> Underwritten (viz)
> Brother Charles Cotton Esq^e
> Broth^r Papillon Ball
> Were regularly passed Masters . . .
>   (*QCA*, IX, p 41)

There can be no doubt that Cotton and Ball had received the three degrees, though the third was highly irregular, having been conferred at a meeting of the Musical Society, not a Lodge.

On 20 May 1725 the Grand Lodge minutes record

> That there be a Lre [Letter] wrote to the foll^g Brethren to desire them to attend the Grand Lodge at the next Quarterly Communication (vizt) [seven names of the principal Founders and officers of the Philo-Musicae.]

The letter was apparently ignored, but the Musical Society had visits from the Junior Grand Warden on 2 September 1725 and the Senior Grand Warden on 23 December 1725 and the Society disappeared early in 1727.

The earliest unimpeachable record of the third degree is in the minutes of Lodge Dumbarton Kilwinning, now No 18 (Scotland). At its foundation meeting on 29 January 1726 there were present the WM with seven MM's, six FC's, and three EA's. At the next meeting on 25 March 1726:

> Gabrael Porterfield who appeared in the January meeting as a Fellow Craft was unanimously admitted and received a Master of the Fraternity and renewed his oath and gave in his entry money.

Porterfield was a Fellow Craft at the foundation meeting of the new Lodge. At the next meeting, he was 'received a Master of the Fraternity and renewed his oath', ie another ceremony; and he 'gave in his entry money', ie he paid for it. There can be no doubt that this was the third degree.

In December 1728, Lodge Greenock Kilwinning at its foundation meeting prescribed *separate fees* for being 'entered as Apprentices . . . passed Fellow-Craft . . . and . . . when raised Master Mason'.

The adoption of the three-degree system was very slow. The earliest record of a third degree in the Lodge of Antiquity, then No 1, was in 1737. From c1733 onwards, there are records of Masters' Lodges usually attached to regular Lodges, but meeting generally on Sundays, for conferring the third degree; but these Masters' Lodges were few in number and ephemeral in character and most of them disappeared within two or three years. No details of their rituals have survived.

An interesting example of the slow adoption of the new system appears in the minutes of the ancient Lodge of Kelso, No 58 (Scotland) whose minutes begin in 1701. On 18 January 1754, three visiting Brethren from the Lodge Canongate from Leith, were invited to act as Master and Wardens in order to demonstrate how Fellow crafts were passed in and around Edinburgh, and two candidates were duly passed by the visiting team.

After the Lodge was closed, the Brethren continued conversing about 'the forms and Practice of this Lodge in particular', when

..... a most essential defect of our Constitution was discovered, viz—that this Lodge had attained only to the two Degrees of Apprentices and Fellow Crafts, and know nothing of the Master's part, whereas all Regular Lodges over the World are composed of at least the three Regular Degrees of Master, Fellow Craft, and Prentice .....

Here, at Kelso, almost thirty years after the trigradal system had begun to come into use, the members of the Lodge had never heard of it! They re-opened the Lodge and the three visitors, with three other Master Masons who were present, conducted the MM degree and raised five Brethren that same evening. (W. F. Vernon. *History of Freemasonry in Roxburghshire & Selkirkshire, p 120*)

Reverting now to 1730, in the *Mystery of Free-Masonry*, which was published only two months before Prichard's work appeared, the same slow development is emphasised in two notes following a catch question!

Q. How old are you? A. Under 5, or under 7, which you will.

NB When you are first made a Mason, you are only entered Apprentice; and till you are made a Master, or, as they call it, pass'd the Master's Part, you are only an enter'd Apprentice, and consequently must answer under 7; for if you say above, they will expect the Master's Word and Signs.

Note, There is not one Mason in an Hundred that will be at the Expence to pass the Master's Part, except it be for Interest. (*EMC*, p 155)

The general contents of this exposure, and of the NB note quoted here, suggest very strongly that the anonymous author was referring only to the second degree in the two-degree system when he spoke of the slow adoption of the Master's Part; but the same comment would have applied, even more forcefully, to the Master's Part in the newly evolving trigradal system.

The point to be emphasised is that 'The Master's Degree' in Prichard's work was still in a very early stage of development. There was no uniformity of practice in the Lodges and no official control of ritual. Most of the Lodges in 1730 would still have been working the earlier system of two degrees and no more; and many of them, especially in the Provinces, had never heard of the third degree. Others, mainly in and around London, were using the new trigradal system at whatever stage of development they had acquired it.

Our study inevitably suggests that the change from two to three degrees was almost certainly the work of Speculative Masons who took the opportunity of extending the moral, religious and philosophical aspects of the Craft by the use of allegory, legend and explanatory materials which brought new life and spirit into the ritual. Thus, the 'Letter G' and the 'Middle Chamber' came into the second degree and the Hiramic legend came into the third. That does not imply that these ritual novelties were new inventions; it is *at least possible that they were traditional materials in Craft-lore*, before the Speculative expansion had begun.

The obvious question arises, 'How, in the absence of official instructions and encouragement, was this great change achieved?' The answer seems to be that no major innovation was involved. The contents of the three-degree system were, in all essentials, the same materials that had existed in the original two, but now in a new arrangement and enhanced by the addition of illustrations and legends which had probably existed long before the changes were contemplated. The actual spread of the new system would have been achieved by plain 'contagion'. One Lodge would make a supposed improvement in its working, and if it proved popular, their work would be copied by those neighbouring Lodges that were able to witness it; and they in turn adopted, arranged and added new materials as they saw fit. Nobody was accused of innovation!

When and where did it begin? It is impossible to answer these questions with any degree of certainty. The evidence of the *Trinity College, Dublin, MS*, quoted above, would suggest Ireland in 1711; but the date seems too early and there is no supporting evidence in lodge minutes, or in contemporary ritual texts. The Mason's Examination, 1723, plus the *Philo Musicae* evidence in 1725, would seem to be more reliable as to date and location, London, with the probability that the latter group were practising a ceremony that they had acquired in the lodge to which most of them belonged, at the Queen's Head Tavern in Hollis Street, London. The indisputable evidence from Dumbarton Kilwinning, in 1726, would seem to be a much stronger claim, but whether the three-degree system actually began there is rather doubtful. Scotland had no Grand Lodge until 1736 and they do not appear to have had the outstanding Speculative members who might have introduced the changes. In England, George Payne, who was Grand Master in 1718, and Dr J. T. Desaguliers, GM in 1719, were the enthusiastic and devoted leaders who might well have been responsible, and there were others, eg Martin Folkes and Francis Drake, who might have helped at a later stage.

Why did it happen? Under conditions of operative masonry practising the two-degree system, there was only one degree for 'Master and Fellow-craft'. *Inside* the Lodge those two classes were equal, both fully trained masons. But *outside* the Lodge, the Master (ie MM) was entitled to operate as an employer, while the FC was only an employee. Inevitably the time would come when there had to be a separate degree for each grade, but under the operative system changes were rare and they usually happened only in response to changing conditions in the mason trade.

In *c*1725 operative masonry was almost at its last gasp. The strict controls formerly exercised by the operative (territorial) Lodges had virtually disappeared and most of the Lodges, both in England and Scotland, were of mixed operative and non-operative membership, with no influence whatever in trade control. The reasons for needing an extra degree had apparently disappeared, but the desire probably remained, and the new conditions were favourable to change.

Another possible reason has already been noted, ie the desire of the English Masons to evade the restrictions implicit in Reg. XIII of the *B of C* which would have limited the Lodges to conferring only the Apprentice degree.

Perhaps the most satisfying explanation is that the changes reflect the earliest results of Speculative influence on the Craft after it had been organised under a Grand Lodge. So long as the cultured elements in the Craft were enjoying their Freemasonry, this kind of expansion was inevitable. It is possible that Reg. XIII may have encouraged their efforts, but the establishment of the Grand Lodge was itself the strongest stimulus.

'MASONRY DISSECTED' – ITS INFLUENCE ON THE RITUAL

It is fitting that the final chapter of this study of Prichard's work should be devoted – however briefly – to a survey of its influence on the Craft ritual. There is no doubt that the book enjoyed a phenomenal success, both immediate and long-term, and all the major historians of the ritual are agreed that *Masonry Dissected* was largely responsible for the stabilisation of the English ritual in its formative years under the first Grand Lodge.

The reason for this success is obvious. In 1730, at a time when Freemasonry was growing in popularity and when Speculative influence was beginning to make itself felt, there was still a total absence of printed versions of officially-approved ritual. *Masonry Dissected*, regardless of the private reasons that had prompted its publication, provided an accessible, soundly-based, and reasonably accurate working, which would enable the Lodges to achieve some kind of standard, incomparably superior to any that had appeared in all the earlier texts, whether in manuscript or print.

After the three pamphlet editions in October 1730, and the pirated newspaper versions in the same month, there were at least nineteen further editions up to 1760, when the next series of English exposures began to appear. There were, indeed, four or five rival exposures published during those thirty years, all of them worthless catch-pennies. Indeed, there are simply *no records of new developments* in English ritual during the thirty-year gap, from 1730 to 1760 and throughout that period Prichard's work held the field.

It was translated into French by an anonymous writer, who published it in 1738 under the title *La Réçeption Mystérieuse* after having added his own comments, with a reprint of the *Réception d'un Frey-Maçon*, the first of the French exposures, originally published in 1737. All these parts were joined together as the first chapter of a book which also contained several chapters on European history etc, of no Masonic interest. Surprisingly, the title-page gave Samuel Prichard's name as the sole author. The compiler was not a Freemason and that explains a number of curious and often amusing errors in translation. It was also translated into German and Dutch in 1738 (*EFE*, pp 9–39).

When the best of the French exposures began to appear in the1740s we begin to see some of the long-term effects of Prichard's work. *L'Ordre des Francs-Maçons Trahi* (the *Trahi*) was first published in 1745, fifteen years after *Masonry Dissected*, and it serves as an excellent illustration of what was happening. Its catechism, now substantially expanded by many new items that had come into French practice during the intervening years, was still basically Prichard's work. In fact, two questions and answers out of every three in the *Trahi* were directly taken from *Masonry Dissected*, either word-for-word, or with French embellishments; and the translation was far better than that in *La Réception Mystérieuse*. The Hiramic legend, which had first appeared in *Masonry Dissected* in the course of answers to a dozen or so questions, was now the subject of a long narrative recital, and the *Trahi* also contained a valuable description of the floorwork and procedures of the ceremony. But when those new materials are stripped away, the basis is still Prichard's work.

The *Trahi* achieved no fewer than seventeen editions in French, up to 1781. It also appeared in German in 1745 under the title *Der Verrathene Orden der Freimaurer*, with three more German impressions in that year and three further editions in 1758, 1763 and 1778. The influence of all these French and German editions on European ritual must have been incalculable.

In England, after the thirty-year gap, the new streams of exposures began to appear in 1760 and 1762 representing both Moderns' and Antients' practices; their catechisms still contained a great deal of Prichard's work, though so much new material had come into use that the original nucleus becomes less obvious. A certain amount of French influence had also remained and it is interesting to read the *English* descriptions of the procedure of the third degree, punctuated by a couple of paragraphs describing the corresponding procedure in the French Lodges.

Many more expansions and changes were to take place before the English ritual was standardised in 1813, but those are strictly beyond the scope of our present study. Nevertheless, the student who will take the trouble to compare his modern ritual with that of Prichard in 1730 will often be astonished to see how much has survived.

6

FREEMASONRY IN THE USA

AMERICA – FIFTY STATES and fifty separate, sovereign Grand Lodges!

On my first visit, in 1960, I started at Montreal, Canada, then south to New York, Boston, and Washington; then right across country to San Francisco, Fresno and Los Angeles. It was a seven-week Masonic Lecture tour and holiday combined, and I gave my Prestonian Lecture to enormous gatherings of Masons in all those cities, covering more than 7,000 miles within the American continent. When I returned to London after that splendid Masonic holiday, the DC of my Mother Lodge said, 'You must tell us all about it at dinner; and we can give you ten minutes.'

Apart from the usual letters of introduction, my principal equipment for the tour consisted of an insatiable curiosity, and a sufficient knowledge of English Masonic practices to enable me to ask the right sort of questions so that I could make a reasonable assessment of our differences. I met and spoke to literally hundreds of Masons from EAs to Grand Masters, and Brethren you should know that Grand Masters are ten a penny in the USA. The explanation is simple. We, in England, choose the best man we can find, usually a cousin of the King or the Queen, and we re-elect him every year for as long as he lives, or as long as he wants the job. In the USA, not so! Most of their Grand Masters are elected for one year only; a few elect for two years and even less to serve three. The result is that every year regularly, there are some 25 brand-new second-hand Grand Masters thrown onto the market. When I said 'ten a penny' I was exaggerating; but you may prefer the American 'a dime a dozen'.

On that first visit, I saw many things that I liked very much, and some that horrified me; but I never stopped asking questions. As a lecturer, it is probable that I was meeting the best types of American Masons, men with a real love for the Craft and a serious interest in its background. I can never forget that in Los Angeles I addressed a large gathering of Masons in a huge two- or three-storey Masonic centre that they had built with their own hands, working voluntarily in their spare time and without pay, under a hired architect and with a practical team of builders, who ensured that the work was well and truly done, and I was proud to be associated with brethren of this calibre.

But, of course, the following impressions do not pretend to be a complete survey, nor can they possibly be true of the whole Craft in the USA. I have simply tried to describe something of what I saw, emphasising our differences in practice, with a critical eye for what seems strange to us, and wholehearted praise where praise is due. American Masons are warm, friendly folk, good hosts, good company, and eager to be helpful, and if my words appear to accentuate certain peculiarities, I must plead that they were written without malicious intent, knowing full well that there is much we can learn from them.

THE BACKGROUND

The first thing that is obvious to every English Mason who visits the USA is that their Freemasonry is vastly different from ours. Indeed, he might be forgiven for saying that it is nothing like ours at all. In the first place, Masonry in the USA is not for father alone, but for the whole family.

For father there are the usual three 'Blue' degrees, and then all the rest running right up to the 32° (The 33° is by selection and invitation; in fact, an honour, rather than a degree).

For mother, there is the Order of the Eastern Star, the Order of Amaranth, and several others less well known.

For boys, aged from 14 to 21, there is the Order of De Molay, named after Jacques de Molai, the last Grand Master of the medieval Knights Templar.

For girls, aged 13 to 20, there is an Order called Rainbow, and another called Job's Daughters, and all these are, in a very special and peculiar sense, Masonic.

All this will seem strange to English ears and must be explained. The plain fact is that when we, in England speak about Women and Freemasonry, we have been spoiled, because automatically we think of the two Orders very respectably established here, both claiming that they wear the same regalia, and use the same ritual as their husbands; and they are, of course, taboo.

For the situation in the USA I quote from the 150th year *History of the Grand Lodge of Louisiana*, a regular Grand Lodge. After 19 chapters of straight history, the next is headed 'Bodies Identified with Freemasonry in Lousiana' and that is followed by a list, including:

> The Order of the Eastern Star,
> The Order of the Rainbow, for Girls,
> The Order of De Molay.

Bodies Identified with Freemasonry is a clear definition of their close relationship with the Craft.

Eastern Star, founded in the USA is the largest fraternal organisation in the world to which both men and women may belong. A genuine Masonic relationship is an essential pre-requisite; male members must be Master Masons in good standing, and a lady Candidate must be mother or wife, sister or daughter of a Freemason. Eastern Star is not quasi-Masonic; they have their own ritual, based on five Biblical heroines, and they are doing magnificent work for Hospitals, Orphanages, Crippled Children, as well as the lesser charities within their own membership. In addition, they count it a duty and a privilege to serve the Craft in every way, eg catering, social, and charitable works.

Rainbow and De Molay require only Masonic sponsorship for joining. Rainbow, as a training ground for the girl who would like to follow mother into Eastern Star. De Molay is best described as an apprenticeship for Speculative Masonry. All this is unusual to us in England, and although it may seem wrong for a Grand Officer to say so, I like it, and I believe that it works! It has obvious advantages. Father knows where mother is on her night out, and vice versa. The fathers help the mothers in their 'Masonry', and the mothers help the fathers in theirs, and both look after the children's organisations. Whether all these efforts have any marked effect on juvenile delinquency rates in the USA would be very hard to say, but I am firmly convinced that this *family approach* to the Craft can do nothing but good.

A nice example of this family spirit occurred in Massachusetts where I lectured to an assembly of some 500 brethren, and over 460 of us sat down to dinner afterwards. It was in an enormous hall, with a stage at one end, on which the Lodge Organist was playing light music throughout the dinner. The tables were arranged Top-table and sprigs (as in England), and everyone except the Officers was dressed in the utmost informality. But all the Officers were in meticulous dinner-dress and throughout the evening we were served by waitresses immaculately dressed in white from head to foot. It was a pleasant, unpretentious meal, and all was going splendidly when, suddenly, the SW far away in the right-hand corner of the room stood up and began to dance with one of the waitresses along the gangway between the sprigs! I was sitting at the right of the WM, and I leaned over to him and whispered. 'Worshipful Master, I thought I had seen almost everything in the Craft, but this I have never seen. Does it happen very often?' He turned to me with a smile and said, 'I hope it does; the lady he is dancing with is his wife. Tonight we are being waited on by our wives. . . .' They were Eastern Star, with 460 at dinner! (I was unable to find out if the husbands help with the 'washing-up', but kitchens are highly mechanised in the USA).

With this kind of background, the objectives in the Craft tend to take on a rather different aspect from ours. Generally, they do not go in so strongly for the maintenance of large Masonic Institutions, as we do. There are, indeed, many splendid institutions, but the emphasis is mainly on the social side, parties, outings and celebrations of one kind or another. A great deal is done by way of homes and equipment for crippled children. Masonic 'Blood-banks' are a big feature, the blood being for ultimate use by Masons and non-Masons alike. There are some Masonic hospitals, and a number of homes for 'senior citizens'. Nobody grows old in the USA; if they are lucky enough to live that long, they become 'senior citizens', and in those jurisdictions that aspire to the maintenance of institutions, it is usually the 'senior citizens' who get first care.

Finally, I must not omit from this description of the background to the Craft, the all-too-obvious fact that *almost everyone wears a badge*, usually a 'lapel-badge', and one sees all sorts of Masonic symbols ranging up to the 33°, with the 32° and 'Shriners' predominating. All this might seem to be a piece of pardonable male vanity and in the vast majority of cases it is nothing more. But the badges tend to become a temptation, and the Masonic visitor to the USA will not need to look far before he realises that they are all too often used for business.

Of all things likely to shock an Englishman, this, I think, must be the most distasteful, and though I am sure that many brethren in the USA find these practices as objectionable as we do, but one has the impression that they have grown accustomed to them, and that is a great pity.

Many of the Grand Lodges publish monthly magazines which report the main Masonic events in their jurisdictions, as well as messages from the Grand Masters and other interesting articles. The pages of the text are generally interleaved with advertisements and in 1960 it was quite common to find that the publicity for the smaller firms included items which were blatant examples of Masonry being used for business:

(Hotel) Bro. A.... B..... General Mgr., X.... Y.... Lo. No. 6666.
(Travel Agent) C.... D...., President. Member of P.... Q.... Lo. No. 777.
(Furrier) E.... F...., Past Master S.... T.... Lo. No. 8888.
(Haulage) G.... H.... Bros. Inc., Members of M.... N.... Lo. No. 9999.

All the above are actual examples; only the names and Lodges have been masked, and all this in official Grand Lodge publications! Those journals are much more circumspect today.

I have heard the situation stated in a somewhat different form. One of my American friends told me, 'I wear the badge (a Shriner's badge, incidentally), to show that I'm proud of my Masonry. As long as I wear it, I'd never do anything to disgrace it; in fact, when I do business with a man whom I recognise to be a Brother, I always try to give him a bigger order than I would otherwise'. All this is true, I am sure, but where is there a commercial traveller among my friend's suppliers who could resist wearing a badge under such conditions?

During a more recent visit to the USA at an informal Masonic party in Providence, Rhode Island, I teased my hosts about this custom of wearing Masonic badges for the wrong reasons, and when I had finished talking, one of the brethren said, 'It is all very well for you to talk about our using Masonry for business, but it is not always like that. Quite often, we have to try to take an order from a Roman Catholic, and then the badge is a liability – not an asset.' I had to agree with him but, privately, I am convinced that it is easier to remove the badge than to change your customer's religion! The RC ban against the Craft has now been removed, hopefully for ever.

LODGE MEMBERSHIP

Judging by our standards in England, where average membership is around 80 per lodge, American lodge memberships are extraordinarily high. Consider, as an example, Washington, DC, the capital and the centre of government; it is virtually a city without industry. It has about fifty lodges in all, four of them with memberships of 1,100, 1,200, 1,400, and 1,500 respectively! And these enormous memberships to be found in all the large cities in the USA. It is, of course, impossible to strike *average figures* as between lodges in the small villages and those in the large towns, because they would be misleading. But in any of the cities, one might expect the general run of lodges to range from 400 to 800 members, with several others running into four figures.

At the time of my first visit to the USA, I was already Secretary of two lodges, and I was naturally puzzled as to the reasons for these (to us) fantastic numbers. There appear to be several reasons, and I dare not commit myself as to their order of importance:

(a)   Maintenance costs are very high for Lodges and lodge buildings in the USA, and this leads to some curious results. In some cities, when a new lodge is to be founded, it is not uncommon to find that the existing lodges raise objections, because they regard all future Masons in their territory as their own 'reserve pool', which will help swell their own membership in due course, and thus help them with their maintenance charges, and their balance sheets. In effect, the Masons themselves are opposing the formation of new lodges! (See the note on this subject in 'Wither are We Travelling?' by M W Bro Dwight L. Smith, PGM, and Grand Secretary of the Grand Lodge of Indiana, in *AQC*, vol lxxvi, p 41).

(b)   Most USA jurisdictions have curious regulations relating to what they call Single, Dual, or Plural membership. Some Grand Lodges allow only Single membership, ie, a Brother may belong to only one Craft Lodge and no more. Others allow Dual membership, usually permitting their members to belong to one lodge inside the State and one outside. Only very few Grand Lodges permit their members the same privilege as we enjoy here of Plural membership, ie of joining as many lodges as we please. It seems possible that, in some indirect way, these regulations have the effect of channelling vast numbers of

Masons into a comparatively small number of lodges, and that leads to large memberships.

I realise that this may be faulty reasoning, but there is no doubt as to the facts, ie, that in many jurisdictions, *if Lodge memberships are to be kept reasonably low*, there are simply not enough Lodges to take the vast numbers of men who want to join.

There are other reasons which are almost national characteristics:

(c)   The Americans are great 'joiners': they like to be in on everything.
(d)   They admire big numbers and mass production.

But it is possible that there is still another reason for the large numbers? I found that in many jurisdictions, it is customary for the Secretary to receive $1.50 annually per head for every member! (As a former Secretary of the QC Lodge, with over 12,000 members, I must say that the idea appeals to me enormously!)

Before this paper went into print, I had it checked by a high-ranking Brother in USA, and the only item on which he faulted me was on this $1.50 per head. 'Harry' he said, 'this is wrong. Many Lodges pay a fixed honorarium. My own Lodge, for example, pay their Secretary $100 a month, $12,000 a year'. 'Good', I said, 'and how many members have you got'? 'Oh. Ours is only a small Lodge, with 400 members.' So they pay $3.00 a head, and that still looks good to me. I do not for one moment suggest that Secretaries are tempted to tout for members; I merely record the differences in our respective practices.

Of course I was anxious to know how the American Lodges achieve these enormous memberships, and the opportunity came when I visited the Grand Secretary's office in Boston, Massachusetts. Among many interesting papers that were given to me was their Year Book, containing all the statistics for the preceding year, and thumbing through the pages casually, I came to the section which summarised their Annual Returns. There were many pages of figures but at the very end of the list, there was one set of figures that caught my eye. They were the details for the very last lodge that was consecrated just before the year book was printed, and at the time of this return the lodge was only 11 months old. At that age (11 months), this infant lodge had a membership of 174; during the 11 months, it had Initiated 54 brethren; it had Passed 49, and Raised 45 brethren. Mass production in a really big way!

The lodges usually meet once a month (for ten or eleven months in the year) for their 'Stated' or regular meetings, and every week, or fortnight, for 'Emergent', 'Special' or work meetings. Attendances are well below the 40 per cent we might expect at the Stated meetings, and even less at the 'work' meetings, which are, in effect, the factories where Masons are turned out by mass production. This may sound cynical, but I believe it is a fair statement of the situation that exists in the larger Masonic Centres in the USA.

Arising from all this, perhaps the most frequent question I have been asked in England is, 'With memberships of 800 to 1,500, how can a Mason ever become Master of a Lodge? Surely he could never live long enough'. The answer is that it is easy. All he needs to do is to express a desire to 'go on', or to 'get in line' as the Americans say, and the path is wide open for him. It is the great tragedy of Craft Masonry in the USA that vast numbers of those who join – simply use Craft as a springboard to the Scottish Rite. To be WM of a 'Blue' lodge may be very pleasant, but it is not nearly so important as to become a 32° Mason and a 'Shriner', with all its attendant advantages (mainly social). As a result, the Craft is neglected, in favour of all sorts of side degrees.

Among the Grand Officers who see and deplore what is happening, this is a source of constant anxiety, frequently expressed in forthright statements. It is a disease whose presence is known and understood, but the remedy, unfortunately, is still to be found. Talk to any American Mason for five minutes, and the chances are that he will show you his wallet containing a whole 'concertina-full' of Dues Cards witnessing the number of 'Masonic' organisations to which he belongs. There will seldom be more than one (or two) Craft Lodges among them: the rest are all side degrees, that are helping, unintentionally, to sap the Craft of its vitality!

THE SCOTTISH RITE AND THE SHRINE

The Ancient and Accepted Scottish Rite is perhaps the most powerful 'Masonic' organisation in the USA, and it is the principal and most popular route towards the 32° and the 'Shrine'. There is an alternative route, via the so-called York Rite. The finest Masonic buildings and the largest Temples are those of the Scottish Rite, and when I lectured to exceptionally large numbers of Masons, the meetings were all held in Scottish Rite Temples.

They are, in fact, beautifully appointed theatres, wired for sound, with stages, scenery and props, wardrobes, dressing-rooms, and elaborate stage-lighting. The degrees are usually conferred in clusters, ie, a set of perhaps three or four degrees will be given the first two or three being 'communicated' or recited, and one, the most important, being actually performed or 'conferred'. The work is done by a team of Officers working as actors in a play. I am told that in some jurisdictions professional teams are used and they are paid for their services.

In England the journey to the 30° of the Scottish Rite would take a lifetime, and the 32° is a rare and exceptional honour. In the USA a Master Mason can acquire the 32° in one day! I quote from a circular published by the SR bodies in Houston, Texas:

ONE DAY REUNION IN HOUSTON
'The Rest of the Way in One Day' . . . 14 May 1977. The Total Fee for the Class $155.00. (Bank financing is available . . . $13.50 per month for 12 months).

Over, 1,250,000 Master Masons seeking further light in Masonry, have taken the inspiring degrees offered by the Scottish Rite, and are now active members . . .

Being a Scottish Rite Mason does not mean that you abandon your Blue Lodge. On the contrary, we require our members to maintain good standing in their home Lodge and urge that they attend and support their Blue Lodge activities . . .

Candidates will become Members in Good Standing After these Essential Degrees, and May See the Other Degrees Exemplified at a Later Date . . .

On these big occasions there will usually be 400 candidates, seated in the front rows of the auditorium. The degrees are gorgeously costumed plays, mainly biblical, and one candidate only is selected from those present to take part in the 'performance'. He is actually 'in the ceremony', but all the candidates take their Obligations together and make the requisite 'responses'. In effect, the selected candidate receives the degrees on behalf of his colleagues – and they get theirs by a kind of artificial insemination.

Many of my close friends belong to the Scottish Rite, and I would not want to be misunderstood in what I write about it. Broadly speaking, it opens up the paths to a wider knowledge and understanding of the Craft itself, but to a much larger degree, of the many 'fringe studies' which may be said to spring from it. Of over four million Masons in the USA more than one in every four belongs to the 32°, and that is an amazingly high proportion. It is here that the trouble lies, not because there is anything wrong with the Scottish Rite, but rather because of the reason why the brethren join them.

I have mentioned 'Shriners', and must say a few words about that organisation. Its full title is 'Ancient Arabic Order Nobles of the Mystic Shrine', and it is strictly and in every sense a non-Masonic Order, but a Brother must be a 32° Scottish Rite Mason (or a York Rite Mason of a similar grade), before he is eligible to join it.

But the 'Shrine' is a thing apart: it is an Order devoted to the social pleasures and good works. At the centre of some twenty of the largest cities in Canada and USA, you will find a large and handsome cluster of buildings, under the sign, 'the Shriners' Hospital for Crippled Children', and they serve children of every colour, race and creed, whether their parents are connected with the Craft or not. In 1959 there were eighteen Orthopaedic Units and three Burns Institutes; there are more today, and all doing marvellous work, which is spectacular, wholly praiseworthy, and deserves emulation. The administration of their hospitals is very sensible, too; they find the land, they build the hospitals, equip them splendidly and ensure their maintenance. All this is wholly admirable, but the other side of the coin is perhaps not so bright.

On the social side, they provide, I quote:

'Your local Shrine Club, Country Club facilities and activities, Ladies' Nights, Parties, Participation in Irem Temple Uniformed Units, and all the Wonderful World of the Shrine'.

Inside the same folder is a picture of a little girl walking with crutches, and one leg in irons; heartbreaking.

Their funds are collected from dues, circuses, ball games and other sources, in (what would seem to us) extraordinary fashion. They stage great processions, with gaily decorated 'floats', bands of music, parades of groups in fancy dress, as well as their own drill teams, bands and 'chanters', and their members, wearing their uniforms that look like those of the French Zouaves, surmounted by a heavily ornamented fez, as headgear. The object, in short, is to persuade the public to open its pockets. Of course, they support their benevolent works out of their own pockets, too, but to our strait-laced views on

Masonic charities being maintained only out of Craft funds, the 'Shriners' methods are rather strange, though undoubtedly effective.

The Conventions appear to be a grand excuse for a good time in the broadest sense of the term and 'Shriners' are commonly referred to as the 'playboys of the Craft'. But the strongest criticism I have heard about them concerns their admission ceremonies, which depending on one's point of view, might be described as amusing and even Rabelaisian. It may be that some of the stories I have heard about them are in the same class as the 'nanny-goat and red-hot poker' tales told about the regular Craft.

As an institution, I gather that the 'Shrine' comes under the control of the Grand Lodge of its territory, and it has to follow the edicts of the Grand Lodge and the Grand Master. Indeed, my informant reports a case within his own memory when a whole 'Divan' (Cabinet) of Shrine Officers was replaced by edict of the Grand Master, because of some infraction. Generally, however, it seems that the title 'playboys of the Craft' is well deserved, and their good works and social advantages go hand-in-hand with a somewhat colourful reputation.

Statistics are liable to misinterpretation, and I try to avoid them here. But an examination of the detailed charts relating to Craft memberships in the USA show quite clearly, that during the past three years there has been a small but regular fall in membership of Craft Lodges; yet the 'Shrine' membership increases each year!

CRAFT RITUAL

There are a number of different Craft rituals in use in the USA, generally exhibiting only minor variations and, broadly speaking, they are very similar to ours in England. Yet, in a very curious way, the visitor who knows his ritual will find that the American versions sound strangely old-fashioned, repetitive, and somewhat fuller and older than ours. Surprisingly, this is true; although the Americans got their ritual from Britain, their ritual is, in fact, older than ours, and that makes an interesting story.

As you probably know, our present ritual was virtually standardised at the time of the union of the rival Grand Lodges, in 1813, when the 'Antients' and the 'Moderns' ultimately came together to form the United Grand Lodge. For several years before that date, committees of learned brethren had been sitting, trying to evolve a revised form of the ritual that would be acceptable to both sides.

The results of their labours, very satisfactory to us nowadays, did not meet with the wholesale approval at that time. Many changes had been made and a great deal of symbolical material had been discarded. Indeed, it might almost be fair to say that in cleaning up the ritual, the baby had been thrown away with the bath-water!

American Masonic workings owe their origins, unquestionably, to England, Scotland and Ireland, but the stabilisation of their ritual was done by an American, Thomas Smith Webb, who, although he wrote very little of it himself, may well be described as the father of American ritual.

In 1792 Webb, a printer by trade, settled in Albany, NY, and soon afterwards he made the acquaintance of John Hanmer, an English Freemason who was a keen ritualist and apparently very knowledgeable about the Preston system. Webb, though barely 22 years of age, had already been a Freemason for nearly two years, and their mutual interests drew them together. This was the period when the English Masonic ritual was at its highest stage of development. Hutchinson and Calcott had published their works; Preston was in his prime, and the 1792 edition of his *Illustrations of Masonry* had just appeared. This was the eighth edition, as popular and successful as its predecessors, and it was almost a Bible to the English Craft. Webb took the book, retained sixty-four pages of Preston's work intact, word for word, cut out a few minor items and rearranged others, and published it in 1797 under the title, *Freemasons' Monitor or Illustrations of Freemasonry*. Within twenty years the ritual in England had been altered, curtailed and polished up (some said – almost beyond recognition), but not so in the USA; they preserved it.

Look at some of our oldest Tracing Boards and you will find pictures of the Scythe, Hour-Glass, Beehive, Anchor, etc, which once had their proper places as symbolic portions of our ritual. They have disappeared from our Tracing Boards and from the ritual; but in America they are still in use to this day, depicted on the Boards and explained in their 'Monitors'. And so, it is fair to say, that their ritual, though it came from us, is actually older than ours, and it is not merely 'old-fashioned', but also more discursive, and by reason of their lectures, much more explanatory than ours, especially of the symbolical meaning of their procedure.

But apart from the things we have lost, their ritual material is essentially the same as ours, and easily recognisable. Their signs and secrets are the same as ours, except that they use the Scottish sign for the EA. Their second degree is more elaborate than ours. Their third is basically the same as ours, but because they perform the drama as if it were a play, treating the candidate as though he was really HA, the result is occasionally rather rough and frightening, especially in those lodges that pride themselves on the realism of their performance.

The manner in which the Americans safeguard their ritual is also interesting. In England our Grand Lodge views the ritual as a 'domestic matter', ie a majority of the brethren in any lodge may decide which 'named' form of ritual shall be worked, and unless the lodge was guilty of some serious breach, the Grand Lodge would not interfere. In the USA the very reverse is the case. Each Grand Lodge prescribes the ritual that its lodges shall work, and usually the Grand Lodge prints and publishes the 'monitorial' or explanatory portions of the rituals, too. Ten out of the forty-nine Grand Lodges also publish the esoteric ritual, in code or cipher, but this is forbidden in the others. Moreover, to prevent innovations, the Grand Lodges protect their forms of working by the appointment of officers, called Grand Lecturers, whose duty is not to lecture, but to ensure that the groups of lodges under their care adhere to the official workings. They do this by means of official demonstrations called 'Exemplifications', and during my first visit, I was lucky enough to see both first and second degrees rehearsed in this way.

The procedure is simple; each Grand Lecturer has perhaps eight to fifteen lodges under his care. On the appointed day, all the Officers (including Treasurer, Secretary, Stewards, etc), are ordered to attend in one of the Grand Lodge Temples, or at a central Masonic Temple, and attendance is compulsory. The officers of the most senior lodge will take their places, and they start to rehearse a ceremony, without interruption. After perhaps ten minutes, the Grand Lecturer will walk to the centre of the lodge, comment on the work and correct any errors that were made, and the next lodge in order of seniority will take over and continue. This is done until all the lodges have been rehearsed.

In some jurisdictions the organisation and procedure is different. The Grand Lecturer has a team of Grand Inspectors under him, each in charge of perhaps five Lodges. Each Lodge, in turn, is host to the other four, and only the 'host' Lodge gives the 'exemplification', while the others look on. Ultimately, the Grand Lecturers are all responsible for the accuracy of the 'work'.

The exemplifications I saw in Boston required a necessary period of adjustment to Bostonian English, but after that, I would gladly give them full marks; their work is splendid. It is proper, perhaps, to add a little tailpiece to this chapter, which gives an insight to the American approach to their Masonry. I am told that in several, if not most, of the USA jurisdictions, the Grand Lecturers are paid for their services!

RITUALS AND MONITORS

Grand Lodge practices, in regard to books of the ritual, differ from State to State. In Pennsylvania and California, for example, no written or printed ritual is permitted. All tuition is, as they say, 'from mouth to ear', ie the Officers and candidates must attend at rehearsals or work-meetings until they have memorised their work, simply by listening to it over and over again. In some jurisdictions each officer is responsible for training his successor, privately, not at rehearsals. The Ritual material is usually divided up into two categories:

1. 'Monitors' which print non-secret portions of ritual and procedure, symbolic lectures, etc, all in plain language.
2. The 'Rituals' proper, which are printed (in ten states), in some sort of cipher, with . . . dots . . . in the usual places.

Books in both categories are supposed to be rather difficult to obtain, but one has the impression that this is merely a case of knowing where to look. The Monitors need not concern us here, but the Rituals are interesting. There appear to be four different ciphers that are mainly used. One of the most popular, is a kind of 'geometrical' code, made up of straight lines, curves, angles and symbols, which look very difficult, but are, in fact, fairly easy to break down.

In many jurisdictions, a two-letter code is used; usually the first and last letters of each word, but occasionally the first two letters of each word. These two codes are fairly difficult to read until one begins to have a fair knowledge of the 'expected' word; but as soon as the phrases become at all familiar, the two-letter codes are quite easy to read.

Most difficult of all is the one-letter code, in which only the first letter of each word is used, and this is absolutely terrifying, almost impossible to read until one has acquired a real knowledge of the ritual.

From the Officers' point of view, all this is simply a matter of patience and regular attendance, but for the candidates it is another story. Here in England, the Candidate for Passing has to learn the answers to twelve questions, usually printed on cards in plain language, with perhaps one or two words omitted. For Raising he learns another nine answers, and he is through.

In the USA Jurisdictions, these examinations are called 'Proficiency Tests', and they must be a really worrying experience. In Rhode Island, for example, the EA, passing to FC, has to answer about seventy-seven questions, with the Obligation, by heart, before he can pass his test; the FC must answer some forty questions and the Obligation from memory, and the MM, *after he has taken his third degree*, another forty or so, again with the Obligation by heart. Then, and not until then, does he become a real member of the lodge. Then he is allowed to sign the Register, and enjoy all the privileges of membership, including a Masonic Funeral if he wants it.

All this would be difficult enough if the questions and answers were printed in plain language, but they are not. In those jurisdictions where no printed rituals are permitted, the candidates must attend 'Classes of Instruction', usually under the care of the JD or SD, until they have learned their work, 'from mouth to ear'. Elsewhere they learn their work from the cipher books. I have a set of the 'Proficiency Tests' as used in Rhode Island, in their one-letter code. They are simply terrifying. I have been a Preceptor for many years, and I find them difficult to read. Heaven knows how the candidates manage – but they do.

Here, I believe, it is fair to say that American Masons, after passing their 'Proficiency Tests' in all three degrees, acquire a much wider knowledge of the ceremonies, and especially of their symbolical meaning, than our candidates get in England. Their patience and industry are more than justified.

VISITING A LODGE IN THE USA

It is impossible to describe the practices of fifty separate Grand Lodges in a short Paper of this kind. To deal with such a subject in detail would require several large volumes. In all that has been written thus far, and especially in the chapter below, the reader will please remember that practices vary from one Grand Lodge to another. I have simply tried to give my impressions based upon the different territories in which I visited.

The Lodge will be opened at perhaps 7.30 pm, directly into the Third Degree. All business is conducted in the Third Degree (except Initiation and Passing). There may have been a meeting earlier in the afternoon for degree work, and that would have been followed by a break from 6.30 pm to 7.30 pm for dinner, a simple and informal meal, without any toasts or speeches. 'Table-work' as we know it in England, is almost unknown in the USA except on special occasions.

At 7.30 pm the Minutes and private Lodge business will be dealt with; at 8 pm the Lodge will be ready to receive its individual guests. Delegations, and perhaps their Deputy District Grand Master, the local Grand Lodge Officer, who has generally some ten to fifteen Lodges under his care.

Most of the Brethren and Visitors, including Grand Lodge Officers, will have picked up a plain white apron from a pile outside the Lodge door, and will enter, wearing no other Masonic clothing, except possibly a breast jewel. Americans, perhaps because of the vagaries of their climate, are very informal about Masonic dress, and the visitor need not be surprised at light-coloured suits, brown shoes, and truly atrocious neckties; but the Officers of the Lodge are usually immaculate in dinner dress, with their full Lodge regalia, and their aprons are often very ornate by English standards.

The layout of the Lodges is not quite like ours in England but, of course, practices will vary in different jurisdictions – I merely describe the best-equipped Lodges that I saw during my many visits. The Temples are large, with the altar in the middle of the floor. As one might expect with 'mass-production Masonry', the altars are enormous, perhaps 8 ft by 6 ft, with kneeling stools on all four sides; a fine altar-cloth, a huge Bible with broad ribbon markers, and a spotlight above the altar shines directly on to the Bible. The three lesser lights (three handsome tall candlesticks) are placed at three corners of the altar. The precise positions of the three lights seemed to vary in different Lodges, and on this point there appears to be no absolute uniformity.

The WM, wearing a top hat, sits in the east, his chair framed in a handsome architectural 'feature' between two pillars, at the head of a flight of seven steps which run along the eastern wall of the Lodge room. He sits 'open to the Lodge' without any pedestal in front of him, but a little low table is at his right hand, just large enough to hold a gavel. The JW sits similarly framed, at the head of a flight of three steps, and the SW has five steps. The Treasurer and Secretary are seated separately in the NE and SE corners respectively, in heavy cash desks with grilles, ornamental cages, rather like those used for bank cashiers thirty or forty years ago. The floor is covered with carpet, usually of a normal household design – not the black-and-white chequered 'pavement' that we know.

The visitor entering the Lodge will be escorted to a point nearest the altar, where he halts to salute first the WM, then the JW, and then the SW. The salute, which I cannot describe here, is always *the position of the hands at the moment of taking the Obligation:* but the EA sign in America is the Scottish 'Due Guard' (which can best be described as the postion of the hands when taking the Obligation in the Royal Arch).

In giving the salute, the visitor will have turned full circle towards the Master who stands to greet him. The Marshal (our DC) will now introduce the visitor by name, giving his Lodge number, rank, etc, and the WM removes his top hat, and holding it at his breast, welcomes the visitor by name, and if he is a Master or Past Master, the WM will offer him the 'courtesy of the east'. This is an invitation to the Guest to sit on the Master's right hand, a courtesy which I accepted gladly. But I was surprised to notice that the majority of American visitors (even including Grand Officers) bowed their thanks and remained in the body of the Lodge. This puzzled me very much, until I realised that I had overlooked one item of the Lodge furnishings. Along both sides of the Lodge, spaced at fairly close intervals, there is a row of large and handsome 'Club' ashtrays – and they are not there for ornament! There are no ashtrays in the east, and this probably explains the visitors' reluctance to sit there. I was told, somewhat shamefacedly, that there is no smoking during the degrees, but I suspect that my informant had his fingers crossed. All this is, of course, very horrifying to us, but one becomes accustomed to almost anything, and, as a strong smoker, I realise that there is a great temptation to stay within reach of the ashtrays. But in fairness, it must be emphasised that smoking in the Lodge room is permitted only in certain American jurisdictions, not in all of them.

The last business of the evening is the confirmation of the Lodge accounts for that day's work, and perhaps this is why the Secretary and Treasurer are kept immured in their corners until the accounts have been passed.

The Americans are very efficient in matters of stage management. The Marshall carries a short ebony baton, perhaps 18 inches long, with handsome silver mounts, and he escorts the WM or the Chaplain down to the altar for all prayers and obligations, while all the lights gradually dim down to darkness, so that only the spotlight is left, shining directly on to the Bible. So, too, after the Lodge is closed, the Marshal organises the 'Salute to the Flag'. A procession of Officers is formed, and a huge flag is brought into the Lodge under escort. It is borne towards the altar, the lights dim down, and only the spotlight is left shining on the flag, while the assembly sings, 'My Country, 'tis of Thee'.

Yes. They really are different.

7

MORE LIGHT ON THE
ROYAL ARCH

THESE NOTES MUST begin with an apology, because it is fairly certain that some of the points to be made will seem surprising, if not actually rather shocking. I need only add that they will be explained as simply as possible and in the light of the best that is known in modern Masonic scholarship.

The Royal Arch made its first appearance in England during the 1740s. We may assume that the seeds of this new ceremony were germinating for several years before we have records of it, but we cannot date the *practice* of the Royal Arch earlier than c1740.

THE REASONS FOR THE RA

If the question is asked, 'Why did the Royal Arch appear?', the answer is that a further ceremony, or a separate 'Fourth Grade', was inevitable, and this can best be explained by our knowledge of the evolution of the three Craft degrees.

The system of apprenticeship made its first appearance in England in the 1200s and a number of legal decisions confirm that in the 1400s apprentices were still the chattels of their masters, ie they were not 'free' and would not have any status in a lodge. This suggests that the earliest single admission ceremony into the Craft (as described all too briefly in the early versions of the Old Charges) was for the fellow-craft, the fully trained mason.

In 1598 and 1599 we have minutes of two Scottish Lodges showing two degrees in practice. The first made an apprentice into an 'entered apprentice' and was usually conferred after he had served about three years of his indentures. The second degree of those days was usually conferred about seven years later and that made him a 'fellow-craft', ie a fully trained mason.

A hundred years later, in 1696, we have the earliest Scottish ritual for those two degrees, and the second is described as 'Master or fellowcraft'. Inside the lodge those two grades were equal, both fully-trained men. Outside the lodge the FCs remained employees, but those who could pay the requisite fees and take up the duties of citizenship were able to set up as Masters, ie as employers. Sooner or later it was inevitable that there would be a demand for a separate degree to distinguish the Masters, and the third degree appeared in England around 1724–25. By 1730 it was widely known, though not so widely practised.

At this stage all three working grades within the Craft were covered by separate ceremonies; only one grade remained unrepresented in this fashion. There was still no distinguishing degree for the men who had presided in a Lodge, ie, for the Masters of Lodges, and inevitably a ceremony appeared around 1740.

This is, of course, an over-simplification of the whole story and it represents my own opinions, but they are based entirely on historical foundations and the dates mentioned here are supported by documentary evidence.

EARLY DEVELOPMENT OF THE ROYAL ARCH

As to the development of the RA ceremony, there is every reason to believe that it was designed, originally, for Masters of Lodges or for men who had passed the Chair, and although there is some difference of opinion as to the interpretation of the evidence on this point, there is, in fact, a great deal of valuable evidence to support this view. In 1744, Dr Fifield Dassigny published a book with an enormous title, *A Serious and Impartial Enquiry into the Cause of the present Decay of Freemasonry in . . . Ireland*, and, speaking of the Royal Arch, he described it as '. . . an organis'd body of men who have passed the chair'.

Twelve years later, Laurence Dermott, Grand Secretary of the Antients' Grand Lodge, wrote scornfully of those '. . . who think themselves Royal Arch Masons without passing the Chair in regular form . . .' (*Ahiman Rezon*, 1756, p 48). But in those days, when Masonry was not nearly so widespread as it is today, a restriction of this kind – had it really been enforced – would have made the new ceremony almost impossible, because there would never have been enough candidates to keep it alive; so, at a very early date, we begin to find evidence of the introduction of a kind of artificial 'Chair Degree' in which prospective members of the RA were given a sort of imitation Installation in order to qualify them to go on to the RA.

Minutes for the early period of the RA (ie c1740 to 1760) are exceedingly rare and uninformative, but there is a record of an emergency meeting at Bolton in 1769, at which three men were successively installed as Master, and afterwards the actual Master of the Lodge was reinstalled. At Mount Moriah Lodge, now No 34, London, it was resolved in June 1785, '. . . that Bro Phillips shall pass the Chair upon St John's Day in order to obtain the Supreme Degree of a Royal Arch . . .' At the Philanthropic Lodge, Leeds, now No 304, the minutes for May 1795, record that 'Bro Durrans past the chair in order to receive the Royal Arch'. Numerous records of a similar character make it evident that a 'fictitious passing the chair' ceremony was being widely practised in the second half of the eighteenth century.

When the rival Grand Chapters were united in 1817, the 'chair-degree' was officially abolished, but it continued to be worked in many places until the 1850s.

To this day, in many of the American jurisdictions, the entrusting which forms a preliminary to the RA is a brief ceremony which contains recognisable elements of our Installation work.

PLACE OF ORIGIN

It is impossible to say, with certainty, that the RA took its rise in any particular country, but it seems likely that the ceremony came into England from Ireland. Several of the earliest references to the RA are undoubtedly Irish, and when the rival Grand Lodge, the 'Antients', was founded in 1751, largely by immigrant Irishmen, it recognised the RA as a more-or-less essential adjunct to the normal Craft degrees.

There is, however, another possibility, that the ceremony originated in France, where a great number of Masonic innovations and expansions made their appearance in the early 1740s. In particular, there is an interesting reference in the *Sceau Rompu*, an exposure dated 1745, to lodges founded by the Crusaders who practised a ceremony commemorating the Israelites who worked at the rebuilding of the second Temple 'with trowel in hand and sword by their side'. Several similar items of evidence support the view that certain characteristic features of the RA ceremony, by whatever name, were already known on the Continent at an early date, but this cannot be taken as proof of origin. Amid a host of new degrees that began to appear in France in the following decades, the Royal Arch as a ceremony or degree in its own right remained unknown.

THE ROYAL ARCH UNDER TWO GRAND LODGES

The first Grand Lodge, the 'Moderns', gave no official recognition to the Royal Arch in the early years of its development in England. It was practised, nevertheless, in several Moderns' lodges, though it was not regarded as an integral part of the Craft degrees. Royal Arch Chapters did not yet exist as separate bodies for controlling the new grade, and there was, of course, no supreme controlling authority.

In June 1766, Lord Blaney, Grand Master of the 'Moderns', was exalted in a new Chapter entitled The Grand and Royal Chapter. That was the first step towards the formation of a Moderns' governing body for the Royal Arch. In that year, Lord Blaney issued a 'Charter of Compact' by which the new Chapter became 'The Excellent Grand and Royal Chapter', which controlled the Royal Arch of the 'Moderns' under a variety of names, until 1817. That was the beginning of an era of progress and prosperity for the Order under the Moderns, and a large number of Royal Arch Chapters were formed.

The 'Antients', founded in 1751, had always counted the Royal Arch as a regular part of Craft Masonry, under the control of their Grand Lodge. The ceremony was conferred in their lodges with full approval of their Grand Lodge, though many of its members were not Royal Arch Masons; they saw no need for a separate governing body. Finally, greatly impressed by the success of their rivals, the Antients created a nominal Grand Chapter in 1771, a shadowy body, without powers, virtually under the control of their Grand Lodge. Their Book of Constitutions, *Ahiman Rezon*, contained no regulations for the government of the Royal Arch, and their first code of RA regulations was not compiled until 1794, more than forty years after their Grand Lodge had come into being.

Throughout the existence of the rival Grand Lodges and Grand Chapters, no attempt was made to control or standardise the rituals that their Chapters were using and, as with Craft ritual, there must have been substantial variations of practice in different parts of the country until the 1780s or 1790s.

SOURCES AND RITUAL OF THE ROYAL ARCH

For the *background of the English Royal Arch ceremony* we have two sources, both of great antiquity:

(1) The return of the Israelites from Babylon and the building of the second Temple, based on Ezra. Nehemiah etc., in the Old Testament.

(2) The legend of the discovery of the vault, the altar, and the Sacred Word. This dates back to the writings of the early historians and Fathers of the Christian Church.

The Bible fixes the date and circumstances in which the legendary discovery of the vault took place. The vault legend is the drama which enshrines the esoteric and deeply religious teachings that are the essence of the ceremony. We may be sure that, in greater or less detail, these sources provided the background of the Royal Arch admission ceremony from its earliest times.

The study of the actual ritual of the RA presents major difficulties, because we lack the splendid run of early ritual texts such as we have for the Craft degrees. In the earlier decades of the Royal Arch, as in early Craft practice, substantial parts of the work would have been in the form of catechism. The ritual documents that survive begin in the 1760s, with more detailed texts towards the end of that century.

Precise dating from ritual always raises problems. When we find a dated text containing new information, we may be satisfied that it represents the practice at that date, but we cannot be sure when it first came into use. The following notes may serve as examples illustrating the difficulties.

There is a French manuscript, date *c*1760, in the Grand Lodge library, which makes reference to a word 'on the Triangle'. This is confirmed in another French text in *c*1765, and we find it again in *c*1784, in an English version of similar material, the *Dovre MS*, which was used by a Moderns' Chapter in Norway.

The earliest text that we have, describing the language of that word is the *Tunnah MS*, of *c*1794, which indicates that it was a compound word in three languages, Hebrew, Chaldee and Arabic. Several later texts, none earlier than *c*1804–10, give the languages as Syriac,

Chaldee and Arabic. All these documents make it clear that there was another 'word', as early as c1760, and we shall come to that shortly. Strangely, the Hebrew characters at the corners of the 'triangle' are not to be found in any of our ritual documents until after the 'standardisation' in 1834.

Apart from overt Christian allusions, later removed, it is clear that in c1792, and perhaps a little earlier, the ceremony of Exaltation was in much the same pattern as it is today, but our present-day Historical and Symbolical Lectures were still in the form of catechism.

There is evidence of the ceremonial Installation of the Principals in the 1790s, but esoteric material relating to those ceremonies does not appear until c1810–12, and Passwords leading to the Chairs are not found until after 1834.*

In studying the sources of the RA ritual we find several interesting passages in early Craft documents which suggest that the Royal Arch, in its early decades and certainly before 1760, borrowed or absorbed certain features that were probably current in early Craft usage. They come under two main headings, first, the 'Ineffable Name', and next, the 'Secret Shared by Three'. Both are sufficiently important to deserve attention.

THE INEFFABLE NAME

There are in all seventeen Craft ritual texts from 1696 to 1730; only three of them refer, more-or-less clearly, to the Ineffable Name of God, 'Jehovah'. The clearest is in *The Institution of Free-masons*, dated c1725.

It runs:

Q   Who rules & governs the Lodge & is Master of it?
A.   Iehovah the Right Pillar. (*EMC* p 84)

The original printed version, from which this was copied, is *The Grand Mystery of Free Masons Discover'd*, 1724, where the relevant passage runs:

Q   Who rules and governs the Lodge, and is Master of it?
A.   *Irah,*
     Iachin,   } or the Right Pillar.

(*E.M.C.* p 78)

---

* I am deeply indebted to E.Comp. John M. Hamill, Librarian of Grand Lodge, for the ritual details quoted here, and for valued help besides.

The word *Irah* is a puzzle. I believe it is only half of a Hebrew place-name, '*Iehovah Ireh*' where Abraham prepared to sacrifice his son, Isaac, at God's command. The Angel stayed his hand. A ram was sacrificed instead 'and Abraham called the name of the place *Iehovah Ireh*. (*Gen.* 22, vv. 11–14). It means 'The Lord will see' or 'provide'.

The third mention is in a printed broadsheet, published in Dublin in 1725, *The Whole Institution of Free-Masons Opened*. It is a brief exposure of words, grips and catechism, much of it worthless, but interspersed with passages of Christian interpretation. The final paragraph begins as follows:

> Yet for all this I want the primitive Word, I answer it was God in six Terminations, to wit I am, and Johova is the answer to it, and Grip at the Rein of the Back . . .

(EMC, p 88)

The 'six Terminations' may perhaps refer to the six letters in the Name 'Iehova'. The 'Grip at the Rein of the Back' seems to suggest that the Ineffable Name was used in connexion with the Points of Fellowship, which are described earlier in the same text; but there the 'Points' are associated with different words.

It must be emphasised that in the earliest group of ritual documents, 1696 to 1730, the Ineffable Name *appears only in the three texts quoted above*; the remaining fourteen have no hint of it. It is therefore impossible to ascertain whether, or how widely, that Name was actually used in the Craft ceremonies of that period.

From 1725 onwards the Name, Jehova, disappears from the English ritual texts and from English Craft usage. We find it next in the valuable stream of French exposures which began in 1737, during the great thirty-year gap in new English developments 1730–60, while Prichard's *Masonry Dissected* of 1730 held the field against all opposition.

Prichard's third degree had become the basis of the European MM degree, and the French in particular had added their own improvements. There, in *Le Catéchisme des Francs-Maçons*, 1744, we find the first brief description of the opening of a Master's Lodge, with a fine description of the floor-work of the third degree and the first illustration of the 'Floor-drawing' for that ceremony. (*EFE*, pp 96–9).

The main feature in that design is a coffin-lid on which there is a sprig of acacia and below it is the word 'Jehova', always described as 'the former word of a Master', (*ancien mot du Maître*). The explanatory text usually adds that 'the word was changed after the death of Adoniram' out of fear that 'his assassins had caused him to divulge it'. In the French rituals Adoniram was 'the architect of the Temple of Solomon'.

L'Ordre des Francs-Maçons Trahi, 1745, was the best of the French exposures during the following decades, and its 'Floor-drawing' was a greatly improved design. But it repeated these Jehova details word for word in its many editions up to 1786. It was also translated into German and Dutch from 1745 onwards. (*EFE*, pp 247–69).

Le Sceau Rompu, 1745, claimed in its opening pages, that Masonry was descended from the 'Crusader Princes' who planned 'to rebuild the Temple of Jerusalem . . . in a spiritual sense' and 'took the name of 'Knights Free Masons' (*Chevaliers Maçons libres*.) The several chapters in the book are more concerned with Masonic practices than with exposing the ritual. There is no mention of Jehova as 'the former word of a Master' but the text follows *Le Catéchisme* in saying that 'the Masters agreed, out of fear that the Masters' word had been revealed . . . that . . . the first word that would be uttered, should serve in future for Masters'.

The unknown author of *Le Sceau Rompu* did, however, include an interesting novelty in his MM catechism. After Adoniram was 'interred in the Sanctuary of the Temple', we find:

Q. What did he [Solomon] order to be placed on his Tomb?
A. A gold Medal, in triangular form, on which was engraved the word Jeova [sic]. Which is the name of God in Hebrew. (*EFE*, pp 205, 225).

Le Catéchisme, in its second edition, was published in 1747. It was now entitled *La Desolation des Entrepreneurs Modernes du Temple de Jerusalem*, and much longer than the original. It included Jehova as the 'former word of a Master', but it also added the triangular 'Medal in gold' on Adoniram's tomb. (*EFE*, p 331).

I have quoted these important French texts only to show that the ineffable Name, 'Jehovah', so rarely used in the early English ritual texts, had now become firmly established in the French and other European Craft Rituals as the 'former word of a Master'.

Its next appearance in English Masonic usage was in the Royal Arch.

THE TRIBLE VOICE—THE SECRET SHARED BY THREE

The *Graham MS*, 1726, is one of the most interesting of our early ritual documents. It begins as a catechism of some thirty questions and answers, followed by a collection of legends, mainly about Biblical characters, each story with a kind of 'Masonic twist' in its tail.

One of the answers in the catechism speaks of those 'that have obtained a trible Voice by being entered passed and raised and Conformed by 3 serverall Lodges . . .'. At first glance, this seems to be no more than a complex reference to the three-degree system, which was coming into practice at that time. But among the legends, there is one that indicates a further meaning. (*EMC*, pp 90–1).

That story deals with Bezaleel, the wonderful craftsman, architect of the Tabernacle, the mobile Temple of the Israelites during their forty years in the wilderness. Two younger brothers of an unidentified King Alboyin were so impressed by his skill that they asked that Bazaleel should instruct them 'in his noble science'. He agreed on condition that they would never reveal his teachings 'without another to themselves to make a trible voice'. The text says 'they entered oath' accordingly, and he taught them the 'theory and practice' of Masonry.

Later, after the death of Bezaleel.

> the inhabitance there about did think that the secrets of masonry had been totally Lost . . . for none knew the secrets thereof Save these two princes *and they were so sworn at their entering not to discover it without another to make a trible voice . . .* (*EMC* pp 93–4).

These brief extracts from the legend show that the 'trible voice' in the *Graham MS*, implies *secrets shared by three, and communicable only by three*.

Four years later, *Masonry Dissected*, 1730, contained the earliest version of the Hiramic legend and there was no hint of a secret shared by three. Hiram, challenged by his attackers, counselled 'time and patience' and he was slain. A substitute word was adopted, and the ceremony was complete in itself.

In the several French versions, 1744 to 1757, and in their later editions, Adoniram being challenged, said that he 'had not received the Word in such a manner'. He was murdered and 'nine Masters' were sent to search for him. They knew the 'former Word of a Master' and fearing he had been forced to divulge it they agreed that the first word uttered on raising the corpse should be the Master's Word.

In all these versions, English and French, there is no hint of a secret shared by three, and the ceremony is complete in itself. When the new series of English exposures began to appear again in 1760 and 1762, the texts had been greatly expanded (and the Royal Arch had been in existence for some fifteen years at least). The two most important texts were *Three Distinct Knocks*, 1760, giving the ritual of the new rival Grand Lodge, the 'Antients', and *J & B* 1762, with the ritual of the original Grand Lodge, the so-called 'Moderns'. In the points under discussion they are identical.

The three ruffians seek to obtain the 'Masters Word and Gripe' so that 'they might pass for Masters in other Countries, and have Masters Wages'. Hiram, when challenged, says he did not receive the word in such a manner, counselling time and patience, but now, for the first time, he continues:

> . . . for it was not in his Power to deliver it alone, except Three together, viz. Solomon, King of *Israel*; Hiram, King of *Tyre*; and *Hiram Abiff.*

Earlier versions of the third degree were clear and simple. A word 'lost', a substitute found, and the ceremony was deemed complete. This note in *Three Distinct Knocks*, 1760 (paraphrased in *J & B*, 1762) was the first item in print confirming what had been in regular practice for perhaps twenty years or more, ie the link between the third degree and the Royal Arch. It was the Royal Arch that provided the framework for a ceremony in which the 'lost word' could be communicated, but only by three participants. But the quotation is good evidence that *the Craft ritual had been modified or 'tailored' to fit with the Royal Arch legend as its completion.*

The *Graham MS*, 1726, had first mentioned the 'trible voice' in the course of one of its legends, but it never became actual practice in any English *Craft* degrees. Absence of early Royal Arch ritual texts makes it impossible to say precisely when it was first introduced, probably in the 1740s, but whatever the date, the secret shared by three made its first appearance *in actual practice* in the Royal Arch.

THE VAULT LEGEND

Reference has already been made briefly to the legend of the Vault, the Altar, and the Sacred Word, which provide the scenic background to the Royal Arch ceremony as well as the religious elements of its teachings. Several crypt or vault legends seem to have made their appearance in the spate of new degrees that were coming into use in the eighteenth century. Here, we are only concerned with those which may have been the source of what became the early Royal Arch legend in England.

The works of several writers are involved, all telling much the same story in their own style. Probably the oldest of these was written by Ammianus Marcellinus, cAD325–393. He was a Greek, of noble birth, the son of Christian parents. As a young man, he entered the Roman army, serving in high office under Constantius II, and later under his successor, the Emperor Julian, 'the Apostate'. In old age, he retired to Rome, and wrote a valuable history of the Roman empire, in Latin, from AD 96 to 378, forming an excellent continuation of the works of Tacitus. Of the original thirty-one books the first thirteen are lost; the surviving eighteen cover the years from 353 to 378. The Ammianus version of our RA legend appears there, perhaps the most interesting of all, because the events relating to the Vault legend took place in Julian's reign, and Ammianus actually served with Julian in the Emperor's last two campaigns.

Another History of the Church, containing the Julian legend, was produced by Philostorgius, a Greek historian (born cAD 364). That work is now lost, but an epitomy of it was made by Photius, who became Patriarch of Constantinople in AD 853. This became the basis of yet another lengthy version in Latin, in the *Ecclesiastical History*, by Nicephorous Callistus, in the early fourteenth century.

Finally, in 1659, Samuel Lee published his *Orbis Miraculum*, in which he gave what was probably the *first English version* of the legend, citing Nicephorus Callistus as his source.

All these versions are concerned with the Emperor Julian's attempt to rebuild what would have been the fourth Temple of the Israelites in Jerusalem. That failed because of earthquake, or fire, or falling stones. How the events relating to the projected fourth Temple came to be adopted as the background to the Royal Arch, which deals with the rebuilding of the second Temple, under Cyrus and Darius, must remain something of a mystery.

There seems to be no doubt, however, that the Julian legend was still attracting attention in the eighteenth century, and it appeared again in the *Histoire Ecclesiastique* by Claude Fleury (b 1640; d 1723).

That version of the story was actually quoted by Louis Travenol in his exposure of the ritual under the title *La Désolation des Entrepreneurs du Temple de Jerusalem*, 1747. This was a much revised and expanded version of his excellent *Catéchisme des Francs-Maçons* of 1744, virtually a new book. It contained many pieces borrowed from contemporary Masonic works, including a fragment from *Le Sceau Rompu*, 1745, which had opened with a chapter tracing the history of Masonry back to the Crusaders, and the 'Knights Free-Masons' (mentioned above).

Travenol was a better than average writer on Masonic subjects, and he knew where to look for his material. He criticised the 'restorers' who intended to rebuild the Temple 'after the example of Julian, the Apostate' in order to refute '. . . the prophecy of JC [Jesus Christ] that the Temple was destroyed for all time'. In support of this belief he added a lengthy footnote to his text, giving the whole of the Ammianus Marcellinus version of the legend, from Claude Fleury's *History*. That was the first version of the Julian legend to have been published in a Masonic exposure.

For all these reasons, the Ammianus version holds a high position in the documentation of the Royal Arch ritual, and it is reproduced here (translated from the French) side by side with Samuel Lee's version from his *Orbis Miraculum*.

THE UNION AND RITUAL UNIFORMITY

The union of the two Grand Lodges in 1813, led naturally to a union of their Royal Arch bodies, which was achieved on 18 March 1817. Among the new regulations was one that we take for granted nowadays, ie that every Chapter unattached to a lodge was to unite itself with a regular Craft lodge. It was to take that lodge's number, and to hold its meetings at separate times from the lodge. This led to many problems and difficulties, especially when the Chapter could not find an eligible mate, and had to link itself with a lodge in another town.

The troubles passed eventually, but there was still a long delay before any attempt was made at ritual standardisation. The first moves towards that end were begun in the early 1830s. A Committee was appointed by Supreme Grand Chapter. The work seems to have been dominated by the Rev G. A. Browne, sometime Grand Chaplain of the United Grand Lodge, who was singled out at one of the meetings with special thanks for his services. In November 1834, the ceremonies were rehearsed and approved by Supreme Grand Chapter, and a Chapter of Promulgation was formed in 1835, for six months only, to work as a Chapter of Instruction and, in particular, to ensure uniformity of practice throughout the Order. It demonstrated the newly-approved forms of the Installation and Exaltation ceremonies in a whole series of meetings held from May to August 1835, and in November 1835, to avoid misconception, the Grand Chapter '. . . resolved and declared that the ceremonies adopted and promulgated by special Grand Chapter on the 21 and 25 of November 1834, are the ceremonies of our Order which it is the duty of every Chapter to adopt and obey'. *Domatic, Aldersgate, Standard* and several other versions are all descended from the RA ritual of November 1834.

INNOVATIONS

The changes and innovations that were made at this time may be said to represent the final stage in the development of the RA ritual, and, rightly or wrongly, it is customary to award praise or blame to the Rev G. A. Browne for the results of the Committee's labours. He perfected the RA Installation ceremonies, which had probably existed for many years before his time, but without any set form of words. He transformed the Catechisms and gave them their new shape as the three Principals' Lectures. He was almost certainly responsible for the introduction of the Letters at the angles of the T . . . with their extraordinary combinations and translations or interpretations. Whoever was responsible for this part of the work, and whatever their motives may have been, the results were lamentable.

In studying the evolution of the ritual, Craft or RA (or any other), one must make allowances for evolutionary changes, for the retention of archaisms, and for occasional historical errors and anachronisms. The RA ritual exhibits all these minor defects and it needs no expert eye to notice them. Like an ancient work of architecture which reveals the skill of many hands in different periods, so that old and new are united in a harmonious whole, the RA ritual, over all, is an inspiration. But one small portion of it is open to really serious criticism, *viz*, the explanation of the Letters at the angles of the T . . . and there is *urgent need* for revision.

Unfortunately, the defects are not easily recognised because, in this portion of the RA ritual, so much depends on a useful working knowledge of Hebrew. In addition to this language barrier, which affects the vast majority of our Brethren, there is also the inherent difficulty of discussing the subject adequately in print.

During this part of the ceremony we are told that *every combination* of the letters makes a word; that *all the words* have reference to the Deity or some Divine attribute: that certain Hebrew *words* (spelt wrongly) have specific meanings; that three *pairs of words* have particular meanings. Not one of these statements is correct, and some of the explanations that follow are so crude as to be downright offensive.

In an attempt to convey some idea of the faults that mar the ritual at this point, the relevant passages are reproduced here, as they appear in the *Domatic* working. (*Aldersgate* and *Metropolitan* are virtually identical with Domatic in this section. The Oxford working is much shorter at this point and contains fewer errors. It also has a long and interesting Note, which indicates that the compilers were aware of the defects, though apparently powerless to remedy them.)

Text

The characters at the angles of the triangle are of exceeding importance, though it is *immaterial* where the combination is commenced, as *each has reference* to the Deity or some Divine attribute. They are the 1, 2, and 3 of the Hebrew, corresponding to the 1, 2 and 3 of the English alphabet.

Comment

Immaterial is nonsense! It is only necessary to glance at the letters to see the absurd result if the combinations are made in the wrong order.

This is simply not true. There are in all twelve possible two-letter and three-letter combinations. Of the twelve, only three make words that could possibly be used for our purpose. The rest are either not words at all, or they mean things which are quite irrelevant.

Text

Take the 1 and the 2; they form 1-2, which is Father.

Comment

Correct. (The only correct statement in the whole piece.)

Text

Take the 2, and 1, and the 3; they form 2-1-3, which is Lord.

Comment

No; this is a childish mis-spelling. The word we use cannot be spelt correctly with these letters. Had it been spelt correctly, it would mean 'Lord, master, or owner', generally a 'human' noun, not a divine one'. In that spelling, it would also be the name of a Phoenician (heathen) god; so that our use of the word in this sense is very near to blasphemy.

Text

Take the 1 and the 3; they form 1-3, which is *Word.*

Comment

It does not mean *Word*; it means 'God', or it means 'not'.

Text

Take the 3, and 1, and the 2; they form 3-2-1, which signifies Heart or Spirit.

Comment

These three letters do *not* signify Heart or Spirit. This is another infantile mis-spelling.

Text

Take each combination with the whole, and it will read:
12/213 = Father Lord
13/213 = Word Lord
312/213 = Spirit Lord

Comment

In this whole set of six words (or three pairs), *only the first word is correct.* For anyone who understands Hebrew, the rest is awful!

There is a view, not uncommon perhaps, that since the vast majority of the Brethren do not understand the words at all, there is no need to worry about a few trifling points of spelling and interpretation. For those of us who value our Masonry, the answer is simple. The prime justification for the existence of the Craft in its present-day form lies in the quality and importance of its teachings. If any of us happened to hear a school-teacher telling a child that the letters D O G spell 'God', we would be justly angry. Yet we allow something almost as bad in this Hebrew portion of the RA, and it passes without notice, simply because so few of the listeners have any knowledge of the subject.

The lessons that we draw from the letters on the T . . . in this portion of the RA ritual are of the utmost importance, because they are designed to crystallise the spiritual meaning of the whole ceremony within a few simple words. We are at fault, both in the 'words' themselves and in the 'explanations' we give to them, and the following is an earnest attempt to furnish a simple and trustworthy explanation of *pure* Hebrew words, with an interpretation that is wholly in keeping with the teachings that lie at the very roots of our RA ceremonies.

The characters at the angles of the triangle are of exceeding importance because the three words which we compose from them may be said to epitomize the Teachings of this Supreme Degree.

They are the 1, 2, and 3 of the Hebrew, corresponding to the 1, 2, and 3 of the English alphabet.

The 1 and the 2 together form the word 1-2, which means Father, and reminds us of our close and intimate relation to Him as His children.

The 1 and the 3 together form the word 1-3, which means God. This word, in the original Hebrew, is seldom used by itself, but normally in conjunction with those attributes which may help us to envisage His glory. So, for us, the word 1-3 means God, the Architect, the Almighty Creator, whose mercy and loving kindness are beyond human comprehension.

The 3 and the 2 together form the word 3-2, which means Heart or Spirit, and is used here to remind us of our duty towards Him, whom we are to serve 'with all our heart and with all our soul and with all our might'. With all our heart, as His children; with all our soul, from a deep conviction of His infinite goodness and power; and with all our might, because our service to Him can never be complete in thought and words alone. Such, my newly exalted Comps., is the explanation we give . . .

Eventually, I addressed an inquiry to the Grand Secretary of the

Grand Lodge of Israel, to ascertain what letters are used in this part of the Royal Arch ceremony, as practised nowadays in Israel. I am delighted to report that (out of the twelve possible combinations of letters) they use exactly the same three 'two-letter words' that are recommended here, with the interpretations, Father, God and Heart.

It will be observed that the familiar passage, 'Father-Lord, Word-Lord . . .', is now omitted, partly because the three letters do not fit that interpretaion (and never did). Another reason is because the interpretation is strictly Christian and Trinitarian, and it is, therefore, not in full accord with the official modern views on purely sectarian ritual.

But for those who would wish to retain this passage, I am indebted to E Comp R. A. Wells, Scribe E of Domatic Chapter of Instruction, No 177, who has produced an admirable and concise version of the earlier forms. It is, of course, understood that the following paragraph bears only an 'interpretational' connection with the original three Hebrew letters and their 'words':

> In former times these characters in conjunction with the triangle have been explained as—Father Lord, Word Lord, Spirit Lord, according to the teachings of the First Epistle of St John (chap. 5, v. 7): 'For there are three that bear record in heaven, the Father, the Word, and the Holy Ghost; and these three are one.' Such, my newly exalted Comp., is the explanation we give of . . . etc

8

THE LETTER G

THE LETTER G, which is conspicuously displayed in many Lodges under the jurisdiction of the Grand Lodge of England (and in numerous other jurisdictions, too), has the curious, if not unique, distinction of being a Masonic symbol which does not have the all-important characteristic of universality. All the others, the working tools, the greater and lesser lights, the pillars, etc, which form an intrinsic part of our *method of teaching*, convey the same lessons to Masons of every race, colour or creed, and in every language. The G, as it is explained in the majority of English-language rituals, bears its interpretation primarily in English alone (and only by accident in other tongues, such as German, etc).

As a starting point, we may note that in the majority of English Rituals the G is referred to in the lecture on the second TB as meaning God, TGGOTU.

During the Closing in the 2nd Deg. it is mentioned again, as follows:

WM   Bro JW, in this position, what have you discovered?
JW   A Sacred symbol.
WM   Where situated?
JW   In the centre of the building.
WM   To whom does it allude?
JW   To God, the GG of the Universe.

But these are, so to speak, the modern refinements of ancient practice, and, as we shall see, there is a great deal of evidence in the Old Charges and in eighteenth century ritual documents to suggest that the G represented the science of Geometry, which always had a special place in the Craft; and so the questions arise:

How and where did the G come into Masonic practice?

What does it represent; God or Geometry, or both?

What are the modern practices in regard to the G?

180

To understand the nature of the problems, we go back to the sources of our earliest Masonic documents, the MS Constitutions or 'Old Charges'.

EVOLUTION OF THE 'SEVEN LIBERAL ARTS OR SCIENCES'

The ancient Greeks propounded the idea of a 'circle' of arts and sciences as a necessary preliminary for Greek youth before proceeding to professional studies, but the precise contents of their curriculum is unknown, although our seven were apparently included among them.

The Roman *artes liberales* covered much wider ground, including the arts of gymnastics, war, generalship, politics, jurisprudence and medicine, etc. They were apparently not grouped into a fixed cycle such as the later grouping of the 'Seven', and, from the point of view of the Roman gentry, there would never have been any kind of connection between the liberal studies and their practical applications. Thus, the association we find in the Ancient Charges between geometry and masonry would not have occurred to them; the crafts were deemed to be vulgar, and Seneca even excluded painting, sculpture and marble-working from the 'liberal arts'.

An early Roman attempt at codification by Varro, in the second century BC, has not survived. Martianus Capella, of Carthage, wrote his *Septem Artes Liberales* some 600 years later, cAD 420, in which the arts were for the first time numbered seven. Cassiodorus (c480–c565) produced a work on the same subject which became one of the standard treatises of the Middle Ages. Boethius was the first to divide them into two groups containing the four mathematical sciences, Arithmetic, Music, Geometry and Astronomy, and the three literary arts, Grammar, Rhetoric and Logic, though he dealt with only the first four.

By the time of Isidore, Bishop of Seville (AD 600–36), the seven liberal arts were the recognised introduction to all knowledge, though he included many other sciences in his curriculum. His definition of the seven became the model for later encyclopaedists:

There are seven liberal arts. First, grammar, that is, skill in speaking. Second, rhetoric, which on account of the grace and fluency of its eloquence is considered most necessary in the problem of civil life. Third, dialectic, also called logic, which by subtle discussion divides the true from the false. Fourth, arithmetic, which contains the causes and divisions of numbers. Fifth, music, which consists of songs and music. Sixth, geometry, which comprehends the measures and dimensions of the earth. Seventh, astronomy, which contains the law of the stars.

There were, indeed, differing views in the Middle Ages as to which of the seven sciences was the most important, but the two oldest Masonic MSS, and all the later versions, stress the idea that Geometry was the foundation of all knowledge.*

> Marvel not that I say all sciences live only by Geometry – for there is no art or handicraft wrought by men's hands but what is wrought by Geometry . . . Geometry is the science that all reasonable men live by . . .†

Although the words differ in the various texts, this same theme is repeated regularly in the MS Constitutions, and when the texts reach the point at which Euclid comes into the traditional history, the story takes a curious twist and we find that he is reported to have taught the art of building, and that *he gave it the name of geometry, now universally called Masonry*. The following quotation is typical:

> And then this worthy Doctor [Euclid] . . . taught them ye Science of Geometrie & practise to worke in stones all manner of worthy work yt belongeth to buildings Churches Temples Castles . . .

and later:

> Euclid was ye first yt gave it ye name of Geometrie the wch is now called Masonrie throughout all this nation . . . (*York No 1 MS. c*1600‡).

Thus the science of geometry and the craft of masonry become virtually synonymous in our oldest Masonic documents, and this particular theme is developed so regularly and with such emphasis that there can be no doubt that this was the basis of at least one meaning of the letter G when it was subsequently introduced into the ritual (and furnishings) of the Craft.

The references to God in the MS Constitutions are more formal. Most of the texts begin with a brief invocation or prayer:

> Thanked be God our Glorious Father and founder and former of heaven and earth . . .§

---

* The foregoing is a brief précis from the chapter of the Seven Liberal Arts in Knoop, Jones & Hamer's *The Two Earliest Masonic MSS* (Manchester University Press, 1938), pp 24–6.
† *Cooke MS, c*1410, lines 99–105 and 127–28. Knoop, *op cit*, pp 74–5. I reproduce the text in modern language.
‡ *The Yorkshire 'Old Charges' of Masons*, Poole & Worts, p 114 *et passim*.
§ The *Cooke MS, c*1410.

Frequently the invocation is of a trinitarian character, but in either form it is simply to be understood as an 'opening prayer' and there is no particular Masonic significance in it. The name of God also appears regularly in the first of the 'Points' addressed to all Masons at their entry to the Craft, when they were adjured to love God and Holy Church, and their master and fellows, etc. Here too, though it reappears in every version of the Constitutions, it is a very proper but rather formal opening to the whole code of Points that follow it. The name of God is venerated, but it does not receive the kind of emphasis which would entitle us to deduce that it might have inspired our early brethren to symbolise it in any particular way.

Nothing that has been written thus far should be construed as a suggestion that the Masons of c1400 were already using the letter G as a symbol, either for God or for geometry. The point is that the word 'geometry' had a special connotation for them; and so long as that idea remained (as it did for several hundred years), it was inevitable that when the first glimmerings of symbolism began to make their appearance in the Craft, the significance of geometry would be emphasised in some way. Within the same texts, however, the name of God receives more normal and formal treatment, so that we are driven to the conclusion that when the G symbol first appeared in Craft usage, it was not in allusion to God, but to Geometry, ie to the science which was deemed to be the very foundation of the Craft.

THE G IN EARLY ENGLISH RITUAL DOCUMENTS

Our next source of information lies in the catechisms and exposures, starting in 1696, which furnish our earliest evidence on the ritual of their time. The oldest of the series, the *Edinburgh Register House MS* of 1696 (and the three related versions), contain no information on our subject; but the *Sloane MS*, dated c1700, has an interesting reference to the 'Blazing Star', and although those words may appear irrelevant at this point, they assume some significance when the whole body of evidence is collated.

Q. How many Jewles belong to your Lodge?
A. There are three the Square pavem^t the blazing Star and the Danty tassley*.

---

* *EMC*, pp 47–48. 'Danty Tassley' is a corruption of Indented Tarsal, 'the border round about' the Lodge, as Prichard describes it; or possibly a corruption of perpentashler.

A number of catechisms (both manuscript and printed) have survived from the years up to 1730, but the Blazing Star does not reappear in any of them until Prichard's *Masonry Dissected*, which was first published in October 1730:

Q. Have you any Furniture in your Lodge?
A. Yes.
A. What is it?
A. *Mosaick* Pavement, Blazing Star and Indented Tarsel.
Q. What are they?
A. *Mosaick* Pavement, the Ground Floor of the Lodge, Blazing Star, the Centre, and Indented Tarsel the Border round about it. [*EMC*, p 162.]

A later version, the *Chesham MS*, c1740, is identical on this point*, and these three texts are the only English documents of this class which refer to the Blazing Star up to 1740. We shall deal with the significance of this symbol and the manner in which it was depicted at a later stage in this study, but for the moment our main interest in it arises because Prichard's exposure deals with two completely separate elements, the Blazing Star and the Letter G. The former appears in the Enter'd 'Prentices' Degree, but Prichard's numerous references to the G are all included in his 'Fellow Craft's Degree'.

If the letter G was indeed part *of the ritual* in the earlier *pre-Grand Lodge* era, which I am inclined to doubt, it seems probable that it had fallen out of use for a time, because there is no trace of it in the numerous catechisms and exposures, English and Scottish, in the years from 1696 to 1730.

Prichard's FC Degree is a catechism of some thirty-three Questions and Answers, followed by a rhymed 'examination' and a form of 'greeting'. We reproduce only those portions which relate to the G:

Q. Are you a Fellow-Craft?
A. I am.
Q. Why was you made a Fellow-Craft?
A. For the sake of the Letter G.
Q. What does that G denote?
A. Geometry, or the fifth Science.
[Several questions leading to 'the Middle Chamber'.]

---

* *Ibid*, p 174. As this text is virtually an exact copy of Prichard, we ignore it in the later discussion.

Q. When you came into the middle, what did you see?
A. The Resemblance of the Letter G.
Q. Who doth that G denote?
A. One that's greater than you.
Q. Who's greater than I, that am a Free and Accepted Mason, the Master of a Lodge?
A. The Grand Architect and Contriver of the Universe, or He that was taken up to the top of the Pinnacle of the Holy Temple. [An early version of our GAOTU.]
Q. Can you repeat the Letter G?
A. I'll do my Endeavour.

                    The Repeating of the Letter G

Resp[onder] In the midst of *Solomon*'s Temple there stands a G.
           A Letter fair for all to read and see,
           But few there be that understands
           What means that Letter G.

Ex[aminer] My Friend, if you pretend to be
           Of this Fraternity,
           You can forthwith and rightly tell
           What means that Letter G . . .
           [Nine lines are omitted here]

Resp.   By Letters four and Science Five
           This G aright doth stand
           In a due Art and Proportion,
           You have your Answer, Friend.

NB – *Four Letters are* Boaz. *Fifth Science Geometry.**

This is all that Prichard has on the subject, but before examining the significance of his text we quote from several other interesting documents.

The *Wilkinson MS* is a catechism, much shorter than Prichard's, which belongs to the same period; indeed, it was dated by Knoop as *c*1727, three years before Prichard, but that is not certain.

Q. What is the Center of yr. Lodge?
A. The Letter G.
Q. What does it signify?
A. Geometry. [*EMC*, p 130.]

This is all that the *Wilkinson MS* has on the subject of the G;

---

* *Ibid*, pp 165–67.

though far less detailed than Prichard, the information it gives tends to confirm Prichard's fuller version.

Another catechism of *c*1740, now lost, is *A Dialogue between Simon and Philip*. It contains only three questions on the G, but it also has an interesting pair of diagrams:

Phil. Why was you made a Mason?
Sim. For the sake of the Letter G.
Phil. What does it signifye?
Sim. Geomitry.
Phil. Why Geomitry?
Sim. Because it is the Root and foundation of all Arts and Sciences.

And a note relating to this Q. and A. explains: 'You may Observe why G is placed in the midle [*sic*] of the Lodge.'

To complete the information from the *Dialogue*, the two diagrams are reproduced here:

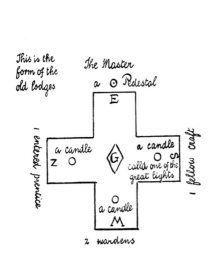

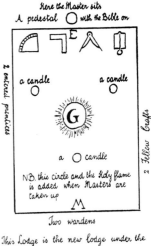

From the *Dialogue between Simon and Philip*, *c*1740. 'This is the form of the old Lodges.' Note the G in a diamond.

From the *Dialogue between Simon and Philip*, *c*1740. 'This Lodge is the new Lodge under the Desaguliers regulation.' Note G in a circle, irradiated.

Among the explanatory notes in this text there is one which describes the layout of the Lodge, and it clearly belongs to the diagrams:

> The Lodge's* . . . is commonly made, with white tape nail'd to the Floor round as you see,† the Letters E for East and S for South &c are made of thin Silver or Tin very thin, And likewise the letter G† at the top in the now constituted Lodge's is a Quadrant, a Square, a pair of Compasses and Plum line placed at the top of the Lodge . . .

The cruciform sketch of the Lodge is probably imaginary. The tape and nails and the tin are confirmed in other contemporary documents.

Two further references to the G and the Blazing Star must be mentioned here, although they do not come from catechisms. During the early decades of the eighteenth century there were a number of newspaper articles on the subject of Masonry, including items written in its defence, exposures, jibes at the Craft, and advertisements. One of these, under the title 'Antediluvian Masonry', appeared in 1726. It was simply a skit on the contemporary Craft, though it was probably written by someone who had first-hand knowledge of contemporary practices:

> There will be several Lectures on Ancient Masonry, particularly on the Signification of the Letter G, and how . . . the Antediluvian Masons form'd their Lodges, shewing what Innovations have lately been introduced by the Doctor and some other of the Moderns with their Tape, Jacks, Moveable Letters, Blazing Star, &c . . .‡

The *Westminster Journal* of 8 May 1742, contained an illustrated account of a procession of Mock Masons which had taken place in London on 27 April, some two weeks earlier. The writer describes the procession in full detail, and gives information on the Craft and its symbols, including a valuable reference to the Letter G and the Blazing Stars:

> The Letter G,
> Signifying Geometry, or the fifth Science, and for the sake of which all Fellow Crafts are made. This Letter G is the Essence of the Fellow Craft's

---

* The word 'Lodge' is used here in the sense of Tracing Board, ie. the 'floor of the Lodge'.
† The text runs exactly as shown, but I believe it would read correctly if new sentences began at these two points.
‡ Knoop, Jones & Hamer, *Early Masonic Pamphlets*, pp 192–94. The date 1726 is uncertain, but the item must have appeared between 1724 and 1731.

Lodge: For being placed in the Middle of the Blazing Star, which is the Center of the enter'd Prentice's Lodge, it then is a Fellow Craft's Lodge.*

Fellow Crafts are subsequently referred to as 'Letter G Men'. The procession had been organised by two prominent Masons in retaliation for some difference with the Grand Lodge, and there is good reason to believe that the details given in the newspaper report were an accurate description of some of the customs of that period.

To summarise the evidence from the documents quoted:

I. THE BLAZING STAR

The Blazing Star was known in c1700 (*Sloane MS*), and probably widely known in 1726, but neither text gives any symbolic explanation. Prichard calls it part of the 'Furniture' of the Lodge and says it is 'the Centre'. (Not 'at the centre' or 'in the centre'; simply 'the Centre'.)

Both texts imply that it appears in a first degree Lodge, and the account in the *Westminster Journal* states specifically that it is 'the Center of the enter'd Prentice's Lodge'.

The Dialogue does not mention a 'Blazing Star', but its two diagrams may be relevant. One shows a G enclosed in a diamond, and we may perhaps assume that it belongs to the EA Lodge, but the implication is uncertain. The other shows a G in a flaming circle, and a note within the sketch says: 'NB this circle and the Holy Flame is added when Masters are taken up.' Still not very helpful, except that there is a clear association of the 'flame' with something Holy. The diagrams and the text indicate all these items in 'the middle' of the Lodge.

II. THE LETTER G

It appears for the first time in a ritual text in Prichard, 1730, which states that a Mason is made a Fellow Craft for the sake of the Letter G, and that the G means Geometry. *Wilkinson* confirms that the G means Geometry, and that it is in the centre of the Lodge; the *Dialogue* says that the Cand. was *made a Mason* (*not* a Fellow-Craft) for the sake of the Letter G; both texts appear to be incomplete on these points, but the *Dialogue* diagrams also support the idea that the G is in the centre of the Lodge, and both texts are confirmed by the *Westminster Journal*.

---

* The practice of adding the G, as described in the above paragraph, is used to this day, in some German Lodges, for altering the EA Tracing Board to FC.

III. THE G IN THE MIDDLE CHAMBER

Prichard's text is the only one, of those quoted hitherto, that carries the symbolism of the G a stage further in his questions relating to the middle chamber, and now the symbol has a divine connotation. The reference to the Pinnacle of the Holy Temple is purely Christian, but now the G specifically denotes 'the Grand Architect and Contriver of the Universe'.

The rhyme 'Repeating of the Letter G' tends to confuse matters. It reverts to the 'geometry' meaning of the letter G, which is now placed *in the midst of Solomon's Temple*.

The details in the *Westminster Journal*, 1742, are particularly helpful at this stage. They confirm that the G means geometry and belongs to the FC, and here, for the first time, we have a precise combination of two separate symbols, so that the G 'placed in the Middle of the Blazing Star' transforms the EA Lodge into a Fellow-Craft's Lodge.

Clearly, Prichard's text gives the fullest and, in certain respects, the only information; the other documents do not refute Prichard – indeed, they all tend to confirm his statements. On Prichard's data, we may agree:

(1) The G belongs to the FC.
(2) It means Geometry.
(3) When the G appears in the middle chamber is means 'Grand Architect', and certainly has some divine connotation.
(4) The Blazing Star (thus far without a G) is part of the Furniture of the Lodge, and in those places where it is used it certainly forms part of the EA Lodge.
(5) The 'Blazing Star' in Prichard, with his G for the FC, and perhaps another for the 'middle chamber', certainly denote two separate symbols and possibly three.
(6) The *Westminster* combination of the *G with the Blazing Star* is the earliest clear evidence of combined practice *in regard to these two symbols*. This kind of 'combination' was by no means unusual, *eg*, 'The Three Pillars' combined with 'Three Lights', and the 'Two Pillars' combined with 'Two Globes'.
(7) The tin or silver G in the *Dialogue* confirms that it had passed beyond the stage of a mere verbal test-question or rhyme, and was by this time a visible and tangible symbol. Prichard is a

possible confirmation; 'Antediluvian' and *Westminster* make it certain.

THE LETTER G: BEFORE OR AFTER 1730

In a note on the ritual of the pre-Grand Lodge era, I suggested that if the Letter G had formed a part of the Masonic ritual before 1717 (and indeed before 1730), it had probably fallen out of use, because there is no trace of that symbol in all the ritual documents from 1696 to *c*1730. But there is another possibility that deserves consideration here, *ie*, that the G symbol for Geometry first came into use in *c*1730.

An examination of the whole collection of some sixteen ritual texts that have been discovered prior to the Prichard and *Wilkinson* texts of 1730 shows that, despite their numerous variations, there is a little nucleus of what may be called 'original material' that is common to all of them. Outside this nucleus, some show mere nonsense-variations; others show definite developments indicating substantial growth in the subject-matter of the ritual and procedure. But the nucleus is there, in each case as a kind of verbal measure of the trustworthiness of each text, and none of these documents has any reference, however remote, to Geometry or the Letter G.

From 1730 onwards we have seen that Prichard, *Wilkinson*, *Chesham*, the *Dialogue* and other sources all include the G theme and give it some prominence. We know, indeed, that the year 1730 marks the beginning of a great new era in ritual development, including the spread of the trigradal system and the general adoption of a much-enlarged catechism. In both these advances, Prichard's work must have played an important part, although there is no justification for believing that he invented them. The real importance of his work lies in the readiness with which it was adopted, as witnessed by the vast number of editions that were published in England and in French, German and Dutch translations, and by the fact that it was adopted almost word for word as part of the longer and more elaborate Continental exposures of the 1740s.

In all these later versions, as we shall see, the Letter G appears, primarily with its Geometry connotation, and with subsequent expansions of symbolism, some of which have already been noted.

Thus, in trying to assess the degree of credence we may give to either of the two possibilities, we have on the one hand the theory that the G was already *in the ritual* and that it had disappeared before 1730. This is extremely doubtful.

All the evidence as to the evolution of Masonic ritual suggests gradual growth from a small nucleus, with subsequent expansion, rearrangement and embellishment; and the possibility that a symbol of major importance had been dropped out of the Craft ritual before 1730 is, therefore, wholly unacceptable.

The alternative theory is that the Letter G was introduced into the Craft around 1730, based on the ancient tradition that Geometry and Masonry were synonymous. On the evidence already adduced, and on that which is to be examined below, this comparatively late introduction seems to be highly probable, and the wider interpretation of its symbolism, which is apparent in Prichard and in all the later texts, tends to confirm this late introduction and to refute the possibility of its earlier existence.

THE SYMBOLISM OF THE BLAZING STAR

Before we proceed further with our study, we may pause to consider the symbolical significance of the Blazing Star, which seems to have had a fairly continuous – though occasionally tenuous – connection with the Letter G.

The *Sloane MS* of *c*1700, which was the earliest text that mentioned the Blazing Star, did not discuss its symbolism, but apparently it was not intended to refer to one of the heavenly bodies. The Sun appears in this text in response to another question, and later texts that bear on this question all support the view that the Blazing Star is not one of the threefold group, sun, moon and stars, but a completely separate symbol.

Many of the early catechisms contain references to the sun, generally with some allusion to 'lighting the men to work'. A few texts have a question on the number of lights in a Lodge, which elicits the answer 'Twelve' (in four triads), including the 'Sun, Moon and Master Mason', but Prichard's text was the first that had 'Sun, Moon and Master Mason', as well as the Blazing Star.

Whether the latter was a piece of purely verbal symbolism, or was represented by a drawing or tangible emblem, its symbolical explanation presents a problem. It may have been a Christian symbol, *ie*, a forerunner of that 'Bright and Morning Star' which came into the ritual at least fifty years later. *Le Maçon Démasqué* of

1751, below, likens it to the 'columns of fire', and also to the 'Sun and the universe', but it adds a note of deep religious symbolism, describing it as 'the centre, whence comes the true light'.

The frequent association of the Letter G with the Blazing Star raises the question as to whether the G 'unadorned' is a symbol in its own right, or whether it should always be irradiated or combined with a Blazing Star.

Did the G acquire its rays of light because of its divine connotation? Did the 'unadorned' G symbolise Geometry; and were the radiations added in order to give it a religious, instead of a scientific, meaning?

There seems to be little doubt that the G was originally without radiations, and even the few texts already cited suggest that the blaze of light may have been introduced either in deference to the sanctity of the symbol or by combining it with a completely separate Blazing Star.

An examination of the further evidence that is available will show – I fear – that none of these questions can be answered with any degree of certainty.

EVIDENCE FROM THE FRENCH EXPOSURES

Hitherto we have dealt only with British (or English) documentary sources of information on the letter G. So far as ritual texts in English are concerned (*ie*, catechisms and exposures), the years from 1730 to 1760 are virtually a blank. Prichard's exposure was regularly reprinted during that period, and in England it held the field. Whatever ritual changes there were, they did not appear in print.

In france and Germany, however, beginning in 1737, there was a steady flow of exposures which grew rapidly into a flood. Several of these were worthless catchpennies; some, however, were more serious and, in the absence of truly reliable sources of information, it must be agreed that they afford useful light on the ritual developments of their time.

We preface our extracts from the foreign texts with a few words from an involuntary exposure by John Coustos, who, in his confession to the Lisbon Inquisition on 21 March 1743, referred to the Letter G, and his words were transcribed in the Inquisition records. They add little to our knowledge of the subject, but they are a useful indication of widespread practice:

The floor of the said Lodge has a design in white chalk wherein are formed several borders serving as ornament, together with a shining Star with a 'G' in the middle signifying the fifth science of Geometry to which all officers and apprentices should aspire . . . (*AQC*, lxvi, p 114, which contains a misprint, 'Geography'.)

Allowing for the fact that the European Freemasonry of that period was of English origin, it is not surprising that most of these works owed a great deal to Prichard, especially in their catechisms; but their expansions of material and their narrative descriptions of the ceremonies and other details went far beyond anything that had previously appeared in English documents.

Several of these Continental exposures also contained sketch plans showing the supposed layout of the 'Lodge' for the various degrees. These plans were generally a combination of two separate themes: (a) Diagrams showing the position of the Officers, altar, steps, etc; (b) Charts showing a collection of tools, symbols, etc, belonging to a particular degree, the combination forming a kind of elaborate and detailed tracing board.

We examine here the *textual* evidence from the Continental exposures; the illustrations will form the subject of a separate note, below.

Le Catéchisme des Francs Maçons, 1744, contains a catechism of over eighty questions and answers, and the author admits that a few of them have slipped his memory. So far as our immediate quest is concerned, he is, however, very helpful. Unlike Prichard, he names the Blazing Star as one of the *Ornaments* of the Lodge (where the English texts call it 'Furniture'), and the word 'Ornaments' persists in all the French texts. Following Prichard, he says that the EA was made FC for the sake of the Letter G, *ie*, Geometry, the fifth Science. Then, after a few Q. and A., leading to the subject of the 'Middle Chamber':

Q.   When you entered [the middle chamber] what did you see?
A.   A great Light in which I perceived the Letter G.
Q.   What does the Letter G signify?
A.   God, that is to say DIEU, or one who is greater than you.

It is only in the last two Q. and A. that the *Catéchisme* shows a development beyond the Prichard text which was its source. Prichard's middle chamber contained only 'The Resemblance of the letter G'. The *Catéchisme* has a 'Great Light containing the G' [*ie*, a combination of the G with the Blazing Star], and, as though to assure us of the English origin of the text, the answer to the last question says that the G means God, 'which means DIEU in English'.

The *Sceau Rompu*, of 1745, contains a splendid catechism, and in regard to the G, etc, it follows almost identically the pattern of *Le Catéchisme*, including, in the middle chamber, 'A great light in which I was able to distinguish the letter G'. Finally, this text declares that the G '. . . signifies the name of God in Hebrew'. [It does not.]

L'Ordre des Francs-Maçons Trahi is perhaps the most important exposure of this period because of the evidence it furnishes of contemporary expansions in ritual practices. It has the 'Blazing Star', and the Cand. is made FC by the Square, the Letter G and the Compasses', and 'For the [sake of] the Letter G'.

Later, in reply to the questions, 'Have you been paid?' and 'Where?', the MM replies, 'Yes . . . in the Middle Chamber'. There is no question of any peculiarly celestial light in the Chamber, but the Letter G, for the MM, goes back to the *Catéchisme* definition, 'God, which (in English) means Dieu'.

The illustrations in this book are of great interest. Among them are two 'Plans' of an EA/FC Lodge, which are, in effect, symbolical charts or Tracing Board covering the first two degrees.

One of these pictures is entitled 'The Correct Plan of a Lodge for the Reception of an EA-FC'. The other Plan (which had originally appeared in *Le Catéchisme des Francs-Maçons*, 1744) is incorrect (according to the author of the *Trahi*), and is sub-titled, *As Published at Paris, but inexact.* The two drawings are much alike, but the faulty picture omits the Sun, Moon and the Door to the Middle Chamber. Apart from these omissions, the main difference between the two pictures is in their arrangement of the letter G.

The incorrect picture shows a Five-pointed Blazing Star with a G at its centre; the correct picture has the Blazing Star, *without the G, but a large G appears (unnumbered and unindexed) above the Door of the Middle Chamber.* (See illustrations).

The *Trahi* also contains a most interesting and unusual Footnote relating to the 'Steps':

> . . . it must be noted that the Author of *Le Secret des Francs Maçons* has forgotten to point out that the first step is made from the west door to the Square; the second, from the Square to the Letter G; and the third, from the Letter G to the Compass; the feet always in the form of a Square.*

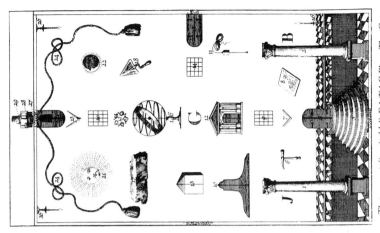

The correct ('*veritable*') EA/FAC Plan. The G is now completely separated from the Blazing Star.

The EA/FC 'Plan'. Note the G in a Blazing Star, but this plate is marked '*inexact*'.

This seems to imply that the G may have been a 'tangible' symbol on the floor of the Lodge.

Le Nouveau Catéchisme, of 1749, contains all the same 'G material', excluding the footnote, but the Letter G now stands for

* The author of the *Trahi* had openly pirated the whole of the *Secret des Francs Maçons* (1742) and used that text as the first part of his book, admitting that the *Secret* was very accurate in all but trifling matters of detail.

GOT [*sic*], which is '. . . the name of God in Hebrew'.

Le Maçon Démasqué, 1751, has a narrative section, which parallels and enlarges on its catechism, but generally both sections preserve the main items of their predecessors. In the catechism the Blazing Star serves 'to light the middle chamber'. The candidate is still made FC for the sake of the Letter G, but when the Master asks what that letter means, the answer contains an interesting expansion:

A. Three things, Glory, Grandeur and Geometry, or the fifth Science. Glory for God, Grandeur for the Master of the Lodge, and Geometry for the Brethren.

These 'Glory and Grandeur' definitions are, so far as I am aware, the first attempt to find new meanings for the G beyond those that were already well established.

Later, in reply to the question, 'Who is greater than I?, etc:

A. It is God Himself, whose name, God in English, is represented by that Letter.

The narrative portion dealing with these matters is described as a 'Demonstration of the Tracing Board' (*Demonstration de Tableau*), and it contains, among numerous symbols, a Blazing Star with a G in the centre (as in the *Catéchisme* 'Plan' of 1744).

The Board is a combination-piece for EAs and FCs, and the explanation follows in close detail the Q and A of the catechism, thus furnishing an interesting and early example of the transition of the ritual from Question and Answer to the 'explanatory' recitations, or Lectures.

One further expansion appears in the Lecture, when the Blazing Star '. . . goes before us like the Column of fire which shone [*brilla*] to guide the people in the wilderness'.

Only one more text need be noted here, the *Réceuil Précieux* . . . of 1767, and all the *Démasqué* definitions are preserved in it practically word for word. The *Réceuil* contains a great deal of symbolical expansion, but, so far as our particular study is concerned, only the Blazing Star shows a new interpretation, being described in one case as 'The symbol of the Sun and the universe', and elsewhere, following the *Démasqué*, it '. . . is the centre, whence comes the true light'.

This curious link between the Blazing Star and the Sun is unusual, but we shall find it again later on.

POSITION OF THE G IN RELATION TO THE DEGREES

Another matter that may best be discussed at this stage is the situation of the G, with its relevant symbolism, *almost invariably within the second degree*. This involves one of the major questions in the evolution of the Masonic ceremonies, *ie*, the rise of the three-degree system.

To summarise the subject very briefly, it may said that, with only one exception,* all the evidence of our early ritual-documents indicates that, in the period 1696–c1723, only two degrees were known in the Masonic ceremonies, one for the EA and one for the FC, or Master. At that stage one may fairly assume, from the evidence, that the EA ceremony was based on a two-pillar theme, and the FC (or Master) ceremony had the FPOF as its nucleus.

In 1724, or very soon afterwards, the three-degree system began to make its appearance, and by the time Prichard's exposure was published – and soon after its publication – the third degree was widely known, though not widely practised. A comparison of the ritual-texts before the change took place, and after, shows beyond all reasonable doubt that the third was not a new degree tacked on to the former two. On the contrary, the third in the new system contained all the elements that had existed in the former second degree. In effect, it seems certain that the new system was achieved by a splitting-up of the first degree into two parts, leaving one portion as the first and embellishing the remainder so as to form a new second. The process of development was gradual, and during its course all three grades were expanded. But if any of the three ceremonies may be described as new, that adjective belongs properly to the second degree.

It is from Prichard (and from his European imitators and 'improvers') that we may deduce the nature of the 'new' portions of the FC degree, since we know already that the pillar material was a simple transfer from the first degree. Prichard's was the first exposure that contained the 'Middle Chamber' theme and the new emphasis on the G with its related symbolism. Indeed, it seems likely that this was, at that time, the only new material in the second degree.

We shall probably never know whence he obtained it, but it was readily accepted in England and the European countries, and it

* The *Trinity College, Dublin, MS, c1711,* allocates separate secrets to three grades, but it has nothing on the letter G in any of its meetings.

reappeared regularly in Prichard's later editions and in the principal Continental exposures during the next forty years.

THE ENGLISH EXPOSURES OF THE 1760s

After the spate of Continental exposures, there began, in 1760, a new stream of those publications in England. The English ritual practices were by this time fairly well stabilised, and this is borne out by the general similarity of the texts. A few of them also contain useful lists (or mentions) of lodge equipment, and 'Plans' or Tracing Boards resembling those in the Continental exposures of the 1740s.

So far as our particular inquiry is concerned, the English texts of the 1760s yield no further information beyond that furnished by the earlier Continental group. Indeed, the English evidence is of such a negative character as to suggest that the Letter G and the Blazing Star no longer occupied positions of importance in the ritual, and were in course of being abandoned completely. The texts are reviewed here briefly, but only in regard to our theme.

Three Distinct Knocks, 1760. (At least four editions before 1780.) Contains EA questions on the Liberal Arts, including Geometry, but there is no mention of the Letter G. The FC portion has questions on the Middle Chamber and the Pillars, but no mention of the Blazing Star or the G, or any points relevant to our study.

Jachin & Boaz, 1762. (At least 16 editions before 1780.) Far the most popular text in the whole group, and there is reliable evidence that it was used in the Craft very much as the 'little blue books' are used today. Everything that has been said about *TDK*, above, applies equally to *J. & B.*, and when we consider the wide circulation that this book enjoyed, the negative evidence of the missing G and Blazing Star assumes an importance far greater than would be attached to the same circumstance in connection with a little-known text. The point is that if those symbols were in wide general use in the Craft Lodges of that period, *J. & B.*, with its numerous editions, would almost certainly have depicted and described them.

From the 1776 edition onwards, *J. & B.* contains an oval frontispiece in which the lodge symbols and furnishings are beautifully illustrated. The 1800 edition has an octagonal engraving containing all the same symbols in a new arrangement, but the G and the Blazing Star are missing from all these illustrations. It may be significant that from 1776 onwards a new symbol, 'The All-Seeing

Eye' (described as the Eye of Providence), appears, in a blaze of light, which might bear an *inferential* relationship both to the G and the Blazing Star.

Hiram, 1764, and *Shibboleth*, 1765, are both void of all reference to our two symbols. *Tubal Kain*, 1767, is a mere copy of Prichard's *Masonry Dissected*, reprinting his material word for word, so that it offers nothing new and is probably not representative of its period.

Solomon in All his Glory, 1766. (At least five editions up to 1780.) This was an acknowledged translation of the French *Maçon Démasqué*, of 1751, though that title is not mentioned. The Blazing Star is described in the Introduction as 'the torch which enlightens them' (*ie*, the Brn.). The FC ceremony, as in the *Démasqué*, has the explanation of the *Tableau*, which contains the Blazing Star with the G in the centre, the flames referring to the 'Pillar of Fire' – in fact, all the *Démasqué* material, both in narrative form in the Lecture, and in Q and A form in the catechism.

The *Tableau* of this FC ceremony contains the Blazing Star with the G at its centre in both the 1766 and 1768 editions. The 1777 edition shows the Star in precisely the same position, but without the G. In all cases the numbered chart relating to the *Tableau* describes item No 19 as 'The Flaming star', and the G is never mentioned. It is rather doubtful if *Solomon*, etc, represents the English Masonic working of this period.

Mahhabone, 1765. (At least three editions up to 1780.) A compilation that borrows considerably from Prichard, *J. & B., Hiram* and *Solomon*. Its first series of catechisms, supposedly 'Antients' ' working, are, like *J. & B.*, void of all reference to our theme. Towards the end of the book, however, there are three further catechisms, under the heading 'Modern Masonry', and the EA section refers to the Blazing Star which 'enlighten'd the Middle Chamber', and the FC portion combines the G with the Blazing Star, saying that the G denotes Glory, Grandeur and Geometry.

The second edition of 1766 has a beautifully-designed frontispiece, and here the Blazing Star is shown with the G at its centre. Again, the key to the picture refers to the Star, but does not mention the G.

The survey, above, covers all the principal exposures of the 1760s. It must be remembered, of course, that none of them was an official publication. On the contrary, they all owed their existence to some breach of Masonic secrecy and they must be treated as fundamentally

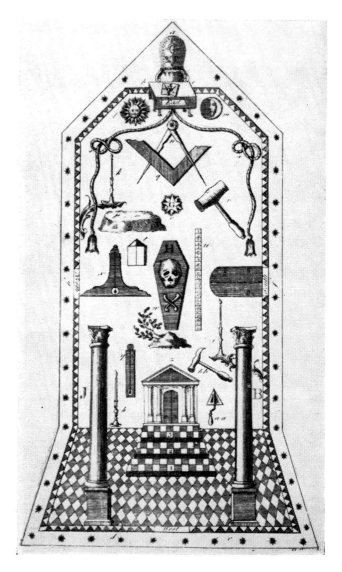

Frontispiece to *Mahhabone*, Second Edn, 1766.
Note the G in a Blazing Star.
(Reproduced by kind permission of the Board of General Purposes.)

unreliable sources. Unfortunately, we are compelled to examine them because no other evidence is available and we have to assess their reliability in the light of what we know of subsequent developments. For all these reasons the conclusions we draw from them are always tinged with some shade of doubt.

It is clear, however, that the whole group of these English texts of the 1760s affords no evidence at all of any expansion in the ritual practices in regard to the G or the Blazing Star. The two documents which would appear to have maintained former practices are clearly copies of the earlier versions, and neither of them achieved the circulation of *TDK* or of *J. & B.*, so that it is unlikely that *Solomon* or *Mahhabone* can have had any material influence on the ritual of their day.

If we exclude those two texts, it becomes evident that during the period 1740–70 the G and the Blazing Star had substantially diminished in their importance as a part of the ritual. The 'Tracing Board Frontispieces', and other items to be noted later, all tend to show that these symbols were not lost entirely, but the negative evidence, from texts that are known to have achieved a high degree of popularity, cannot be ignored, and it seems reasonable to infer that even in those lodges where the two symbols were displayed they had virtually disappeared from the actual words of the ritual.

THE POCKET COMPANIONS AND THEIR SUCCESSORS

In addition to the various exposures which achieved great popularity in England during the eighteenth century, another, more respectable, class of books made their first appearance in 1735, under the generic title of Pocket Companions. The size of Anderson's *Book of Constitutions* probably made it an awkward piece to be carried to and from lodge, and, when it went out of print in 1734, William Smith (whose identity has not been established) compiled and published the first *Pocket Companion*. It was practically a miniature version of Anderson's *B of C*, containing his 'history' – with additions, the Prayers, Charges, Regulations and Songs.*

These little books proved so popular that some twenty-five editions

---

* Anderson, in his *B of C*, laid great stress on Geometry, *eg*: '. . . Adam . . . must have had the Liberal Sciences, particularly Geometry, written on his Heart . . .' His work is full of allusions to the science, with a fantastic list of its supposed practitioners, including Noah, Abram, Moses, etc. His work might well have encouraged the introduction of the letter G, but his text affords no evidence that the symbol was in use in his day.

appeared within the next forty years. When Preston's 1775 edition of his *Illustrations of Masonry* appeared, with its more varied contents, it quickly took top place in this particular field, so that the demand for the Pocket Companions began to shrink and very few editions were published after 1780.

The G appears in only one of the *Pocket Companions*, the *Book M*, published at Newcastle in 1736, and now very rare. Its reference to the G is so cryptic as to suggest that it may have had a purely esoteric significance. (In the Irish Installation ceremony there is a note which states specifically that the G does not mean God, or Geometry, but that it has an esoteric meaning.)

THE EXPOUNDERS AND EMBELLISHERS

In 1769, Wellins Calcott, perhaps the first of the 'illustrators' of the Masonic ritual, published his *Candid Disquisition*, a series of moral and ethical articles on the Craft, with a collection of Lectures delivered by well-known Brn on various Masonic occasions. The work contained not a single reference to the letter G or its symbolism.

In 1775, William Hutchinson published his *Spirit of Masonry*, a collection of pieces, called Lectures, on the spiritual and symbolical aspects of the Craft. Lecture VIII, on Geometry, begins:

> It is now incumbent upon me to demonstrate to you the great signification of the letter G, wherewith lodges and the medals of masons are ornamented.
>
> To apply its signification to the name of GOD only is depriving it of part of its Masonic import; although I have already shewn that the symbols used in lodges are expressive of the Divinity's being the great object of Masonry, as architect of the world.
>
> This significant letter denotes Geometry, which to artificers is the science by which all their labours are found; and to Masons . . . proof of the . . . wisdom of the power of God in his creation.

Lecture IX deals with the Master Mason's Order and the lessons implicit in the MM ceremony:

> As the great testimonial that we are risen from the state of corruption, we bear the emblem of the Holy Trinity, as the insignia of our vows, and of the origin of the Master's order. This emblem is given by geometricians as a demonstration of the Trinity in Unity.

An illustration accompanies the text, and it is reproduced here, with another from the title-page to the same work, which has the All-Seeing Eye at the centre of the G.

From Hutchinson's *Spirit of Masonry*, 1775.

At left: From the title-page. Note the 'Eye' within the G.

At right: From Lecture IX, on the 'Master Masons' Order'.

This work clearly gives a place of importance to the Letter G, but it indicates that a curious change of emphasis had taken place. All previous writers, no matter what interpretation they gave to it, had first stressed that it represented Geometry, etc. Hutchinson says:

> To apply its signification to the name of GOD only is depriving it of part of its Masonic import . . .

Evidently, by 1775, some interpreters had begun to relate the symbol to the Deity alone, and Hutchinson was trying to restore the earlier practice, *ie*, God and Geometry. The Trinitarian link between the G and the 'Master Mason's Order' is, so far as I am aware, without contemporary parallel.

William Preston was by far the greatest influence on the symbolical expansion and interpretation of the ritual. His *Illustrations of Masonry* ran through innumerable editions, and the Lectures, in which the results of his studies were framed in Question and Answer form, were the ancestors of those in use in many modern workings today.

In his *Illustrations* of 1775 (and later), he made numerous references to 'Geometry, or Masonry, originally synonymous terms'. He enlarged on its 'moral advantages' and on the spiritual and scientific studies to which it gives rise, but, rather surprisingly, he made no reference in this book to the letter G as a symbol, nor to the Blazing Star.

In the Grand Lodge Library, however, there is a MS, No 16540 (dated by its watermarks 1807–10), which is supposed to be in Preston's own handwriting. If not, it was certainly copied out by someone who had access to Preston's material. Here we have the lengthy explanations framed in Q and A, some being traditional, and others, to say the least, unusual. The candidate is passed FC not 'for the sake of the letter G', but 'for the sake of G^y . . . because G^y and M^y were synonymous terms.

But in the section dealing with the Middle Chamber, Preston gave his imagination full rein:

1. In this Chamber, what struck the admiration of the candidate? On entering . . . the splendour of the scene . . . The counsel [*sic, ie,* Solomon's Council] arrayed . . . pageantry . . .
2. To what was the attention principally [*sic*] directed? The figure which first struck the attention, at the entrance was the sacred sign, richly emblasoned, and surrounded by a glory. In this figure the holy name of G was inscribed in letters of gold.
3. Where was it placed? In the center of the Chamber.
   Why? To represent the Supreme Judge of the World . . .
4. . . . struck with the sublimity of the object, prostrate on the ground they fell in humble and profound adoration . . . Recovering . . . & viewing with fixed eyes the symbol of the deity through the emblem of his power . . . etc.

We know that Preston meant well; other comment is superfluous. Although there is good evidence that large parts of this text were used in at least one London lodge in the 1780s and later, I have been unable to trace if the portions quoted from the Middle Chamber Lecture, above, were actually used. So far as I know, it has not survived into present-day practice, and I cannot believe that it was widely practised in Preston's day.

We have now traced the letter G through all the principal written and printed ritual sources up to the late 1780s. Despite the emphasis laid on the symbol by Prichard in the 1730s, and by the Continental catechisms in the 1740s and later, it is clear that the English stream of texts of the 1760s were ignoring this theme, and there is little evidence in the 1780s of its being used in the course of the admission ceremonies. Hutchinson's and Preston's quotations both belong probably to the special occasions when zealous expounders of the ritual demonstrated what could be done with an essentially simple theme. But I do not believe that any of the florid pieces quoted for this later period represents the type of symbolical explanation of the letter G current in the lodges at that time.

I am inclined to accept the hint, in Hutchinson, that the G was now revered as a sacred symbol, rather than a scientific one, and Preston, in a rather fantastic manner, tends to confirm this.

No doubt this religious interpretation was fostered and encouraged by the G that was displayed in many lodges, first as a drawn or movable letter on the 'Floor-drawing', then as a painted letter on the Tracing Boards, and later perhaps as a more or less ornate irradiated symbol hanging in the centre of the lodge or over the Master's Chair. But its *ritualistic* importance had, almost certainly, declined, except perhaps in a few rare lodges where ritual practices were expanding beyond the bare mimimum.

THE G AND THE BLAZING STAR AS TANGIBLE SYMBOLS

The 'Antediluvian' skit, with its reference to Movable Letters and Blazing Stars, is perhaps one of the earliest pieces of evidence of the gradual change from merely verbal to visible symbols. The lodges, during the early decades of the eighteenth century, must have been sparsely furnished, especially as regards strictly Masonic equipment.

Lodges meeting in small taverns could not be expected to own very much in the way of movable furniture. Three candlesticks and a Bible, with a few collar-ribbons and jewels, were doubtless the first essentials. The remaining symbols were probably drawn, more or less expertly, on the floor of the lodge, either with chalk and charcoal or tape and pins, and supplemented later by metal templates, as described in the *Dialogue*. During the 1740s many lodges were already using ready-made 'floorcloths' that could be rolled up and stored in a small space, and these were the prototype of our present-day Tracing Boards.

In the 1730s and 1740s a few well-to-do lodges were beginning to spend substantial sums on equipment, and from this time onwards we find lodge records of purchases of candlesticks, floorcloths and jewels, etc, while the exposures list such items as pillars, wardens' columns, wands, globes, etc – in fact, much of the paraphernalia of a modern lodge. Still later, in the 1770s and 1780s, the early lodge inventories that have survived confirm this gradual evolution, which had, in fact, begun some 30 or 40 years before.

So it is in this period, c1740 to c1780, that we may look to find evidence of the G as an item of lodge furnishings, as a pendant from the ceiling of the lodge-room, or as a template on the floor, or as part of the design of the Tracing Boards. But here, except in regard to Tracing Boards, our search yields only meagre results – in fact, almost a complete blank.

In those days, when candles were the only means of illumination, the idea of the Blazing Star on the G as an actual blaze of light may be ruled out as a physical impossibility. The 'light' from those items was largely symbolical.

A close search of early lodge histories and inventories* has failed to reveal even a single case of the G or the Blazing Star as a ceiling pendant. Perhaps the murky lighting and low-ceilinged rooms made such pieces impracticable. Whatever the reason, there is no trace of them in the period up to 1780, and the verbal references noted in the ritual-texts must also be deemed symbolical.

As regards cut-out letters and templates, we have the reference to metal cut-outs in the *Dialogue*, c1740, in the 'Antediluvian' text of 1726, with possible confirmation in the *Westminster Journal*, and this somewhat dubious evidence is supported by a record of the Lodge of Relief, No 42, Bury, where 'brass emblems, BJ and G' were in use since 1771. There is no note of when they were purchased.†

An inventory made by the Marquis of Granby Lodge, No 124, Durham, in 1775, begins with 'The Letter G and a Slate'.‡ This entry poses a problem. It is, of course, possible that these two items had nothing to do with each other; but the note in the *Westminster Journal*, 1742, in which the G was added to the Blazing Star to

---

* Particularly the papers on English, Irish and Scottish Lodge Inventories and Furnishings, by Bro. C. Marshall Rose, in *AQC*, lxii, lxiii and lxic, as well as many individual lodge histories.
　† E. B. Beesley, *Mas. Antiquities in E. Lancs. Lodges*, p 148; also Drawing, *AQC*, xxix, p 304.
　‡ Wm. Logan, *History of Freemasonry in Durham (and) the Marquis of Granby Lodge, No 124*, p 17.

Floor Cloth, dated 1764, of the Lurgan Lodge, then No 394 (GL Ireland).

transform the EA lodge into an FC lodge (quoted *ante*, p 175), suggests that there was a link between the Slate and the G.

My guess is that the Blazing Star was drawn on the slate for the EAs, and when a second deg. was to be given, the Letter G, in shiny metal, or in diamanté (like many eighteenth century jewels), was laid in the centre. This is the only explanation I can give which combines these two items *in line with recorded practice*.

An inventory of the Royal Sussex Lodge of Hospitality, Bristol, now No 187, taken in 1816, but representing pre-Union equipment, lists a

Star and Silver

without indication, however, as to whether this represented one item or two.*

An inventory of the Moira Lodge of Honour, No 326, in 1813, recorded '1 Letter G in Tin', and as this was one of many tin pieces recorded in their possession, Bro Powell was of opinion that these were templates used for 'Drawing the Lodge'.† But because all the items were carefully and recognisably painted, I concur with Dring's opinion that the pieces were actually used as *mobile portions of the tracing board*, *ie*, not as templates. Though these pieces belong to the period 1809–13, they were certainly in imitation of much earlier practices.

I have omitted from this collection of *tangible* G's the many collar jewels, in plate and pierced silver, which were much worn by Masons in the eighteenth century. The Grand Lodge Museum has a splendid collection of them, dating from *c*1760 onwards, and they are excellent examples of the silversmith's art, containing beautifully carved and etched collections of 'working tools', usually enclosed within a large G, which more or less frames the whole design.

While noting the existence of these jewels, which surely indicate a substantial interest in the letter G, it is proper to point out that the interest appears to have been 'decorative' rather than 'ritualistic'.

It has not been possible to prove, for example, whether the jewels belonged to a particular grade, and it seems possible that they were worn by anyone who could afford them. This view is supported by the introductory note in the 1776 edition of *J. & B.*, which speaks of the

---

* From photostat supplied by Bro Eric Ward.
† *AQC*, xxix, pp 299 and 321.

Three pierced silver jewels of the eighteenth century.
Left – late eighteenth century. Centre – c1760. Right – dated 1755.
(By kind permission of the Board of General Purposes.)

'Regalia and Emblematical Figures . . . represented in the Frontis-piece'. The latter is drawn as an oval '. . . Medallion, in Imitation of those Medals, or Plates, that are common among the Brotherhood. These Medals are usually of Silver, and some have them highly finished and ornamented so as to be worth ten or twenty Guineas. They are suspended round the Neck with Ribbons of various Colours, and worn on their Public Days of Meeting, at Funeral Processions, &c, in Honour of the Craft . . .'.

So far as I have been able to ascertain, there is no evidence of these jewels being used as 'presentation-pieces' (ie, for services rendered), and there is no evidence of any symbolical explanation belonging to them.

ILLUSTRATIONS IN THE EXPOSURES AND OTHER MASONIC SOURCES

Both the English and Continental exposures of the eighteenth century afford another useful source of information on our subject in their illustrations depicting lodge symbols and equipment. They are usually set out in more or less formal designs, rather like crowded Tracing Boards.

Within the period up to 1780 there were many other publications, *eg*, Books of Constitutions, Song Books, Pocket Companions, disquisitions on the Craft and prints illustrating the ceremonies. There are also a few very early lodge 'Cloths' or Tracing Boards, and various jewels and pieces of furniture, which come in towards the end of our period, and from most of these sources we have illustrated selected items that have a bearing on our theme.

The illustrations are not intended as a complete collection – if, indeed, such a collection were possible – but because we have only shown items which contain the G, they may give rise to some misunderstanding. It is therefore necessary to emphasise that several important works, in which we might have expected to find the symbol displayed and explained, do not have it.

SURVEY AND CONCLUSIONS

Having examined the evidence that is available on our subject up to c1780, the inferences and some tentative conclusions are now briefly summarised. The present-day practices in regard to the G and

Frontispiece to Cole's *Constitutions*, 1728/9. Note the G in the head of the arch (at right of central figure).

the Blazing Star are not relevant here, since our prime object is to trace the rise and early development of those practices.

c1390. The importance of Geometry in the oldest documents of the Craft. The G symbol, from its earliest beginnings, must have represented Geometry. It acquired extended meanings later, but never lost its original basic connotation which it probably had, amongst Masons, long before any stabilised forms of ritual had begun to appear.

*c*1700. The first appearance of the Blazing Star in a ritual text which does not mention either the G or Geometry (the *Sloane MS*). It may have been a Christian survival, and its constant position, 'in the centre', confirmed in most of the later texts, suggests that it was a Divine symbol.

*c*1727–30. In the ritual, the Blazing Star for the EA; G for the FC; and it now has two connotations, Geometry and God. G is always at the centre of the lodge: whether ceiling or floor is uncertain, but the latter seems more probable.

*c*1726–40. The G as a 'cut-out' letter, a three-dimensional symbol. It is sometimes irradiated, and then it is perhaps a combination of the G and BS. A suggestion that the combination turns an EA Lodge into an FC Lodge; and another possibility that the combination (in some places) may belong to the MM.

*c*1744–51. On the Continent, in the ritual, the Blazing Star is one of the ornaments of the lodge (*ie*, of all grades). G is still associated with the FC, and still means Geometry. G is usually associated with a Great Light (in the Middle Chamber), and there and then it always has a Divine connotation. From 1751 it has further interpretation, *ie*, Glory, Grandeur (and Geometry). Evidence suggests the appearance of the G and the BS, separately or combined, as *illustrations* on the Floor, or on the Tracing Boards, *ie*, not as three-dimensional symbols.

*c*1760–66. English evidence suggests that the G and BS are falling out of use *in the ritual*. Useful evidence to show that they appeared on Tracing Boards, and that they were being combined into one symbol, *ie*, an irradiated G, or a Blazing Star with a G at its centre. Very scanty evidence of their use as tangible symbols, so rare indeed as to suggest that they were not used generally.

*c*1775. A scarcity of textual references suggests that the G is not being explained in the ritual. Hutchinson's note that the G does not mean God alone seems to imply that the 'Geometry' meaning had faded, and that the Craft had begun to accept an interpretation similar to that which is in use today.

Finally, a note on design. Most of the early diagrams of the Blazing Star, whether by itself or as a 'frame' for the G, are in the form of a pentalpha, *ie*, a five-pointed star. The triangle as a 'frame' for the G is apparently a later development, and, in addition to the example quoted earlier, there is an interesting example in the Kirkwall Scroll,

A modern German Tracing Board for the EA Degree.

which is perhaps c1770. (See *AQC*, x, p 79.) The G in the six-pointed star (or Shield of David) is also late and far more rare, probably belonging to the period c1760 to 1780.

THE G IN MODERN PRACTICE

The following pages represent a brief sketch of present-day practices in regard to the Blazing Star and the letter G. This is not intended as a truly comprehensive survey (even of the numerous rituals practised in England alone). The data given here for England,

Ireland, Scotland, some of the European countries and USA jurisdictions may serve as an indication only of the developments in this particular portion of our ritual during the past 250 years.

ENGLAND

In England it is perhaps fair to say that *Emulation*, with its numerous imitations and derivatives, represents the rituals most widely practised.

Emulation, 1st Deg. The Blazing Star appears in the lecture on the First Tracing Board and in the First Lecture, Section 5. It is one of the ornaments of the lodge, and is described (in both cases) as follows:

> The Blazing Star, or Glory in the centre, refers to the Sun, which enlightens the earth, and by its benign influence dispenses its blessings to mankind in general.

The Blazing Star is illustrated on the Emulation 1° TB as a seven-pointed star within a circle, the latter being irradiated, and there is no G at the centre. The Sun, Moon and Stars are shown separately on the TB, so that, although the Blazing Star is supposed to 'refer us to the Sun', both symbols are illustrated, and in the First Lecture, Section 3, there is a series of questions dealing with the Sun, Moon and Master of the Lodge.

Emulation, 2nd Deg. In the Second Lecture, Section 2, the candidate is passed FC 'for the sake of Geometry or the fifth science, on which Masonry is founded', an explanation that goes right back to Prichard, 1730. Geometry and its virtues are discussed at some length, both here and in Section 4, but the G is not mentioned at this stage. In the Lecture on the Second TB, and in the Second Lecture, Section 5, the Middle Chamber is said to contain 'certain Hebrew characters, which are now depicted in a FC's L by the letter G', and the G is said to denote 'God, the Grand Geometrician of the Universe; to whom we must all . . .', etc.

The Emulation 2nd TB depicts the G in the middle of a 'Shield of David' (*ie*, two interlaced triangles), the whole being irradiated, and forming a kind of pictorial allusion to Psalm 84, v 11, '. . . for the Lord God is a sun and shield', and those words actually appear in the 1736 Newcastle Pocket Companion, *The Book M.*

It must be emphasised, however, that the 'Lectures' and the

explanation of the Tracing Boards are heard only rarely in the vast majority of Lodges, and the Letter G, with or without the Blazing Star, does not appear on any of the 'standard' Tracing Boards that are in use in the nineteen Temples at Freemasons' Hall, London.

As regards 'tangible' symbols, just as with the forms of the ritual, there is no uniformity of practice in England. In the London area, which contains some 1,650 Lodges, it is rare to see the letter G or Blazing Star displayed either in the east or hanging from the centre of the ceiling.

In the Provinces, especially the N and W of England, variations of practice appear to be more marked in proportion to the distance of the lodges from London. Still, in the majority of rituals, the explanation of the letter G follows the 'Emulation' pattern, but, unlike London practice, the G is usually visible as a more or less ornate cut-out letter hanging in the centre, and occasionally it appears as a carved or moulded ornament on the ceiling. The Blazing Star is generally in the east, usually as a luminous transparency above the Master's Chair.

Bro Wm Waples, writing of the Lodges in County Durham, says:

All North-Eastern Lodges have a 'G', and the seven stars in the ceiling, except the Phoenix Hall (1785), No 94, Sunderland, which has a Triangle with the letter G inside it. The apex of the Triangle points to the east, and the whole is surmounted with a radiant sun *eighteen* feet in diameter.

Most old Lodges still use the Star in the East, generally above the Canopy, or Master's Chair. This Star is switched on for a moment at that point in the 3rd when the cand is asked to '. . . lift your eyes to that Bright Morning Star . . .'

SCOTLAND

The G is displayed in every Scottish Lodge, but not in the Grand Lodge. It usually hangs *above the Altar, in the centre of the Lodge*, but it is frequently found in the east, over the Master's Chair.

The Scottish Masonic ritual generally resembles the standard English workings in many respects, although it is much more elaborate and 'explanatory'. In their lecture on the First TB, the Blazing Star is 'Emulation', word-for-word; and the lecture on the Second TB, speaking of the letter G in the Middle Chamber, also follows Emulation precisely, with its definition, 'denoting God, the Grand Geometrician . . .'.

But the Scottish ritual does not lose sight of the original meaning of the G. The Second TB Lecture is followed by a Charge, and then by another lengthy piece (partly in the form of Q and A) entitled 'The Middle Chamber Lecture'. Its final paragraph begins:

> My Brother, we have now arrived at a place representing the Middle Chamber of KST. *Behold the letter G suspended in the E; it is the initial letter of Geometry*, the first and noblest of sciences.

(From information supplied by Bro G. S. Draffen, of Newington, MBE, P Dep GM of GL of Scotland.)

IRELAND

The Irish ritual and procedure is perhaps the most interesting formulary, because it shows a distinct and *deliberate* departure from the more normal practices outlined above.

As regards the letter G *on display*, there appears to be no complete uniformity of practice. Official information is that the letter G is not displayed in Irish Lodges, and, from another reliable source, 'the letter G is practically ignored in Ireland!' But this applies only to the first three degrees, and the evidence collected from correspondents seems to indicate that the G was deliberately removed from those ceremonies in order to give it a special prominence at a higher stage.

> . . . the letter G is displayed in both our Lodge Rooms in Cork. It forms part of a symbol over the Master's Chair, comprising a Square and Compasses and the G intertwined.
>
> It is not referred to, at any time, in any of the three degrees, or at any time explained in any way. We always understood it to represent the initial letter of the word of the Installed Master, but even when giving this degree in a Conclave, it is not usually referred to by drawing the new Master's attention to it, although I once heard an Installing Officer state that the G in the PM's Jewel did, in fact, refer to that word, and not to God.
>
> I have never heard it suggested that it could be connected with Geometry.
>
> (From an officer of the Prov GL, Munster.)

The Standard Irish PM Jewel is a 'gallows' square and compasses, enclosing the letter G, and numerous early examples have survived from the late eighteenth century. The G on the Jewel (as noted in an earlier chapter) is by no means a novelty. Many beautiful examples are to be found in the English Grand Lodge Museum, but those are not associated with any particular degree or status; the G in the Irish Jewel belongs specifically to the Installed Master and PM, and this is borne out by the following extract from the Irish Installation ritual. It is an explanatory passage, which is recited immediately after the new WM has received the Master's word:

> You will find the Scriptural reference to that word in a marginal reference in the . . . Old Testament . . . and it is to this word and not to the Name of the Deity nor to the science of Geometry that the latter refers.

This extract provides the basis for my suggestion that there has been a deliberate change from the normal symbolism. The Irish working gives the Master's word without interpretation, and then it takes the trouble to emphasise that the letter G does not mean God or Geometry, etc – a rare example of a recognised Masonic ritual pronouncing, by implication, that other workings are not correct on a particular point.

The suggestion of deliberate change is strongly supported by the Lurgan Floorcloth, a single sheet containing emblems for all three Craft degrees. (See page 207.) It was painted for the Lodge in 1764 and thus provides good evidence of early practice. The Square and Compasses, under the central arch, enclose an irradiated Sun, without the G. The letter G appears quite separately and boldly at the centre of the picture, and it is clearly intended as one of the symbols belonging to the degrees, and not to the IM or PM.

But the transfer of the G, in Irish practice, seems to have gone even further, for it appears in several Irish Royal Arch documents, usually in the form of an irradiated Sun with a G at its centre, immediately below the Keystone. (See Lepper and Crossle, *Hist of GL of Ireland*, vol i, p 338.)

GERMANY

> The G appears in the centre of the Blazing Star (a pentagram) on the 'tapis', *ie*, the Tracing Board of the 1°. In the 2° it is in the centre of a six-pointed star (hexagram), still on the 'tapis'. In the MM degree it appears in a transparent hexagram, in the East. In the first degree it means God; in the second, Geometry; in the third, as a hint to Golgotha.

(From information supplied by Bro R. Ebel, of Oldenberg, Germany.)
(See Page 213, Tracing Board for the EA Degree.)

THE NETHERLANDS

The letter G, always in a five-pointed Blazing Star, appears on the Tracing Board in all Dutch Lodges, lying in the centre of the floor. It also appears, again in a Blazing Star, in an illuminated transparency, above the Master's chair, but only in the second and third degrees. It is illuminated after the candidate has completed his five perambulations in the 2°. It is also mentioned in the opening of the Lodge in the 2° and in the Catechism of that degree. (See remarks, below.)

In the present (official) Craft ritual, no particular explanation of the letter G is given. Older workings (*ie*, the ritual of 1865, which was influenced by the English Craft workings after 1815, and also by the Hamburg ritual of Schröder) give the explanation as 'God, the Great Geometrician of the Universe'.

In the opening ceremony in the Second Degree, the following dialogue is contained:

WM: Bro SW, are you a Fellow Craft Freemason?
SW: I am acquainted with the letter G.

The same question and answer are found in the Catechism of the Second Degree, which is read between the WM and a Fellow Craft, after the Ceremony of Passing. In this Catechism, the WM puts the following questions to the Bro who is giving the answers:

WM: What is the meaning of that letter?
FC: It is a symbol of the Eternal Source of all Perfection.
WM: Where did you see that letter G?
FC: In the centre of the Blazing Star.
WM: What does that Star denote?
FC: The Light, which shines on our path, even in the deepest darkness, and which originated with the Great Architect of the Universe.

This part of the ritual is of modern origin, and not ancient practice, although it is part of the official ritual of our Grand Lodge.

The explanation of the letter G has been the subject of much speculation. Some authors have stated that the 'original' letter G is the Hebrew *gimel*, which has the form of a square, but no such letter has ever been found in older illustrations.* The G is often explained by our 'Kabballistic' Brethren (there are, unfortunately, still too many of them) with the use of the symbolism of numbers; more

---

* I can find no trace of the Hebrew 'gimel', either as a square or a right-angle.

serious Brethren have thought of 'Gnosis',† as the immediate insight to the 'hidden mysteries of Nature and Science'. The philosopher G. J. P. G. Bolland, who was not a Freemason, wrote a book on the Blazing Star in connection with ancient Greek philosophy, and explains the symbol as the principle of 'Generation'.

Personally, I am of the opinion that the letter G should not be explained at all in Masonic ritual; it is meant to have a certain 'allusive' value, and the road to various explanations should be left open.

(From Bro Dr D. C. J. van Peype, of Leiden.)

NEW YORK (USA)

The Blazing Star is mentioned in the First Degree as one of the three ornaments of the Lodge. No further description is given, except that it is 'in the centre'.

The letter G appears in the Second Degree where the SD addresses the Candidate (after the Entrusting) as follows:

> My Brother, we have now arrived in a place representing the Middle Chamber of KST. Behold the letter G suspended in the East; it is the initial of Geometry, the first and noblest of sciences, and is the basis on which the superstructure of Masonry is erected . . .'. (Followed by a dissertation on what may be learned by means of Geometry.)

Later the WM reverts to the G:

> My Brother, the letter G, to which your attention has been directed on your passing hither, has a still higher and more significant meaning. [The WM uncovers, and all rise.] It is the initial letter of the great and sacred name of God, before whom all, from the EA in the NE corner to the WM in the E, should most humbly, reverentially, and devoutly bow.

CONNECTICUT (USA)

Bro James R. Case, Grand Historian, Connecticut, writes:

1. In Connecticut, the letter G is displayed in the lodge room and occasionally on the outside of the lodge hall or temple.
2. Within the lodge room it usually appears above the Master's chair, and may be flat on the wall, set out or suspended from the ceiling, depending on whether built in or added, etc. It may also be seen

---

† 'Gnosis' is defined in *OED* as 'a higher knowledge of spiritual things'.

occasionally as a decoration, or one of the figures on the altar, base of the columns, or where not. It shows on the old 'wall charts' [*ie*, Tracing Boards] for the FC degree.

3. The G appears in all sorts of combinations – within a star, within rays of light, within the square and compasses, within a triangle, etc. It is usually lighted and frequently wired, so that it is illuminated when the great lights are displayed or when the lodge is declared open.

4. The letter G is mentioned in the FC degree as the initial of Geometry and further explained as an allusion to the Sacred Name, etc.

5. The Blazing Star is mentioned in the monitorial lecture of the EA degree, where it appears in the centre of the mosaic pavement and once was said to be commemorative of the star which appeared in the east to guide the wise men to the place of the Nativity. But it is more often explained as the hieroglyphic representation of Divine Providence on which we rely for the blessings and comforts of our lives checkered with good and evil.

[Iowa practice is almost identical with the above, apart from a slight variation in the symbolism of the Blazing Star. *HC*]

SCANDINAVIA

The G is displayed in the FC degree, in the middle of the Tracing Board, which, in the Swedish Rite, is placed in the middle of the floor of the Lodge. Further in the west, there is a G in a transparency, *ie*, illuminated.

In the MM Degree, the G appears in the E, above the head of the WM. In both these degrees it is explained as Geometry.

(From Bro E. H. B. Birkved, Copenhagen, Denmark.)

Finally, an interesting note from Bro J. M. Harvey, of Sao Paulo, Brazil:

In the Portuguese edition of *Emulation Working*, published by the Grand Orient of Brazil in 1920, the Second Tracing Board ends with the words, 'que aqui estam representados pela letra D significando Deus, o Grande Geometra do Universo'.

Thus, the letter G becomes a D for the Masons in Brazil.

POSTSCRIPT

Doubtless there are many other variations of practice and interpretation that have arisen during the centuries. All are interesting, and some are surprising. This essay was written in an attempt to ascertain whence the practices arose and how they developed. It was not designed to show that a particular symbol or a certain form of words is right, and that others are therefore wrong. There is a great need for a proper tolerance in such matters. We may regret that certain symbols and phrases have tended to disappear from practice, or that their importance and symbolism has been enlarged or altered far beyond their original significance. Within the vast boundaries of Masonry universal there is room for every shade of interpretation, and I believe the Craft is strengthened and enriched by these variations and by the absence of uniformity.

9
KIPLING AND THE CRAFT

THE CENTENARY YEAR of Kipling's birth would seem to be justification for adding yet one more to the vast number of papers that have already been written on this subject.

The need for this further essay was first made apparent to me when – in my capacity as Secretary of the Lodge and Editor of the *Transactions* – I began to receive inquiries from Brethren as far away as Vancouver and Singapore, asking for materials and information which might help them to complete their own papers on Kipling, and I found, to my surprise, that while our library contains a great deal of relevant material, there has never been a paper on Kipling in our *Transactions*.

I approached four Brethren in turn, each with vastly better qualifications for this task than any that I could muster – but without success; and eventually the work fell to me. My diffidence was increased when one of the Brethren with whom I discussed the project said: 'What, another paper on Kipling and Freemasonry! Let's hope it will be the paper to end all papers on that subject!' Coming from a middle-aged man who had been a lover of Kipling's works since childhood, this remark puzzled me, but he would not enlarge on it.

When I started to read the papers that had already been written, I began to understand, and, although he may not have so intended, he had indeed provided the best of reasons for yet another piece. On the subject of Kipling's Masonic writings, each of the earlier papers had covered the ground more or less thoroughly, with suitable quotations, comment and interpretation. But on Kipling's Masonic career and background, there was a kind of uniform haziness, a screen of uncertainty and inaccuracy as to dates and details, which could hardly have been more effective if he had been born 500 years ago; here, it seemed to me, was the real justification.

In regard to Kipling's Masonic writings, it is hoped that the brief selections quoted will suffice to point the way towards the pleasures that are in store for the would-be reader of the tales and verses from which they are drawn. So far as the main events of Kipling's Masonic career are concerned, I will only say that every effort has been made to check the facts and to quote the proper authority for the statements that are made here. I have been fortunate enough to find useful pieces of hitherto unpublished material, and these, with original minutes and records, are quoted wherever possible. Where sundry details still remain unconfirmed, the absence of confirmation will be properly noted.

ACKNOWLEDGEMENTS

I must acknowledge my indebtedness first and mainly to Charles Carrington's famous work, *Rudyard Kipling, His Life and Work* (London, Macmillan, 1955), which has furnished the principal biographical data in my paper.* Next, to Bro R. E. Harbord, President of the Kipling Society of England, for the loan of valuable papers and for furnishing the two Kipling portraits reproduced in the paper. In addition, I owe him my special thanks for his kindness in reading the proofs of the paper and the corrections and data he supplied in the course of that task. My thanks likewise to another member of the Kipling Society, Bro Capt D. M. Penrose, Secretary of *Societas Rosicruciana in Anglia*, who provided the details of Kipling's admission to that body.

Finally, my thanks are due to Bro Col R. J. Wilkinson, Librarian of Mark Grand Lodge, and to the numerous Secretaries of Craft Lodges who added to – or confirmed – information already known; to Bro A. R. Hewitt, Librarian and Curator to the Grand Lodge, for unstinted help; and to the Board of General Purposes for their permission to reproduce a portion of Kipling's work as Secretary of his Mother Lodge.

RUDYARD KIPLING'S PARENTS AND FAMILY BACKGROUND

John Lockwood Kipling was born on 6 July 1837, the eldest son of

---

* Subsequent references to this book are marked C.C.

a Methodist minister. Despite an unhappy schooling at a boarding school near Leeds, he grew up to be a man of wide reading and he early developed a deep interest in the Arts and Crafts movement, one of the results of the Great Exhibition of 1851. In 1861 he was employed as a sculptor during the building of the Victoria and Albert Museum, but his interest in the arts expressed itself equally well in painting, in prose, and in a craftsman's skill with tools. At the age of 22 he settled in Burslem to gain experience in pottery-designing, and there he met his future wife, Alice Macdonald, daughter of the local Methodist minister. They were married in London in 1865.

The Macdonalds were a large and remarkable family, five sisters and two brothers, who, by their own talents and by marriage, had established themselves as an artistic and literary circle in London. The Rosettis, Swinburne and William Morris were among their friends. One sister married Edward Burne Jones; another married Edward Poynter. Both men became members of the Royal Academy and Baronets; Poynter was later a President of the RA.

At the time of his marriage, John Lockwood Kipling was very poor, but he had managed to obtain an appointment as principal of a new art school at Bombay, and the couple left for India soon after their wedding. It was a country where they had neither friends nor influence. Hope, health and a zest for his work were John Lockwood Kipling's principal assets, but he was a good-humoured and very likeable man.

HIS CHILDHOOD

Joseph Rudyard Kipling* was born at Bombay on 30 December 1865, and in that bustling, thriving city he spent the first five years of his childhood, his world bounded by the limits of his parents' bungalow garden, where he played with modelling-clay and the sculptor's chips from his father's studio.

His most frequent companion was Meeta, a Hindu servant, from whom he acquired such a competent knowledge of the vernacular that he often had to be reminded to speak English when with his parents.

In March 1868, the family visited England for a brief spell, and

---

* Rudyard, the name of the place where his parents had first met.

there, three months later, Kipling's sister 'Trix' (Alice) was born. In 1871 they came to England again for a six-month furlough, and before the parents returned to India they made arrangements – customary with Anglo-Indian families – to leave the children in England for their education.

Rudyard, aged nearly six, and Trix, aged three, were boarded at the home of a retired sea captain at Southsea. Their new guardians, automatically promoted to the status of 'Uncle and Aunty', were total strangers; indeed, John Kipling had chosen the couple from a newspaper advertisement. There is some speculation as to why the children were not boarded with any of their relatives, and it seems possible that the reason was partly because John Kipling's independent spirit would not let him seek favours from his wealthier 'in-laws'; but it may simply have been because the latter were fully occupied with their own families.

The five years that Rudyard and Trix spent at Southsea, though they appeared to be living in modest comfort, were a period of wretchedness and misery that left their mark, on the lad especially. 'Aunt Rosa' was doubtless a good woman, but harsh, tyrannical and unsympathetic. At the age of six, Rudyard had not yet learned to read or write, and in the years that followed he became a restless, clumsy, unruly and unresponsive lad. When he did learn to read, a whole new world must have opened for him, and he read everything that came within his reach. He talked constantly about the characters in his books and suffered the worst of all punishments when deprived of his reading.

His eyesight became affected, resulting in a series of bad monthly reports from the day school which he attended, followed by further punishments. But a long time passed before it was realised that the lad's eyes were so weak. Glasses were ordered and he was forbidden to risk further eyestrain by reading. The next few months were the worst of all for the boy. The story, 'Baa, Baa, Black Sheep' (published later in *Wee Willie Winkie*), is a wholly biographical piece, and it describes this period of their lives as Kipling remembered it, with pitiable effect. If it was in any way exaggerated, that may be readily explained as a child's-eye view, but it must have been a fearful experience for him to have recalled it as he did.

There came, at last, a happy day in March 1877, when his mother arrived from India and the two children were taken off to a farm at

Loughton, Essex, where they had a wonderful holiday under their mother's care – in preparation for Rudyard's admission to a public school.

SCHOOL AT WESTWARD HO!

The United Services' College at Westward Ho! in Bideford Bay, North Devon, was founded in 1874 by a group of Army officers who sought to give their sons a gentleman's education at fees within their means. It was chosen by John Kipling because its headmaster, Cormell Price, was a friend of his – and he was already Uncle 'Crom' to the young Rudyard.

The school was in its fifth year when Kipling joined it, its discipline stern, if not harsh. Most of his fellows were soldiers' sons, and both they and their environment were distinctly rough and ready. Kipling's defective sight rendered him unfit for most of the school sports or for holding his own against heavy-handed or quarrelsome boys – and he soon learned to avoid trouble by his tact and friendliness. But there is good evidence that he found his fellows tough, and the settling-in period was not a happy time, as we see in a letter from the boy's mother to Cormell Price, dated 24 January 1878:

> This morning I had no letter from Ruddy – yesterday I had four. It is the roughness of the lads he seems to feel most; he doesn't grumble to me – but he is lonely and down. I was his chum, you know, and he hasn't found another yet. I don't encourage the rain of letters; I discourage it – at the same time knowing that both his father and I have really an unusual twist for scribbling, and think no more of it than of talking . . . The lad has a great deal that is feminine in his nature, and a little sympathy from any quarter will reconcile him to his changed life more than anything. . . .

Despite the lad's facility with his pen, his mother was clearly ready to believe it was an hereditary trait rather than a native skill!

Very gradually, the separation from his mother and sister were compensated for by the friends he found in this new male society.

At twelve he was short for his age, chubby, with an aggressive chin, the heavy black eyebrows which so distinguished him in later life, and bright blue eyes behind thick glasses which he wore only when he was not reading.

In 1878, John Lockwood Kipling was in charge of the India section of the Paris Exhibition, and Rudyard was taken over to Paris for a memorable holiday with an English friend from another school. John Kipling was quick to realise his son's good qualities, but he was still unable to refrain from judging him by adult standards, although 'Ruddy' was not yet thirteen years old. On 15 June 1878, John Lockwood Kipling wrote to Cormell Price:

> I find Ruddy a delightfully amiable and companionable little chap, but the way in which he only half apprehends the common facts and necessities of daily life is surprising. Vagueness and inaccuracy, I fear, will always bother him & they take curious forms . . .
>
> If there is anything in him at all, the steady stress of daily work in which exactness is required should pull his mind together a little. But I should think he will always be inclined to shirk the collar and to interest himself in out of the way things. . . .

But the boy's interests were widening, greatly encouraged by 'Uncle Crom', in whose company, during the holidays, he met and was thoroughly at home with artists and writers. His own reading had become diversified and adult, and he had the useful faculty of digesting the essence of a book in a matter of minutes.

When the opportunity came for him to share a study with two other boys, George Beresford and Lionel Dunsterville (M'Turk & Stalky) joined him and unwittingly became the pattern for the adventures enshrined in *Stalky & Co.*

A particular influence on Kipling at this time was William Crofts, his teacher for Latin and English Literature, who helped to broaden his reading, which now ranged very widely indeed. Defoe, Fielding, Smollett, Dickens and Thackeray had been the basis of his early reading at Southsea. At Westward Ho! Milton, Tennyson, Longfellow, Emerson, Mark Twain and Bret Harte, Carlyle, Ruskin and Browning, and Landor's *Imaginary Conversations* were all studied and discussed to the point where Kipling was able to write verse and tales in the style of any of his favourites. In the last two years of his schooling, 'Uncle Crom' gave Kipling the run of his library without pressure or prohibition, leaving him free to range over hundreds of volumes of verse, drama and prose in English and French. Now 'the Head' began to take a close personal interest in Kipling's studies. In

---

* Extracts from a collection of 18 autograph letters from 3 July 1874, to 3 March 1899, all addressed to Cormell Price, Kipling's headmaster and friend. They were sold at Sotheby's auction rooms on 1 December 1964, by Price's son. At the time of writing the purchaser is unknown. The extracts here are from the Sotheby sale catalogue.

1881 his parents had arranged for the publication of a collection of his verses under the title, Schoolboy Lyrics – all unknown to their author. Kipling, absorbed in his reading and writing, was clearly destined for some kind of literary career. Whether this first publication was a simple piece of family pride, or whether they foresaw a successful literary career for their son, it is certain that before the end of that year they had made their decision, and this is shown in a letter from John Lockwood Kipling to Cormell Price:

Lahore, 23 October 1881.

. . . Now a boy living in India has curiously few chances of going wrong—and especially living with his own people. I must confess from what I have seen of Ruddy it is the moral side I dread a breakout on. I don't think he is the stuff to resist temptation.

It has occurred to us that the regular daily work of a newspaper would furnish by no means a bad occupation and I doubt not I could get him engaged on the *Civil & Military Gazette* here. And on the whole I am inclined to think that the easy-going general interest he is ready to take in all sorts of things, though the plague of his masters, who think he could do so much better if he would only work—is after all one of those affairs of temperament & constitution which nothing can change, and must be made the best of. Journalism seems to be specially invented for such desultory souls. . . .

A few weeks later John Kipling wrote to another friend that he proposed to

bring Rudyard out to India next year, and get him some newspaper work. Oxford we can't afford. Ruddy thirsts for a man's life and a man's work.

Nevertheless, his last year at school was a happy time for Rudyard. Beresford and Dunsterville were his inseparable companions and they were the leaders of taste in the school. Their exploits included all sorts of pranks in breach of school regulations, smoking, poaching and excursions out of bounds; but they never blundered into serious mischief, and Kipling found time – in addition to his studies – to write several poems for the *College Chronicle* and some articles for a local newspaper.

John Kipling was still troubled about his son's character and abilities, as may be seen in the following extracts from his letters:

Lahore, 17 June 1882.

. . . And if Ruddy does not learn conciseness, and the way to begin to consider a question—the mere fluency & facility of yarning he possesses will be of but little use. I am inclined to think he will learn his work in harness better than anywhere else. . . .

> Simla, 1 September 1882.
> . . . It is impossible of course not to see the faults of the boy's qualities – with others more serious . . . Alice says I am unduly harsh in saying, Ruddy must be a journalist because he won't fit himself for anything else . . . But though far from triumphant about him, we cannot but see that he has some of the qualities necessary for his craft. . . .

Rudyard's last 'school' summer holiday was spent at Rottingdean with a host of Macdonald cousins, and partly at Skipton with his Kipling grandmother. He sailed for India on 20 September 1882, alone, in drizzling rain and seasick.

LAHORE AND SIMLA, 1882-1887

After four weeks at sea, with an exciting stop at Port Said which made a deep impression on Kipling's imaginative mind, he arrived at Lahore in October 1882, happy to be back in the atmosphere of his childhood.

Lahore, a low-lying, ancient walled city full of the sights, sounds and smells of Asia, was connected by a broad boulevard to its newer European quarter, which housed some seventy British residents. Outside the city, at a distance of some four miles, was Mian Mir, a military cantonment housing a Battalion of British Infantry and a Battery or more of Artillery. John Kipling was Principal of the Mayo School of Art and Curator of the Lahore Museum, and for the first few days after his return Rudyard helped in the Museum, where his father had established a notable collection, relating to Indian arts and archaeology, that was much used by the students.

In November 1882, Rudyard, nearly 17 years of age, started work as 'Assistant Editor' on the *Civil & Military Gazette*, a local newspaper owned by two Englishmen, who were also the proprietors of the *Pioneer* at Allahabad – a journal of national status. Both of them were close friends to John and Alice Kipling, who were frequent contributors to the *Pioneer*, and there can be no doubt that this friendship had helped in procuring Rudyard's appointment.

The editor, Stephen Wheeler, was the only other European member of the staff, and, as he was often sick with fever, Kipling frequently carried the responsibility of overseeing the 170 Indian printing hands. Wheeler kept him hard at work on news-agency telegrams, preparing their contents as copy for each edition which went to press at midnight. Kipling mastered the technical work without difficulty and his schooling had already prepared him for the strictly-controlled style of his literary work, which must have involved a severe restriction on his own native exuberance.

In 1883, aged 18, he already had his own quarters in his parents' bungalow, a personal servant, a bay pony and a trap in which he drove to the office, which consisted of two wooden sheds near to the city. John Lockwood Kipling wrote to a friend in 1883:

> Ruddy is getting on well, having mastered the details of his work in a very short time. His chief, Mr. Wheeler, is very tetchy and irritable, and by dint of his exertions in patience and forbearance, the boy is training for heaven as well as for editorship. I am sure he is better here where there are no music-hall ditties to pick up, no young persons to philander with . . . All that makes Lahore profoundly dull makes it safe for young persons. . . . (C.C., p. 50, quoting from the Kipling Papers, the property of Mrs. George Bambridge, Kipling's daughter.)

During the hot weather of 1883 his parents went for several weeks into the Hills, and Kipling was unbearably alone in the house with the Indian servants. Then he stayed for 30 days at Simla with James Walker, one of his employers.

Simla was virtually the centre of government from May to October, housing the Viceroy and his staff, with the best and gayest of Anglo-Indian society, as well as the place-seekers and fortune-hunters. It was, according to John Kipling, 'full of pretty girls' and, of course, the wealthier matrons, who stayed there for several months, though their husbands had to be satisfied with only their month or sixty days of leave. Simla was a hill-town whose steep slopes left no room for good roads. All the houses were built on the slopes and in constant danger of slipping down the hillsides during the rainy months of July and August. Yet that was the brightest time for Simla, when the Europeans most needed refuge from the fever-ridden plains.

In August, Kipling was back at work in deserted Lahore, where a dozen men represented the whole European community, the remainder being away in the Hills with their families.

He was a none-too-popular honorary member of the Punjab Club (doubtless because he was too young for full membership) and there he dined and spent most of his evenings. After the paper had gone to press he wandered for hours through the alleys of the old city until the cool of dawn brought some relief.

In January 1884, his mother brought Trix back to India from England, and the next four years were Kipling's happiest years in India. Trix, an attractive and intelligent girl, made up the devoted and close-knit 'Family Square', as Alice Kipling called it, which was perhaps the best formative influence on Rudyard's character.

Soon he was commissioned as special reporter on public events, and in March 1884, he went to Patiala State, in the train of Lord Ripon, the Viceroy, where he greatly enjoyed princely hospitality and turned in some very successful newspaper work. Here, incidentally, he had his first experience of Indian bribery when he rejected a choice of banknotes, a concubine, or an Arab horse, which were offered him if he would use his newspaper's influence on behalf of one of the Indian princes. Wherever he went, people, scenes, objects, actions and behaviour were noted, observed and stored in his extraordinarily receptive memory, as always, to reappear at some future date in his stories and verses.

His one unhappy moment during this year was the end of his first love affair. At the age of 16, while in England, he had met Flo Garrard, a lovely, sophisticated girl, who was another paying guest with Trix at 'Aunty Rosa's'. Their meetings must have been infrequent and secret, but, when Rudyard left England in 1882, the attachment was so far advanced that they considered themselves engaged. She was a year or two older than Rudyard, and when, in July, 1884, she wrote breaking off their 'understanding', he must have been deeply hurt, though undoubtedly it was the best thing that could have happened. Eighteen months later he wrote to one of his English aunts asking her to find out if Flo Garrard was happy, and she held her place in his memory for many years. This theme of a young man in India and his girl at home was frequently repeated in his later stories.

The year 1884 brought cholera to Lahore, where the European community had eleven cases and four deaths out of the population of seventy. The family were at Dalhousie, a more economical hill-station than Simla, and Rudyard joined them for a month, during which he and Trix together wrote a volume of verse parodies,

Echoes, published later by the *Civil & Military Gazette*. The book had a fairly good reception and Rudyard's articles were also beginning to attract attention, though he used different pen-names for his contributions to the down-country journals.

In March 1885, he was at Rawalpindi for the first big event under Lord Dufferin, the new Viceroy, when his political articles and reportage began to win him credit as a well-informed journalist.

Lord Dufferin's first summer at Simla, 1885, was a turning-point in the social life of the Kiplings. He was a traveller, scholar and wit; his wife a great lady who strengthened her husband's hand, and their daughter was a pupil in John Kipling's sketching class. Lady Dufferin soon brought the Kiplings into the Viceregal circle of friends, and in no time their son, Lord Clandeboye, had become attached to Trix, now an acknowledged beauty and an accomplished actress and dancer. The young man was packed off to England before matters could become too involved, but the two families remained good friends. Rudyard was at Simla as a journalist on duty, and his employers insisted that he must learn to dance and partake fully in the social life, a hint which he accepted wholeheartedly.

In 1885 the family produced a 'magazine' which was subsequently published in the *Gazette* under the title *Quartette*, and it contained the first two stories which Rudyard, in later time, thought worthy of preservation in his collected editions – one, *Phantom Rickshaw*, a Poe-like study of hallucination; the other, *Morrowbie Jukes*, a venture into the unknown world of Indian life, far removed from his normal journalistic world. About this time, too, he fell in love again, with a daughter of the military chaplain at Mian Mir, but this time the affair had no depth or duration and he came through it unharmed.

Kipling was now nearly 21 years old, an untidy, abrupt fellow, cheerful, exuberant and with abounding energy, quick in repartee and witty. He had a great zeal for his chosen profession, working hard enough for three, and he was singularly happy within the 'family-square', but he still had an uneasy social manner. Some of these traits are manifestly irreconcilable, and it seems that they were born of a natural shyness or diffidence which disappeared on close acquaintance. Everyone who knew him well found him a likeable and even a loveable character.

In April 1886, aged 20 years and 3 months, Kipling entered the Craft.

KIPLING'S EARLY YEARS IN THE CRAFT

One of the many papers on Kipling, 'Bro Rudyard Kipling and His Masonic Verse',* speaks of Kipling's father as *Bro* John Lockwood Kipling, and this is the only case I have found which suggests that Rudyard may have had a *family* connection with the Craft. It is extremely doubtful if there was any such link. Kipling never mentioned it, and, allowing for the deep affection he had for his father, it is certain that he would have noted the fact either in his letters or his writings. There is likewise no mention of any kind of *family link* to be found. Kipling was proposed for initiation into Lodge Hope and Perseverance, No 782 (EC), by a military friend, Col Oswald Menzies, at that time President of the Punjab Dist Bd of General Purposes; he was seconded by another member of the Lodge, Bro C. Brown.

In his little autobiography, *Something of Myself*, pp 52–3, written towards the end of his life, he gives his own modest account of his admission:

In '85 I was made a Freemason by dispensation (Lodge Hope and Perseverance 782 E.C.) being under age, because the Lodge hoped for a good Secretary. They did not get him, but I helped, and got the Father to advise, in decorating the bare walls of the Masonic Hall with hangings after the prescription of Solomon's Temple.

Here I met Muslims, Hindus, Sikhs, members of the Araya and Brahmo Samaj, and a Jew Tyler,† who was priest and butcher to his little community in the city. So yet another world opened to me which I needed.

Kipling was wrong in his dates. The following is a transcript of all the minutes relating to his admission in the records of the Lodge Hope and Perseverance, 1886–87:‡

[INITIATION]

MINUTES of the Proceedings of the Regular Meeting of Lodge of Hope and Perseverance, No 782, EC, Held at The Masonic Hall (Anarkali), Lahore, India, on Monday, the 5 April 1886.
Worshipful Master: W. Brother G. B. Wolseley.

---

* By Bro Marcus Lewis, PAGDC (ENG), PDGW (Natal).
† The Tyler of the District Grand Lodge of the Punjab, and of the Lodge of Industry, No 1485, meeting at Lahore, was a Bro E. I. Manasseh, almost certainly a Jew. I have been unable to trace the name of the Tyler of No 782, but it is extremely likely that it was this same Bro Manasseh.
‡ From a copy made of the original Minutes prepared by Bro W. L. Murray-Brooks, of Lodge de Loraine, No 541, of Newcastle-upon-Tyne, a member of the Kipling Society. Subsequent quotations from his transcripts of the minutes are marked (MB). Reproductions of his notes are marked (MB/N).

Item on
Agenda

3. The Ballot was taken for Mr Joseph Rudyard Kipling, aged 20 years
    2½ months, Assistant Editor, 'Civil & Military Gazette', and
    residing at Lahore, a candidate for Initiation.
    PROPOSED by W Bro Col. Menezes
    SECONDED by Bro C. Brown
    which proved unanimously favourable.
    DISPENSATION from District Grand Master authorising his
    Initiation as a minor was then read.

4. THE CANDIDATE, Mr Joseph Rudyard Kipling, was then
    admitted and initiated in due form into the Mysteries and Secrets of
    Ancient Freemasonry, The Worshipful Master giving the Degree.

                                            (Signed) O. Menezes, PM

[PASSING]

At the Regular meeting on Monday, 3 May 1886.
Worshipful Master: W Bro Col O. Menezes.

3. BRO KIPLING being a Candidate for the Second, or Fellowcraft,
    Degree, was duly examined in the First, or Entered Apprentice,
    Degree and being found proficient, was allowed to retire for
    preparation.

4. THE LODGE was then opened in the Second Degree.

5. THE candidate was then re-admitted and passed to the Second
    Degree in due and ancient form.

[RAISING]

At the Regular Meeting on Monday, 6 December 1886 [the Lodge
having been in vacation in the interim].
Worshipful Master: W Bro Col G. B. Wolseley.

3. BROTHER RUDYARD KIPLING being a Candidate for the High
    and Sublime Degree of a Master Mason, was then examined by the
    Worshipful Master according to ancient custom, and having proved
    proficient, was allowed to retire, while

4. THE LODGE was opened in the Third Degree.

5. ON the Candidate being re-admitted, he was raised to the Third
Degree in due and ancient form.

'The Minutes recording his raising are actually entered in the Minute Book in Kipling's own handwriting, he having acted as Secretary to the meeting at which he was raised – perhaps a unique position.' (MB/N.)

Entered in April 1886; Passed in May; Raised in December, the Lodge having been closed in the interim period, which included the hot months. It is perhaps typical of Kipling that within a few months of his Raising he gave a Lecture in his Mother Lodge on the 'Origin of the Craft First Degree', and four months later he lectured again on 'Popular Views on Freemasonry'. (The first Lecture was on 4 April 1887; the second on 4 July 1887.) (MB/N). What a great pity that the texts of both talks have disappeared!

There is no record of the source of Kipling's Masonic knowledge and it is extremely doubtful if his Lodge possessed a Masonic Library. The military Lodge at Mian Mir was an even less likely source. The only Masonic journal then published in the Punjab was the *Masonic Record of Western India*,* a monthly magazine of some 40 pages *octavo*, printed at Allahabad, which gave brief items of Masonic news from all parts of the world, with fuller details from the English Quarterly Communications and fairly full reports of Indian Masonic matters, all these being interspersed with brief articles, poems and stories more or less related to the Craft. Some of the earlier volumes of this little journal may have furnished Kipling with his material, but that is pure speculation. Yet, if Kipling at 21 was anything like the successful author of later years, betraying in his tales a full grasp of all the technical information belonging to his subject and eagerly inserting the odd details that show how he delighted in his mastery of them, it is certain that he did not undertake his Masonic Lectures without a good grounding.

He was recorded as Secretary, *duly elected*,† at the regular meeting on 10 January 1887. He was invested with his collar of office at the February meeting, 'appointed PM Steward' at that meeting, and he attended every monthly meeting up to and including 1 August 1887.‡ He pursued every branch of the Craft that was within his reach with his customary zeal. He was advanced in the Mark Degree in Fidelity

* Subsequent references to this journal are marked *M.R.W.I.*
† Secretaries are not elected nowadays.
‡ MB/N.

Mark Lodge, No 98, at Lahore, on 14 April 1887, and was elevated in Mt. Ararat Ark Mariners' Lodge, No 98, on the same day.*

Of his love for Freemasonry there can be no doubt, especially when we see how often it crept into his later writings; yet it is strange that he left practically no personal records of his Lodges, or of his friendships in the Craft.

The Lodge of Hope and Perseverance, No 782, was constituted in 1858 (as No 1084), meeting in the 'Lodge Rooms', Lahore. At the time of Kipling's Initiation it had some 25 or 30 members, largely made up – as one might expect in the India of that time – of soldiers, civil engineers, civil servants, doctors, men attached to various branches of the post and telegraph services and to the police. The total Masonic population of the Punjab State, under the District Grand Lodge, English Constitution, was 650 (approx.) in some 20 Lodges, an average of 30 members per Lodge. These low numbers, combined with the high incidence of illness, home furlough and unavoidable long-distance travel in a large and developing country, must have caused all sorts of difficulties in the continuity of management of the Lodges. This was remedied in No 782 in 1887, a year after Kipling's Initiation, when the Lodge amalgamated with Lodge Ravee, No 1215, which was in difficulties owing to insufficient membership; No 782, the stronger Lodge, absorbed the weaker. The Grand Lodge Ravee returned its Warrant.

The well-known passage in *Something of Myself*, in which Kipling wrote, 'Here I met Muslims, Hindus, Sikhs, members of the Araya and Brahmo Samaj . . .', may be true in substance, but it tends to create the impression that Hope and Perseverance was a heavily 'mixed' Lodge, with a high proportion of members from the native population. This was probably quite unintentional, but one of Kipling's letters to *The Times* in 1925 (forty years after his Initiation) seems to support the suggestion, and it contains, incidentally, a notable error of fact:

> . . . I was Secretary for some years of Hope and Perseverance Lodge, No 782, Lahore, which included Brethren of at least four creeds. I was entered by a member of Bramo Samaj, a Hindu, passed by a Mohammedan, and raised by an Englishman. Our Tyler was an Indian Jew.
>
> We met, of course, on the level, and the only difference anyone would

---

* Dates and details confirmed by Mark Grand Lodge.

notice was that at our banquets some of the Brethren, who were debarred by caste rules from eating food not ceremonially prepared, sat over empty plates.*

The Lodge minutes prove that the details of Entry are certainly incorrect, and those of Passing are probably wrong, too. A reference to the Initiation minute, above, will show that it ends with the words '. . . the Worshipful Master giving the Degree'. The WM on the night in question was W Bro Col G. B. Wolseley, C.B, PDistDepGM, certainly not a Hindu, and he presided at Kipling's Raising, too. The WM at the Passing was Col Oswald Menzies, who had proposed him. There is no record in the minutes of any other Brother taking the Chair for the 2° and 3° ceremonies, and it seems very likely that the '. . . Hindu and . . . Mohammedan . . .' were either the results of faulty memory or the creatures of a fertile imagination.

It is certain that the ability of Europeans and Asiatics to meet 'on the Level' in the Lodge Room, without distinction of class or colour, race or creed, had made a very deep impression on Kipling, as witness his poem *The Mother Lodge*, which was founded on that theme, and this may well explain the momentary lapse in the accuracy of his memoirs. The records show that there were, in fact, at least four non-European Brethren in the Lodge at that time, as follows:

Bikrama Singh†	Profession not stated
Mohammed Hayat Khan†	Assistant Commissioner‡
Protal C. Chatterjee, M.A.†	Pleader† In the Law Courts (?)
Gopal Das†	U.C.S. (?)

The Kipling file in the Grand Lodge archives contains the Annual Return made to the Dist G Lodge of the Punjab by the Lodge of Hope and Perseverance on 31 December 1886. The Lodge had evidently been suffering from Secretarial troubles at that time,§ and

* This letter was also printed in the *Freemason* (London), 28 March 1925, and our transcript is from that journal. The Grand Lodge Kipling file contains a copy of another letter from Kipling to a correspondent in S. Africa, which repeats these details almost word for word. The letter was offered for sale to the Grand Lodge Library, but was not purchased, as there was reason to suspect it as a forgery. For that reason, we do not reproduce it here.
† Names recorded in the Annual Return to the Dist Grand Lodge.
‡ Professions as recorded in the Grand Lodge Register.
§ A Minute of the Bd of GP of the Dist GL of the Punjab, dated 25 August 1886, shows that the Lodge had not yet made its Return for the preceding 30 June. (*M.R.W.I.*, vol. xxiii, p. 305.)

this particular Return is especially interesting, because it was compiled and signed by Kipling himself, as Acting-Secretary, only eight months after his Initiation and less than four weeks after his Raising!

Kipling's Return shows a total of twenty-four members in the Lodge, including the four named above, but his Return is certainly incomplete. B. C. Jussawalla, a merchant, joined the Lodge in 1884, and was still on the Roll five years later, but he does not appear in Kipling's Return. Dr Brij Lal Ghose, RB, Assistant Surgeon, joined the Lodge in 1879 and there is no record of his resignation, but he, too, is omitted from Kipling's Return, though he is regularly shown in high office at meetings of the Dist Grand Lodge and its Committees during the period of Kipling's association with the Lodge.

It is strange that Kipling left practically no record of his personal impressions and recollections within his own Lodge. Stranger still, perhaps, that none of the Masonic allusions in his verse and prose can be deemed strictly autobiographical. In later years, after he had achieved world fame, he avoided all discussion of his private affairs with strangers and shunned that kind of publicity like the plague. This facet of his character arose directly from the success which made him a target for all who could profit from his words. But that was not the case in his youth, when he was still shy, ill-at-ease and finding it very difficult to settle into the adult society of Lahore. For a youngster in that frame of mind, to be received as an equal in the Lodge was indeed an unforgettable experience, and when, towards the end of his life, he wrote about his Initiation: 'So yet another world opened to me, which I needed', he was referring not so much to Freemasonry, the Craft itself, but to the little group of Brethren who had opened their doors to him.

He made it his business to learn about the Craft, because, as a writer, that kind of approach was second nature to him. That he found it in every way admirable is constantly revealed in his writings; but his zeal for the craft was not centred in its organisation or its ritual, and one may doubt if he would ever have reached the Chair, even if he had had an opportunity to do so. There seems to be no doubt, and his subsequent record confirms the fact, that his real love for the Craft was based on the welcome that he found in it and upon the rich variety of characters whom he met in the Lodge.

On 10 January 1887, a few days after his election as Secretary, he is recorded as 'J. Rudyard Kipling, Secy of No 782', a visitor at the meeting of the Dist Grand Lodge at Lahore (*M.R.W.I.*, vol xxiii, pp 450); a month later he served in that capacity at a meeting of the Permanent Committee of his Lodge. It is reasonably certain that he found time to visit the Lodge at Mian Mir (St John the Evangelist, No 1483), where two of the members were Surgeon Capt Terence Mulvaney and Lieut Learoyd, RA, whose names are immortalised in *Soldiers Three*. The remainder of his career in the Craft was sadly interrupted by the calls of his profession – but that is another story.

LITERARY SUCCESS AND RESIGNATION FROM THE LODGE

In the summer of 1886, Kipling joined his family at Simla, where (by reason of Lord Clandeboye's attachment to 'Trix') he moved into the Viceregal circle and found numerous friends among the rising young men of the Viceroy's staff, which led to a natural and noticeable increase in his status as a journalist.

On his return to Lahore, in the cool months of 1886–7, he began to write the verse and stories that brought him to fame. Wheeler, his chief at the *Gazette*, had allowed him no scope for the imaginative writing that he wanted to do; but now, broken in health, the editor was retiring, and Kay Robinson, assistant editor of the *Pioneer* at Allahabad and a good friend to Kipling, was to take over Wheeler's position. Kipling was delighted and the new arrangement began to show immediate results. Copying a journalistic feature that had proved very successful during his time on the London *Globe*, Robinson set Kipling to write a series of regular weekly articles for the *Gazette*. They were to be short topical pieces of high local interest and limited to 2,000 words, an ideal discipline for Kipling and one that he greatly enjoyed. The best of them are preserved today in his *Plain Tales from the Hills*.

In the course of his journalistic duties he was ready to take all sorts of risks in the lowest quarters of the town, and he had already developed an uncanny skill in quickly absorbing local colour, a skill which became one of his principal assets as a writer. It was said that he knew more about the shady side of life in Lahore than the police, more about the regiments and the life at Mian Mir than the Officers themselves; but his curiosity ranged over every field.

In 1887 he sold a collection of his verse, of local and topical interest, under the title *Departmental Ditties*, to a Calcutta publisher, for 500 Rupees. They were inclined to be shocking and cynical, attracting considerable attention in India, but the only review in the London Press found them merely 'quaint and amusing', perhaps because they were too closely related to the narrow themes of civil service and military life in India. His friends, and Robinson especially, were beginning to urge him to spread his wings and seek a wider public in London, but he was happy in his Lahore-Simla surroundings, treating his employment on the *Gazette* as a kind of seven-year apprenticeship to his profession.

During the summer of 1887, Kipling's employers were arranging to transfer him to the staff of the *Pioneer* at Allahabad, and the minutes of the Lodge of Hope and Perseverance, No 782 (in Kipling's own handwriting), record the following:

3.   The Secretary having announced his impending departure to Allahabad as a reason why he should be relieved of his office, W Bro J. J. Davies rose and said:
'Worshipful Sir and Brethren,
     'We have all heard with deep regret the intimation made by our Bro Secretary that we are soon to lose his services as Secretary of this Lodge. Those of us who have watched his conduct since his initiation feel sure that he has before him a successful Masonic career, for the thoroughness with which he conducted his duties was prompted by a lively interest in his work and by a keen desire for a deeper insight into the hidden truths of Masonry.
     'Bro Kipling has also contributed towards the welfare of the Lodge by the series of Lectures which he delivered to the Brethren, which was of a nature both interesting and instructive, while his courteous disposition has won for him the general esteem of the Brethren. He has been all that a Secretary should be, and it is with regret that I hear the Lodge is about to lose the services of one whom I feel sure will yet be an ornament to his Lodge and a bright light in the Masonic Circle.
     'I feel sure that all the Brethren will join me in wishing Bro Kipling success in his future life and to express a hope that circumstances will permit him to occasionally visit the meetings of his Mother Lodge.'
     Bro Kipling returned thanks for the kind allusions made to his success as Secretary and for the good wishes expressed by the Brethren present. He said he would always remember with pride and affection the meetings he had attended at Lodge Hope and Perseverance whereby he had formed friendships which would leave a lasting

impression on his memory. He would take every opportunity that offered of attending the meetings of his Mother Lodge.

(Signed) E. C. Jussawallah.*

At this stage Kipling cannot have had any idea that his departure would be anything more than a temporary break in his Masonic career, and until that time he had certainly discharged all his duties, and more, with a praiseworthy zeal.

He lived a bachelor life at the Allahabad Club, but he soon found good and interesting friends, notably Prof S. A. Hill, a Government meteorologist, and his wife. In a letter to her sister in Pennsylvania, she described Kipling as short, dark-haired, balding and fortyish (he was only twenty-two), with a heavy moustache and thick glasses, a scintillating and animated story-teller, and equally interesting in more sober conversation.

The *Plain Tales* met with immediate success in India, where many of their thinly-disguised characters were readily recognised. A French edition† was also well received, but the work remained unnoticed in London. For the *Pioneer*, Kipling was now travelling a good deal and was writing a series of articles, the *Letters of Marque*, afterwards issued as the first part of Vol. 1 of *From Sea to Sea*. He began to write fiction for the Week's News and for other journals – work which was all too quickly written and accepted by undiscriminating publishers and public. Six volumes of short stories were issued in 1888 (later contained in *Soldiers Three* and *Wee Willie Winkie*). They brought him, for the first time, a bank balance of £200 in advance royalties, and established his reputation as a writer whose works ranged over civil service, military, native and society life. They were sketches and impressions as much as stories, in which character-studies and local colour were as important as the tales themselves.

Busy though he was, Kipling still found time for his Freemasonry, and there is a record of his attendance at the Installation meeting of Lodge Independence with Philanthropy, No 391, at Allahabad, on 22 December 1887, when Sir John Edge, Chief Justice of the NW Provinces, was installed before an enormous assembly. (*M.R.W.I.*,

---

* Reproduced from MB. The minutes are signed by Bro Jussawallah, whose name had been omitted from Kipling's Annual Return to the Dist Grand Lodge. Kipling is entered as Secretary in the Records of the Regular Meeting of 7 November 1887, but the minutes are not in Kipling's handwriting. (MB/N.)

† The French edition appeared later.

---

vol xxiv, p 345.) In March 1888, when he believed that he was permanently settled in Allahabad, he wrote to his Lodge at Lahore as recorded in the Minutes:

> At the Regular Meeting on Monday, 2 April 1888. Worshipful Master: W Bro Koenig.
>
> 9. Read the following letter from Bro RUDYARD KIPLING dated Allahabad, 22 March 1888:
> 'Dear Sir and Worshipful Master,
>
> 'It is with great regret I have to inform you that I am now permanently transferred to Allahabad and therefore forced to abandon any active connection with my Mother Lodge. I write to ask you to forward a Clearance Certificate to enable me to join 'Lodge Independence with Philanthropy' at this Station, and also to send my Grand Lodge Certificate to the Master of that Lodge when it arrives. I have of course no intention of withdrawing my name from the Lodge Roll and shall be obliged if you would have me put down as an Absent Brother.
>
> 'I send herewith Rs 24 PM, subscription and shall always look back with keen pleasure to my Masonic life in "Lodge Hope and Perseverance", and, if at any time, I can do anything to further its aims and objects, am entirely at your disposal. Convey my warmest and most fraternal regards to the Brethren and
>
> Believe me
> Yours faithfully and fraternally,
> (Sgd.) RUDYARD KIPLING.'
>
> 10. THE SECRETARY was directed to comply with Bro Kipling's request and to reply to his letter thanking him warmly for his kind offer and expressing regret that his altered circumstances has deprived us of his valuable assistance and genial companionship.
>
> (Sgd.) F. Koenig, WM   (MB)

It seems certain that Kipling fully intended to pursue his Masonic career in his new environment, while remaining on the Roll of No 782 as an 'Absent Brother' (probably a status equal to 'country-membership'), but that was not to be. He was recalled to duty at the *Civil & Military Gazette* and there followed a brief spell at Lahore, deputising for Robinson, who was absent on sick-leave. It is recorded that he attended, for the last time, at his Mother Lodge, No 782, in May 1888, acting as Inner Guard.* (MB/N.) The heat of the summer months became intolerable and Kipling went off for a three-week

---

* This was apparently his first and last 'floor-office'.

stay at Simla, which was doubly enjoyable because he had already made up his mind to go to England. He returned to Allahabad, where his pleasure in the company of the Hills (he had been living with them during most of 1888) was marred by Mrs Hill's sudden and serious illness. On her recovery she decided to convalesce at her home in Pennsylvania, and, on hearing this, Kipling resolved to travel east-about to England, going with them to America, *en route.* Introductions to friends in the USA were showered on him.

He joined the Lodge Independence with Philanthropy, No 391, at Allahabad, on 17 April 1888.* At that time it was the fourth largest Lodge under the District Grand Lodge of Bengal, with 35 members. The largest Lodge had only 50 members, and the records show that several Bengal Lodges were in abeyance and others were having great difficulty because of their small memberships. (*MRWI*, vol xxiv, p 449.) No 391 was a 'mixed' Lodge with a substantial proportion of non-European members,* and it is fairly certain that Kipling would have been very happy there, but his active participation in the work of the Lodge lasted, in fact, less than a year, because of his projected trip to England. (He never returned to Allahabad, and resigned from the Lodge on 31 December 1895).*

In February 1889, he went home to Lahore for a farewell visit, and soon afterwards went down to Calcutta. The March 1889, minutes of Hope and Perseverance record:

> At the Regular Meeting of the Lodge held on Monday, 4 March 1889. Worshipful Master: W Bro F. Koenig.
> 8. THE WORSHIPFUL MASTER stated that he had received a card from Bro RUDYARD KIPLING stating that he was leaving the Province permanently and wished to resign. Directed that it be acknowledged with regret. (MB)

Kipling resigned from his Mark and Ark Mariner Lodges three months later, on 30 June 1889.†

On 9 March 1889, he went aboard the S.S. Madura with Prof and Mrs Hill for the beginning of a happy holiday, enlivened by the society of his friends. His time was filled by his unending interest in the mechanism of the ship and in the men who kept it moving, as well as the yarns of the variegated travellers in the bars and smoking-

---

* From the Grand Lodge Registers.
† Information confirmed by Mark Grand Lodge.

rooms. They passed through Rangoon, Penang, Singapore, Hong Kong, and stayed a whole month in Japan, each halt making an indelible impression on his photographic mind and leaving a store of colour, sights and sounds that enriched so much of his later work. They left Japan for San Francisco, and there, in the course of newspaper interviews, Kipling carelessly let fall various items of too-ready and immature criticism of American affairs, which made him an unpopular target in the American press.

The Hills left him at San Francisco to finish their journey by train, and Kipling remained in the care of Mrs Carr, a friend of his mother, who introduced him into wealthy and influential society, and to professional men, journalists and writers, who found him a boon companion. After a few days he went off for a fishing holiday to Portland, Oregon, and then into British Columbia, where a smart piece of salesmanship left him owning a plot of land in Vancouver City which was certainly not worth what he had paid for it.

Writing articles all the while for his paper, he travelled leisurely across America until he arrived eventually at the little town of Beaver Falls, Pa., where Mrs Hill was living with her parents. Kipling stayed with the family for two months, and there he met Mrs Hill's young sister, Caroline Taylor, a plump and cheerful girl. Continuing his travels in the Eastern States, his closer acquaintance with the country and its people brought him to a real liking for what he saw and a somewhat jingoist view of the importance of the 'Anglo-Saxon all round the world'. The appearance of several favourable reviews of his works must have pleased him greatly, but at this period a pirated version of *Plain Tales* was published in the USA, the first of a whole series of similar outrages, which, allowing for his poverty at the time and his inability to obtain legal redress, was an understandable source of exasperation.* An introduction to Henry Harper, head of the New York publishing house, led to an interview which was quickly ended by Harper's brutal rudeness. Happily, 'He never had to ask a favour of an American publisher again.' (*C.C.*, p 132.)

Meanwhile, carrie Taylor had decided to go to India with her sister, and at the end of September 1889, all four, the Hills, Carrie

---

* It is interesting to read in the *Masonic Record of Western India* for October 1887 (vol xxiv, pp 272–5), a bitter article by Bro R. F. Gould, the great historian, and a Founder of the Q.C. Lodge, protesting that his life work, *The History of Freemasonry*, had been similarly treated by unscrupulous American publishers.

and Kipling, took ship for England, arriving in London in early October. There, Kipling left his friends to take a short holiday in Paris. On his return to London he moved into two rooms at the foot of Villiers Street, overlooking the embankment, only a few doors from the London office of the *Pioneer*. Mrs Hill and Carrie helped him to settle in before they went off to India.

Kipling had few friends in London, and he was lonely, short of money and too proud to ask for help. His letters to Mrs Hill at this time betray his loneliness and nostalgia for India, which persisted long after he had won his place in London literary circles. His letters to Carrie show that he was falling in love with her, not surprising, perhaps, in view of his lack of young feminine company during those important years. Andrew Lang, who had reviewed some of Kipling's earlier work, took him to the Savile Club, the haunt of editors and writers, and this resulted in an introduction to Sampson Low, who arranged to publish an English edition of his six volumes, but on rather unfavourable terms. More useful introductions came to him through Wheeler, his former chief at Lahore, now on the staff of the *St James's Gazette*, and from Mowbray Morris, editor of *Macmillan's Magazine*. Wheeler took him to Sidney Low, who later described his first evening with Kipling, at Sweeting's in Fleet Street, where, with very little persuasion, Kipling began to talk of India and his travels, and soon had half the room as his audience. Two of his poems, both under pseudonyms, were published by Macmillan, and soon he counted the best of literary London among his friends.

Trix, now married, visited him in London in February 1890, and was shocked to find him in poor health and low spirits. He had met his first love, Flo Garrard, by chance in London, and had realised that she still meant a great deal to him. Perhaps his attachment to Carrie was of too rapid a growth to withstand their separation, or its roots may have been too shallow. Whatever the reasons, his estrangement from her was complete by this time. He resumed his courtship of Flo Garrard, without hope of success, because she was interested in nothing but her own career as an artist. He confided all this to Trix, but his only refuge was in his work, which he pursued '. . . with a sort of fury'.

His visits to his aunts and cousins were rare and pleasurable interludes, though they introduced him into good society where – as usual – he was made much of. Publishers' doors were being opened to him and he had enough commissioned work in hand to be assured of a modest livelihood. A splendid review of his works in the London *Times* in March 1890, described him as a writer who had 'tapped a new vein, and . . . worked it out with real originality'. It led to a Kipling boom in London, while the re-issue of his early works in America went on more strongly than ever. Kipling had arrived! He was twenty-five years old, with a collection of prose and verse behind him, including *Plain Tales from the Hills* and the *Departmental Ditties*, which had made his reputation from India to America.

He sent a cryptic telegram to his parents announcing his success and inviting them to come to England. The message was a gem of its kind; it ran: 'Genesis xlv, 9, 10, 13.' The first of those verses reads: 'Haste ye and go up to my father and say unto him, Thus saith thy son Joseph; God hath made me lord of all Egypt; and come down unto me, tarry not.'

Nothing could have been more apposite, and his choice of the quotation reveals a very useful knowledge of the Bible.

In May 1890, his parents came to London and the 'family square' was happily re-united. It is strange that this – the period of his first real taste of success – was the time when he published *The Light That Failed*, which contained the story of his involvement with Flo Garrard, and much autobiographical material, yet tinged with occasional bitterness and cruelty, wholly out of keeping with his character.

MARRIAGE AND FAME

Around 1890, Kipling met Wolcott Balestier, a charming and talented young journalist – turned publisher – who had captured literary London. Balestier, an American, with a sure foresight of the young author's potentialities, set himself to make friends with Kipling, and he succeeded, despite Rudyard's justifiable distrust of publishers – especially American. Soon there was talk of their collaborating in a novel, which appeared about two years later as *The Naulahka* – a book based on America and India – which gave them both good opportunity for their individual talents. As agent for an American publishing house, Balestier actually persuaded Kipling to write a happy ending to *The Light That Failed* – a commercial move which nobody else in Rudyard's circle could have achieved.

Balestier's family visited England to share in his success and

Kipling visited them often; but it was in Wolcott's office that he first met Caroline Balestier, Wolcott's sister – a quiet, competent and forceful young woman, who made such an impression on Kipling's mother that she instantly predicted, without enthusiasm, but correctly, as it transpired, 'That young woman is going to marry our Ruddy.'

Kipling's health was very bad at this time and he was troubled with constant recurrence of malaria and dysentery, with mental exhaustion resulting from the great pressure of work since his arrival in England. On medical advice he took a short voyage to America with one of his Macdonald uncles, Kipling travelling under the name of J. Macdonald for the sake of privacy. The stratagem failed; his eyebrows and moustache made him too easily recognisable, and when he found that his arrival was already publicised in New York – knowing he was not fit to face the intrusion of reporters – he returned immediately to England.

In July 1891, he stayed with the Balestiers at their home in the Isle of Wight, and it is fairly certain that by this time he and Carrie had come to an understanding – which was not made public, however. In August, still in pursuit of health, he set out on a voyage round the world. He made a brief and pleasant stay in Cape Town, where he met Cecil Rhodes, who ultimately became a great friend. On to New Zealand and Tasmania, Australia and back to Colombo, with a train journey of four days and nights through India to Lahore, where he arrived for a Christmas reunion with his parents.

But soon after his arrival he received a cable from Caroline to say that Wolcott had died of typhoid while on a business trip to Dresden. Kipling did not stay for Christmas and managed to get back to England in 14 days, a notable feat at that time. Meanwhile, Carrie had taken charge; '. . . a little person of extraordinary capacity who will float them all successfully home', said Henry James in one of his letters, paying tribute to her '. . . force, acuteness . . . and courage'.

Kipling arrived in London in January 1892, and they immediately arranged to marry within eight days, by special licence. An influenza epidemic was raging, and only one cousin, 'Ambo' Poynter, attended (as best man), with Henry James, Edmund Gosse and William Heinemann as the only friends present at the ceremony at All Souls', Langham Place. The newly-weds parted at the church door, because Carrie had to nurse her mother. Their wedding party was a small family lunch held two days later.

From this time on, Kipling's story cannot be told or read without the constant reminder of this masterful and devoted woman in the background. She watched his health, shielded him from intruders, kept his accounts, managed their homes and their many moves, and bore him three children. All that was, of course, in the future, but it is noteworthy that the majority of writers on the Kiplings are agreed that it was he who got the best of the bargain.

Rudyard was now comfortably off, with £2,000 in the bank and with many publishers' contracts in his pocket, and the couple set off for a honeymoon voyage round the world, Kipling taking the final chapters of *The Naulahka** to prepare them for the press *en route*.

As part of their tour they stopped off at Brattleboro', Vermont, headquarters and home of the Balestier family, staying a few days with Carrie's younger brother, Beatty Balestier, and his wife. Beatty conveyed a 10-acre plot of the family land to them for a nominal sum, and they continued their trip through Chicago to Canada, Kipling paying his way by his travel sketches, which were now far more profitable than on his first American visit. Reporters sought him constantly and were kept at bay by Carrie, now his business manager. And so, on to Japan and Yokohama, where their joyous holiday was rudely interrupted by the failure of Kipling's bank, with the loss of his life's savings, nearly £2,000.† They were stranded in Japan with only their return tickets, some £10 sterling and 100 dollars in a New York bank. Lack of cash was no longer a serious worry, because there was a ready and constant demand for everything Kipling wrote, and hospitality was showered on the young couple everywhere. They stayed another three weeks in Japan, but cancelled the remainder of their honeymoon.

Back to Vermont, where, in a house rented at 10 dollars a month, with a Swedish maid at 18 dollars per month, they lived in spartan simplicity for a year.

In April 1892, the *Barrack-Room Ballads* were published; they were three times reprinted in that year and fifty times more in the next thirty years. As usual, a pirated edition had appeared in the USA before the authorised English edition came out in 1892! But

* This was the title of the book, but when, a little later, the Kiplings built their own home in Vermont, they named it correctly, Naulakha.
† The bank eventually paid all its depositors.

Kipling did very little new writing in their honeymoon year. *The Naulahka* began to bring in a useful and rapidly-growing income and money was flowing in rapidly from Kipling's earlier work. Now much of their time was spent in planning, with a New York architect friend, a new house that was to be built on their 10-acre plot.

The Kiplings visited the Balestier family often and they were much attached to Beatty's little daughter, but Beatty himself, a gay, extravagant and intemperate fellow, did not get on well with his sister Carrie, who treated him as an irresponsible boy, doling out his share of *Naulahka* dividends in petty sums, as a deliberate means of controlling his extravagance.

Before the new house was ready, their first child, Josephine, was born in December 1892. That year was also made happy for them by a visit from John Lockwood Kipling, Rudyard's father, now retired, and the two men went off for a trip into Canada, leaving Carrie to prepare and supervise the removal into their new home, 'Naulhakha'.

Father and son got on famously together, and Rudyard, as always, was ready and glad to have his father's help, which was quite invaluable in artistic and certain technical matters. This was the period which gave rise to the *Jungle Books* – the best-sellers of all Kipling's works. Now, after a period of comparative rest and with the assurance of real prosperity, Kipling had again got into his stride with the 'return of a feeling of great strength'. At this time he wrote some of his most notable verse and ballads – work which would have brought him fame if he had not achieved it already. He could now command $100 per thousand words, a very high rate in those days, and Scribner's paid him $500 for his dramatic poem, *M'Andrew's Hymn*.

After a brief holiday in Bermuda, Rudyard and Carrie crossed to England in 1894, moving into a house at Tisbury, Wiltshire, where Rudyard's parents had settled in retirement. In their frequent visits to London, the Kiplings were lionized and fêted. Back to the light, quiet and peace of Naulakha, they lived comfortably with their little daughter, enjoying the society of a few close friends. Rudyard noted in Carrie's diary, in December, 1894, that he had earned $25,000 (£5,000), a great sum in those days.

The interminable intrusions of summer-visitors, sightseers and journalists eventually drove Carrie to sell her husband's autographs at $2.50 each for charity, in the hope of avoiding the nuisance – but that was misinterpreted as a publicity device, and it attracted abusive comment.

Early in 1896 the Kiplings took a six-week holiday in Washington, DC, while Carrie recuperated after a furnace accident. There they were made welcome in the very best of American society, but Kipling, on a visit to the White House, was disgusted by the company he met among President Cleveland's associates. This disenchantment was largely compensated for by the close friendship he formed with 'Teddy' Roosevelt.

On their return home, a serious money quarrel arose between Carrie and her brother over his careless stewardship of the house during their absence, and the two families were no longer on speaking terms – a real discomfort because they were such close neighbours. Meanwhile, the Anglo-American dispute over the Venezuela-British Guiana borders led to a great deal of bad feeling on both sides of the Atlantic, and the Kiplings began to plan a return to England; but that had to be deferred, as Carrie was expecting the birth of her second child. Their daughter, Elsie, was born in February 1896.

Kipling was busy meanwhile on *Captains Courageous*, an all-American story in characters and setting, which grew largely out of his friendship with Dr Conland, their family physician. The rift with the Balestiers had widened and about this time Beatty was made bankrupt. The newsmen swooped, scenting a story, but Kipling refused to be interviewed. 'American reviewing is brutal and immoral . . . Is it not enough to steal my books without intruding on my private life?'

During the winter he played golf in the snow, with red balls, and learned to ski – on the first skis in Vermont – sent to him by Conan Doyle. Later in the year he took up the fashionable sport of cycling, and in May 1896, an accidental spill on a road near his home led to a face-to-face meeting with Beatty, who, in an ungovernable rage, threatened to shoot Kipling. Very unwisely, Kipling laid information against his brother-in-law for threatening to kill him, and Beatty was arrested next day. The ensuing court proceedings brought the Kiplings the most frantic and unwelcome publicity, which was aggravated by Rudyard's impulsive and ill-advised behaviour throughout the whole of this trying period. The case was adjourned for trial, but nothing came of it because they left the USA before it came up for hearing. They had had four happy years in Vermont, but the miseries of the family quarrel finally drove them back to England, where they arrived in September 1896, staying at a rented house near Torquay.

TORQUAY AND ROTTINGDEAN

It was a barrack of a house after the beauty and comfort of Naulakha, but there was compensation in the visits they had from their family and friends. John Lockwood Kipling set up a studio in their coach-house, moving over from Tisbury to help his son with a projected illustrated edition of his works. Living not far from Dartmouth, Rudyard was invited to cruise with the Channel Squadron, and – always an avid collector of the data that might form the background to his stories – he began zealously to master navel and engine-room techniques.

Kipling had maintained his membership of Lodge Independence with Philanthropy, No 391, Allahabad, since 1888, but he resigned on 31 December 1895. It had been his only Lodge during those years, and, so far as all known records go, he became an unattached Brother, remaining in that status for the next four years. The details of his subsequent Masonic affiliations are given below.

In the winter of 1896 he did not do very much work, although he was now feeling much better (doubtless because of his distance from the troublesome Beatty). He was elected to the Athenaeum at the age of 31, their youngest member, and on the night of his admission he dined there with Cecil Rhodes, Alfred Milner and the Editor of *The Times*. Two months later, with Carrie expecting the birth of their third child, Rudyard began to look around in Kent and Sussex for a new home, and in June 1897, they moved into North End House, Rottingdean, at the centre of a large group of relatives – and accessible to their friends. It was Queen Victoria's Diamond Jubilee year and the publication in *The Times* of his *Recessional* attracted admiration far surpassing Kipling's earlier triumphs. Now his name was being voiced as a possible Poet Laureate.

Their Third child, a son, John, was born in August 1897, and, at Christmas, Kipling wrote in Carrie's diary that this year was "In all ways the richest to us two personally". In January the happy pair embarked for a winter holiday in South Africa, which opened a new sphere of interest for Kipling. It was followed soon afterwards by a summer cruise for Rudyard with the Channel Squadron, which proved a great personal triumph for him.

This year saw the publication of his poem, *The White Man's Burden*, another triumph. It was the first appearance in print of that now-famous phrase, one of a whole series of verses with a strong imperialistic tone, typical of some earlier Indian verse, but always urging the sense of responsibility and duty that ought to over-ride all tangible reward.

In February 1899, they set off on a visit to New York – Carrie to see her mother, and Rudyard to deal with a copyright dispute which led to a long, expensive and fruitless lawsuit. Unwisely, they had decided to take the three children with them and, after a fearful crossing, arrived at their New York hotel with all the children ill from whooping-cough. Carrie herself fell ill, but she shook it off for the sake of the children. Dr Conland arrived from Vermont, bringing the news that Beatty was threatening to sue Kipling for $50,000 for malicious arrest. Josephine, the eldest child, developed pneumonia and was sent off to Long Island in the care of Conland; Elsie also showed symptoms, but soon recovered; while John, the baby, became ill with bronchitis. Family and business worries proved too much for Kipling, and he, too, succumbed with an inflammation of the lungs which rapidly deteriorated – so that he became delirious and dangerously ill. The news could not be kept from the press and traffic outside their hotel was blocked by crowds of sympathisers. Letters and messages flowed in from all parts of the world and the hotel lobby was crowded with reporters. Prayers were said for Kipling in the churches and people were seen to kneel before the hotel doors to pray for him. Never – even for Royalty – had there been such a spontaneous proof of affection and admiration. Carrie, despite all her courage and competence, was desperate, and Frank Doubleday, the New York publisher and their dear friend, neglected his own affairs to act as secretary and manager for Carrie while she looked after the children.

On 4 March, Kipling was at last declared out of danger, though still very ill, but two days later Josephine died. Many Months passed before Kipling was fully restored to health – but neither he nor Carrie ever recovered from the shock of Josephine's death. In May, Kipling was fit to return to England under orders to take a six-months' rest, and Doubleday, with his wife, made the journey with them and did not leave them until they were settled back in their own home. Andrew Carnegie wrote offering them the use of a small house in the Scottish Highlands, and there Rudyard mended slowly and settled down gradually to work again.

On 4 October 1899, doubtless as a result of his residence in Scotland, Kipling was elected an Honorary Member of Lodge Canongate Kilwinning, No 2 (SC), and – rare honour – he was made Poet Laureate of the Lodge (1905–8), thereby joining a distinguished band of Brethren of whom Robert Burns was the first, in 1787–96. There is no evidence, unfortunately, of his visiting the Lodge, but ill-health and family troubles would explain that.

In October 1899, *Stalky & Co.* was published, adding a new facet to his fame because it was so obviously autobiographical, but it met with a mixed reception and, as a picture of school life, many critics found it distasteful. Kipling was now at the height of his fame; social invitations were showered upon him – and mainly refused. It had been a sad and bitter year for them, and they needed quiet and seclusion.

THE SOUTH AFRICAN WAR: KIPLING THE IMPERIALIST

In September 1899, on the eve of the Boer War, Kipling published a poem, *The Old Issue*, in which he urged that the quarrel with Kruger was a fight for liberty and against tyranny. Some part of this must have had its roots in a native imperialism which was an inherent part of his background; but there is no doubt that it was also inspired by his unbounded admiration for the Empire-builders, the men with the machines and tools, the road-makers, the bridge-builders and the engineers.

When the war was declared he started the Soldiers' Families' Fund, and his poem, *The Absent-Minded Beggar*, set to music by Sir Arthur Sullivan, helped to raise nearly a quarter-of-a-million pounds for the fund. Never a seeker after limelight, he now shunned publicity, and when Harmsworth, of the *Daily Mail*, wanted to give the poem and its author publicity in aid of the fund, Kipling wrote asking that his name should be kept out.

> The verses are fetching money in a wonderful way – thanks to your management – but don't make so much of their author. (CC p 304)

In January 1900, he left with Carrie for a trip to South Africa, including a tour of the Military Hospitals, and he was there just in time to welcome Rhodes on his release after the raising of the siege of Kimberley. Rhodes spoke of his plan to build a house at Groote Schoor for artists and writers who would stay there as his guests, and offered them the house when ready. Carrie accepted enthusiastically and went off with the architect to select a site.

At the Battle of Paardeberg, Kipling went up to the Modder River rail-head on an ambulance train, returning with a trainload of wounded men, his first direct experience of the horrors of war. There is an interesting note regarding Kipling's visit to Bloemfontein in the *Transactions of the Authors' Lodge*, vol v, p 226. It speaks of Conan Doyle's services during the South African War, when he was Medical Officer to the Langham Field Hospital. He was '. . . one of the brethren who formed the never-to-be-forgotten Emergency Lodge held at Bloemfontein in company with Bro Rudyard Kipling and other notable Masons.' It has proved impossible to trace any further details of this particular Lodge meeting. With the gradual success of the campaign, Lord Roberts resolved to start an Army newspaper and he wired Kipling inviting him to join the staff of the new journal. Kipling accepted a temporary post as sub-editor for the few weeks that remained of his stay in South Africa and wrote a number of pieces for the paper, *The Friend*, enjoying himself enormously in the company of his congenial colleagues. The dry, warm climate suited him and he flourished.

Back at Rottingdean, his writings at this period had a strong political flavour, but towards the end of 1900 he was preparing to publish *Kim*, his last work on India, a task which had engaged him intermittently for some years. It is an adventure story in which the plot is of minor importance, but it furnished the opportunity for a study of an enormous variety of people in circumstances which enabled Kipling to depict the life, colour and atmosphere of his beloved India, and something of the mysticism and the complexities of character of its population.

At the end of 1900 the Kiplings were back in South Africa and moved into 'The Woolsack', the dream-cottage that Rhodes had placed at their disposal, their happiest environment for many years.*
Meanwhile, the war dragged on, bringing many unpleasant shocks,

---

* They wintered there regularly with the children from 1901 to 1908.

despite the general success of Lord Roberts' campaign after the opening disasters. Kipling, deeply touched by the losses that had been suffered through the inexperience of the soldiers and the inefficiency of their officers, wrote *The Army of a Dream*, a vision of England trained and prepared for war, with an awakening at the end reminding the readers that the men who might have made this possible had thrown away their lives in the recent holocausts.

A year later, in December 1901, his poem, *The Islanders*, pursued the theme still further, as a plea for less interest in sport and more in national service and defence. His reference in that poem to 'flannelled fools and muddied oafs' aroused great criticism and antipathy, but Kipling was never afraid to say what he thought.

In March 1902, Rhodes died, and Kipling wrote the verses which are inscribed on his tomb. Rudyard had lost a great friend, more especially one whose hopes for the outcome of the war coincided with his own, of a land settled by the men who would bring a new prosperity. His war poems, soldier ballads and stories of this period often reflect this feeling.

Later in 1902 the Kiplings settled in at their best and happiest home in England, 'Bateman's', at Burwash, in Sussex. By this time they had bought their second car, and motoring adventures and misadventures appear frequently in some of Rudyard's stories of this period.

The war ended, and the inevitable reaction that followed it enabled Kipling to relax at 'Bateman's'. After the publication, in 1903, of his book of South African verse, *The Five Nations*, he began to apply himself to his writing in a new and more controlled style. There was no longer any hurry to publish and he held his work back, cutting and revising until he was fully satisfied. His genius ranged from far-seeing science fiction to children's tales and his work took on an even wider variety – occasionally with a kind of obscurity – yet with a breadth of vision and appeal that kept him high on the list of the world's story-tellers.

The Conservative landslide in the General Election of 1906 and the subsequent elections in South Africa were a great blow to the Kiplings, and they made their last stay at the 'Woolsack' in April 1908.

KIPLING THE POLITICIAN: THE WORLD WAR

It seems strange that Kipling, whose conscientious mastery of intricate technical matters enabled him to write with facility on all sorts of subjects, could never bring himself to 'write to order'. This may have been one of the reasons why he never became Poet Laureate; it certainly prevented him from taking any kind of public office that might limit his freedom to write and say what he thought. He refused Parliamentary constituencies, and he refused two invitations to travel in the Royal entourage on State visits to India. A Knighthood (KCB) had been offered him, and refused, in 1899. The KCMG was similarly refused in 1904.

He did, however, accept academic honours, and in 1907–8 he and Carrie spent much time in travelling to ceremonial occasions at the Universities, including a trip to Canada to accept a doctorate at McGill. That trip was combined with a lecture-tour to Canadian Clubs, in which he continued to expound a facet of his Imperialist ideas – exhorting them to understand and accept their responsibilities.

In 1908 he was awarded the Nobel Prize for Literature, a great honour which carried, in those days, a grant of some £7,700.

In July 1909, Kipling joined the Societas Rosicruciana in Anglia, a purely Christian society, open to Master Masons '. . . of high moral character . . . [and] . . . of sufficient ability to be capable of understanding the revelations of philosophy, theosophy and science, possessing a mind free from prejudice and anxious for instruction . . .' This brief quotation sufficiently demonstrates the range of studies which fall within the Society's nine grades and it shows that Kipling was ready to explore far beyond the normal range of Masonic study.

One of the conditions of entry is that the Candidate must be 'a *subscribing member* of a Regular Lodge under the Grand Lodge of England or under a jurisdiction in amity therewith . . .' and Kipling described himself as a member of Lodge Hope and Perseverance, No 782, although he had resigned from that Lodge in 1889!

The Application Form also contains the motto, chosen by Kipling for that occasion, 'Fortuna non virtute', a modest note which may be freely translated, 'By good Fortune, not by Merit'.

The Authors' Lodge, No 3456, was founded in 1910, and apparently Kipling was invited either to be a founder or to attend the Consecration. He was unable to be present, and the report of the Consecration (*Freemasons' Chronicle*, November 1910) records that letters were received from Kipling and many other prominent authors of that period, sending their greetings and good wishes.*

A careful check of the *Transactions of the Authors' Lodge* reveals that he made no contributions to their work, but he is listed as an Honorary Member of the Lodge in the *Transactions*, vol iv, which cover the period 1918 to 1928. There is no record of the precise date of election.

Kipling's mother died at Tisbury in 1910, followed early in 1911 by his father. Though he was devoted to his parents, he had seen less of them in recent years, being fully occupied with his work and in the tight circle of his own family. One wonders if this may have been due to a possible coldness between Carrie and her mother-in-law.

From 1909 to 1914 his active interest in right-wing Conservative politics kept him fully occupied. His dislike of Liberal policies, strikes and the troubles in Ireland provided him with ample ammunition, and he wrote no longer as a spokesman for the 'little man' or the 'underdog', but as a propagandist for the Tory Party. He was a friend of Baden-Powell, and became a Commissioner and an active supporter of the Boy Scout movement, as well as of the National Service League, the latter an unpopular cause in those days. In May 1914, a wild and intemperate anti-Liberal speech to 10,000 people at Tunbridge Wells brought him a great deal of adverse publicity, bringing embarrassment to himself and to his own party.

When war was declared, young John Kipling, not yet 17, went up to London to offer himself for a Commission, but his weak sight prevented this. Kipling thereupon wrote to Lord Roberts, and with his influence the lad was nominated to their friend's own regiment, the Irish Guards. The Kiplings, with their daughter Elsie, were busy meanwhile at 'Bateman's' on work for the Red Cross and for the Belgian Refugees. Rudyard now began a tour of the Military Hospitals and training Camps in England, writing articles for the *Daily Telegraph* and stories based on incidents of the war.

The family made frequent trips to London, where John could come in from his barracks to meet them.

In August 1915, Rudyard was invited to visit the French Armies in the field. He met Clemenceau, Briand and General Nivelle, and had a warm reception everywhere, being easily recognised, because his works were as well known in France as in England. On his return,

* Confirmed in *Trans. of Authors' Lodge, No 3456,* vol i.

there was an invitation from the Admiralty to Kipling to write about the Royal Navy – apparently in the hope of satisfying the Allies of the activities of the 'Silent Service'. He made visits to the Dover Patrol and the Harwich Flotilla, and, on returning home, fell ill with gastritis.

On 2 October 1915, a telegram arrived from the War Office reporting that John was wounded and missing after the Battle of Loos. After a few days, Kipling returned to his work, the only anodyne, while awaiting further information. Two years passed before they had the full story. The lad had been shot through the head in action when his Company forced its way into a gap between Hill Seventy and Hulluch. After the agonised years of waiting and incessant inquiries, the parents, numbed and broken, sought refuge more than ever within themselves, with Elsie as the only comfort left to them.

Kipling made several visits to quiet sections of the Front, to the Grand Fleet in Scottish waters, and to the Naval establishments at Dover and Harwich. Apart from his war journalism, his best work of this period consisted of Naval songs and ballads. In 1917 he began work on a History of the Irish Guards, his son's regiment, and, in the same year, made a visit to Italy to collect material for the story of the Italian campaign, *The War in the Mountains*. In this year, too, he wrote 'In the Interests of the Brethren', by far the best of his Masonic writings, rich in sympathy and full of understanding of the needs of the men who were actually fighting in the war.* Following the confirmation of the death of his own son, one may imagine his anguish when he wrote of the principal character, L. H. Burges, of Burges and Son, '. . . but Son had been killed in Egypt'.

In September 1917, he was invited to join the Imperial War Graves Commission, of which he was a diligent member for the last 18 years of his life; indeed, it was he who chose for them the inscription, 'Their Name Liveth for Evermore.'

> . . . never before had war exacted such a terrible toll of death; never before had a permanent organisation for the care of their graves been needed in peace-time . . . among the graves under its care were those of men and women of many nations and of many religions . . . and by the nature of its task it [had to be] free from religious partiality.†

---

* Published in *Debits and Credits* in 1926.
† From *Thirty-five Masters. The Story of the Builders of the Silent Cities Lodge, No. 4984*, by W Bro C. G. Wyndham Parker, L.G.R.

The newly-formed Commission made its Headquarters just outside St Omer, and in January 1922, a Lodge was consecrated at St Omer as No 12 on the Register of the Grande Loge Nationale Indépendante et Régulière pour la France et les Colonies, Françaises (now the GLNF). Among the founders of the Lodge was Rudyard Kipling, and it was to his inspiration that the Lodge owes its name, 'The Builders of the Silent Cities', which so beautifully expresses the vocation of its members, 'whose sympathetic labour it is to construct and maintain permanent resting places for . . . the valiant dead of the British Empire who fell in the Great War'.

The first two Initiates of the Lodge were Major-General Sir Fabian Ware, Vice-Chairman and Chief Horticultural Officer of the Commission, and Captain J. S. Parker (from whose son's work these notes have been reproduced). As a tribute to Kipling, the Lodge adopted a modified form of the 'Sussex Working' of the Third Degree; Kipling was then a Sussex man and it was believed to be his favourite 'working',* but, in fact, his interest was in the Commission itself, rather than the Lodge, though he retained his membership of No 12 until his death.†

He was invited to become one of the Rhodes Trustees (for the Rhodes Scholarships at Oxford), an honour which he accepted willingly because both he and Carrie had taken a deep interest with Rhodes in the scheme when he was planning it. On 28 June 1918, the Motherland Lodge, No 3861, was consecrated at Freemasons' Hall, London, '. . . to signalise . . . the coming together of the English speaking family of nations to fight side by side on behalf of liberty and right, against wrong and oppression'. Kipling had been invited to attend, but he is listed among the Brethren who sent letters of apology. According to custom, the Consecrating Officers were made Honorary Members of the Lodge and presented with Founders' Jewels. 'A similar honour was conferred on' [various distinguished visitors, as well as] 'Bro Rudyard Kipling (who had personally selected for inclusion in the souvenir of the meeting a verse from his *Song of the Native-born*).' (*Freemasons' Chronicle*, 20 July 1918, pp 28–30.) The Secretary of the Lodge reports that, despite the Honorary Membership, there is no record of Kipling ever visiting the

---

* One may wonder, indeed, when R.K. found time to acquire a 'favourite working', for there is virtually no evidence of his attendances at Lodges after his first departure from India.
† Confirmed by the Secretary of the Lodge.

Lodge, or of his taking any practical interest in it thereafter.

War work and war journalism kept Kipling busy, leaving him little time for his ordinary literary work, and his best work of this period is in verse, especially those pieces which were highly critical of the errors and mismanagements of the war. When it was ended, Carrie wrote in her diary, 'a world to be remade . . . without a son'.

FINALE

The family returned to 'Bateman's' as to a refuge – Rudyard in poor health, and Carrie a diligent guardian and a constant shield against intruders. But theirs was not a hermit existence. There was a constant stream of visits from their closest intimates; John's army colleagues came, and the children of their relatives and friends. Airmen came to visit and to discuss the world air-routes that Kipling had predicted so long before. Stanley Baldwin, his cousin, serving under Bonar Law's Government, came to offer him 'any honour he will accept', but he steadfastly refused.

In December 1921, he was offered the Order of Merit, an honour in the King's personal gift, tendered in a charming letter from Lord Stamfordham. Refused, it was offered again in 1924 and refused again, but the King's admiration for Kipling and his work was not harmed by this stubborn independence.

In 1920 the family resumed their motor-tours in France, giving Kipling an opportunity to make personal inspection of more than 30 cemeteries under the War Graves Commission, on which he reported and advised. They also paid a visit to Loos to identify the spot where John had died.

In 1921 they went to Paris, where Kipling accepted a Doctorate of the University of Paris, and was fêted as a national hero by the social and political leaders of France. In 1922 they accompanied the King and Queen on their pilgrimage to the War Cemeteries, and Rudyard had the opportunity of a long private conversation with the King. Thereafter, his work on the Irish Guards being finished, the customary exhaustion followed and he was troubled again with gastric illness, which had been an intermittent source of discomfort for many years. He settled down at Batemans, a listless and bedridden invalid – with no interest, even in politics.

During this period the *New York World* published details of a supposed interview with Clare Sheridan, reporting Kipling's views on

Anglo-American relations, and that he had charged that America had come into the war too late and withdrawn too soon, with other observations equally unpalatable to the friends of both countries. It is possible that Kipling had indeed aired his views during an informal and private tea-time visit by Clare Sheridan to Burwash. If so, his words were certainly 'off-the-record'; but they became front-page news in the world Press, to Carrie's great distress, because her husband was too ill to deal with the matter. It was also a great embarrassment to the Government, at a time when relations with the USA were delicate. Eventually, Kipling sent a notice to the Press saying that he had not given an interview and denying that he had said the words attributed to him.

A severe recurrence of his illness led to a surgical operation, followed by several months of convalescence and a sea trip to Cannes, where he gradually recovered his health and began work again. At this period he wrote *The Janeites*, another 'Stalky' story, and several war stories, published in 1926 as *Debits and Credits*. Fashions had changed since his last book had been published some nine years before, and the new book had small success at first, though it steadily moved into favour afterwards. His zeal for compression, generally a virtue in a story-writer, when carried to extremes often made his work obscure and cryptic. Another volume of stories (published in 1932) was clearly the work of a tired and ageing invalid.

In 1926 he was awarded the Gold Medal of the Royal Society of Literature – an honour shared only with Scott, Meredith and Hardy. A year later, somewhat to Kipling's displeasure, the Kipling Society was formed, with General Dunsterville, 'Stalky' himself, as its first President. Much of the family's time in the next years was spent in motor-tours and voyages in search of sunshine.

In 1925 the War Graves Commission opened a new Head Office in London and many of the senior members of No 12 (France) found themselves transferred to England. This led to the formation of a London Lodge under the same title as its sister Lodge in France. Builders of the Silent Cities Lodge, No 4948, was consecrated in December 1927, and Kipling, still deeply interested in the work of the Commission, was one of its founders. But there is no evidence that he attended the Consecration or that he ever attended or took active part in the work of the Lodge. (He resigned in 1935, shortly before his death.)

Rudyard's last serious work was done in the early months of 1932, and now, as though he knew that the sands were running out for him, he began to tidy up, arranging a new volume of *Collected Verse*, as well as *A Pageant of Kipling*, a collection of verse and prose selected for the American market.

He supervised the preparation of the sumptuous Sussex Edition of his works, and then began to write *Something of Myself*, the bare framework of an autobiography, which tantalisingly ommited most of the most important people and incidents in his career.

In the summer of 1935 the Kiplings went off together to Marienbad (for Carrie's sake), and in the autumn Rudyard was busy with Hollywood agents, arranging for the filming of several of his stories.

In January 1936, Kipling replied to an invitation from the Secretary of the Authors' Lodge:

> Bateman's,
> Burwash, Sussex.
> January 2, 1936.
>
> Dear Brother Spalding,
>   Thank you very much indeed for the Lodge invitation for the 15th, but I'm sorry to say that each year I pass from the labour of fighting the English climate to the refreshment, more or less, of the South of France, and by the 15th I ought to be there in whatever sunshine this mad world has to offer.
>   Please convey my regrets to the Brethren, and
>   Believe me,
>   Fraternally yours,
>   (Signed) RUDYARD KIPLING.
>   (*Transactions of Authors' Lodge*, vol. vii, p 162.)

Early in January 1936, they were spending a few days at Brown's Hotel in London, prior to a projected trip to Cannes. On the night of 13 January, Rudyard suffered a violent haemorrhage; he lingered a few days and died on 18 January 1936, soon after his 70th birthday.

He lies buried in Poet's Corner at Westminster Abbey.

Is it fair – or even possible – to sum up in few lines the Masonic character of a man who had led such a full, busy and successful life? The constant interruptions in his career, his necessary mobility as a journalist, and his travels, his early marriage and his subsequent wanderings, all contributed towards his inability to make 'progress' in the Craft. Yet his zeal for Freemasonry was proclaimed in his writings time and time again. It has been suggested that as a creator of word-images his was not the kind of temperament to be troubled with the learning of ready-made ritual, but his writings show, constantly, that he had mastered a great deal of Masonic ritual during the bare three years of his Masonry in India.

When he wrote his wonderful Masonic tale, 'In the Interests of the Brethren', he was, indeed, an Honorary Member of Lodge Canongate Kilwinning, but he had been a non-subscribing Mason for some 20 years, yet nothing could better display his affection for the Craft or his knowledge of its background, and, perhaps most important of all, his love for humanity.

There was in his character a kind of native vehemence which prompted him occasionally to express himself in hasty words – that he must have regretted – yet it was that same vehemence which brought the blazing light of sympathy into his writings, which taught him how to defend the under-dog, which helped him to write with insight and understanding for children, as well as adults, over fields of literature unequalled by anyone before or since his day.

Generally – and all his Masonic writings seem to support this view – he was a 'practical' Mason, keenly aware of the practical usefulness of the Craft in bringing men together in service and good deeds; yet in *Kim* – and in some of his poems – he showed a genuine awareness of the spriritual aspects of the Craft.

PART II

FREEMASONRY AND MASONIC ALLUSIONS
IN KIPLING'S WORK

The extracts that follow do not pretend to be a complete catalogue or collection of all the Masonic allusions in Kipling's prose and verse. Indeed, it is doubtful if such a comprehensive collection would be possible, because many of them hinge on a mere turn of phrase, or association of ideas, where it is difficult to be certain of the writer's intentions. Nor is there any attempt here to make a study of Kipling's qualities as a writer. The extracts are presented, primarily, to show the many and various ways in which he expressed his ideas about the Craft, to indicate the diversity of purpose with which they were written, and to give some idea of the fascinating items of high

Masonic interest which await the reader who has not already discovered them for himself.

Occasionally the allusions are wholly Masonic in character, so that the background, the story and the theme (or moral) are all centred on some aspect of the Craft. Often the Masonic references are bold and clear, yet without any particular relevance to the story, which would have been equally complete without them. In such cases the allusions seem to have slipped into the text almost involuntarily, as though Kipling could find no better way of expressing himself, even though he must have known that their full significance might only be apparent to a tiny fraction of his readers. These references reflect an inner compulsion which is, itself, a measure of his love for the Craft.

In contrast to the direct allusions, relevant or not, the most difficult items of all to trace are the tricks of phrasing – the odd word or two which have their origins or parallels in Masonic ideas and lines of thought – although the words themselves do not belong to any specific Ritual or Lodge procedure.

All the extracts presented here fall into one or other of the categories outlined above. Previous writers have presented the same material more or less at random, usually on the basis of personal preference. They are reproduced below, as far as possible in chronological order, with only enough comment to enable the reader to grasp their implications, but with larger notes on matters that deserve special attention.

Many of the pieces appeared originally in newspapers, etc, but it would be extremely difficult for the reader to locate them in that form. The dates and book titles that are given in each case represent the main work in which the items were first collected and published.

———————

The Man Who Would Be King (*Indian Railway Series*, 1888) (*Wee Willie Winkie*, 1895) is generally accounted one of the best of Kipling's stories. It is told by a journalist (presumably Kipling himself) who falls into conversation, on a train journey, with an entertaining vagabond, Peachey Carnehan, who is planning a blackmailing visit to a native ruler. Warned off by the journalist, Carnehan asks him to deliver a message to another loafer at a railway-junction at some distance. The conversation runs:

'I ask you as a stranger – going to the West', he said, with emphasis. 'Where have you come from?' said I.

'From the East', said he, 'and I am hoping that you will give him the message on the Square – for the sake of my Mother, as well as your own.'

Englishmen are not usually softened by appeals to the memory of their mothers, but for certain reasons, which will be fully apparent, I saw fit to agree.

The journalist delivers the message – which is only the arrangement for a rendezvous – and he puts the matter out of mind. Several months later the two scamps walk into his office and introduce themselves as 'Brother Peachey Carnehan and Brother Daniel Dravot', and they unfold a plan to go into Kafiristan, in North-West Afghanistan, where they propose to drill the natives and set themselves up as Kings. The night is spent in studying maps and perfecting plans for the journey, which is full of danger on every hand, and the two soldiers of fortune go off.

Two years later Carnehan, the unrecognisable and crippled wreck of a man, crawls into the narrator's office, and tells the story of their journey. The two adventurers did reach Kafiristan, where the natives believed them to be gods.

Now the story takes a curious twist, based on the idea – commonly held among Masonic travellers and students of folk-lore during the past hundred years or so – that many primitive and civilised tribes in the Near and Far East use signs and symbols which are known and used in Speculative Masonry. Dravot, by some accident, makes this discovery, and the rest of their story, apart from its tragic end, is almost pure Masonry:

'Peachey', says Dravot, 'we don't want to fight no more. The Craft's the trick, so help me!' and he brings forward that same Chief . . . Billy Fish, we called him . . . 'Shake hands with him', says Dravot, and I shook hands and nearly dropped, for Billy Fish gave me the Grip. I said nothing, but tried him with the Fellow Craft Grip. He answers all right, and I tried the Master's Grip, but that was a slip. 'A Fellow Craft he is!' I says to Dan. 'Does he know the Word?' 'He does', says Dan, 'and all the priests know. It's a miracle! The Chiefs and the priests can work a Fellow Craft Lodge in a way that's very like ours, and they've cut the marks on the rocks, but they don't know the Third Degree, and they've come to find out. It's Gord's Truth! I've known these long years that the Afghans knew up to the Fellow Craft Degree, but this is a miracle. A God and a Grand-Master of

the Craft am I, and a Lodge in the Third Degree I will open, and we'll raise
the Head Priests and the Chiefs of the villages.'

'It's against all the Law', I says, 'holding a Lodge without warrant . . .'

'It's a master-stroke o' policy', says Dravot. 'It means running the
country as easy as a four-wheeled bogie on a down grade. We can't stop to
inquire now, or they'll turn against us. I've forty Chiefs at my heel, and
passed and raised . . . they shall be . . . The Temple of Imbra will do for
the Lodge-room. The women must make aprons as you show them. . .'

The most amazing miracles was at Lodge next night . . . I felt uneasy,
for I knew we'd have to fudge the Ritual . . . The minute Dravot puts on
the Master's apron . . . the priest fetches a whoop and a howl, and tries to
overturn the stone that Dravot was sitting on. 'It's all up now', I
says . . . Dravot never winked an eye, not when ten priests took and tilted
over the Grand-Master's Chair . . . The priest begins rubbing the bottom
end of it to clear away the black dirt, and . . . he shows all the other priests
the Master's Mark, same as was on Dravot's apron, cut into the stone. The
old chap falls flat on his face at Dravot's feet . . . 'Luck again', says
Dravot . . . 'they say it's the missing Mark that no one could understand
the why of. We're more than safe now.'

Using the butt of his gun as a Gavel, Dravot declares himself
'Grand Master of all Freemasonry in Kafiristan in this the Mother
Lodge o' the country, and the King of Kafiristan equally with
Peachey!'

Overwhelmed by their success, Dravot decides to take a wife from
among the tribe and the transition from the status of gods to mere
mortals proves to be their undoing. The tribe revolts, with results that
are dreadful to read, but splendidly told.

In a very different vein is *The Rout of the White Hussars* (*Plain
Tales from the Hills*, 1888). It is a light-hearted and slightly cynical
tale of a very proud Cavalry Regiment in India, whose Colonel, a
new man, self-willed and bumptious, decides to 'cast' the Drum-
Horse, the idol of the Regiment. One of the Subalterns buys the
horse against the Colonel's wish, on the pretext that he would not
want the beast ill-treated by a future owner, and mollifies him by a
promise that the horse will be shot. A different horse is substituted,
shot and buried with suitable honours.

The Colonel, aware that his obstinate action has aroused great
resentment in the regiment, decides to make the men 'sweat for

their . . . insolence', and orders a Brigade field-day.

At the end of a gruelling day the White Hussars are preparing their horses for stables to the traditional accompaniment of the regimental band. Suddenly, silhouetted against the sunset, the men see a lone horse, with a sort of grid-iron mounted on its back, approaching the band. There is a neigh, and the piebald is immediately recognised as the dead Drum-Horse of the White Hussars; the grid-iron is, in fact, a skeleton, riding between kettle-drums draped in black! Panic seizes the men and their horses; the regiment – for the first time in its history – breaks and runs. The Drum-Horse, disgusted by the behaviour of his old friends, trots up to the steps of the Mess, where the Colonel discovers that the whole affair is a practical joke – and the skeleton has been fastened into the saddle with wire.

The regiment gradually filters back, and the Masonic sting of the story is in its tail. A week later the Subaltern who had bought the Drum-Horse.

> . . . received an extraordinary letter from someone who signed himself 'Secretary, *Charity and Zeal*, 3709, EC', and asked for 'the return of our skeleton which we have reason to believe is in your possession' . . . 'Beg your pardon, Sir', said the Band-Sergeant, 'but the skeleton is with me, an' I'll return it if you'll pay the carriage into the Civil Lines. There's a coffin with it, Sir.'

Need we ask what the Lodge was doing with a skeleton and a coffin?

One of Kipling's many military tales of this period is *With the Main Guard* (*Soldiers Three*, 1890). The story is told by Mulvaney, the wild Irishman, of an adventure with his first regiment, the blackguardly Black Tyrones. They are ordered out on a punitive expedition against Pathan tribesmen, and the regiment, attacking, is jammed into a narrow defile. Some fierce hand-to-hand fighting ensues.

> 'Knee to knee!' sings out Crook, wid a laugh whin the rush av our comin' into the gut shtopped, an' he was huggin' a hairy great Paythan, neither bein' able to do anything to the other, tho' both was wishful.
> 'Breast to breast!' he says, as the Tyrone was pushin' us forward closer an' closer.
> 'An' hand over back!' sez a Sargint that was behin'. I saw a sword lick

out past Crook's ear like a snake's tongue, an' the Paythan was took in the apple av his throat like a pig at Dromeen fair.

'Thank ye, Brother Inner Guard', sez Crook, cool as a cucumber, widout salt . . . I wanted that room.' . . .

Masonry was strong in all ranks of the Indian military Lodges, but here the Masonic crosstalk is a gratuitous introduction born of Kipling's own enthusiasm; the tale would have read just as well without it. He used the same theme, in verse, a few years later, in *With Scindia to Delhi* (*Barrack-Room Ballads*, 1893), to describe another battle:

'. . . There was no room to clear a sword – no power to strike a blow, for foot to foot, ay, breast to breast, the battle held us fast . . .'

A Masonic poem, beautiful in its theme as in its clear simplicity, is *My New-Cut Ashlar* (*Life's Handicap*, 1891). It is the prayer of a craftsman who hopes that his work may be found worthy in the eyes of the Great Overseer. But the symbolism is not for Masons alone, and the two last lines are a plea and a promise of dedication:

MY NEW-CUT ASHLAR (*Life's Handicap*, 1891)

My new-cut ashlar takes the light
    Where crimson-blank the windows flare.
By my own work before the night,
    Great Overseer, I make my prayer.

If there be good in that I wrought,
    Thy Hand compelled it, Master, Thine –
Where I have failed to meet Thy Thought
    I know, through Thee, the blame was mine.

. . . One stone the more swings into place
    In that dread Temple of Thy worth.
It is enough that, through Thy Grace,
    I saw nought common on Thy Earth.

Take not that vision from my ken –
    Or whatsoe'er may spoil or speed.

Help me to need no aid from men
That I may help such men as need!

THE WIDOW AT WINDSOR (*Barrack-Room Ballads*, 1892)

An early poem which used Masonic phrases to express Kipling's ideas on a non-Masonic subject was 'The Widow at Windsor'. It describes the soldier's views of the might and power of Queen Victoria, but in none-too-respectful language. Yet, to the trooper, the British Empire is 'the Lodge' that stretches from the Tropics to the Pole:

Hands off o' the sons o' the Widow,
　Hands off o' the goods in 'er shop,
For the Kings must come down an' the Emperors frown
　When the Widow at Windsor says 'Stop'!
　(Poor beggars! – we're sent to say 'Stop'!)

Then 'ere's to the Lodge o' the Widow,
　From the Pole to the Tropics it runs –
To the Lodge that we tile with the rank an' the file,
　An' open in form with the guns.
　(Poor beggars! – it's always they guns!)

The poem ends with a play on the Tyler's Toast:

Then 'ere's to the sons o' the Widow,
　Wherever, 'owever they roam.
'Ere's all they desire, an' if they require
　A speedy return to their 'ome.
　(Poor beggars! – they'll never see 'ome!)

In the same collection, *Barrack-Room Ballads*, 1892, one of Kipling's poems which achieved great fame was *The Ballad of East and West*, the story of an Afghan raid on a Border fort, in which the Colonel's valuable mare is stolen – and recovered. Despite the opening line of the poem

Oh, East is East, and West is West, and never the twain shall meet, it tells the tale of worthy foemen and the story is told at a rollicking pace – one can almost hear the clatter of hooves. Towards the end of the poem the narrator, realising the bravery of the enemy, finds that they, too, are men of quality:

They have taken the Oath of the Brother-in-Blood on leavened bread and salt:
They have taken the Oath of the Brother-in-Blood on fire and fresh-cut sod,
On the hilt and haft of the Khyber knife, and the Wondrous Names of God.*

In the last lines, the Colonel's son rides back to the fort with the son of the Afghan chief at his side, as friends, and the whole theme of the poem is enshrined in the one line,

And to have come back to Fort Bukloh where they went forth but one.

No strong Masonic allusions here, but an expression of Kipling's views on the infinite possibilities of the Brotherhood of Man.

Perhaps the best known and best loved of Kipling's Masonic poems, also produced at this period, was *The Mother-Lodge* (*The Seven Seas*, 1896), 'which he wrote in a single morning'.† Nothing could better express the profound impression that the universality of the Craft had made on Kipling's mind. The poem is no mere catalogue of the men of different Asiatic races who sat side-by-side in Lodge. There is a special emphasis on the Aden Jew and the Roman Catholic, with a proper respect for the problems of caste; and Kipling shows the unique atmosphere of the Lodge when he says that each man could talk of the God he knew best in an environment of brotherhood and understanding. It is the picture of an Indian Lodge of Kipling's day, and it is good to know that the characteristics that he admired so much have remained to this day.

* This reference to the Names of God has been used as the flimsy basis for the suggestion that Kipling was a member of the Royal Arch. There is, in fact, no evidence of any kind in support of this argument.
† C.C., p 213.

THE MOTHER-LODGE (*The Seven Seas*, 1896)

There was Rundle, Station Master,
    An' Beazeley of the Rail,
An' 'Ackman, Commissariat,
    An' Donkin' o' the Jail;
An' Blake, Conductor-Sergeant,
    Our Master twice was 'e,
With 'im that kept the Europe-shop,
    Old Framjee Eduljee.

Outside – Sergeant! Sir! Salute! Salaam!
Inside – Brother, an' it doesn't do no 'arm.
We met upon the Level an' we parted on the Square,
An' I was Junior Deacon in my Mother-Lodge out there!

We'd Bola Nath, Accountant,
    An' Saul the Aden Jew,
An' Din Mohammed, draughtsman
    Of the Survey Office, too;
There was Babu Chuckerbutty,
    An' Amire Singh the Sikh,
An' Castro from the fittin'-sheds,
    The Roman Catholick!

We 'adn't good regalia
    An' our Lodge was old an' bare,
But we knew the Ancient Landmarks,
    An' we kep' 'em to a hair;
An' lookin' on it backwards
    It often strikes me thus,
There ain't such things as infidels,
    Excep', per'aps, it's us.

For monthly, after Labour,
    We'd all sit down and smoke
(We dursn't give no banquits,
    Lest a Brother's caste were broke),
An' man on man got talkin'

Religion an' the rest,
An' every man comparin'
Of the God 'e knew the best.

. . . Full oft on Guv'ment service
This rovin' foot 'ath pressed,
An' bore fraternal greetin's
To the Lodges east an' west,
Accordin' as commanded
from Kohat to Singapore,
But I wish that I might see them
In my Mother-Lodge once more!

KIM (1901)

Kim, one of Kipling's few full-length novels, is the story of the orphan son of Kimball O'Hara, colour-sergeant and afterwards a railway gang-foreman in India. After the death of his wife he took to drink and opium, and within three years he died, 'a poor white', leaving the infant Kim to be brought up by a half-caste woman. The child's only legacy from his father

> . . . consisted of three papers – one he called his *ne varietur* because those words were written below his signature thereon, and another his 'clearance-certificate'. The third was Kim's birth-certificate . . .

These the half-caste woman had sewn into a leather amulet-case, which the lad wore about his neck. In moments of opium exaltation the father used to prophesy that those papers would make a man of the youngster, and that he would one day join his father's regiment. But Kim grew up a waif, fending for himself, the 'Little Friend of all the World', and far more at home in native dress and the iniquity and filth of the native quarters than among white folk.

At the age of 13, Kim, already a keen-eyed, intelligent adult, meets an old man – formerly the Abbot of a Tibetan monastery – now a wandering lama or Holy Man, who is making a mystical pilgramage to see the 'Four Holy places' before he dies. Kim befriends him, becoming his servant, guardian and devoted slave, begging food and alms for him on their journeyings.

Their many adventures are told against the teeming background of

Indian native life. One night Kim blunders on a military camp, an advance part of his father's old regiment. He does not know their name, but recognises the regimental flags, 'a red bull on a green ground', which his father had described to him. Wandering through the camp, he is seen by the Padre, who grabs him, believing he is a native thief. In the struggle the cord of Kim's amulet-case is broken and the Padre discovers the three papers. He calls Father Victor, the Catholic priest, and during the interrogation that follows they discover that Kim is the son of a former soldier of the regiment, and that the priest had actually attended at O'Hara's wedding.

The Padre, who is Secretary of the Regimental Lodge, recognises the *ne varietur*.

'We cannot allow an English boy – Assuming that he is the son of a Mason, the sooner he goes to the Masonic Orphanage the better.'

Father Victor urges that they must consult with the lama. A long argument ensues, with Kim all eager for instant flight, but the Churchmen want him to be brought up and educated as a Sahib. English education in India costs money, and the lama – to Kim's dismay – is anxious to know how much. Father Victor answers:

'Well . . . the regiment would pay for you all the time you are at the Military Orphanage; or you might go on the Punjab Masonic Orphanage's list . . . but the best schooling a boy can get in India is, of course, St Xavier's in Partibus at Lucknow . . . Two or three hundred rupees a year.'

The lama asks for the name of the school and the amount to be written down for him – and, through his monastery, he arranges to provide the necessary funds. Kim goes off to St Xavier's for three years, much against his own will at first, and suffering the 'exile' only out of affection for the Holy Man.

Kim, who had already shown a natural aptitude, is to be groomed for the Indian Secret Service, but at the end of his three years he rejoins the lama, so that they can complete their former pilgrimage.

The story, rich in adventure and colour, contains several Masonic references, too numerous to be quoted at length. But it is not merely an adventure tale. The theme of the holy pilgrimage, which runs through the book from start to finish, is certainly of greater Masonic significance than the actual references to the Craft. It has its origins in Asiatic religion and mysticism, but no thoughtful Mason can read the

book without feeling that this theme of a spiritual search and purpose
– though couched in unfamiliar phrases – is the very stuff of Masonic
ideology and symbolism. Nowhere, in all his Masonic writings, did
Kipling approach more closely or more effectively to those aspects of
Freemasonry.

A poem, *The Palace* (1903), is purely Masonic in character, but it
contains an element of mysticism and is, for that reason, open to wide
interpretation. Its principal theme is, perhaps, the lesson that even in
decay a craftman's work, done to the best of his ability, will hold a
message of faith and encouragement to unborn generations – 'After
me cometh a Builder. Tell him, I too have known'.

THE PALACE (*The Five Nations*, 1903)

When I was a King and a Mason – a Master proven and skilled –
I cleared me ground for a palace such as a King should build.
I decreed and dug down to my levels. Presently, under the silt,
I came on the wreck of a palace such as a King had built.

There was no worth in the fashion – there was no wit in the plan –
Hither and thither, aimless, the ruined footings ran –
Masonry, brute, mishandled, but carven on every stone:
'After me cometh a Builder. Tell him, I too have known.'. . .

. . . When I was a King and a Mason – in the open noon of my
pride,
They sent me a Word from the Darkness – They whispered and
called me aside.
They said – 'The end is forbidden.' They said – 'Thy use is fulfilled,
'And thy palace shall stand as that other's – the spoil of a King who
shall build.'

I called my men from my trenches, my quarries, my wharves and
my shears.
All I had wrought I had abandoned to the faith of the faithless
years.
Only I cut on the timber, only I carved on the stone:
After me cometh a Builder. Tell him, I too have known!

By far the best tale that Kipling ever told – from a Mason's point of view – is *In the Interests of the Brethren* (*Debits and Credits*, 1926). The story is set in London, towards the end of World War I, where the anonymous narrator – after a couple of accidental meetings – runs into the principal character for the third time, behind the counter of a tobacconist's shop of which he is the proprietor: 'Lewis Holroyd Burges, of "Burges and Son" . . . but Son had been killed in Egypt'. For men fond of pipes, cigars or snuff, the shop is a collector's paradise, and Burges is quite a character, too. He is one of a small group of Brethren, leaders in a Lodge of Instruction (attached to Lodge Faith and Works, No 5837) which, because London is the hub of the war-time world, has now opened its doors on its regular evening and for two afternoon sessions each week, the latter mainly for the benefit of the maimed and wounded brethren in the nearby hospitals.

The fame of this Lodge of Instruction – in a converted garage – has spread, so that it has become a wayside halt for soldiers and seamen passing through London – and for any who can 'prove themselves'.

The narrator arranges to accompany Burges that evening. The examination of Visiting Brethren is conducted with charity; most of them have no 'papers', and some lack arms or hands, or even the ability to speak coherently. The officers for the ceremony are chosen from amongst the visitors and they are encouraged to 'work' without correction or interference. Later, a team of 'regulars' demonstrate the same work while the guests relax.

There is no story – just a picture of worn and weary men withdrawn for a few brief moments, from the terrors of a world in chaos, into a haven of peace and sanity, where the teachings of Brotherhood acquire a new and poignant meaning against the background of their sufferings.

A simple banquet follows each evening meeting, provided by the leaders, and no visitor is allowed to pay. The table-talk gives Kipling the opportunity to point the moral and to show what Freemasonry could really mean to men under stress – for this is no ordinary Lodge of Instruction, but an ideal; it is an appeal to the Craft to awaken to its responsibilities.

'A man's Lodge means more to him than people imagine . . . When I think of the possibilities of the Craft at this juncture, I wonder . . . There ought to be a dozen – twenty – other Lodges in London every night; conferring degrees too, as well as instruction. Why shouldn't the young men join? They practise what we're always preaching . . . We must all do what we can. What's the use of old Masons if they can't give a little help along their own lines?'

No brief summary could possibly do justice to this evocative and fascinating piece, told with a real economy of words and yet with such profound sympathy and perception. For anyone who lived in those troubled days it is a sad reminder; but for the Mason reader this simple tale has a special fascination. It breathes the true spirit of Freemasonry in every line, and it is a piece of inspired craftsmanship that will never become dated and never go out of fashion.

Every writer about Kipling has perforce commented on the massive grasp of technical and background detail displayed so readily in his writings. 'In the Interests of the Brethren' is the one piece that shows to the full his background knowledge of Masonry, and, although he has condensed his remarks in a few brief words, we can read his attainments between the lines.

'. . . a carefully decorated ante-room hung round with Masonic prints. I noticed Peter Gilkes and Barton Wilson, fathers of "Emulation" working, in the place of honour; Kneller's Christopher Wren; Dunkerley, with his own Fitz-George book-plate below and the bend sinister on the Royal Arms; Hogarth's caricature of Wilkes, also his disreputable "Night"; and a beautifully framed set of Grand Masters, from Anthony Sayer down.'

One wonders how many Masons there are – even among those who practise *Emulation* – who know that Gilkes and Barton Wilson were among their great leaders, or how many had ever heard of Dunckerley? Only a student who had read his life story could possibly know that he was an illegitimate son of George II, and that he affected the Royal Arms with a bar sinister. Kneller's 'Christopher Wren' and Hogarth's 'Night' are known to the world at large, but how many Brethren – even if they know Hogarth's leering caricature of John Wilkes – would know that he, too, was a Freemason; and how many are there who could name Anthony Sayer as the first Grand Master.

Here, in one paragraph, Kipling demonstrates a basic knowledge of Craft history far beyond the average – but perhaps the most interesting piece comes a few lines later:

'There are some more in the Lodge Room. Come and look. We've got the big Desaguliers there that nearly went to Iowa.'

It would be difficult, perhaps, to determine which precise portrait of Desaguliers is mentioned here, but the reference to Iowa betrays specialist knowledge. The Grand Lodge of Iowa was founded in 1840, and around 1850 it began to collect rare items, of Masonic books especially, which have made their library into one of the best collections of its kind in the English-speaking world. Not one English Mason in ten thousand would be expected to know this, yet Kipling threw in this little detail simply to emphasise the importance of the picture in question. How he got his information is a puzzle, but there is a possible clue. When the Kiplings left Vermont after the trouble with Balestier (*ante*, p 229), they settled in Torquay, Devon, for some two years, 1896–97. Torquay was the home of that great Masonic scholar and bibliophile, W. J. Hughan, a founder of the Quatuor Coronati Lodge, who served the Grand Lodge of Iowa for a number of years as adviser in the acquisition of their collections. He was made Senior Grand Warden of the GL of Iowa in recognition of his services. It is more than likely that he met Kipling and discussed matters of mutual interest with him. This is, of course, pure speculation, but, wherever Kipling got his information, he was one of only a handful of men in the whole world who could speak on the subject with knowledge.

The poem, *Banquet Night*, is simply a colourful piece of Masonic high spirits, urging the Brethren to 'Forget these things', *ie*, the troubles of the world outside, and rejoice in fraternal fellowship.

BANQUET NIGHT (*Debits and Credits*, 1926)

'Once in so often', King Solomon said,
  Watching his quarrymen drill the stone,
'We will club our garlic and wine and bread
  And banquet together beneath my Throne.
And all the Brethren shall come to that mess
As Fellow-Craftsmen – no more and no less.

'Send a swift shallop to Hiram of Tyre,
   Felling and floating our beautiful trees,
Say that the Brethren and I desire
   Talk with our Brethren who use the seas.
And we shall be happy to meet them at mess
As Fellow-Craftsmen – no more and no less.

'Carry this message to Hiram Abif –
   Excellent Master of Forge and mine:
I and the Brethren would like it if
   He and the Brethren will come to dine
(Garments from Bozrah or morning-dress)
As Fellow-Craftsmen – no more and no less.

. . . The Quarries are hotter than Hiram's forge,
   No one is safe from the dog-whip's reach.
It's mostly snowing up Lebanon gorge,
   And it's always blowing off Joppa beach;
But once in so often, the messenger brings
Solomon's mandate: 'Forget these things!
Brothers to Beggars and Fellow to Kings,
Companion of Princes – forget these things!
Fellow-Craftsman, forget these things!'

———————

The whole quotation relating to Kipling's admission into the Craft has been given earlier. One sentence is repeated here, for two reasons:

'. . . Here I met Hindus, Muslims, Sikhs, members of the Araya and Brahmo Samaj, and a Jew Tyler, who was priest and butcher to his little community in the city'.

These words – quite apart from their autobiographical interest – help to focus attention on two aspects of Kipling's quality, both as an author and as a Freemason.

He speaks of the Jew, who was priest and butcher to the Jewish community of Lahore, and in that sentence he reveals his searching nature as a writer who made it his business to study every facet of his subject before putting pen to paper. Soldiers, guns, horses, sailing ships, lighthouses, engines, railways – all these and a hundred other themes were his stock-in-trade, described and characterised with the sáme infinite care which he devoted to his individual heroes and heroines. So, too, with the Jew Tyler!

The Jews have been wanderers for 2,000 years, and whenever they begin to settle in a new place their first concern (which arises primarily out of their religious needs) is to congregate. They need a 'priest' to lead them in prayer – often a difficult task because there are relatively few who can read the ancient Hebrew. They need a 'shochet' (ie, a slaughterer) who can prepare poultry and animals according to the forms prescribed in Jewish law; and the 'shochet' is usually a 'mohel' too, and thereby qualified to perform circumcision, as prescribed in Holy Writ. These three are the first 'officers' in every Jewish community, and if the congregation consists of only a few souls, invariably one man has to double-up for all duties. So the slaughterer is also the 'butcher and priest'; and since his income from those duties is always very small, he usually has to find some sort of additional employment too. He might become dues-collector or secretary to some little charitable organisation, or, if the opportunity offered, he might become Tyler to several Lodges. This little sentence is a near-perfect example of Kipling's insight.

It also draws attention to another and less attractive aspect of Kipling's character, since it is almost the only case in which he wrote of a Jew (or 'the Jews') without betraying his rooted aversion. This was the one 'blind-spot' in Kipling's Freemasonry, and the reader who delves will find that his ideas on the 'Brotherhood of Man' could comprehend all of humanity, except the Jews and the Chinese!

10

WOMEN AND FREEMASONRY

A Brief Entertainment For Masons And Their Ladies

DEAR LADIES, my talk tonight is addressed mainly to you, and I shall be speaking about 'Women and Freemasonry'; not all women, but only a few who tried to get in, with one or two who succeeded and several famous ladies who managed, somehow, to find a place in Masonic history.

Our troubles really began in 1723, when Dr James Anderson published his *Book of Constitutions*, the first rule-book of the first Grand Lodge. In Rule *III* of his 'Charges of a Freemason' he wrote:

> The Persons admitted Members of a Lodge must be good and true Men,
> . . . . of mature and discreet Age, . . . *no Women* . . . (My italics.)

That Rule aroused great curiosity among the ladies, and very soon we begin to hear dozens of stories of women hidden in grandfather clocks, in attics, in cupboards or behind panelling, in order to learn those secrets about which their menfolk were so cautious. True or false, we do not know, but some of them were certainly true.

My first story is about a famous French lady who did not need to hide. I must explain that we, the English, planted Freemasonry in France in 1725, where it soon became an elegant pastime for the nobility and gentry. The Duke of So-and-So would hold a Lodge in his own home, where he was Master for as long as he wished, and whenever the fancy took him, he would make a few Masons among his friends.

Ten or twelve years were to pass before the Craft had spread widely among the lower levels, merchants and tradesmen, and by that time Lodge meetings were being held in taverns and restaurants. In 1736–37 the French government finances were very shaky, conditions in the country were bad, and a fear arose, in Court circles, that the secret meetings in Lodges might be used for plots and conspiracies against government. In 1737 an Edict was proclaimed at Paris, by the Chevalier René Herault, Lt General of Police, prohibiting the taverns and restaurants from giving accommodation to Masonic Lodges, under severe penalties. Several taverns were closed up for six months and their owners were ordered to pay heavy fines – but the Edict was unsuccessful. Masonry in France had started in private houses; when Police measures became uncomfortable, the Lodges went back into private houses and the Police were ignored.

Herault, enraged by his failure, decided that he could do much more damage to the Craft if he could bring it to ridicule. He was sure that if he could make the Masons a laughing-stock, he would put them out of business altogether. He visited one of his girl-friends, a certain Mme Carton, who is usually described as a dancer at the Paris Opera. The truth is that she belonged to a much older profession and it would be fair to say that she slept in the best beds in Europe. She was then a mature lady in her fifties and she had a daughter in the same line of business. I have to be careful in what I say about these two ladies, because one of our own Grand Masters was said to be entangled with the mother, or the daughter, or both! But all this was common news at that time.

Herault asked her to obtain the Masonic ritual from one of her clients and pass it on to him, so that he could publish it in one of the naughty newspapers, in the hope that it would put an end to Freemasonry in France. She did obtain a copy of the ritual from one of her lovers and Herault published it: but for all the damage that it did to the Craft, he might just as well have dropped it in the Seine! The Craft in France continued to flourish. I need not discuss the actual text, except to say that as we read it, there seems to be no doubt at all that the gentleman who dictated it had his mind on much more wordly matters at that time!

In a rather different vein is the story of 'Mollie, the chambermaid' who was employed at a tavern in Canterbury, England, where a military Lodge met regularly in 1754. Mollie was a fine strapping wench, greatly interested in her customers, and determined to find out what they did at their Lodge meetings. In pursuit of her plan, she climbed into the attic above the Lodge-room and made a small hole in the floor, which was the lath and plaster ceiling of the Lodge.

Then, one day, after a meeting had begun, she went up into the attic and knelt down to see and hear what was happening. She must have found it all extremely interesting because, in the excitement, she forgot to stay at a safe spot and moved to kneel between the joists. Soon the thin lath and plaster began to give way and there is a famous picture – a printed engraving – showing the wrong end of Mollie coming through the ceiling, feet first, with lots of lingerie and large expanses of Mollie, while the Masons stand aghast, watching their unexpected visitor! True or false, we do not know, but the engraving must have made a small fortune for the artist.

A somewhat similar tale, with a different ending, is told about a Mrs Bell, who was landlady of the Crown Inn at Newcastle, where a Lodge of the 22nd Regiment met regularly. The story goes that she broke open a door, but there are no details of what she heard and saw. All we know is that there was a lengthy advertisement in the *Newcastle Chronicle* of 6 January 1770 saying that Mrs Bell 'having found out that secret is willing to make it known to all her own sex . . .'. The story was probably a hoax.

There is a well-documented story, which is almost certainly true, concerning the Hon Elizabeth St. Leger, daughter of Viscount Doneraile, who regularly held a Lodge at his own home, Doneraile Court, County Cork, Ireland. Some time between 1710 and 1713 there were repairs being done on one of the walls of the room used for Lodge meetings, for which purpose a large section of panelling had been taken off the wall, leaving open brickwork which had been temporarily covered by leaning the loose panel against that wall, when the workmen had departed on that particular evening.

Elizabeth, then aged about seventeen, had gone into their library, adjoining the Lodge room, started to read a book and had fallen asleep there. She awoke, to hear, and even to see, some part of the ceremonies. When she realized what had happened she attempted to leave the library, but was seen in the outer hall by the family butler who was on duty there, in the capacity of Tyler. One version of the story says that she fainted. The acting-Tyler reported to the Lodge and this brought the Viscount and his sons into the Hall. Leaving Elizabeth in the care of the butler and some of the Brethren, the members of the family returned to the Lodge and after lengthy discussion it was resolved that – as a matter of honour – she should allow herself to be initiated.

Elizabeth agreed and she was made a Mason (or Masonette?) receiving the Two degrees current at that time. She died in 1773 aged 80, having held 'such a veneration for Masonry that she would never suffer it to be spoken of lightly in her hearing'. There are several well-known portraits of her, including one wearing a 'trowel jewel', and her descendants still own what is supposed to have been her original Masonic apron.

We return now to France, where the Craft spread very strongly from the 1740s onwards, with all sorts of novelties and extravagances beginning to appear. Perhaps the best of these new creations were the 'Lodges of Adoption', a system under which perfectly regular Craft Lodges would adopt mixed Lodges of ladies and gentlemen of good society, who worked a kind of imitation Masonic ceremony, usually followed by a dinner and ball. These highly social Adoptive Lodges became very popular and there is a good story about one of them, in which all the characters can be identified.

In 1802, Brother the Baron Cuvelier de Trie was giving a Fete of his Lodge of Adoption. But *before* the Fete, his Craft Lodge, Les Freres Artistes, decided to hold an ordinary Lodge Meeting. After the Lodge had opened, among the visitors waiting to enter was a Cavalry Officer, not a member of the Lodge. The 'outer-guard' asked him for his Certificate and the Officer handed him a folded sheet which was sent into the Lodge un-opened.

The paper was read to the Lodge by the Orator, and it proved to be a Commission as ADC issued to Madame de Xaintrailles, wife of General de Xaintrailles. She was a heroine of the French Republican Revolution who had won her Commission at the point of the sword. The Brethren were astonished and proud to have such company. She was well known to have courage and all the manly vitrues, having served several important missions which needed discretion and prudence, as well as bravery.

The Lodge resolved that she should be initiated as a man, not in Adoptive Masonry, but in real Masonry, and a message was sent out to her, inviting her to accept initiation in the regular Lodge. Her answer was very simple: 'I am a man for my Country, I will be a man for my Brethren'. She was initiated with proper modesty, and from that time often assisted in the work of the Lodge.

My last story from the pages of Masonic history, is vastly different. Charles d'Eon de Beaumont was born in France in 1728, into a good family of nobility in Burgundy. He was educated at Paris, passed with distinction in Law and Literature, and was licensed to practise in Civil and Canon Law. He was appointed Royal Censor on History and Literature and he published many essays and reviews, especially on Historical finance. Throughout his youth and middle age he had only one hobby, fencing, and he was accounted to be one of the five best swordsmen in Europe.

In 1755, Louis XV sent him on an important mission to St. Petersburg, where he achieved a brilliant success, and he was appointed Secretary to the French Embassy at St. Petersburg. In 1757, he was sent on another Royal mission to Vienna, again with outstanding success, and he was awarded a Commission in the Dragoons. He served with bravery in the Seven Years War and was twice wounded.

In 1763, at the end of the war, he was appointed Minister Plenipotentiary and Secretary to the French Ambassador in London. He served continuously in the Peace negotiations with England, where he became very popular and was trusted even by his English enemies. Louis XV awarded him the Royal and Military Order of St. Louis, and thenceforward he was known as the Chevalier D'Eon.

Back in France, he was at the top of the political tree, but his success made enemies for him. Throughout his life, this brilliant man had one extraordinary disability – he had the face and figure of a woman. Eventually, he was displaced from Office and in 1768, aged 40, he came to England, bringing his valuable Secret Service papers with him, and for the next three years or so he lived well in good Society. Louis XV, and later Louis XVI wanted him to return his papers, and the parliamentary Opposition in England offered to pay him £40,000 for them (because it was believed that they contained plans for a French invasion of Britain). But D'Eon refused all offers.

Meanwhile, his French enemies had begun to spread rumours that D'Eon was a woman, rumours which rapidly spread to England. This was the great age of gambling in England and very soon enormous wagers were being laid on his sex. On all sides he was being pestered by gamblers to prove whether he was a man or a woman, and, of course, none of the bets could be settled without his co-operation. Bookmakers and professional speculators began to issue 'Policies', enforceable at law and in 1771 it was said that there were £120,000 worth of wagers depending on D'Eon's willingness to prove their case, either way. D'Eon, harrassed and horrified, disappeared for two months, but he returned to London in 1771, to make a sworn declaration before the Lord Mayor that 'He had no part in these bets, and had refused £25,000 to prove his sex judicially.'

D'Eon always claimed that he was a man and throughout his life he kept perfect records of his expense accounts. They show that he was Initiated as a Mason in London in May 1768; he was J. W. of the Lodge of Immortality No 376, meeting at the Crown & Anchor tavern in the Strand. The accounts also show the sums he paid for visitor's fees and for his Masonic Jewel.

But gamblers gave him no peace, and in 1777 there were fresh rumours that D'Eon was going back to France. This brought matters to a head. William Hayes, a London surgeon, had wagered a 100 guineas against Jacques, a Broker, who was to pay him 700 guineas if D'Eon was proved to be a woman. That wager, in the form in which it had been drawn up, was a perfectly legal document and Hayes started a lawsuit against Jacques, which came to trial, in July 1777, before Lord Mansfield, in the Court of the King's Bench. D'Eon had nothing to do with the wager or the lawsuit.

Two lying witnesses were brought in to give evidence. Dr Le Goux, a surgeon, swore that 'he had professionally examined *Mlle* D'Eon . . . .'. De Morande, a journalist, swore that 'he had slept with her'. D'Eon was adjudged a woman and the bets were paid. This was too much for D'Eon. He accepted a substantial pension from Louis XVI to return to France, *but the condition was imposed, that he would live the rest of his life as a woman and never resume man's clothing.* He lived first in a Convent, and finally in a home for ladies of gentle birth. He died in 1810 and was buried as *Mlle. la Chevaliere* D'Eon. Nevertheless an autopsy, at his death, by an independant surgeon and in the presence of many of his English friends, proved beyond doubt that he was really a man.

Many more stories might have been included here, but the few that I selected, were chosen mainly for their variety. Before I finish I ought to say a few words about Women and Freemasonry today. On that subject, it would be fair to say that we, in England, have been spoilt. When we talk about Women and Freemasonry in Britain we are compelled to discuss the two Orders firmly established here, both claiming that they use the same ritual as their husbands. They wear the same Masonic clothing, and even go so far in copying us that they

call each other 'Brother'. Inevitably, they are taboo. I must add that
both are very respectable societies, doing useful social and charitable
work, but they are not for us; Masonically, we may not recognise
them.

In the USA especially, Freemasonry has strong social and family
implications. The two best-known Women's Orders are 'Eastern
Star' and 'Amaranth'. Both permit male membership. In addition,
there is 'De Molay' for boys from age 14 to 21: 'Rainbow' and 'Job's
Daughters' for girls in similar age groups, and all these Orders are, in
a very special sense, Masonic. Indeed, the majority of USA Masonic
jurisdictions recognise them as 'Bodies identified with Freemasonry'.
The De Molay boys are admitted by a highly moral and picturesque
ceremony. Their Order may be best described as an apprenticeship
for Speculative Masonry, and I am assured that similar compliments
may be paid to the girls' Orders.

It must be emphasised that none of these Orders use our Masonic
ritual. As an example, 'Eastern Star' uses a ritual based on five
Biblical heroines and they make no attempt to copy our Freemasonry. Perhaps the best explanation I can give of their relationship to the
Craft is to ask you to think, for a moment, of your Church or
Synagogue and of the Ladies' Guild that serves it in every way it can.
They do a great deal of magnificent work in serving the Lodges, not
in copying them, and I have seen some fine examples of the help that
they give in catering, social and charitable works. This kind of 'family
Masonry' has many advantages. Father knows where mother is on
her night out, and *vice versa*; and both are able to take a direct
interest in the children. So far as a foreign onlooker may judge, I
must say it all looked very good to me.

Eastern Star is recognised by the Grand Lodge of Scotland, and the
co-operation of the ladies is highly appreciated, especially in the
smaller towns and villages where their assistance with catering is
helping to keep the Craft Lodges alive.

The United Grand Lodge of England does not recognise the
Order, but it is being established here, very gradually. One reason for
this slow development is that the list of Officers in an Eastern Star
Lodge is not complete without two male Officers (Worthy Patron and
Worthy Treasurer, I believe,) who must be regular Masons. No
English Mason is able to assist them in this way and the ladies usually
have to find Scottish Masons who could take those Offices.

Difficulties arise when two regular Masons are not to be found. In such cases, I am told, that Headquarters will grant them a Dispensation by which two of their ladies are allowed to become gentlemen for that purpose! It shows, at least, that these nice people are ready to take a great deal of trouble to achieve their praiseworthy objectives.

And so, for my final words, I quote our own Grand Master, HRH The Duke of Kent; speaking of the Freemasonry of which he is the titular, active and popular head, he said:

> How pleasant it is to work with nice people, to live with nice people, and to sleep – with a contented mind!

11

THE EVOLUTION AND RITUAL OF THE THIRD DEGREE

NOTE

This essay is not a study of present-day ritual or practice. The textual and procedural items which are discussed here represent only the practice claimed – in surviving documents – to have been in use in their day. From first to last we are only concerned with documentary evidence relating to the Masonic ritual from 1696 to 1762. We have taken no account of the massive changes that appeared towards the end of the eighteenth century, and of the revisions adopted at the union of the Grand Lodges in 1813, when our present-day usages were more-or-less standardised for England.

THIS ESSAY IS an off-shoot of my *600 Years of Craft Ritual (AQC, 81)* which was a broad history of the ritual from its beginnings up to the time when it was revised and virtually standardised at the union of the rival Grand Lodges in 1813. Here we shall be dealing with problems arising in the development of the Third Degree, historically the most interesting of all three. As before, I promise that there will be no 'fairy tales' and I shall give the names and dates of every document by which the arguments may be proved.

Our earliest evidence on an admission ceremony into the Mason trade comes from the Old Charges which begin with the *Regius MS*, *c*1390. They were the earliest 'constitutions' or rule-books for the Operative Lodges, and the *Regius, without describing a ceremony*, indicates the importance attaching to the mason's oath:

> And all shall swear the same oath of the masons,
> Be they willing, be they loth.

That was the key that would open the door into the Craft, and later versions of the Old Charges contain the actual words of a simple oath of fidelity to the King, the trade and the Master.

In our third version of the Old Charges, the *Grand Lodge No 1 MS*, 1583, we have the first piece of new information on the admission ceremony. It is an instruction, often in Latin, sometimes in English, which appears immediately before the actual regulations, and it runs (in translation):

> Then one of the Elders shall hold out the book, and he or they shall lay their hand upon the book and the following regulations shall be read.

This was the earliest posture for the Obligation and it appears regularly in most of the later versions of the Old Charges.

There was no question of 'degrees'; the oldest documents indicate only a single ceremony, almost certainly for the Fellow-Craft, ie, the fully trained mason.

TWO DEGREES

In the early 1500s, new Statutes of Labourers in England begin to recognise the status of apprentices, and in 1598–99 we have Lodge regulations and Lodge minutes in Scotland proving that there were two degrees in practice, the first which made an apprentice into an entered-apprentice; the second for the *master* or *fellow-craft*. Inside the Lodge, Master and Fellow-craft were equal, both fully-trained men. Outside the Lodge the Fellow remained an employee and the Master, having paid the requisite fees and undertaken the responsibilities of citizenship was allowed to set up as Master, an employer.

We have no details of the actual ceremonies until the 1600s when we find a new version of the mason's Oath:

> There is sev^{r}all words & signes of a free mason to be revailed to y^u wch as y^{u}will answ: before God at the Great & terrible day of Judgm^t y^u keep Secret & not to revaile the same to any in the heares of any pson but to the M^{rs} & fellows of the said Soceity of free Masons so helpe me God, xc (*Harleian MS No 2054, c*1650. Gould, II, p 114).

'Several words & signs', plural, imply more than one degree; but they also indicate that the ceremonies were beginning to take something of their modern shape, ie, an obligation followed by the 'entrusting' with words and signs.

The oldest actual descriptions of the two ceremonies of those days appear in the *Edinburgh Register House MS*, of 1696, and its two sister texts of *c*1700 and *c*1714. In addition they each contain a catechism of fifteen or sixteen questions for the E.A., and three or four for 'the master or fellow-craft'. That was the title of the second degree in the two-degree system. [*E.M.C.* pp 31–4].

All three texts are authenticated by the 'Haughfoot fragment' of ritual, dated 1702, thereby providing the earliest trustworthy ritual texts of those days, and a yardstick by which we may judge the reliability of later documents of this kind.

A brief description of the EA ceremony may be helpful here, illustrating the style of the admission procedures. There is no mention of any preparation of the Candidate. He was made to kneel 'and after a great many ceremonies to frighten him' (horseplay?) he took up the bible, laying his right hand upon it. After he 'promised secrecie', the Oath was administered, in which he vowed that he would never reveal what he would 'hear or see at this time, whether by word nor write . . . nor draw it with the point of a sword, or any other instrument upon the snow or sand, nor . . . speak of it but with an entered mason, so help you god'.

He was taken out of the Lodge by the 'youngest mason' and (after further horseplay) he was taught the 'due guard . . . [ie] the sign, postures and words of his entrie'. He returned to the Lodge made 'a ridiculous bow' and the EA sign, and recited the 'words of entrie' which included a promise of faithful service, under penalty of having his 'tongue cut out . . . and . . . buried, within the floodmark', followed by the EA sign again.

Finally, the 'youngest mason', acting as a kind of Deacon, whispered 'the word' in the ear of his neighbour, who whispered it to the next man, and so on round the lodge until it came to the Master, who gave it to the Candidate. A biblical note indicates that the EA ceremony *was based on two pillars*. The catechism would have followed, but the answers cannot have been given by the Cand., because he had had no opportunity to learn them. The texts continue:

'But to be a master mason or ffellow craft there is more to be done . . . none suffered to stay but masters'.

There was no horseplay for the senior degree. The original oath of secrecy was administered anew and the Candidate was taken out of the lodge by the 'youngest master, to learn the postures and signes of fellowship'. Returning, he made the Master-Sign (not described) and recited the same 'words of entrie' as the EA (but omitting three words). Now, 'the youngest Master' whispered 'the word' in the ear of his neighbour, each passing it on in a 'rotational whisper' until it reached the Master.

Now the Candidate 'put himself into the posture he is to receive the word', giving a greeting to the 'Honourable Company', in the kind of wording he would use when visiting another Lodge. Then, without details of the 'posture', which will appear later:

> . . . the master gives him 'the word' and gripes his hand after the masons way which is all that is to be done to make him a perfect mason'.

All three texts describe their second degree with the same brevity, *omitting any mention of the actual 'word(s)'* or any description of 'the sign(s)'. *Only 'the postures' are described in detail in the F.C's catechism.* They are the oldest version of the Points of Fellowship and they are important.

Q 1. 'Are you a fellow craft. Ans. Yes
Q 2. How many points of fellowship are ther. Ans. fyve. viz. foot to foot, Knee to Kn[ee] Heart to Heart, Hand to Hand and ear to ear. Then make the sign of fellowship and shake hand and you will be acknowledged a true mason.

These scanty details from the senior degree of the two-degree system are the starting-point for our study of what later became the third degree. *There is no legend of any kind, nor any indication as to the meaning of the 'Points', or their purpose.* Apparently they were simply the posture in which the 'word(s)' were communicated. Despite the brevity of these texts, obviously compiled as *aide-memoires*, it is evident that the 'Points', with the 'word' that accompanied them, formed the original core of the second degree of those days.

We have seventeen texts in all, from 1696 to 1730, most of them belonging to the two-degree system *and the Points of Fellowship appear, in better or worse detail, in fourteen of them.* This indicates widespread use, not only in Scotland but, as we shall see, in England and Ireland too, and although these earliest records of the 'Points' appear in documents belonging to the late period of operative

Masonry, there is little doubt that they came into use in the middle or late 1500s, long before we find them in our oldest ritual texts.

Among the remaining texts not yet mentioned, there are four which contain the Points of Fellowship (sometimes called 'proper' points) exactly as in the three Scottish versions cited above, still without a single word of additional information on the subject [*E.M.C.*, pp 79, 85, 105, 154.] In the following summary of the remaining texts up to 1730, we deal only with those that show new developments relevant to our study. In effect, we shall be watching the ritual as it grows.

The Sloane MS c1700. An English text, contains a new form of the oath 'without . . . Equivocation or mentall Resarvation', a lengthy catechism and a fantastic collection of modes of recognition by signs, words, grips and other tricks, some of them absurd. Then:

> Another they have called the masters word and is Mahabyn which is allways divided into two words and Standing close With their Breasts to each other the inside or Each others right Ancle Joynts the masters grip by their right hands and the top of their left hand fingers thurst close on ye small of each others Backbone and in that posture they Stand till they whisper in each others eares ye one Maha – the other repleys Byn.
> [*E.M.C.* p 48]

Here we find the earliest version of the second-degree word, *omitted from the three Scottish texts*, already clearly debased. Apparently the word was 'halved' for use as a test, the oldest example of halving in the Masonic ritual. The posture is described as though the writer was watching the procedure at a distance and did not know the precise details. The 'hand in back', variously described, appears in several later texts. The *Sloane MS* still has no hint of a third degree but some of the others are more helpful.

HINTS OF THREE DEGREES

The Trinity College, Dublin, MS 1711, an Irish text, begins with a set of eleven Q. & A., all perfectly normal, except that there are not as many as there should be, which suggests bad memory, or faulty copying. Then there is a brief catalogue of words and signs with separate details for 'Master, fellow-craftsman, and Enter-prentice'. This is clearly a hint of three degrees in practice, the first of its kind, but not to be trusted until we have Lodge minutes. I quote only the information relating to the Master:

The Masters sign is back bone, the word Matchpin . . . Squeese the Master by ye back bone, put your knee between his, & say Matchpin.

The 'Points of Fellowship' are not named, and it is obvious that the writer, ignorant of the formula, described the postures as though watching them at a distance. [*E.M.C.* p 70].

'A Mason's Examination', 1723, was the first Masonic printed exposure published in a London newspaper, *The Flying-Post or Post-Master*, 11 April 1723. It begins with several paragraphs favourable to the Craft, but the few words on ceremony are sadly incomplete. Thus, immediately after a passage relating to the EA, we find:

> After this the Word *Maughbin* is whisper'd by the youngest Mason to the next, and so on, till it comes to the Master, who whispers it to the entered Mason, who must have his Face in Due order to receive it: Then the entered Mason says what follows:
> An enter'd Mason I have been
> *Boaz* and *Jachin* I have seen:
> A Fellow I was sworn most rare,
> And know the Astler, Diamond and Square;*
> I know the Master's Part full well,
> As honest *Maughbin* will you tell.

This piece of rhyme clearly implies separate secrets for three grades, EA, Fellow, and Master.

> Then the Master says:
> If a Master-Mason you would be,
> Observe you well the *Rule of Three*;
> And what you want in Masonry,
> Thy *Mark* and *Maughbin* makes thee free.

The catechism that follows is very similar to the earliest Scottish texts, but there is a novelty:

> Q. How many Points be there in Fellowship?
> A. *Six*: Foot . . . Knee . . . Hand . . . Ear . . . Tongue . . . Heart . . .

The new sixth item, Tongue . . ., is interesting, as we shall see later. Finally, in a curious collection of modes of recognition, there is a passage enlarging on the 'back bone' theme in the *Sloane* and *Trinity College, Dublin, MSS*. [*E.M.C.* pp 71–5].

---

* Astler = Ashlar. Diamond probably means a diamond-hammer, ie an operative mason's tool.

The Whole Institutions of Free-Masons Opened, 1725, was a broadsheet printed in Dublin. A brief catechism, including unusual and mildly religious Q. & A., is followed by a passage on 'your first . . . second . . . and third word' as though referring to three grades. That is not stated, and some of the words are nonsensical. Thus:

> Your first word is J . . . and B . . . is the answer to it and Grip. . . . Your 2d word is *Magboe* and *Boe* is the answer to it, and Grip at the Wrist. Your 3d Word is *Gibboram, Esimberel* is the Answer and Grip at the Elbow, and Grip at the Rein of the Back, and then to follow with the five Points of *Free Masons* fellowship, which is Foot to Foot, Knee to Knee, Breast to Breast, Cheek to Cheek, and Hand to Back . . .

Later:

> . . . *Magboe* and *Boe* signifies Marrow in the Bone, so is our Secret to be Concealed.

The *Magboe* and *Boe* probably belong to the Maha-Byn, Matchpin and Maughbin family of words all equally debased, but now for the first time we have a supposed meaning for the words, ie, 'Marrow in the Bone'. There is no legend or explanation that might justify the suggestion that the 'Marrow' phrase is a translation, and it is generally assumed to be a mnemonic.

The final paragraph begins with a puzzling sentence:

> 'Yet for all this I want the primitive Word, I answer it was God in six Terminations, to wit I am, and *Johava* is the answer to it, and Grip at the Rein of the Back'.

The grip, in this case, seems to suggest that the Name, Johova, accompanied the F.P.O.F., but that is doubtful. The sacred Name appears in only one other English ritual text, *The Institution of Free Masons, c*1725, as follows:

> Q. Who rules & governs the Lodge & is Master of it?
> A. Iehovah, the right Pillar.

In both texts it is virtually impossible to say in which degree that name belonged. [*EMC* pp 87–8].

The Grand Mystery Laid Open, 1726, is another broadsheet of no particular interest in our study. It does not mention the 'Points of Fellowship', but it gives *six* 'Spiritual Signs' which are 'Cabalisttical', and lists them as 'Foot to Foot . . . Knee to Knee . . . Breast to

Breast, Hand to Back . . . Cheek to Cheek . . . Face to Face'. Bro Poole (*AQC* 50 p 6) described this print as 'a pure freak, with nonsensical names for anything and everything'. [*EMC* pp 97–8].

By this time, 1726, there are lodge minutes showing the three-degree system in practice in England and Scotland, though its adoption was rather slow. We have several versions of the Points of Fellowship and four different versions of the supposed 'word' that accompanied them. But we still have no indication of why they were used, and no hint of a 'legend'. Now, in 1726, we begin to find details relating to those missing items.

The Graham MS, 1726 is headed:

The Whole Institutions of Free-Masonry Opened And Proved By The Best Of Tradition And Still Some Referance To Scripture

It begins with a 'Sallutation' or greeting, followed by a catechism of some thirty Q. & A. which include much religious interpretation. Finally, a question on the 'Babbalonians' leads into *a collection of legends* relating mainly to Biblical characters.

One of them tells the story of three sons who went to their father's grave to try to discover 'the vertuable secret which this famieous preacher had'. They opened the grave, found the body 'all most consumed away' and eventually raised it 'setting ffoot to ffoot knee to knee Breast to breast Cheeck to cheeck and hand to back and cryed out help o ffather . . .'

Then, not knowing what to do they 'Laid down the dead body again', and one son said 'here is yet marow in this bone': the second said 'but a dry bone' and the third said 'it stinketh'; so *'they agreed for to give it a name as is known to free masonry to this day'*. That 'name' is not mentioned in the text, which finishes the story with a few words of purely religious interpretation [*EMC* pp 92, 93. My italics. H.C.]

Here is the earliest legend of a 'raising' within a Masonic context. The 'points of fellowship' are not so described, but this is the first text which explains that they were actually used for raising a dead body. Most interesting of all is the fact that this legend (or fragment of legend) so soon to be associated with the builder of Solomon's Temple, had no connection with him at all. The old gentleman in the grave was Father Noah and the three sons were Shem, Ham and Japhet.

The *Graham MS* does not mention two degrees or three, but one answer in his catechism speaks of those

> . . . that have obtained a trible Voice by being entered passed and raised and Conformed by 3 severall Lodges . . . [*op. cit.*, pp 90–1].

The word 'conformed' is a puzzle, but there can be no doubt about 'entered passed and raised . . . by 3 severall Lodges . . .' ie three separate ceremonies.

The 'trible voice' is mentioned again in two notes concerning 'Bazalliell' the great craftsman who built the Ark of the Covenant for the Israelites in the wilderness. He had become so famous that

> . . . the two younger brothers of the fforesaid king alboyin disired for to be instructed by him [in] his noble asiance [science] by which he wrought to which he agreed conditionally they were not to discover it without a another to themselves to make a trible voice so they entered oath and he tought them . . . [the theory and practice of] masonry . . .

Later, at the end of the same legend, but after Bazalliell's death:

> . . . the inhabitance there about did think that the secrets of masonry had been totally Lost because they were no more heard of for none knew the secrets thereof Save these two princes and they were so sworn at their entering not to discover it without another to make a trible voice . . . [op cit, pp 93–4].

The mention of secrets 'lost' by the death of one of three participants and the clearly-implied requirement of three participants before the lost secrets could be 'discovered' is a direct parallel to versions of the Hiramic legend which re-appeared in English ritual documents in 1760, thirty-four years after Thomas Graham had written them.

There is no further reference to the 'vertuable secret' in the Noah legend, but secrets are the central theme of another 'Bazalliell' note which appears in the *Graham MS*, between the two extracts concerning 'Bazalliell' quoted above.

> . . . then was masons numbered with kings and princes yet near to the death of Bazalliell he disired to be buried in the valey of Jehosephate and have cutte over him according to this diserveing [i.e. an epitaph] which was performed by these two princes and this was cutte as follows

Here Lys the flowr of masonry superiour of many other companion to a
king and to two princes a brother.
Here Lys the heart all secrets could conceall,
Here Lys the tongue that never did reveal.

[ibid., pp 93–4].

In this extract we find again an extraordinarily close parallel to a
facet of the Hiramic legend in the epitaph to 'the heart all secrets
could conceall . . . the tongue that never did reveal'. The significance
of all this material so closely allied to the themes of the Hiramic
legend, full four years before we have any details of the legend itself,
has yet to be satisfactorily explained. There is no evidence to suggest
that Thomas Graham invented the stories – they do not even have the
shape of stories, being virtually without beginning or end. A far more
plausible explanation is that he was simply collecting materials
currently available in the folk-lore of the Craft, or perhaps the
fragments of stories that had been current among masons in earlier
days.

   The Wilkinson MS c1727 was compiled or copied in 1746 or later,
but Bro Knoop and his colleagues were of the opinion that its
contents indicate that it is a copy of a lengthy E.A. catechism of
*c*1727. Here we are concerned with only one answer in the catechism:

   Q. What is the form of your Lodge?
   A. An Oblong Square
   Q. Why so?
   A. the manner of our Great Master Hiram's grave.

If that answer was in existence anywhere before 1730, it was the
first hint of a *Hiramic* legend in Craft ritual.

THE FIRST RITUAL OF THREE DEGREES

Masonry Dissected, by Samual Prichard, was published on 20
October 1730. It was a 32 page pamphlet, price six-pence, the *first
exposure of the ritual of three degrees*, and it must have caused a
sensation. There were three Prichard editions 'Printed for J.
Wilford'; a reprint in a London newspaper, *Read's Weekly Journal*;
another (in two parts) in the *Northampton Mercury*, and a pirated
pamphlet edition by J. Nichols, London, all within fourteen days!
Douglas Knoop and his colleagues, writing in 1943, mentioned thirty
numbered editions printed in England and eight in Scotland.

Prichard had been a member of a regular 'Constituted Lodge' and was probably well known to senior officers of the Grand Lodge. In his introductory pages he displayed a useful knowledge of the Craft of his own day and he left several clues proving that he had had access to a version of the Old Charges that was being copied for Lord Coleraine, Grand Master in 1727–28. Soon after that was finished, in 1728, an incident had occurred – trivial or serious, we do not know – but it turned him against the Craft and he betrayed his Obligation.

His book was condemned in Grand Lodge on 15 December 1730 'as a foolish thing not to be regarded' and he was styled 'an Imposter'; but his work was, nevertheless, incomparably superior to any of its predecessors and it became a major influence in the standardisation of English ritual during the next thirty years.

Prichard's pamphlet begins with an oath, sworn before a London magistrate, that it is 'a True and Genuine Copy in every Particular'. Then a 'Dedication . . . To the Rt. Worshipful and Honourable Fraternity . . .' followed by four pages about the Craft including a note about 'Quarterly Expenses' which may have been connected with his betrayal.

The main text is in the form of a catechism which was clearly *not* designed as a complete description of the floor-work or ritual, but for rehearsal at table after the completion of a ceremony, in order to explain or enlarge on features of special interest. Here, we begin with brief notes on his EA and FC catechisms leading up to a closer study of his 'Master's Part *Masonry Dissected: Enter'd 'Prentice's* Degree.

Ninety-two Q & A, including many that had appeared in the earlier texts, but now substantially expanded. They indicate the preparation of the candidate 'slipshod . . . bare-bended knee . . . Compass extended to my naked L . . . B . . .'. A perambulation leads to a splendid Obligation including three sets of 'penalties' for the EA, in language far superior to a similar Ob. that had appeared in the *Mystery of Free-Masonry* two months before.

There are questions on the composition of a Lodge, its Dimensions, Covering, Furniture, Jewels, Lights, Signs, Tokens and Perfect Points of Entrance. Finally the EA degree contains *two* Pillar-names, one of them 'lettered'.

The Fellow-Craft's Degree
Thirty-three Q. & A. largely composed of material that had never

appeared in any of the earlier texts. In the first few answers the candidate says that he was 'made a Fellow-Craft . . . for the sake of the Letter G', denoting Geometry. (Later it denotes the 'Grand Architect and Contriver of the Universe'.) The candidate affirms that he has 'travelled East and West' and worked 'in the Building of the Temple', going through 'the Porch' to reach 'the middle Chamber' where he saw 'Two great Pillars'. There are several questions on their dimensions, ornamentation, on the 'winding Stairs' and the door of the Chamber, where a Warden demanded the 'Sign, Token and a Word'. These are described in a note which ends with the name of one Pillar.

The Master's Degree

This, the earlier version of the Third Degree and of the Hiramic legend, consists of only thirty Questions and Answers. It is reproduced here in full:

The Master's DEGREE

Q. Are you a Master-Mason?   A. I am; try me, prove me, disprove me if you can.

Q. Where was you pass'd Master?   A. In a Perfect Lodge of Masters.

Q. What makes a Perfect Lodge of Masters?   A. Three.

Q. How came you to be pass'd Master?   A. By the Help of God, the Square and my own Industry.

Q. How was you pass'd Master?   A. From the Square to the Compass.

['From the Square to the Compass' acquires a special significance in later texts of the 1740s.]

Ex. An Enter'd 'Prentice I presume you have been.

R.   Jachin and Boaz I have seen;
A Master-Mason I was made most rare,
With Diamond, Ashler and the Square.

Ex. If a Master-Mason you would be,
You must rightly understand the Rule of Three.
And *M.B. shall make you free: * Machbenah.
And what you want in Masonry,
Shall in this Lodge be shewn to thee.

R.   Good Masonry I understand:
The Keys of all Lodges are all at my Command.

[These lines of doggerel verse closely resemble those in 'A Mason's

Examination' (on p 293 above). That text gave the word 'Maughbin'. Prichard gives the initials M.B., with the word 'Machbenah' in a marginal note. Its explanation does not appear until the final answer in the catechism.]

Ex. You're an heroick Fellow; from whence came you?   R. From the East.

Ex. Where are you a going?   R. To the West.

Ex. What are you a going to do there?   R. *To seek for that which was lost and is now found.*

Ex. *What was that which was lost and is now found?*   R. The Master-Mason's Word. [*My italics, H.C.*]

Ex. How was it lost?   R. By Three Great Knocks, or the Death of our Master Hiram.

Ex. How came he by his Death?   R. In the Building of Solomon's Temple he was Master-Mason, and at high 12 at Noon, when the Men was gone to refresh themselves as was his usual Custom, he came to survey the Works, and when he was enter'd into the Temple, there were Three Ruffians, suppos'd to be Three Fellow-Crafts, planted themselves at the Three Entrances of the Temple, and when he came out, one demanded the Master's Word of him, and he reply'd he did not receive it in such a manner, but Time and a little Patience would bring him to it: He, not satisfied with that Answer, gave him a Blow, which made him reel; he went to the other Gate, where being accosted in the same manner and making the same Reply, he received a greater Blow, and at the third his *Quietus.*

Ex. What did the Ruffians kill him with?   R. A Setting Maul, Setting Tool and Setting Beadle.

Ex. How did they dispose of him?   R. Carried him out at the West Door of the Temple, and hid him under some Rubbish till High 12 again.

Ex. What Time was that?   R. High 12 at Night, whilst the Men were at Rest.

Ex. How did they dispose of him afterwards?   R. They carried him up to the Brow of the Hill, where they made a decent Grave and buried him.

Ex. When was he miss'd?   R. The same Day.

Ex. When was he found?   R. Fifteen Days afterwards.

Ex. Who found him?   R. Fifteen Loving Brothers, by Order of King *Solomon*, went out of the West Door of the Temple, and divided themselves from Right to Left within Call of each other; and they agreed that if they did not find the Word in him or about him, the first Word should be the Master's Word; one of the Brothers being more weary than the rest, sat down to rest himself, and taking hold of a

Shrub, which came easily up, and perceiving the Ground to have been broken, he Hail'd his Brethren, and pursuing their Search found him decently buried in a handsome Grave 6 Foot East, 6 West, and 6 Foot perpendicular, and his Covering was green Moss and Turf, which surprized them; whereupon they replied, *Muscus Domus Dei Gratia*, which, according to Masonry is, *Thanks be to God, our Master has got a Mossy House*: So they cover'd him closely, and as a farther Ornament placed a Sprig of *Cassia* at the Head of his Grave, and went and acquainted King Solomon.

Ex. What did King *Solomon* say to all this? R. He order'd him to be taken up and decently buried, and that 15 Fellow-Crafts with white Gloves and Aprons should attend his Funeral [*which ought amongst Masons to be perform'd to this Day*].

Ex. How was *Hiram* rais'd? R. As all other Masons are, when they receive the Master's Word.

Ex. How is that? R. By the Five Points of Fellowship.

Ex. What are they? R. Hand to Hand[1], Foot to Foot[2], Cheek to Cheek[3], Knee to Knee[4], and Hand in Back[5].

NB *When Hiram was taken up, they took him by the Fore-fingers, and the Skin came off, which is called the Slip; the spreading the Right Hand and placing the middle Finger to the Wrist, clasping the Fore-finger and the Fourth to the Sides of the Wrist; is called the Gripe, and the Sign is placing the Thumb of the Right Hand to the Left Breast, extending the Fingers**

Ex. What's a Master-Mason nam'd. R. *Cassia* is my Name, and from a Just and Perfect Lodge I came.

Ex. Where was *Hiram* inter'd? R. In the *Sanctum Sanctorum*.

Ex. How was he brought in? R. At the West-Door of the Temple.

Q. What are the Master-Jewels? A. The Porch, Dormer and Square Pavement.

Q. Explain them. A. The Porch the Entering into the *Sanctum Sanctorum*, the Dormer the Windows or Lights within, the Square Pavement the Ground Flooring.

Ex. Give me the Master's Word.

R. Whispers him in the Ear, and supported by the Five Points of Fellowship before-mentioned, says *Machbenah*, which signifies *The Builder is smitten*.

NB *If any Working Masons are at Work, and you have a desire to distinguish Accepted Masons from the rest, take a Piece of Stone, and ask him what it smells of, he immediately replies, neither Brass, Iron, nor Steel, but of a Mason; then by asking him, how old he is, he replies above Seven, which denotes he has pass'd Master.* The End of the Master's Part.

---

* The earliest description of a Master's sign.

The new 'word' and its meaning, adopted by the searchers are interesting, and the story implies that both were approved by Solomon. It is important to emphasise that *Prichard's version of the Hiramic legend was complete in itself.* There is never any suggestion that the 'word' was to be treated as a substitute word, or that somewhere there was a lost word still to be found. This is confirmed in the Q. and A. which precede the legend.

> Ex.   What was that which was lost and is now found?
> R.   The Master-Mason's Word.

The popularity and regular reprints of Prichard's *Masonry Dissected* made it practically the 'standard work', and that brought its own penalty. No rival text could hold its own against Prichard and (apart from the 'Charge . . . to new admitted Brethren' which appeared in 1735) there is virtually no evidence of new ritual developments in Britain from 1730 to 1760, a great thirty-year gap. For further information on the ritual during that period we have to go to France. English speculative Freemasonry had been planted there in *c*1725 and it began as an elegant pastime for the nobility and gentry. In the course of the next twelve years or so, it became widely popular.

THE FRENCH EXPOSURES*

The first French exposure was published in 1737 entitled *Réception d'un Frey Maçon*. It consisted of a brief narrative of what might have been a single two-pillar French ceremony of those days. It appeared in English translation in three London newspapers in January 1738, but the contents were so far inferior to Prichard's work that they made no impact on the Craft in England.

The next French exposure was *La Réception Mystérieuse*, 1738. It began with a rather poor translation of *Masonry Dissected* followed by the *Réception d'un Frey-Maçon* (above) and other non-masonic pieces. This book adds nothing to our knowledge of the third degree, but it was the first appearance of Prichard's work in French and that formed the basis of the third degree in the best of the exposures that followed, with interesting French expansions and improvements.

In 1742, the Abbé Perau, sometime Prior of the Paris *Sorbonne*,

---

* All the French texts described here have been published, in English Translation, by the Quatuor Coronati Lodge, London, in the *Early French Exposures*. (Abbrev. *E.F.E.*)

published *le Secret des Francs-Maçons* which gave a very useful narrative description of the French initiation ceremony, the toasting routine, 'Masonic Fire' and the pleasures of the Table. But he apparently mistrusted the French version of *Masonry Dissected*, which had been published in 1738, and his notes on the MM degree are of no great value:

> 'There is, moreover, a sort of drawing [ie the floorcloth] which depicts the tomb of Hiram. The Free-Masons make a great ceremonial lamentation over the death of this Hiram . . . some believe that he was Hiram, King of Tyre . . . they believe that they shed their tears in memory of this Prince who assisted in the building of an edifice which they propose to rebuild . . .'

This is the earliest hint on the floor-cloth of the MM degree but there is no illustration. Continuing, Perau argues that the Masons are not concerned with HKT but with Hiram, the 'excellent Worker in every kind of metal work . . .'

> 'This last reception is nothing more than a ceremony: one learns practically nothing new from it . . . The Masters have no other word to distinguish them from the Fellows, they simply have a custom of embracing, by passing the arm over the shoulder . . . which is followed by the pedestal sign [ie placing the feet in the form of a square].

[*E.F.E.* pp 73–5]

The mention of floor-drawing, and the 'embracing' (probably an oblique reference to the Points of Fellowship) are the only items of interest in Perau's MM degree.

LE CATÉCHISME DES FRANCS MAÇONS, 1744

The first of the really valuable French exposures bearing on the third degree was *le Catéchisme des Francs-Maçons*, published in 1744 by a celebrated French journalist, Louis Travenol, under the pseudonym Leonard Gabanon. The book begins with a dedicatory 'Letter to the Fair Sex', saying that it was published to avenge their exclusion from the Masonic fraternity. Next, a note 'To the Reader' praising Perau's work and arguing that *the Masons do not mourn Hiram, 'the artificer in metals*, but *Adoniram or Adoram* 'who was in charge of the work of building Solomon's Temple' (I *Kings* IV, 6: I *Kings* XII, 18). He adds that there is no trace of the legend in

Scripture, but the Free-masons 'claim that it is taken from the Thalmud'. [It is not! H.C.]

Apart from the actual catechism, the main body of the book is divided into two chapters, the first under the heading 'Summary of the History of Adoniram, Architect of the Temple of Solomon'. It begins with a list of the signs, grips and words allocated to E.A's and F.Cs, to avoid the risk of paying a lower grade the wages of a higher one. 'The Master [= MM] had only a word to distinguish him . . . which was *Jehova*, but that was changed after the death of Adoniram'. This leads to the earliest French version of the Adoniram legend.

The story of the murder follows *Masonry Dissected* very closely, and the major differences in the French legend may be listed briefly as follows:

1. Prichard says Solomon sent 'Fifteen Loving Brothers' to find the body of Hiram and they, being only FC's agreed 'that if they did not find the Word in him or about him, the first Word should be the Master's Word'. *Le Catéchisme* says that Solomon ordered 'nine Masters' to find him, and that they, 'fearing that the assassins might have obtained the word from him . . ., resolved to change it'.

2. This implies that they knew *the original word*, and later items in the text support this view.

3. The word they adopted was yet another version of the same family of words already discussed above, but now it has an entirely new meaning, 'the flesh falls from the bones' (*E.F.E.* pp 85–112).

A few items of minor importance are omitted, though they had appeared in *M.D.* and in its French translation, but they do not affect the *Catéchisme* legend which is far superior to those earlier versions on which it was based.

The next chapter headed 'Reception of a Master', is a splendid *narrative description* of the French third-degree of those days. It is the first and oldest floor-work of the MM degree, all told in minute detail so that we can follow every move. There is no special preparation of the candidate; he is dressed as he pleases, wearing his Apron as a Fellow, flap-up, but he does not carry his sword. Only Master Masons may witness the ceremony. The candidate is accompanied by an Officer known as *Brother Terrible*, who will announce him and put him in the care of the Second Warden when the Lodge door is opened. Meanwhile, they wait outside.

The book also contains two splendid engravings of the floor-drawings, the earliest that had ever appeared in print. The first, '*Plan de la Loge de l'Apprenti Compagnon*', is a combined design for those two grades, EA and FC. The second is the floor-drawing of a Master's Lodge, which is illuminated by lighted candles, three in the E., three S., and three West. The details are as follows:

> A coffin, surrounded by tear-drops.
> On the coffin, a sprig of acacia and the
> word 'Jehova . . . the former word of a Master'.*

> Near the western end of the coffin, a skull and cross-bones.
> Below it, a square, its arms pointing west.
> At the east end, an open pair of compasses, its arms pointing west.
> Three zig-zag lines are drawn, showing zig-zag steps from the square to the compasses.

In readiness for the ceremony, three Brothers stand around the drawing, one in the S, one N, and one E, each of them carrying a roll of paper hidden under his coat.

The WM stands in the East, at an Altar, on which are a Holy Gospel and a small gavel. Both Wardens are in the W, facing the WM. The Orator, Treasurer and another Officer 'to keep order' are dispersed with the Brethren around the Lodge. One Brother stands inside the Lodge door and keeps guard with two swords, one held point upwards, and the other in the left hand, point down.

All having taken their places, the Master makes the Master's sign (the back of the right hand to the side of the forehead, thumb and fingers extended, forming a square, and carrying the thumb so, to the pit of the stomach) saying 'Brn, assist me to open the Lodge'. The first Warden replies 'Come Brn, to Order' and they all make the Master's sign, remaining in that position while the WM addresses the

---

* Jehova, the ineffable Name of God; in Jewish law it is the name which may never be uttered. It appears in several later floor-drawings, with its textual description as the 'former word of a master' (*Ancien Mot du Maître*). That name had appeared in two English exposures of 1725, in both cases in a context so confused that it is impossible to determine where it really belonged, or whether it was actually used. (See p 294 above).

questions alternately to the Wardens, until he announces 'Brn, the Lodge is open'. This is the oldest description of the opening of a Master's Lodge, and of the so-called Master's sign.

It would be impossible to do justice to the description of the ceremony in précis, and the text is therefore reproduced here (from *E.F.E.*, pp 101–3, but divided into paragraphs).

> *Brother terrible* knocks on the door three times three. The Grand Master replies by striking three times three with his small gavel on the Altar which is in front of him. Then the second Warden gives the Master's sign & with a profound bow to the Grand Master he opens the door & says to the Brother who knocked, "What do you want, Brother?" The other replies "It is an Apprentice Fellow Mason who desires to be made a Master". "Has he served his time?" says the second Warden. "Yes, Worshipful", replies the *Brother terrible*. Thereupon, the Warden closes the door, returns to his place, & having arrived there he goes through the same procedure as before . . . [i.e., sign and bow] & addressing the Grand Master, he says, "Very Worthy, it is an Apprentice Fellow who desires . . ." "Has he served his time, do you consider him worthy"? asks the Grand Master. "Yes, Very Worthy," replies the second Warden. "That being so, you may admit him" says the Grand Master.
>
> On these words, the second Warden repeating the sign & bow that he has already made twice before, goes & asks the Brother who is acting as Guard, for the sword that he holds in his left hand: he takes it also in his left, & with his right, smartly opens the door, presenting the point of his sword to the Candidate, & commanding him to take hold of the point in his right hand & to rest it against his left breast, holding it there until he is told to remove it. This done, he takes the Candidate's [left] hand in his right, & in this manner brings him into the Reception Chamber & leads him three times round the Lodge, beginning in the West, all the while in the same posture, except that each time they pass before the Grand Master, the Candidate drops the point of the sword & the hand of his Conductor; & with a bow, he makes the sign of a Fellow. The Grand Master & all the other Brethren reply with the Master's sign. After this the second Warden & the Candidate resume their former posture & continue their route, going through the same Ceremony at every tour.
>
> The last circuit being completed he [i.e. the Cand.] finds himself facing the Grand Master, & between the two Wardens; the second Warden returns the sword to the Brother from whom he took it, & he strikes three times three on the shoulder of the first Warden, passing his hand behind the Candidate. The first Warden asks, "what do you want, Worshipful?" He answers, "It is an Apprentice Fellow Mason who desires . . .." After

this, the first [Warden] makes the Master's sign, and addresses the Grand Master. "Very Worthy, it is an Apprentice Fellow Mason, who desires to be made Master". "Direct him to advance to me as a Master & present him to me", replies the Very Worthy.

Then the First Warden makes him do 'the double Square', which is done by placing the two heels together, toes pointing outward so that they touch the arms of the Square, which is drawn in a Master's Lodge. Then he shows him the Master's steps [la marche de Maître] which is done by travelling the distance from the Square to the Compasses; in three long equal paces, roughly in triangular form [sic]: i.e., on leaving the Square he carries the right foot forwards & slighly towards the South; the left slightly towards the North: & for the last step, he carries the right foot to that point of the Compasses which is on the South side, & follows with the left, the heels together, so that his feet again form a double-Square, this time with the Compasses.* It is necessary to add that at each step, one of the three Brethren I spoke of, who are armed with rolls of Paper, strikes him a blow on the Shoulder as he passes by.

The three steps taken, the Candidate finds himself as a result quite close to, & facing the Grand Master, who takes up his small Gavel, saying to the Candidate, "Do you promise under the same obligation you took when you became Apprentice Fellow, to guard the Master's secret against Fellows, just as you have guarded those of the Fellows against the Profane?" "Yes", says the Candidate. Upon which, the Grand Master gives him three light blows on the forehead with his Gavel, & as soon as the third blow is struck the two Wardens who have been holding him around the waist, throw him backwards so that he lies outstretched on the Coffin which is drawn on the floor: then another Brother comes up & covers his face with a Cloth which seems to be stained with blood in several different places.

This done, the first Warden claps his hands three times, & at once all the Brethren draw their swords, presenting the points towards the Candidate. They all remain a moment in this posture; the Warden claps his hands again three times, all the Brethren sheath their swords & the Grand Master approaches the Candidate, takes him by the index [finger] of the right hand, his thumb pressed to the first large [knuckle-] joint, & making what looks like an attempt to raise him, he allows it to slip through his fingers, & he utters the word *Jakhin*. After this, he takes hold of the second finger in the same fashion, & allowing it to slip as before, he says *Boz*.

---

* These curious steps were apparently unknown until they appeared in *Le Catéchisme*, and they appear in the later French texts. There is no mention of them in English practice, but there is one question in *M.D.* which suggests that they may have been used in England:

Q. How was you pass'd Master?   A. From the Square to the Compass. That is exactly how the French candidate would make his advance to the Master, travelling *from the square to the compass.*

Then he takes him by the wrist, applying his four fingers separated & bent claw-fashion at the joint of the wrist, above the palm of the other's hand, his thumb between the thumb & index [finger] of the Candidate, thus giving him the grip of a Master, & holding him thus by this claw-grip, he orders him to draw up his right leg towards his body, & bend it so that his foot can rest flat on the floor; so that his leg, from knee to foot, is as nearly as possible perpendicular. At the same moment the Grand Master places his right leg against that of the Candidate, so that the inside of his knee touches the inside of the other's, & then he tells the Candidate to pass his left hand over his [the GM's] neck, & the Grand Master, bending down, passes his own left hand around the Candidate's neck, , raising him at that moment & giving him the word *Macbenac*, which is the word of a Master. It 'signifies among the Free-Masons *the flesh falls from the bones*'. [E.F.E. p 98].

Then they remove the blood-stained cloth that covers his head, & he is told in whose memory they perform this Ceremony, & they instruct him in the principal Mysteries, & the obligations of the Mastership; by these means, he will be acknowledged amongst Masons, as a Brother who has passed through all the grades of Masonry, & who needs nothing more, except a perfect knowledge of the Catechism that follows.

Thus the ceremony ends with the recital of the legendary 'History'. The catechism which follows is continuous, ie the questions are not divided into separate groups for each grade. It deals mainly with EA and FC matters and it adds nothing new on the third degree except that the word *Macbenac* is 'lettered'.

To summarise the new material on the third degree in *Le Catéchisme*. In brief, it gives us:

1. The earliest description of the opening of a Master's Lodge, and of the Master's sign consisting of two postures.
2. A detailed description of the actual ceremony, now dramatised by the introduction of three Brethren armed with 'rolls of paper'.
3. The original Master's word 'Jehova'.
4. The 'floor-drawing'.
5. The Master's three zig-zag steps.
6. The 'claw-grip'.
7. A new meaning of the Master's word.
8. The separate legend (or History of Adoniram) recited after the actual ceremony is completed.

The last of the French exposures needed for our present study is *L'Ordre des Francs-Maçons Trahi*, published in 1745 by an unscrupulous anonymous compiler. He stole most of his material, using Perau's *Le Secret* and Travenol's *Catéchisme* for the body of his work adding only a few minor corrections. His main change in the third degree is that the Candidate is allowed to see a 'mock-candidate' raised from the 'coffin-design' before he undergoes the same raising.

The *Trahi* catechism includes interesting expansions of symbolism and there is a new block of several Q. & A. which describe a new sign that had never appeared before and 'Passwords' for Apprentices, Fellows, and Masters, with the reasons for their introduction:

Q. When a Mason finds himself in danger, what must he say & do, to call his Brethren to his aid?

A. He must put his joined hands to his head, the fingers interlaced, & say, Help, ye Children (or Sons) of the Widow.

Q. What do these words mean?

A. As the Wife of Hiram became a Widow, when her Husband was murdered; the Masons, who regard themselves as the Descendants of Hiram, call themselves the Sons (or Children) of the Widow.

Q. What is the Password of an Apprentice?

A. T. . .

Q. That of the Fellow?

A. S. . .

Q. And that of the Master?

A. R. of M. G. . .

These three Passwords are scarcely used except in France, & at Frankfurt on Main. They are in the nature of Watchwords, introduced as a surer safeguard [when dealing] with Brethren whom they do not know.

Some maintain that the Masters also demand of each other the Master's Word, which is *Mak-benak*: but if this is done, it is an error. On the contrary they avoid, as far as possible, the utterance of this Word, which is regarded to some extent as sacred. The only times they use it are, at the Reception of a Master, described above, & when they examine a Brother Visitor who has entered the Lodge in the character of a Master.

There is evidence in the 1738 records of the Portuguese Inquisition that a 'password' was already in use in a Lisbon Lodge, but the extract above was the first appearance of a trio of passwords in an exposure. The discerning reader will realise that with this new sign, words and passwords (as indeed with all the ritual matters throughout this paper) there were substantial changes still to come before and at the Union of the rival Grand Lodges. *The French texts are valuable because they reveal developments during the period 1730–1760 when we have no comparable evidence in the English documents.*

THREE DISTINCT KNOCKS, 1760

The first English exposure following the thirty-year gap, *Three Distinct Knocks*, was published in London in April 1760, with five further issues in the next two years. It claimed to expose the ritual of the rival 'Grand Lodge According to the Old Institutions', the 'Antients', which had come into existence in 1751. The title-page boasted that the author was 'Member of a Lodge in England . . .' and in a lengthy introduction he said that he had attended lodges both 'Modern' and 'Antient'. His book is concerned only with the ritual of the latter, and there are several passages in his text bitterly critical of the Craft in his day.

He speaks well of *Masonry Dissected* 'but it is not half that is used now'. He must have seen something of the French ceremony (described above) because he actually quoted details of the 'mock-candidate' in their third degree. That piece of business does not appear in *T.D.K.*

There are separate catachisms, now *with separate Obligations for all three degrees*, punctuated by a large number of explanatory *NB* notes, giving details of floor-work, or of variations in practice. '*How to open a Lodge*' is described before the EA degree; there are no openings for the FC or MM degrees.

The 'Plan of the Lodge' is now a simple oblong in chalk or charcoal. It has three ruled steps at its western end, on which the EA candidate would take only one step, the FC, two, and the MM all three. No other 'floor-drawings' are mentioned and there is no 'coffin design', and no instruction on the subject of zig-zag steps.

In the preliminaries to the Obligation, the MM candidate will be examined in the EA and FC signs and words, and will be required to give 'the password of a Master', which will qualify him to receive the MM degree. He kneels for his Ob on 'both knees bent bare', his breast and both arms 'naked', his RH on the Bible, his left holding the compass points to his R. & L. B's. The Ob now contains only one 'penalty', my B . . . sever'd in two . . . etc'.

A few more Q. & A. on the EA and FC words and signs and the Master begins the story of Hiram's murder. In this version fifteen FCs plotted to extort the Master's word, so that they might pass for Masters in other countries and 'have a Master's wages'. Twelve of them recanted but three persisted. Those three 'Ruffians' are now named (for the first time) *Jubela, Jubelo, Jubelum*. The text implies, as in the earlier French versions, that the candidate plays the part of the victim during the dramatic performance of the ceremony. One major novelty in *T.D.K.* appears when the first ruffian demanded the word, Hiram answered that

> it was not in his Power to deliver it alone, except Three together, *viz Solomon*, King of *Israel, Hiram,* King of *Tyre*; and *Hiram Abiff.*

This is the earliest note in a Craft ritual that the word could only be communicated by *three participants*, a theme closely related to the Royal Arch which had emerged in the 1740s. That provided the framework of a further ceremony in which a 'lost word' could be communicated. The earlier versions, English and French, *were complete in themselves.* Here we have the first indication that *the Craft ritual was being modified or 'tailored' to harmonise with the 'lost word' expansion of the legend*, and 'Jehova, the former word of a Master' does not appear in *T.D.K.*

At the end of the Master's account of the murder the catechism continues:

Mas. After you was thus knock'd down, what was said to you then?
Ans. He said I represented one of the greatest Men in the World, our Grand-Master *Hiram*, lying dead.

Here, the author inserts a long NB note on the weapons used by the assassins (the 24 inch gauge, the square and the setting maul); and he adds two paragraphs describing the French 'mock-candidate' procedure which, he says, is the only difference between French and English practice in this degree).

Now the Master completes his recital of the legend. The twelve FC's who recanted tell their story to King Solomon and he orders them to search for the ruffians. They divide into four groups, travelling N,S,E and W. One party arrives at the Sea of Joppa and, having sat down to rest, one of the searchers hears a 'frightful Lamentation' coming from a cleft in the rock nearby. There, the three ruffians are bemoaning their crime, each wishing he had suffered one of the EA, FC, or MM penalties rather than being concerned in the murder.

They are captured and brought before Solomon, who orders that each must suffer death by the penalty for which he had prayed. The King now sends the same twelve FC's to find the body of Hiram, telling them that,

> . . . if they could not find a Key-word in him, or about him, it was lost; for there were but Three in the World that knew it, and it can never be deliver'd without we Three are together; but now One is dead, therefore it is lost. But for the future, the first occasion'd Sign and Word that is spoke at his [Hiram's] raising, shall be his [ie the Master's Word] ever after . . .

On opening the grave 'they saw their Master lie dead' and

> They lifted up both their Hands above their Heads . . . and said, O Lord my God (which is the grand Sign of a Master-Mason).*

Later, the body is raised on the FPOF and the word (another new version) is 'Mahhabone; that is almost rotten to the bone, which is the Master's Word'.

The catechism, continuing, asks the Candidate to explain the FPOF. None of the earlier texts had ever given any kind of explanaton of the origins and meaning of the complex postures that were involved. The *T.D.K.* 'explanation' might have been truly valuable; in fact it is no more than a piece of shallow interpretation, thus:

> 1st Hand . . . I always will put forth my hand to serve a Brother . . .
> 2n. Foot . . . I will never be afraid to go a foot out of my way to serve a Brother . . .
> 3d. Knee . . . I ought never forget to pray for my Brother . . .
> 4th. B . . . . I will keep my Brother's secret as my own.
> 5th. H . . . to B . . . I will always support a Brother as far as lies in my power.

T.D.K. also contains a chart of the words and passwords up to the MM degree, in English and Hebrew, with their meanings. This chart is unique among the eighteenth century exposures. Unfortunately, the typesetter knew nothing about the Hebrew alphabet and for *Mahhabone* he set up a collection of letters and vowel-points which

---

* The same sign, accompanied by noisy stamping of feet was used as a Salutation, ie *'the Master's Clap'*

read approximately *Ma-cha-ba-ga*, which is nonsense! His explanation, however, is more informative, and is given here in full:

> This signifies rotten, or decayed almost to the Bone.
> It is the Word that is whispered in your Ear at the raising of your Master, and is never to be spoke out; for they receive it as solemn as the Name of God.

Omitting many brief chapters that are irrelevant to our present study, I have given a summary of the *T.D.K.* evidence on English developments in the third degree, which claimed to be the ritual of the 'Antients'.

J & B

In 1762 the first edition of *J & B* was published and it achieved some thirty-four editions before 1800 (including those published in Dublin, New York, Albany, Boston & Philadelphia). A large part of its opening material (relating mainly to Initiation) is borrowed from *A Master-Key to Free-Masonry*, 1760, itself a bad translation of the corresponding section of *L'Ordre des Francs-Maçons Trahi*. But the catechism, which forms the main body of *J & B*, is so close to *T.D.K.* as to imply plagiarism.

My own view is that (apart from changes made by the Moderns in the 1730s to esoteric items in the EA & FC degrees) the ritual of the rival bodies was virtually identical. Indeed, so far as the third degree is concerned, there are only two items in which they differ:

1. *J & B* omits the passage in the MM Obligation in which the candidate vows not to have 'carnal Conversation' with a Mason's womenfolk.
2. *J & B* gives *alternative* words for the MM, ie, 'Mahhabone, or, as in the Modern Lodges, MacBenack, which is the Master's Word'.

And in a later passage:

> 'Mahhabone; or in some Lodges 'Mac Benach.'

A number of new exposures began to appear in England in the 1760s, none of them adding anything of importance in the third degree. The 1770s marked the beginning of the mainstream of *speculative* interpretation and expansion of the ritual so that, by the turn of the century, the English ritual may be said to have been at its shining best.

In 1809, the first major step towards a union of the rival Grand Lodges was taken by the Moderns, and in that year the Lodge of Promulgation was created (with members representing both Antients and Moderns) to revise the ritual and procedures, and bring them to a form satisfactory to both sides. That was inevitable, and among the texts described in the preceding pages many items were changed, others re-arranged, and some were discarded.

Here our main task is to discuss the three principal problems of the third degree of those days, ie, the 'word', the legend itself, and the origin and meaning of the Points of Fellowship.

THE WORD(S)

Originally the word in the third degree was apparently its most secret element and our three earliest Scottish texts, 1696 to *c*1714 give the FPOF etc in plain detail, but the whispered word for the 'Master or fellow craft' is not given at all. The French exposures and later *T.D.K.*, 1744–60 indicate great reticence in its use:

> *Trahi*, 1745 '. . . they avoid as far as possible the utterance of this Word, regarded to some extent as sacred,'
> *T.D.K.*, 1760 '. . . never to be spoke out, for they receive it as solemn as the name of God'.

Their original language was almost certainly Hebrew with three main consonants M, B, N, interspersed with a variety of letters, C, H, K, CH. and TCH, and the resulting words are certainly not Hebrew.

Normally, the accepted English translations might have served as a clue to the correct Hebrew words, but there is such a variety of supposed 'meanings' in the several texts as to make that impossible: and if we cannot be sure of the original Hebrew, the English translations become pure guesswork. We have:

1. Rotten to the bone.
2. Marrow in the bone (in several variations).
3. The body is decayed (or rotten).
4. The flesh falls from the bones.
5. The builder is smitten.

For any of the 'bone' versions there is simply no solution. The

Hebrew word for 'bone' is 'etzem', and that does not fit with any of the eighteenth century MM words. The Hebrew 'mo-ach' means 'marrow'; the Hebrew 'muck' means 'rotten'; but I see no way in which these forms could have been embodied in the surviving MM words.

With item 5, above, we may be on safer ground. 'Boneh' in Hebrew means a builder, and the word 'ha-boneh' means 'the builder', which is very close to the version in *Three Distinct Knocks*, 1760, 'Mah-habone', and perhaps to the *Sloane MS*, which gives 'Maha-Byn', c1700. But the *Sloane* has no meaning for the word, and *T.D.K.* says it means 'almost rotten to the bone', and it cannot mean that! It is likely that 'The builder is smitten' was the accepted English translation in the 1730s, but in that case Prichard's Hebrew 'Machbenah' would be wrong. The nearest we can get to 'The builder is smitten' is 'meth haboneh' which means 'the builder is dead'.

There are two Old Testament names which closely resemble the words in question, but neither of them can be linked in any way with the debased words in the exposures, or with the Hiramic Legend:

Machbanai, who went with David when he fled from Saul, I *Chron* 12,13.
Machbenah, who appears in the genealogy of Judah. I *Chron* 2., 49.

I must emphasise, Brethren, that *we are dealing with the words in use in the eighteenth century, not those in use today*, and there seems to be no definite solution to the problems relating to the true original words. We have to accept that in one form or another they were actually in use during the eighteenth century. One conclusion may definitely be drawn from the fact that their very existence implies that *there must have been some legend, story, or explanation that would justify their use* – and that leads us to the next problem, ie the sources of the Hiramic legend.

ORIGINS OF THE HIRAMIC LEGEND

The story of the building of Solomon's Temple is told at length in *Kings* and *Chronicles* and (in more or less detail) by Josephus and later Jewish historians. But nowhere in these accounts is there any hint of the death of Hiram, the craftsman, or of his murder. Indeed, there is a Rabbinical tradition that the work on the Temple was so holy that none of the workmen died while the work was in progress. The story of Hiram's murder is pure legend, and the masons in the middle ages were certainly familiar with a number of Masonic legends, carefully preserved in the Old Charges, and probably many others, now lost.

One of the oldest, regularly repeated throughout the ages, tells how the four children of Lamech, fearing that the world would be destroyed by fire of flood, carved 'all the sciences' on two pillars, 'one which would not burn, and the other which would not drown'. These were the two earliest pillars in Craft literature. Another little gem tells how Abram went down into Egypt where he taught a worthy scholar named Euclid, who learned all the seven liberal sciences.

The Old Charges give only a few sentences to David, Solomon and his Temple, with regular mention of a mysterious character, whose name varies in almost every version, from Minus Greenatus to Aymon or Anon. The legend says that he worked at the building of the Temple, and it was he who carried the science of building into France, whence it was finally brought into England, with the help of St. Alban! But there is never a hint of anything that could have become the Hiramic legend.

The English 'miracle plays' or 'mystery plays' performed at holiday times by various guilds, were an important feature of religious education in the middle ages. They covered all sorts of subjects from Old and New Testament, but a careful search through the many texts that have survived yields nothing that could have become the basis of the Hiramic legend.

The French versions all agree that the victim was Adoniram (*Kings* VI, 14) who was 'over the tribute' (or levy) for Solomon's Temple. The same man appears as Adoram (I *Kings* XII, 18) in the reign of Solomon's son, Rehoboam, when the people rebelled against Rehoboam's extortions and stoned Adoram to death. In this respect, the French legends are on safer ground, because that murder is recorded in the Bible. *But Adoniram/Adoram had no part in the building work*; the Hebrew words describing his work mean that *he was in charge of the impressment of labourers*.

Finally there is a mass of craft-lore in the building trade, with stories or legends relating to foundation and completion-sacrifices. The latter include stories of architects immured alive in the walls of a completed building, because the owner wanted to ensure that the victim would never create a similar structure. Against this, as a possible source of the legend, we have I *Kings* VIII describing Solomon's dedication of the Temple, when 22,000 oxen and 120,000 sheep served as his completion sacrifice. Moreover, every version of the eighteenth century legend says that HA was murdered, not by Solomon, but by three fellowcrafts.

In short, the Bible, the ancient histories, the Old Charges, the 'miracle-plays' and 'completion sacrifices' are all ruled out as possible sources of the Hiramic legend. Thomas Graham's collection of stories relating to Noah, and especially to Bazalliel, may well have formed the basis on which the more familiar legend was soon developed. But, it must be emphasised that Graham's work, in 1726, was in manuscript; it had never had the wide distribution of a printed publication, and this implies that stories of this kind were probably common knowledge among masons in those days when stories and songs would have formed their main entertainment.

Prichard's 'Master's Degree' in 1730 remains the earliest version we have of the Hiramic legend, almost certainly the result of speculative treatment of stories well known in the craft. There must, indeed, have been some sort of legend or explanation in the early operative days, *when the ceremony for 'Master or fellowcraft' contained no legend, but only the five Points of Fellowship*, and the origin of the Points becomes our next subject.

ORIGINS OF THE POINTS OF FELLOWSHIP

In the course of our study we have examined eighteen texts, English, Scottish, Irish and French, that mention the Points of Fellowship. Six of the latest, from 1726 onwards, appear as part of a legend, the first relating to Noah, and later versions to Hiram the craftsman, or to Adoniram in the French versions. All six describe the actual mechanics of raising a corpse from the grave, suggesting in almost every case, that the participants were trying to obtain a secret from a dead body.

The twelve earlier documents, from 1696 onwards, that contain descriptions of the Points of Fellowship, indicate widespread usage among masons in Britain, *implying that they were strongly established in the two-degree system in operative times, long before we find them in the Edinburgh Register House MS in 1696.*

Despite substantial differences in detail, there is one characteristic that these twelve have in common; *none of them has a word of explanation as to where the Points came from, or what they meant.* Yet there must have been some sort of explanation of the curious postures that were involved, and its total omission from all our earliest texts is a major problem in our search for *the origin* of the Points.

Dealing with the same problem, Douglas Knoop, one of the greatest Masonic scholars of this century, quoted three Biblical examples of 'miraculous restoration of life', in each case by something closely resembling the Points:*

I *KINGS* XVII in which Elijah raised the son of the widow in whose house he lived : v. 21
II *KINGS IV*   in which Elisha revived the child of the Shunamite woman : v. 34
ACTS XX   in which St Paul resuscitated a young man who was taken up dead after a fall : vv. 9–10

They are all interesting, *but the second, with Elisha, gives the story in great detail.* I quote II *Kings* IV, Verse 34:

And he [Elisha] lay upon the child, and put his mouth upon his mouth, and his eyes upon his eyes, and his hands upon his hands; and he stretched himself upon the child; and the flesh of the child waxed warm.

In effect, Brother Knoop was suggesting that the Points are closely akin to what we describe nowadays as the 'Kiss of Life'. We may recall here the two early texts that give *six* Points of Fellowship instead of the usual five:

(a) 'A Mason's Examination' 1723, which adds 'tongue to tongue'.
(b) *The Grand Mystery Laid Open*, 1726, which adds 'face to face'.

Both lend useful support to the 'Kiss of Life' theory.

But Bro Knoop carried his argument a stage further, saying that these Bible stories would have developed in the sixteenth and seventeenth centuries into necromantic practices, ie the art of foretelling the future by means of communication with the dead. At this stage I have to abandon his theory. One may well imagine the kind of person who became involved in 'black magic' after reading these verses in the Old and New Testament. But I cannot accept that

---

* 'The Mason Word', the Prestonian Lecture for 1938, published by the Quatuor Coronati Lodge, London, in *The Collected Prestonian Lectures, vol one* pp 255–56.

they could have affected the whole of the mason craft during several centuries. *We are dealing with operative masonry, long before the appearance of speculative interpretation*, and my own instinct in a problem of this kind, is to look for a more practical explanation.

If the Points ever had a practical purpose, we may perhaps ignore the precise details in which they appeared in the various early versions. Regardless of the exact words, it seems highly probable that *they were taught and used originally* as a means of raising a broken body, or reviving someone who had been killed by a fall in the course of his work.

Accidents of this kind must have been common in operative times, and in searching for early documentary evidence on the subject I went back to the Schaw Statutes of 1598. That was a code of some twenty-two regulations for the management of the mason trade, addressed first to the Lodge of Edinburgh, but 'to be observed by all Master Masons within this realm'. William Schaw was Master of Works to the Crown of Scotland and Warden-General of the Mason Craft. If you can imagine a kind of Grand Master who was at the same time in charge of all the royal palaces, castles and defence works, that was William Schaw, and his regulations governed the daily life of the masons in Scotland both inside and outside the lodge.

Offenders, in most cases, were punished by fines ranging from £10 to £40 Scots money, roughly three weeks to three months wages of a trained craftsman in those days. Reg. 18 in that code was *the first official rule* on Scaffolding and it is reproduced here in modern language and spelling, word-for-word, but three obsolete terms are shown in parentheses:

> Item, that all masters, enterprisers of works, be vary careful to see their scaffolds and walkways (futegangis) surely set and placed, to the effect that through their negligence and sloth no hurt or harm (skaith) come to any persons that work at the said work, *under penalty of being forbidden* (dischargeing of them) *thereafter to work as masters having charge of any work, but they shall be subject all the rest of their days to work under or with another principal master having charge of the work.*
>
> [My italics. H.C.]

This was certainly the strictest rule in the whole code of the 1598 Statutes. *All the others could be satisfied by a fine*. But a Master, *at the peak of his career*, found guilty, after an accident of careless

Scaffolding, *was condemned for the rest of his life never to use Scaffolding again*, except *under or with another principal master.* He could not blame an underling; it was his personal responsibility.

I believe that this explains the origin and purpose of the Points, and it also solves the biggest problem of all, ie *why the twelve earliest versions of the Points are without any kind of explanation.* The masons did not need it. They learned those procedures in the normal course of their training, just as a child learns the alphabet as a preliminary to reading. The Points were simply the masons' *Kiss of Life*, at least as old as their earliest mention in the Bible itself.

12

TWO SHORT-LIVED LODGES

THE SUBJECT matter of this essay is drawn almost entirely from three important papers which were published in the Transactions of the Quatuor Coronati Lodge No 2076. They are:

(1) The Special Lodge of Promulgation 1809–11, by W. B. Hextall, *AQC* 23.
(2) The Lodge of Reconciliation 1813–16 by W. Wonnacott. *AQC* 23.
(3) The Traditioners by J. Heron Lepper. *AQC* 56.

and my essay is little more than a precis of the enduring work of these three scholars, designed to depict an important phase in our masonic history, within the space of a short lecture. I hope that the brevity of this paper will encourage the reader to study the original works, where their industry will find rich reward.

––––––––––––––

The main subject of my essay is the life and work of two lodges which played an important part in our masonic history, although their names are practically unknown. The first was the Special Lodge of Promulgation, which was warranted in October 1809, and closed down in February 1811. The second was the Lodge of Reconciliation which began its work in December 1813 and finished in May or June of 1816. The combined lives of these two lodges was barely four years, yet the effects of their work are manifest in every part of our Craft Ritual today. But the story behind these two lodges really begins some 80 years before they were brought into being.

Not long after its formation in 1717, the first Grand Lodge of England found itself troubled by the publication of the so-called

'Exposures', and by many irregular and clandestine 'makings' of masons. Grand Lodge took simple precautions at first, ordering that proper visitors' books should be kept, and that no strangers were to be admitted into their Lodges unless they were properly vouched for. This action proved wholly inadequate; the nuisance continued unabated, and drastic measures had to be taken. The full extent of those measures is not known, because they were never recorded officially, and our evidence on the subject is largely drawn from later documents; but we do know that sometime between 1730 and 1739, Grand Lodge reversed the order of certain words in the 1st and 2nd degrees. The exact date is unknown.

Unfortunately the Grand Lodge of those days did not possess the widespread powers which it has today, and although many lodges, (and perhaps the majority) loyally accepted the new 'arrangement', it is clear that several lodges, some of them quite important, refused the change, and continued to work in the old traditional manner. Bro Heron Lepper has distinguished these Lodges by the title 'The Traditioners'. *AQC*, 56.

About this time, there were still a number of independent lodges in the London area, which had never acknowledged the authority of Grand Lodge. Their membership was drawn largely from the artisan classes, with a strong Irish element; indeed they are sometimes referred to in contemporary documents as the Irish Lodges. These lodges, owing no allegiance to the Grand Lodge, naturally ignored the 'new arrangement' and continued to work their ritual in its original form.

There is no evidence of an organised opposition. On the one hand there were the lodges under the Grand Lodge with certain dissenting elements in their midst, and outside this organisation there were the unattached lodges, unrecognised by Grand Lodge, and ignoring its authority.

The oppostion (for lack of a better word) seems to have developed very gradually, but it came to a head in 1751, with the formation of a rival Grand Lodge under the title 'The Most Ancient and Hon[ble.] Society of Free and Accepted Masons', soon with ten lodges already established and numbered on its Roll. Boasting always of their strict adherence to the ancient practices, they soon became known as the 'Antients', while the senior Grand Lodge, by contrast, inevitably acquired the rather disparaging title of 'Moderns'.

Under the brilliant leadership of their Grand Secretary, Lawrence Dermott, the 'Antients' flourished and gained adherents far and wide. The rivalry between the two organisations was deep and bitter. Lodges, finding themselves neglected under the bad management of the Moderns, changed their allegiance, and some actually took out new Charters under 'Antient' authority. For the Moderns it was rather a bad time, and it was not until the accession of Lord Blayney as Grand Master, (1762), that they began to recover from their low state. In the course of the next 30 years their condition so far improved, that we find several records of Antient lodges joining up with Moderns, while others converted altogether and took out new Charters, under Modern Constitution.

Throughout this period, however, there were still several 'Modern' lodges which had continued to work in the old tradition, and it seems possible that it was from these lodges, which had so much in common with the Antients, that the first tentative moves began towards promoting a union.

Towards the end of the eighteenth century the rivalry had begun to die down, and in 1797 the first 'official' move was made, in the form of a resolution in the Antients Grand Lodge, recommending that both Grand Lodges should appoint committees to meet with a view to effecting a union.

At this time, the GM of the Antients was the Duke of Atholl with Thomas Harper as his Dep GM. Harper was Initiated in No 24 Antients in 1761. He joined the Globe Lodge in 1787 and Antiquity in 1792, both Modern, and he became Grand Steward in the Moderns Grand Lodge in 1796; all this while he held high office in the Antients Grand Lodge!

The Moderns GM was the Prince Regent (afterwards George IV), with Lord Moira as Acting Grand Master. Nothing came of this first move and in 1801–02 negotiations began again. Harper, the Antients, Dep GM, had been expelled by the Moderns because he refused to break his connection with the Antients, and it is believed that for fear of losing his high office with the Antients, he covertly used his influence to prevent the union. On 6 April 1809 another resolution was put in the 'Antients' Grand Lodge recommending a 'committee to negotiate' and Harper flatly refused it.

By now there must have been considerable pressure within the Moderns' lodges, which prompted them to take a far-reaching and important step towards a removal of the differences that had so long separated the two fraternities.

At the Quarterly Communication on 12 April 1809, the Grand Lodge of England (Moderns) resolved 'That this Grand Lodge do agree in opinion with the Committee of Charity that it is not any longer necessary to continue in Force those Measures which were resorted to in or about the year 1739 respecting irregular Masons, and do therefore enjoin the several Lodges *to revert to the ancient Land Marks of the Society*'. The Committee of Charity was the contemporary equivalent of our Board of General purposes.

The importance of this move cannot be over-estimated, because, in reverting to the ancient and traditional practices, the Moderns not only satisfied the latent opposition within their own ranks, but at one blow they were removing the principal barrier that had separated the rival fraternities for nearly 60 years.

Six months later the Acting Grand Master, the Earl of Moira, issued a Warrant (dated 26 October 1809) constituting fifteen eminent Grand Lodge Officers with other brethren into a lodge '. . . for the better carrying into effect the intention of the said Grand Lodge . . .' in the resolution of 12 April (quoted above). The lodge was to be opened at Freemasons' Hall 'for the purpose of Promulgating the Ancient Land Marks of the Society and instructing the Craft in all such matters and forms as may be necessary to be known by them in Consequence of and Obedience to the said Resolution . . . and require you to appoint days of meeting when you will give such instruction . . . in order that all Masters of Regular Lodges and such other Brethren as you may think proper, may have an opportunity of attending . . .' The warrant empowered the first members to associate others with them from time to time, and it was to continue in force until 31 December 1810, and no longer, ie, fifteen months in all.

The first meeting was held about a month later (21 November 1809). James Earnshaw was elected Master and he appointed two of his colleagues as wardens. The lodge then resolved that it should be entitled 'The Special Lodge of Promulgation' and proceeded to elect 23 additional members (consisting of 11 P Gr Wardens and Prov Gr Masters, 2 Past Masters, and 9 Masters of Lodges), among them HRH the Duke of Sussex who was at that time Rt WM of the Lodge of Antiquity No 1, with his Senior Warden, a certain Bro Bonnor.

Bonnor's inclusion in the team was very significant because the Lodge of Antiquity, though a Modern lodge, seems to have retained its original ritual unaffected by the changes that had taken place 'in or about the year 1739'.

At the next meeting (1 December 1809) Bonnor was made Secretary and the Lodge got down to its real business, which was to ascertain '. . . *what were the Ancient Landmarks which they were required to restore*'.

This question of Landmarks presented an insoluble problem, because they had never been officially defined. Lists of Landmarks suggested by some of our well known students and historians have varied in number from 25 to 54 and to this day, though we refer to the Ancient Landmarks at several important stages of the ritual, we can only hazard a guess as to what they really are.

Had the Lodge of Promulgation adhered strictly to this part of its duties, it might never have finished its labours. Fortunately, they took a more realistic view of their instructions and, at this meeting, the Grand Treasurer outlined the principal points of variation between Antient and Modern practice, and then Bonnor (a member of a Moderns lodge) gave 'an accurate description and recitation of the *Ancient Practice*' in the opening and closing in all three degrees, and 'in the mode prescribed and practiced for communicating and receiving the particular(s) secrets in those several degrees . . .' It must have been an exciting night's work, for the lodge did not close until 12.30 a.m.

We begin to see now the importance of Bonnor's inclusion in the team. Officially, he was a Modern Mason, but the minutes reveal beyond doubt that he had a wide experience of Antient ritual-practice, and it is clear that the lodge was quite ready to accept his description of the differences between the two rites.

At the third Meeting, (8 December) a number of subjects came up for discussion, among them:

Placing of the three Great Lights.
The seating of the Wardens.
Opening in the first degree.
Reading the Ancient Charges at Opening and Closing.
Preparation and admission of the Candidate.
The Ceremony of Initiation.
Calling Off and On.

All these were approved and resolved on, and 'the Lodge was closed in Ancient form'.

At the fourth meeting (13 December 1809), it was 'Resolved that Deacons (being proved on due investigation to be not only Ancient but useful and necessary Officers) be recommended'.

This was quite an innovation for the Moderns, but having at last decided on them, they did not know where to put them. The question was argued and deferred at the next meeting, but a week later two deacons were appointed and their situation in the lodge was confirmed.

About this time, those members of the lodge who were used to 'Antient' practice must have suddenly realised that they were divulging rather a lot of their 'working' to the Moderns, and the lodge resolved (on 18 December) 'We do hereby solemnly engage and obligate ourselves not to reveal improperly any of the Secrets or Mysteries, Forms or Ceremonies, of *Ancient Masonry* which have been or may hereafter be communicated unto us'.

On 22 December 1809, Bonnor outlined a 'Plan' he had prepared for promulgation of the Landmarks, Ceremonies and Forms. It was an elaborate affair based on the appointment of a 'Masonic Professor', a kind of super-preceptor, who would prepare in cypher a complete 'pandect' of the Science of Speculative Freemasonry. The cypher was to be enshrined in an Ark at Grand Lodge, to be used as a kind of Oracle, a solution to every problem, and a perpetual guide to the approved forms of Ceremonial Ritual practice. By a miracle of far-sightedness, the Lodge of Promulgation were able to envisage the dangers of the project, and, very politely, they shelved it for all time.

It would be uninteresting and even monotonous to chronicle the details and repetitions of the work done at every meeting. I have noted only a few of the more important items that came up for discussion, (in addition to those already mentioned).

The Preparation and ceremonial for the 2nd degree.

Completion of the 2nd and working of the third.

The Three Great Lights 'at the entrance'. We have no details on this point, but the minute indicates some difference from our present-day practice.

The mode of advancing to the Master, in the 1st and 2nd degrees.

The situation of the Wardens. JW in the South. (This may have been

a mild victory for the 'Moderns' because our earliest evidence suggests that both Wardens usually sat in the W.)
The Deacons and their duties, 'not as Officers but appendages'.

It was also decided that the candidate for Initiation be 'received by the JD, and after the Invocation, the SD takes charge . . . and conducts him through the ceremony of Initiation'.

On 16 February 1810, it was 'Resolved that previous to the communication of the Test of Merit of a Candidate for the Third Degree, he shall undergo an examination to prove his claim thereunto'. Apparently the Moderns had grown careless in this respect.

The Lodge also discussed the procedure of the third degree and the form of closing the Lodge in the third. On this point, they came to a resolution which is a model of tolerance and broad-mindedness

'. . . that Masters of Lodges shall be informed that such of them as may be inclined to prefer another known method of communication the S— in the Closing Ceremony will be at liberty to direct it so, if they should think proper to do so.'

It seems likely that our use of a double-word in the third degree dates from this time.

At the meeting on 16 March 1810, there was '. . . a conversation respecting the ceremony of Installation'. This was the hint of what afterwards became a major change in Modern procedure, because the Installation ceremony was virtually unknown in their practice.

Another change, perhaps the most important of all, was . . . the restoration of the pass-words to each degree, and the making of the pass-words *between* one degree and another, instead of *in* the Degree.

In the 1740s when we find our earliest documentary evidence on the pass-words they appear in 'reverse order'. In those days each PW was given at the end of the preceding ceremony, and they did not form the basis of a small intermediate ceremony as they do nowadays. This resolution was the basis of our modern practice.

The catalogue is a long one, and two things are abundantly clear. First, that every detail of ceremonial lodge-work was examined and rehearsed, revised and agreed; and if words are to be given their normal meanings, then the minutes show beyond all doubt that on every major point of difference between the Modern and the Antient workings, the Moderns were ready to give way, and adopt Antient practices!

Meetings were held frequently, at weekly and fortnightly intervals, and in addition to discussion and explanatory work, a number of demonstration meetings were arranged to enable the Masters of the Modern lodges to see the changes that were recommended.

At a demonstration meeting in January 1810, fifty Masters of town lodges were present and saw the '. . . whole Ceremony of Initiation according to Ancient Practice.' A fortnight later there was another demonstration meeting, at which a candidate answered the questions leading from the first to the second degree, was entrusted by a Past Master, and was duly passed.

At a meeting in March, a question about the admission of Atholl (ie Antient) Masons, brought a very guarded reply from the Master, but a month later he came out with a bold hint of 'the near prospect of a union with Athol Lodges which probably would lead to fraternal communication and a digested arrangement equally satisfactory to both.'

The Lodge closed down for six months during the summer, and reopened in October 1810, when it was 'Resolved that it appears to this Lodge that the ceremony of Installation of Masters of Lodges is one of the two Landmarks of the Craft and ought to be observed,' and it was decided that those members of the lodge who were Installed Masters should install the Rt WM (Earnshaw) who had never had that pleasure, '. . . and under his direction, take such measures as may appear necessary for Installing Masters of the Lodge.' It is practically certain that the term 'two Landmarks' was an error, and that the words should be 'true Landmarks'.

Three weeks later, (16 November 1809) the Installation meeting took place, and four of the members being themselves Installed Masters, retired to an adjoining room, formed a Board of Installed Masters 'according to the Ancient Constitutions of the Order' . . . and installed Earnshaw as Rt WM of Promulgation and of No 22, and then installed the two Wardens as Masters of their respective lodges.

This was the beginning of an orgy of installation ceremonies, for on 14 December, Earnshaw resigned his office pro tem, so that a Past Grand Warden (one of the elected members of the lodge) might be elected to the Chair and installed on that night. He was installed, and immediately resigned to make way for a third man, who also resigned after installation, so that Earnshaw was able to be re-elected to the Chair '. . . and the lodge was closed in the 3rd degree.'

By now the lodge's time was nearly run out, and on 28 December, Earnshaw informed a demonstration meeting that the MW Grand Master, the Prince of Wales, afterwards George IV, had graciously agreed to renew the powers of the lodge until 28 February 1811, so that they might have time to deal with this *newly-adopted ceremony.*

In January, a small committee was formed to arrange for the ceremony of installing the Acting Grand Master, the Earl of Moira, and two meetings were fixed in January for the purpose of installing Masters of London lodges, '. . . each to bring a certificate that he had served as Warden and been duly elected Master'.

About this time another petition was sent to the AGM asking for an extension of another year in the life of the lodge, but they were given only a few weeks and were requested to finish their labours by the end of March (1811).

The minutes at this point are incomplete. Another 12 Masters were installed on 15 February, and so far as we know that was the end of the Lodge of Promulgation. The minute book closes with an account of the installation of Lord Moira, at which Earnshaw acted as, or deputised for, the Grand Master, while Bonnor apparently performed the actual ceremony, he being designated 'as I. Mr', but even on this occasion three eminent Brethren managed to get themselves installed before the main event took place.

Throughout the whole period since the Grand Lodge of the Moderns had taken their momentous decision 'to revert to the ancient Land Marks', a great amount of work was going on, openly, and behind the scenes, all tending towards a happy solution of the differences which divided the two Grand Lodges.

Despite Harper's refusal (in September 1809) the Antients managed to appoint a Committee two months later (December 1809) to report on 'the propriety and practicability' of a Union, and in 1810, the Moderns' Grand Lodge made another friendly gesture, by rescinding the decree of expulsion which it had made against Harper seven years before.

In March 1810 the Atholl Committee reported very favourably '. . . that a Masonic Union on principles equal and honourable to both Grand Lodges, *and preserving inviolate the Land Marks of the*

Ancient Craft, would in the opinion of this Grand Lodge, be expedient and advantageous to both'. They were clearly determined that the Union should be on their own terms.

This resolution was sent by letter to Lord Moira, who informed the Moderns' Grand Lodge that he had conferred with the Duke of Atholl privately on the subject, and that they were both of opinion that it would be truly desirable to consolidate the two Societies under one Head. The result of this announcement was a most cordial reception of the Antients' resolution, and the Moderns then set up a committee to confer with that of the Antients. The joint committees held their first meeting on 31 July 1810 and, in the course of the next three years, drew up the 'Articles of Union', the document which is virtually the Warrant of Constitution of our present United Grand Lodge. It contains 21 articles in all, among them Article 5, which required the two Grand Masters, *'for the purpose of establishing and securing . . . perfect uniformity in all . . . Lodges . . .'* each to appoint *'Nine Worthy and expert Master Masons . . .'* to meet together as a Lodge, entitled the Lodge of Reconcilation. Article two was the famous declaration '. . . that pure Ancient Masonry consists of three degrees and no more, viz those of the Entered Apprentice, the Fellow Craft, and the Master Mason, including the Supreme Order of the Holy Royal Arch . . .'

The two groups of nine experts were instructed to meet at a suitable place, each group to open a Lodge there, in two separate rooms, according to the practice of their own Grand Lodges, and then to '. . . give and receive mutually and reciprocally the Obligations of both Fraternities . . .' deciding by lot which party should first obligate the other. The meeting took place on 7 December 1813, at the Freemason's Tavern, when the Antients took the Obligation first, and then administered their Ob to the Moderns.

The Duke of Kent and the Duke of Sussex both happened to be in the building to attend a birthday dinner to Lord Moira (Past AGM of Moderns), and they, with a great entourage of Grand Lodge Officers were then introduced, and all who had not been previously obligated, were duly obligated according to Antient form.

During December, meetings were held at about three day intervals, alternately at the Freemasons Tavern (HQ of the Moderns), and at the Crown and Anchor (the Antients). Apparently each group took charge when the meeting was at their own premises; but virtually nothing was done in the way of constructive work except to re-obligate all who offered themselves.

The members were beginning to feel that they were wasting their time, but they were tied by the Articles of Union which prevented them from undertaking their real duty until *after* the Union had actually taken place.

The great day came at last, and on 27 December 1813, the Brn of both fraternities took their places in Freemasons Hall, in such order that they were completely intermixed. The two Grand Masters, the Duke of Kent (afterwards father of Queen Victoria) and his brother, the Duke of Sussex, seated themselves in two equal chairs on each side of the 'throne'. The Act of Union was read, accepted, ratified and confirmed by the assembly, and the new United Grand Lodge of England was constituted. The Duke of Kent then announced that he had only taken the office of Grand Master of the Antient Fraternity in order to facilitate the Union which had been so happily consummated on that day, and he proposed that HRH the Duke of Sussex be elected Grand Master for the ensuing year. This was carried unanimously, and he received the homage of the united fraternity.

The arrangements and instructions for the Lodge of Reconciliation had been ill-timed and ill-prepared, and the United Grand Lodge soon realised that it was completely unable to deal with the flood of requests for guidance in the newly adopted forms of the ceremonies, because, despite the work of the Lodge of Promulgation, nothing had yet been decided *officially* by the new United Grand Lodge, which had now replaced both Antients and Moderns.

A circular was sent out from Grand Lodge on 10 January 1814, inviting lodges in the provinces to send deputations to attend the Lodge of Reconciliation, where they would learn the 'acknowledged forms', but the Lodge of Reconciliation was quite unprepared for this, and a month later the Lodge sent a unanimous resolution to the Grand Master, begging him to notify all the Lodges that they should 'continue to work as heretofore until they received further notice'.

Practically nothing was done for six months, but in August 1814, the work of displaying the ceremonies was started, and at twelve meetings in the next two months, all three degrees with the Openings and Closings, etc, were rehearsed, before deputations of the London Lodges. Meanwhile, the vast majority of the provincial Lodges remained in ignorance of the proposed new forms.

A suggestion was then made, that the Lodges meeting just outside London should team up with their nearest neighbours inside the London area, so as to learn the new work from them, and in this way a number of the near-London Lodges acquired the revised ceremonies at second-hand.

About this time, a determined opposition began – most unexpectedly – in a group of six Antient Lodges in London, who asserted that the Lodge of Reconciliation was not discharging its duties under the Articles of Union. Among many charges that were levelled, was one stating that the lodge '. . . had altered all the Ceremonies and Language of Masonry and not left one sentence standing'. This may have been an exaggeration – in the heat of argument, but the complainers raised some solid objections:

(1) That the new Ob in the 1st degree was not 'strong enough'. There are a number of early exposures which indicate that originally the Ob of the 1st deg. had contained penalties which are associated nowadays with all three ceremonies. If the Lodge of Reconciliation had altered this so that the Ob was left with only the one familiar penalty, we can readily understand why the complainers argued that the Ob was 'not strong enough'.

(2) That under the proposed new procedure, *some part of the secrets* of the second deg. were to be communicated *before* the Cand. was obligated. This probably referred to Cand's. posture when taking the Ob in the 2nd, when in fact he makes a sign which is explained to him later, as part of the entrusting.

(3) Another difficulty seems to have arisen through some ambiguity in drafting the Articles of Union, which left a doubt as to whether the mutually-obligating Brethren were to take only the MM Ob, or all three.

The Lodge of Reconciliation – with the full support of Grand Lodge, dealt very patiently and discreetly with the rebels, and after a struggle which lasted about 18 months the rebellion came to a peaceful end. Goldsworthy, their ringleader, who had been a member of the Lodge of Reconciliation, was replaced very soon after the opposition began, and a number of other Brn were chosen to fill vacancies in the Lodge membership.

Meanwhile (with the exception of the small opposition) the Lodge had practically completed its duties as regards the London Lodges, but the country Lodges were compelled, willy nilly, to continue their normal ritual practices, until they could get official training in the new forms. Another circular was sent out in January 1815 asking the provincial Lodges to send deputations to attend the weekly demonstration meetings at Freemasons Hall, but for many of them the expense and difficulties involved were far beyond their powers. A letter to Grand Lodge from one of the Lodges in Cornwall, is typical of the plight in which these country Lodges were placed.

> '. . . but as we are but a young Lodge . . . and been to a deal of expence, and was at the expence of sending a Brother to London in March last to gain instructions, and who did not receive but little or none. It cannot be expected that we can be at the expence of sending another Brother to attend the L. of Reconciliation to receive the Instructions now offered us, as it will be the means of annihilating the Lodge altogether . . .'

A number of the country Lodges, however, did send deputations, and individual members of the Lodge of Reconciliation played their part in the work, by travelling all over the country, demonstrating and explaining the changes that had been made.

At a Quarterly Communication of Grand Lodge on 23 August 1815, the Obligations in the 1st and 2nd degree were repeated, and it was resolved and ordered that they be recognised as 'the only pure and genuine Obs of these degrees . . .' and the Opening and Closing in the three degrees were also ordered to be used and practised.

On 26 February 1816, there was a special meeting of the Lodge to deal with the work of the Installation Ceremony, and at the Quarterly Communication on Wednesday, 5 June 1816, after alteration on two points in the third degree, the whole of the three degrees, (which had been fully demonstrated on 20 May) were approved and confirmed. The work of the Lodge of Reconciliation was concluded.

When we sum up the work of these two short-lived lodges, it is evident that the principal changes were made by the Lodge of Promulgation, and they were changes *that had to be made* before the Union could be brought about.

The duties of the Lodge of Reconciliation were of a less drastic nature and seem to have been concerned first with minor matters of procedure, and chiefly with the arrangements for disseminating the approved ceremonies to the post-union Lodges.

Strictly speaking, the story of their efforts to establish a uniformity of working, should end here, but there is a postscript which provides a gleam of wry humour to the whole story. When we read of the interminable rehearsals, amendments, and revisions of the ceremonies, and of their final ratification and acceptance by the United Grand Lodge, we might feel justified in believing that they were indeed settled and agreed once and for all. Yet it is a fact that all the rituals practised under Grand Lodge sanction today, Emulation, Stability, with their innumerable descendants and variants, are derived from the so-called *uniformity* which was established in 1816. (The Bristol working has retained a number of pre-union features).

The two oldest Lodges of Instruction are Stability, founded in 1817, and Emulation, 1823. Both of them assert with pride, that among their founders there were famous Preceptors, who had been members of the Lodge of Reconciliation. Their rival claims as teachers of the only authentic ritual have often been bitter, and always *without complete proof*. It is clear now that we shall never know in the fullest detail the exact forms of all the ceremonies that were approved by the United Grand Lodge.

Perhaps it is better so!

13

THE RELATIONSHIP BETWEEN THE CRAFT AND THE ROYAL ARCH

It is declared and pronounced that pure Ancient Masonry consists of three degrees, and no more, Vizt. those of the Entered Apprentice, the Fellow Craft and the Master Mason, including the Supreme Order of the Holy Royal Arch . . .

(Article II of the Articles of Union, 25 November 1813)

THIS EXTRACT FROM the Articles of Union in 1813 defined for all time *the official view* of the newly-created United Grand Lodge on the relationship between the Craft and the Royal Arch. The words were almost certainly in the nature of a formula designed to satisfy the adherents of the newly-united rival Grand Lodges, whose views on the status of the Royal Arch had differed very widely during the preceding sixty years. If doubt remained as to whether the Royal Arch was to be considered as a part of the whole rite or included with the third degree, that question was settled to some extent by a statement that appears in most of the English Royal Arch rituals. The final paragraphs of the Ceremony of Exaltation contain the familiar passage:

. . . You may, perhaps, imagine you have this day taken a Fourth Degree in Freemasonry; such, however, is not the case. It is the Master Mason's completed, for when you were raised to the Third Degree, you were informed that by the untimely death of our MHAB, the secrets of a MM were lost, and that certain substituted secrets were adopted to distinguish all MM, until time or circumstances should restore the genuine. These

335

secrets were lost for a period of nearly 500 years, and were regained in the manner which has just been described to you, somewhat in dramatic form . . .

(Quoted from the *Domatic Ritual of the Royal Arch*. This statement appears (virtually word for word) in the majority of English Royal Arch rituals, including *Aldersgate, Taylor's, Hornsey, Metropolitan, Complete, Standard, Midland* and *Sussex*. The *Oxford Ritual of Royal Arch Masonry* is a notable exception; it makes no mention of a 'Fourth Degree' and it does not claim that the Royal Arch is 'the completion' of the Third.)

For students, however, the words 'It is the Master Mason's completed' create further doubts, primarily, as to the accuracy of the statement. But let us be clear as to what we are questioning. There is no doubt as to the accuracy of the legend of the third degree, or of that which forms the principal theme of the Royal Arch; *both are legends, myths or parables*. They form what may be described as the illustrative bases of the moral teachings of the two ceremonies, and the fact that they are not historically true in no way diminishes their usefulness. Our queries arise only as to the accuracy of the various statements which purport to *define the relationship* between the two ceremonies:

A. If the Royal Arch is the completion of the third degree, are we to understand that the third degree in its present form is incomplete? If so, was it complete in say 1730, before the Royal Arch had come into existence?

B. Is it possible that there was a kind of embryo of the Royal Arch story embodied in the third degree from the very beginning?

C. Did the third degree always contain those elements of 'loss and substitution' which the Royal Arch claims to restore to us in its recovery theme? Does 'lost' in this instance really mean 'lost'?

D. What is the meaning of the word 'completed' in this particular case? Does it imply that a missing section or fragment of the third degree is supplied by the Royal Arch, or is the latter a separate story, or a sequel, which simply takes up where the third degree left off?

These, and many other questions, provide a fascinating field of study for all who are interested in the ritual of the Craft and the

Royal Arch, a study in which those two branches of ritual become entangled. Predictably, there will be more questions than answers, and possibly no definite answers at all. Yet, the search is so interesting as to be sufficient in itself, even if there are no major discoveries to reward us at the end.

Beginning, therefore, on the basis of the officially-expressed link between the Master Mason degree and the Royal Arch, we turn our attention to the third degree in its earliest stages, not merely to search for a link, but in the hope that it may prove to be a possible source as well. Indeed, since the third degree was itself a comparative novelty, belonging to the early decades of the eighteenth century, there would seem to be some justification for the hope of finding useful pointers in the Craft ritual even *before* the trigradal system came into practice.

The prime object, here, is to collect and present the evidence that may have some bearing on the problems already outlined. Our period is a very narrow one, from 1696 to the early 1760s, ie starting with the earliest documents that furnish details of Craft ritual and procedures and up to the mid-eighteenth century, when the Royal Arch had been in practice in Britain for about twenty years.

It must be emphasised that this paper is not a study of present-day ritual, either of the Craft or the RA. It is concerned only with sources and early development, and it takes no account of all the massive accretions and changes that took place both in the Craft and in the RA during more than 200 years beyond the point at which our study finishes.

EVIDENCE FROM THE TWO-DEGREE SYSTEM, 1696 TO c1714

Our earliest evidence on the evolution of the third degree begins, almost a generation before that ceremony came into practice in Britain, with a collection of three manuscript rituals often described as the 'Edinburgh Register House (or the Haughfoot) group' of texts.* Three of them are so closely related as to be virtually identical:

The Edinburgh Register House MS, dated on its endorsement, 1696.
The Chetwode Crawley MS, c1700.†
The Kevan MS of c1714.‡

---

* *EMC*, p 31.
† ibid, p 35.
‡ ibid, p 39.

They all describe the Scottish system of only two degrees, the first for the EA, and the second for the 'Master Mason or fellow-craft'. Within the Lodge they were of equal status, both fully trained men. Outside the lodge the first was an employer, the other an employee. These three texts, despite their extremely interesting contents, would have had to be rejected by responsible students, since they were written in violation of the Masons' oath. They are made valid and respectable, however, by the Haughfoot 'fragment', some five lines (twenty-nine words) in the first surviving page of the Minute book of the old lodge at Haughfoot, 1702–63. Those words are virtually identical with the corresponding portions of the three complete texts listed above and they show that the complete versions are to be trusted as representing the two-degree system that was in use in Scotland until the 1730s at least, and in some cases much later than that.

For the EA degree the Candidate was put to his knees and, after 'ceremonies to frighten him', he took up the bible and the oath was administered. He was taken out of the lodge with the 'youngest mason' who taught him the sign (or due guard) 'postures and words of entrie', which he repeated on his return, ending with the sign and a description of the penalty of those days. He was then entrusted *with two pillar words*, which had previously been communicated in a whisper all round the Lodge. The ceremony was completed with a set of fifteen questions and answers, which were probably rehearsed for the Candidate, because it is clear that he had not had time to learn them.

The ceremony for the 'master mason or fellow craft'* was a very brief affair in Scotland in those days (ie 1696 to c1714). The Candidate repeated the oath of fidelity and secrecy. He was taken out of the Lodge by the 'youngest master' and there instructed in the 'sign, posture and words of entry'. He came back, made the 'master's sign' (which is not described), repeated the 'words of entry' and gave a greeting to the master and brethren. Then the word was whispered by the 'youngest master' into the ear of his neighbour, and so on all round the lodge until it came to the master (of the Lodge) who gave it – with a grip – to the Candidate; there is a separate note which indicates that the word (not mentioned in these texts) was conferred

---

* ibid, p 7, Carr, *AQC* 63, pp 258–59.

in the course of a posture described as the 'fyve points of the fellowship'.

It should be added that all the documents mentioned hitherto are of Scottish orgin. When the English (and Irish) texts begin to make their appearance, from c1700 onwards, they are substantially in agreement with the earlier versions in many respects, so that it would be reasonably safe to say that when the first English Grand Lodge was founded in 1717, its lodges were working a two-degree system roughly similar to that described in the 'Edinburgh group' of texts.

None of the texts already mentioned gives details of the word(s) of the second degree. That information appears for the first time in the *Sloane MS* No 3329, whispered 'half in one ear, half in the other'. There is an extraordinary degree of uncertainty about the word(s) which accompanied the FPOF at this period. All the earliest known versions of the 'words', up to c1744, differ from each other and *it is quite impossible to say which, if any of them, was correct.*

It is generally believed that the word(s) were of Hebrew origin and that the difficulty of pronouncing and spelling a collection of syllables in an unknown tongue may well explain the wide variations in the surviving texts. There is also the possibility that the 'word' was not a word at all, but simply a kind of abracadabra non-word, which had a meaning among Masons, but nowhere else. There was no satisfactory explanation or interpretation of the words in any of the early texts before 1730. There is one case, however, where a kind of interpretation is given, ie 'Marrow in the Bone', as the 'significance' of the words and the same phrase appears in another instance where its purpose is not so well defined. It would be extremely difficult to decide whether the phrase is a translation or interpretation, or if it merely served as a mnemonic. For the purpose of ready identification (and because it will not be necessary to analyse them individually) we describe all the versions in this group – separately or collectively – as 'Marrow word(s)'.

If we adhere strictly – as we must – to the evidence of the texts already mentioned, there was no Hiramic legend *in the two-degree ritual* at this period. None of these early documents mentions Hiram, and there is nothing in the texts, except perhaps the actual posture of the FPOF, to suggest that some such legend or explanation existed, not necessarily Hiramic, to indicate where they came from, what they meant, or why they were used. In 1726 and 1730, we begin to find evidence relating to the FPOF and 'words' which give support to this view.

This is not intended to imply that a legend existed as part of the ritual; the texts available at this date would preclude any such conclusion. The suggestion is simply that the story, or parable, or legend, was a part of the folklore or craftlore of the Mason trade, so well known to them that even a posture, or word, or movement, relating to it would be fully understood by the participants. All this is pure speculation, however, and, in the absence of any specific evidence to justify the existence of a Hiramic legend *in the ritual* in the period 1696 to *c*1725, we must proceed on the assumption that it did not yet exist *as part of the ceremonies of that time.*

Before we proceed to summarise the implications of the two-degree documents described above, it is perhaps necessary to emphasise that within a few years after this period, when the third degree made its appearance *it was not a newly created ceremony; it was the degree of 'Master or fellow-craft', the old second degree of the two-degree system, promoted into third place by a splitting of the old first degree into two parts.* The earliest text that actually described a system of three degrees, ie Prichard's *Masonry Dissected* (*EMC*, p 157) of 1730, shows these details very precisely. It also shows that by this time all three degrees had acquired additional materials, notably the 'Winding Staircase' etc, in the second degree and the Hiramic legend in the third. But two of the essential elements of the 1730 third degree (the FPOF and the 'Marrow words') were clearly from the original second degree of the two-degree system.

To sum up the evidence from the earliest texts of the two-degree system:

(a) The senior degree of the two-degree system contained the Points of Fellowship accompanied by a word or words.
(b) The *Sloane MS* of *c*1700 is the first text that gives details of the word(s) and all the later documents in which those word(s) appear confirm that, despite wide variations in spelling and pronunciation, they fall into the category of 'Marrow words'.
(c) Until *c*1730, there is no trace of a Hiramic legend *in the ritual*; there is no hint of tragedy, or of any loss sustained as a result of the drama and there is no mention of the temporary adoption of any substituted materials 'until time or circumstances might

restore the genuine'. The idea of 'subsequent restoration' was a much later addition to the legend.

In due course we shall find that the words which accompanied the FPOF in the eighteenth century were adopted, or prescribed, in place of *the original Master's word* which was for some reason 'lost', unknown, or unutterable. Here, our only interest in the ritual that later became the third degree is the hope that we may find evidence on its relationship with the Royal Arch.

OTHER RITUAL DOCUMENTS OF THE PERIOD c1710 TO 1730

Apart from the documents already discussed, the remaining ritual texts (catechisms and exposures) of the period 1696 to 1730 are a curiously mixed bag. None of them can compare with the three texts of the 'Edinburgh group' as attempted descriptions of the whole ritual or procedures of the contemporary ceremonies. They are still mainly in the form of Question and Answer, but they usually have the appearance of incomplete collections of notes. Each in turn furnishes evidence of expansions in the two-degree ritual and several of them add interesting and important items of information which have a bearing on the evolution of the trigradal system. In the necessarily brief summary that follows, we shall deal only with points relevant to the present enquiry.

The *Dumfries No 4 MS,* *c1710, is unusual because it begins with a version of the Old Charges, not normally found in connection with ritual documents of the kind under discussion. It mentions Solomon, H.K.T., and 'Hiram . . . master masson of all ye buildings & builders of ye temple . . .' but it contains no hint of what subsequently became the Hiramic legend.

The *Trinity College, Dublin, MS,*† endorsed 1711, begins with a set of eleven questions and answers (almost certainly a fault, since we already have three complete sets of fifteen Q. & A. in the 'Edinburgh group' of texts). Then, instead of continuing, as one might expect, with a description of the ceremonies, this text gives a brief catalogue of the Freemason's words and signs, and this is the earliest text that provides *modes of recognition for three separate grades*, 'Enterpren-

---

* *EMC*, p 50.
† ibid, p 69.

tice', 'fellow craftsman' and 'Master'. For the latter the text describes a posture which must surely be the world's worst description of the FPOF and it gives the word which is supposed to have accompanied the 'posture'. Once more, there is no hint of legend, drama, loss, or substitution, etc, etc. The important point about this text is that its modes of recognition for three separate grades make it the earliest hint of a trigradal system, and it is valuable in showing essential materials originally in the second degree of the two-degree system, now appearing in what may be an embryo of the system of three degrees.

'A Mason's Examination'* is the title given nowadays to the first *printed* exposure, which appeared in a London newspaper, the *Flying Post*, in 1723. It contains a considerably expanded catechism, but its description of only one ceremony is so confused as to be quite worthless. It gives six POF, which now include 'tongue to tongue', and describes a posture, which may be related to the FPOF. There is no hint of a Hiramic legend or anything resembling it and its principal interest as regards our present study is that it contains several lines of doggerel verse in which there is a threefold division of the Mason's supposed secrets and another new version of the Master's word.

The Grand Mystery of Free-Masons Discover'd† is a printed pamphlet first published in 1724. It contains a lengthy catechism without any description of ceremonies. Only one question concerns us in our present study:

Q. How many proper Points?

and the answer is a version of the FPOF. But there is no hint of any word that accompanies it, or of any other details relating to the legend of HA or the third degree.

The Institution of Free Masons,‡ c1725, is a manuscript version of the same text and the FPOF details noted above are identical in both versions. There is one question however, common to both, in which the answers are different:

* *EMC*, p 71.
† *EMC*, p 79.
‡ *EMC*, p 84.

Q. Who rules & governs the Lodge & is master of it?

The Grand Mystery . . ., 1724	*The Institution of Free Masons*, c1725
A. *Irah* + or the Right Pillar *Iachin*	Iehovah the right Pillar

Although the point seems irrelevant at this stage, this is the first appearance of the 'Ineffable Name', Iehovah, in any of these ritual documents.

The Whole Institution of Free-Masons Opened, 1725, is a folio broadsheet, first published in Dublin. It contains *inter alia* a 'Salutation' followed by a rather poor and defective catechism. At the end of the catechism there is a paragraph (not in the form of Q & A) dealing with 'words and the answers to them', thus:

Your 2*d* word is *Magboe* and *Boe* is the answer to it . . .
Your 3*d* Word is *Gibboram Esimberal* is the Answer . . .
. . . and then to follow with the five Points . . .

The text finishes with four paragraphs under the heading:

The Explanation of our Secrets, is as follows:

. . . *Magbo* and *Boe* signifies Marrow in the Bone, so is our Secret to be Concealed. – Tho' there is different opinions of this, yet I prove this the truest Construction. . . .
. . . Yet for all this I want the primitive Word, I answer it was God in six Terminations, to wit I am, and *Johova* is the answer to it. . . .

The 'Marrow' phrase is probably a mnemonic and we shall meet it again. The final extract brings the 'Ineffable Name' into the ritual again, once more in a somewhat confusing context. It will appear, much more clearly, in several later documents.

EARLIEST CONFERMENT OF THE 3°

At this stage, and in order to present the documentary evidence on the evolution and contents of the third degree in chronological order, we turn from the catechisms and exposures to examine the earliest records of the actual conferment of the third degree. The first of these, admittedly of a somewhat dubious character, is in the proceedings of a London musical society, *not a lodge*. The whole story of the society, though extremely interesting, is too long to be recounted here in detail; we must be content with brief extracts. The name of the society was *Philo-Musicae et Architecturae Societas Apollini* (the Apollonian Society for Lovers of Music and Architecture) and their record begins:

> On The Eighteenth Day of February [1725] This Society was Founded and Begun at the Queen's Head near Temple Barr by us the Eight Underwritten Seven of which did Belong to the Lodge at the Queen's Head in Hollis Street, and were made Masons There, in a Just and Perfect Lodge Vizt [two names with a note that they had been made Masons *in the Lodge* on 15 Dec 1724 and two more names of men who had been made Masons *in the Lodge*] . . . on 22 Dec 1724, by His Grace The Duke of Richmond, Grand Master,* who then Constituted the Lodge. Immediately after which Charles Cotton Esq was made a Mason, by the said Grand Master. . . .
>
> . . . And before We Founded This Society A Lodge was held Consisting of Masters Sufficient for that Purpose In Order to Pass Mr Papillon Ball and Mr Thomas Marshall Fellow Crafts . . . Immediately after which Vizt the 18th Day of February AD 1724 [ie 1725 new Style] the Officers of the Society were chosen. . . .

We need only follow the Masonic career of Mr Charles Cotton and the above record shows that he was regularly made a Mason in the 'mother' Lodge on 22 December 1724. He was Passed FC on 18 February 1725, *on the day the Society was founded*,† but whether that happened in the Lodge or in the Musical Society is not clear. The next minute which concerns Charles Cotton's career is in the minutes of the Society:

> The 12th day of May 1725 – Our Beloved Brothers & Directors of this Right Worshipfull Societye whose Names are here Under-written (viz)
>   Brother Charles Cotton Esqr
>   Broth^r Papillon Ball
>   Were regularly passed Masters
>   Brother F. X° Geminiani
>   Was regularly passed fellow Craft & Master
>   Brother James Murray
>   Was regularly passed Fellow Craft
>   Witness . . . (*Q.C.A.* IX, pp 41–2)

There seems little doubt that the Musical Society was 'making'

---

* Grand Master from 24 June 1724 till 27 December 1725.
† Author's italics.

Masons, passing Fellow Crafts and Passing Masters, and their minutes may be trusted as a record – albeit irregular – of the third degree being conferred in May 1725 and, by inference, conferred within a regular environment in the 'mother' Lodge at the Queen's Head in Hollis St., London, in 1724.

This view is supported by the fact that within ten months of the May date there is unbreakable evidence of the third degree in practice, in the minutes of Lodge Dumbarton Kilwinning (now No 18, SC). That Lodge was founded on 29 January 1726 and the minutes record that there were present, John Hamilton, Great Master [sic]* with seven Master Masons, six Fellows of Craft and three Entered Prentices. At the next meeting, on 25 March 1726:

> The Said day Gabriell porterfield [who appeared in the January meeting as a Fellow Craft] By unannimous Consent of the Masters, was admitted and Received a Master of the ffraternity, Who Renewed his oath and Gave in his entry money in the termes of the Constitution.
>
> (From a photostat of the original minute.)

It is necessary to emphasise that while these records are of great importance in our study of the evolution and adoption of the third degree, they give virtually no information at all as to the contents of the ceremony. Dumbarton mentions the renewal of an oath, and nothing more. One could not, indeed, expect lodge minutes, however detailed, to furnish such information, for which, whether trustworthy or not, we still have to go back to the exposures.

SUBSEQUENT DOCUMENTS

Returning now to the exposures, the *Graham MS*† 1726, is one of the most interesting of all these early texts. It begins with a catechism of some thirty Q. and A., including several of a strongly Christian character. Here, and in the later narrative part of the text, there are three extremely interesting references to 'a trible Voice'. The first of these, showing that a three-degree system was already established in England, speaks of those

> . . . that have obtained a trible Voice by being entered passed and raised and Conformed by 3 severall Lodges (ibid, pp 90–1).

---

* The Grand Lodge of Scotland was founded ten years later, in 1736.
† *EMC*, p 89.

HARRY CARR'S WORLD OF FREEMASONRY

The word 'Conformed' is a puzzle, but there can be no doubt about 'entered passed and raised . . . by 3 severall Lodges . . .'

The later references occur in the course of a legend concerning 'Bazalliell' in the reign on an unidentified 'king alboyin'. It says that 'Bazalliell' had become so famous by his building works that

> . . . the two younger brothers of the afforesaid king alboyin desired for to be instructed by him [in] his noble asiance [science] by which he wrought to which he agreed conditionally *they were not to discover it without a another to themselves to make a trible voice* so they entered oath and he tought them . . . (op. cit., p 93. My italics, H.C.).

Later, at the end of the same legend, but after Bazelliell's death:

> . . . the inhabitance there about did think that the secrets of masonry had been totally Lost because they were no more heard of for none knew the secrets therof Save these two princes and they were so sworn at their entering not to discover it without another to make a trible voice. . . . (op. cit., p 94*)

The mention of secrets 'lost' by the death of one of three participants and the clearly-implied requirement of three participants before the lost secrets could be 'discovered' is a direct parallel to much later versions of the legend of HA. The appearance of this theme in connection with 'Bazalliell' suggests very strongly that the Hiramic legend and the RA theme with which it is linked, did not come into our ritual all 'ready-made' as we have it today, but that it was only one of several streams of craft-lore that were eventually shaped and edited to form the central theme of the HA story.

Two further examples of these several streams are to be found in the *Graham MS.* Its compiler did not attempt to describe actual ceremonies. Instead, at the end of his catechism with its religious commentary, he rambled on into a collection of legends concerning various Biblical characters, each story having a kind of Masonic twist in its tail. One of them tells how three sons went to their father's grave

---

* For a more detailed study of 'The Trible Voice – A Secret Shared by Three', see 'More Light on the Royal Arch', pp 163–179.

. . . for to try if they could find anything about him ffor to Lead them to
the vertuable secret which this famieous preacher had . . . so came to the
Grave finding nothing save the dead body all most consumed away takeing
a greip at a ffinger it came away so from Joynt to Joynt so to the wrest so to
the Elbow so they R Reared up the dead body and suported it setting ffoot
to ffoot knee to knee Breast to breast Cheeck to cheeck and hand to back
and cryed out help o ffather as if they had said o father of heaven help us
now for our Earthly ffather cannot so Laid down the dead body again and
not knowing what to do – so one said here is yet marow in his bone and the
second said but a dry bone and the third said it stinketh so they agreed for
to give it a name as is known to free masonry to this day. . . . (op. cit., pp
92–3).

Here is another clear parallel to certain elements of the Hiramic
legend and, incidentally, the first description of an actual raising in a
masonic document. The 'several streams' argument becomes more
sharply pointed when we find that the man in the grave was 'father
Noah' and the three sons who raised him were 'Shem, Ham and
Japheth'.

There is no further reference to the 'vertuable secret' in the Noah
legend, but secrets are the central theme of another 'Bazalliell' note
which appears in the *Graham MS*, between the two extracts
concerning 'Bazalliell' quoted above.

. . . then was masons numbered with kings and princes yet near to the
death of Bazalliell he desired to be buried in the valey of Jehosephate and
have cutte over him according to his diserving (ie an epitaph) which was
performed by these two princes and this was cutte as follows

Here Lys the flowr of masonry superior of many other
companion to a king and to two princes a brother
Here Lys the heart all secrets could conceall
Here Lys the tongue that never did reveal

– now after his death the inhabitance . . . (op. cit., pp 93–4).

The story ends with the extract shown above, beginning 'the
inhabitance . . .'.

In this extract we find again an extraordinary close parallel to a
facet of the Hiramic legend in the epitaph to 'the heart all secrets
could conceall . . . the tongue that never did reveal'. The significance
of all this material so closely allied to the themes of the Hiramic
legend, full four years before we have any details of the legend itself,

has yet to be satisfactorily explained. There is no evidence to suggest that Thomas Graham invented the stories – they do not even have the shape of stories, being virtually without beginning or end. A far more plausible explanation is that he was simply collecting materials currently available in the folk-lore of the Craft, or perhaps the fragments of stories that had been current among masons in earlier days.

The remaining documents between 1726 and 1730 offer virtually no evidence at all on the problems under discussion.

The Grand Mystery Laid Open, 1726* contains a set of *six* 'Spiritual Signs', ie 'Face to Face' added to one of the early versions of the FPOF. It also gives a whole collection of nonsense 'words' and nothing relating to the third degree.

'A Mason's Confession'† printed in the *Scots Magazine* of March 1755–56, claims to represent a working of 1727. It details a version of '*the fellow-crafts* due guard' which is apparently a contemporary form of the FPOF but contains nothing of interest in our study.

It is perhaps appropriate, here, to insert an extract from a Masonic skit, dated c1726, which appeared as an advertisement in a newspaper of that period, under the heading 'Antediluvian Masonry', announcing a series of Lectures:

> There will likewise be a Lecture giving a particular Description of the Temple of Solomon . . .; with the whole History of the Widow's Son killed by the Blow of a Beetle, afterwards found three Foot East, three Foot West, and three Foot perpendicular . . .
>
> (Knoop, Jones and Hamer, *Early Masonic Pamphlets*, p 193.)

There is some slight doubt about the date of this item, 1726, though the learned compilers of the work from which this quotation is drawn took a great deal of trouble to check its accuracy. If the date is to be trusted this is a very early hint of the Hiramic legend in a form which suggests that it may have been *a part of the Masonic ritual* at that date. Another hint of the Hiramic legend *in ritual* appears soon afterwards.

The Wilkinson MS, c1727,‡ is a lengthy catechism which closely parallels a number of questions and answers in the Enter'd 'Prentice's

---

* *EMC*, end Edn, p 97.
† ibid, p 99.
‡ ibid, p 109.

Degree in Prichard's *Masonry Dissected* of 1730; it contains no trace of a second or third degree. But it does contain one answer which sheds the first faint light foreshadowing a Hiramic legend:

Q. What is the form of your Lodge?
A. An Oblong Square.
Q. Why so?
A. The Manner of our Great Master Hirams grave.

That is all; an oblique reference indicating that Hiram – the Master – had made his appearance in the Craft ritual and that his death was in some fashion commemorated too.

'The Mystery of Free-Masonry' was published in the *Daily Journal* on 15 August 1730 and under several different titles, as broadsides. Its appearance was noted in the Grand Lodge Minutes of 28 August 1730.

It has a version of the FPOF but no mention of a word or words that may have accompanied it. It also has a brief comment on the newly emerging third degree which probably gives a reliable impression of the slowness of its adoption:

> Note, There is not one Mason in an Hundred that will be at the Expence to pass the Master's Part, except it be for Interest. (*EMC*, p 155.)

With these exceptions its questions and answers seem to belong to the EA and FC only, and it contains no trace of legend, Hiramic or otherwise.

MASONRY DISSECTED 1730
And so we come to the peak-point of all the early English exposures, Samuel Prichard's thirty-two page octavo pamphlet, *Masonry Dissected*, which was advertised in the *Daily Journal* on 20 October 1730 and first came on sale on that day. The second edition was advertised on the very next day and the third on 31 October, three editions in twelve days. The work had also been reprinted in a London newspaper, *Read's Weekly Journal*, on 24 October and an undated pirated edition (with a mis-spelt title *Masonry Disected*) also made its appearance before the end of that month. The main reason for its success is not hard to find. It was the first exposure that claimed to give

. . . an Impartial Account of their Regular Proceedings in Initiating their

New Members in the Whole Three Degrees of Masonry. viz I. Enter'd
'Prentice, II. Fellow-Craft, III. Master . . .

For some unknown reason Prichard's work does not contain a
narrative description of the ceremonies such as we find in the
'Edinburgh' group of texts. Prichard cast the whole of his exposure in
the form of catechism, supplemented here and there by explanatory
notes under the heading 'N.B.' But even in Question and Answer he
managed to pack some useful floorwork and procedural information
into his 'Enter'd 'Prentice' Degree, eg:

Q. How did he [the J.W.] dispose of you?
A. He carried me up to the North-East Part of the Lodge, and brought me
  back again to the West and deliver'd me to the Senior Warden.

and later:

Q. What did the Master do with you?
A. He made me a Mason.
Q. How did he make you a Mason?
A. With my bare-bended Knee and Body within the Square, the Compass
  extended to my naked Left Breast, my naked Right Hand on the Holy
  Bible; there I took the Obligation (or Oath) of a Mason.

These items in the 'Enter'd 'Prentice Degree' are the more
interesting when compared with the second and third Degrees, both
of which are also in the form of catechism; but they contain nothing
of floorwork or procedure. This deficiency is not altogether
surprising. At this date, 1730, the second degree was still a novelty,
brought about by a splitting of the original EA ceremony into two
parts. Prichard's exposure demonstrates this, showing also that *his*
second degree had acquired some new features (ie materials relating
to the pillars and their dimensions, the winding stairs, the 'middle
chamber' and to the 'Letter G') that had not appeared in any of the
earlier texts.

The third degree was itself a direct result of the 'split' noted above,
which had put the original second degree up into third place.
Masonry Dissected shows quite clearly that the principal features of
the original second degree, ie the FPOF and the word which had
accompanied it (since 1696 at least) were now in the third degree; but
the main theme in this new ceremony was the Hiramic legend. This
is, indeed, the earliest known version of that legend and the two

earlier features (FPOF with the word) had been fitted neatly into the story.

It seems fairly certain that the ceremonies, in their new trigradal arrangement, were not fixed and finalised in the 1730s; on the contrary they were still in the early changing stages of development. There was no 'official' ritual and no guidance on that subject from the Grand Lodge. The private lodges, whether through ignorance or apathy, were slow to adopt the third; hence the gradual rise of Masters' Lodges which specialised in that degree, though there is no evidence that the third degree was the same ceremony in all of them. In the absence of 'official' control of ritual it would be astonishing if they were all alike.

This may explain why Prichard's *Master's Degree* (like his *Fellow Craft's Degree*) is void of floorwork and entirely in the form of catechism. The third degree begins with five simple questions and answers and then continues under the headings Ex.[amination?] and R.[esponse]. The reason for this change, which occurs in both the second and third, is not clear. It may indicate that Prichard was copying from two separate sources; another possibility is that the portions marked Ex. and R. were habitually rehearsed or recited by two other persons, not the Master and Candidate, because it is reasonably certain that the Candidate had no time (on the day of his Passing or Raising) to learn to give the answers from memory.

The following is a brief summary of the 'Master's Degree'. (It is reproduced in full on p 299 above.)

> Ex. You're an heroick Fellow; from whence came you?
> R. From the East.
> Ex. Where are you a going?
> R. To the West?
> Ex. What are you a going to do there?
> R. To seek for that which was lost and is now found.
> Ex. *What was that which was lost and is now found?*
> R. *The Master-Mason's Word.*
> Ex. How was it lost?
> R. By Three Great Knocks, or the Death of our Master *Hiram.*

In the course of the catechism that follows we get the whole of the earliest Hiramic legend, in many respects very similar to the modern version. Hiram, 'at high 12 Noon' went to 'survey the Works' and found there 'Three Ruffians, suppos'd to be Three Fellow-Crafts' at 'the Three Entrances'. One of them demanded the Master's Word', and Hiram replied that 'he did not receive it in such a manner, but *Time and a little Patience would bring him to it*'. He received a blow that made him reel, but he gave the same answer at the next gate, receiving a greater blow, and at the third gate he was slain.

The assassins hid the body until midnight and then carried it to the 'Brow of the Hill' and buried it in 'a Decent Grave'. Hiram was missed the same day and found 'Fifteen Days afterwards'.

> Ex. Who found him?
> R.   Fifteen Loving Brothers, by Order of King *Solomon*, went out of the West Door of the Temple, and divided themselves from Right to Left within Call of each other; and they agreed that if they did not find the Word in him or about him, the first Word should be the Master's Word; one of the Brothers being more weary than the rest, sat down to rest himself, and taking hold of a Shrub, which came easily up, and perceiving the Ground to have been broken, he Hail'd his Brethren, and pursuing their Search found him decently buried in a handsome Grave 6 Foot East, 6 West, and 6 Foot perpendicular, and his Covering was green Moss and Turf, which surprized them . . . So they cover'd him closely, and as a farther Ornament placed a Sprig of *Cassia* at the Head of his Grave, and went and acquainted King *Solomon*.

Solomon ordered that Hiram be decently buried, and that fifteen FC's were to attend the funeral wearing 'white Gloves and Aprons'. Hiram was raised as all Masons are 'when they receive the Master's Word' on the FPOF but when he was 'taken up by the Fore-fingers the Skin came off, which is called the Slip'. (These details of the Slip appear in a long NB note which also describes the Master's 'Gripe' and Sign.)

The last few questions refer, *inter alia*, to the Sanctum Sanctorum, the Porch, Dormer and Square Pavement, and the Master's Word, given in a whisper on the FPOF; the Word now means *The Builder is Smitten.*

I comment briefly only on those items which are of interest in our present study:

> R.   To seek for *that which was lost and is now found.*
> Ex. What was *that which was lost and is now found?*
> R.   *The Master-Mason's Word.* (Author's italics.)

This, the oldest version of the third degree, is the first that contains the legend of HA and the details relating to the Master's [MMs] Word have been neatly fitted into that legend. It is still a 'Marrow' word, making a total of five different versions of that 'word' from c1700 to 1730, all clearly debased.

Here, in the first mention (within a Masonic context) of *a lost word*, we learn that it is already found. The legend, as it unfolds later, tells how the searchers *of their own accord* decided that the first word uttered on the discovery of the body would be the Master's word and, though not so described in the text, this is the earliest indication that the word which accompanied the FPOF was a substitute word.

How are we to interpret the statement

'. . . that which was lost and is now found'?

Evidently, the intention is to confirm that the legend is complete in itself. In 1730, the Royal Arch has not yet come into existence and there is no hint of a ceremony or degree that will discover the word that 'was lost'. There is, indeed, an omission in the legend that needs to be emphasised. When the Three Ruffians demand the Master's Word from HA, there is no hint of the answer which became a kind of standard formula in later versions, ie that 'the Word was known to but three in the world and without the consent and co-operation of the other two, he neither could nor would divulge . . .'

Much has been written on the influence that Prichard's exposure exercised on the English and European ritual of his time. During the thirty years, 1730–60, it was reprinted frequently and it certainly helped to stabilise English lodge practice during those years, to such an extent that, we have no records of new ritual developments in England during those three decades except the appearance of the Charge to the Initiate which was first printed in Wm. Smith's *Pocket Companion*, of 1735. For all other ritual developments during that thirty-year gap our prime source of information is in the French Exposures.

EARLY EVIDENCE OF THE ROYAL ARCH IN PRACTICE

During the ten years or so, from 1743 onwards, there is evidence from Ireland mainly, that the Royal Arch, as a separate degree or ceremony, was already in existence, eg in a description of a St. John's Day procession in December 1743 by members of the Lodge in

Youghall. It is a somewhat cryptic reference, in *Faulkner's Dublin Journal*, 10–14 January 1743–44:

> . . . The Royal Arch carried by two excellent Masons. . . .

D'Assigny's famous reference to the Royal Arch, in his *Serious and Impartial Enquiry into the Cause of the present decay of Free-Masonry in the Kingdom of Ireland*, 1744, p 32, in which he described it as:

> . . . an organis'd body of men who have passed the chair.

There is another note in the same book which implies that the Royal Arch was also known in London, York and Dublin, though it was almost certainly not yet widely known or practised.

An entry, dated 16 April 1752, in the Minute Book of Vernon Lodge No 123, Coleraine:

> . . . At this Lodge Bro. Thos. Blair proposed Sampson Moore, A Master & Royal Arch Mason to be admitted a member of our Lodge.*

The earliest minute recording the actual conferment of the RA is in the minutes of the Lodge at Fredericksburg, Virginia, dated 22 December 1753:

> December 22d 1753. Which Night the Lodge being Assembled was
> present
>
> Right Worshipfull Simon Frazier GM
> Do   John Neilson S Wardn   of Royall
> Do   Robert Armistead Jnr. Wardn   Arch Lodge
> Transactions of the night
>   Daniel Campbell
>   Robert Halkerston   Raised to the Degree
>   Alex'r Wodron   of Royall Arch Masons
> Royal Arch Lodge being Shutt Entered Aprentices Lodge opend . . .
> (Coil, p 265).

Unfortunately, none of these documents gives any hint of the *contents* of the RA ceremony, or of any possible relationship to the Hiramic legend. They have been inserted here simply to show the evolutionary stages of the Royal Arch as a kind of background to the items in the French exposures, to which we now revert.

---

* Lepper and Crossle. *Hist. of the Grand Lodge of . . . Ireland*, Vol I, p 99.

EVIDENCE FROM THE FRENCH EXPOSURES

The stream of French texts began, somewhat inauspiciously, in 1737, with the appearance of a ten-page pamphlet under the title *Réception d'un Frey-Maçon*. It contained several items of Craft admission procedure that had not been mentioned in the earlier English texts, but its contents, which apparently belonged only to the first two degrees, were very badly confused and there was nothing in the text relating to the third degree or to our present study.

The next exposure in France was *La Réception Mystérieuse*, published in 1738. It was an avowed translation of *Masonry Dissected*, plus a plagiarised copy of the 1737 *Réception d'un Frey-Maçon*. From this time onwards we can trace the influence of Prichard's work in many of the French exposures; but there were notable expansions. The legend of HA (or Adoniram as he was usually named in the French rituals) took on a new two-part form, ie a narrative description of the ceremony, and a completely separate version of the legend also in narrative form. Within the period of our particular study there were five exposures of special interest, dated respectively 1744, 1744, 1745, 1747 and 1751.

Le Catéchisme des Francs-Maçons, 1744, by Louis Travenol, a celebrated French journalist, writing under the pen-name Leonard Gabanon, was the earliest of the French exposures to give a description of the third degree as practised in France at that time. It begins with the legend under the heading 'Summary of the History of Adoniram, Architect of the Temple of Solomon'. The story tells how Adoniram had so many workmen to pay that he could not possibly recognise them all and 'to avoid the risk of paying an Apprentice the wages of a Fellow, or a Fellow the wages of a Master' each group was to be distinguished 'by different words, signs, & grips'. There follows a description of the modes of recognition for Apprentices and for Fellows, and then:

> The Master [= MM] had only a word to distinguish him from those I have been discussing, which was *Jehova*, but that was changed after the death of Adoniram.
>
> (*The Early French Exposures*, p 96.)

The rest of the legend follows, in much greater detail than Prichard's text, but the story is quite clearly an amplified version of his work, though now entirely in narrative form. *Le Catéchisme* also contains the two earliest engravings of the 'floor-drawings'; one, a combined design for the EA and FC lodge, and the other for the Master's Lodge. The latter is a very simple picture of a coffin-lid on which is a sprig of acacia and the word Jehova, 'the former Word of a Master' (*Ancien mot du Maître*). It had appeared in two English texts of *c*1725, in a confusing context, leaving some doubt as to where they belonged or how they were used. Here we have, in *Le Catéchisme*, the first clear statement, confirmed in several later texts, that Jehova was '*the former Word of a Master . . . changed after the death of Adoniram*'.

There is another interesting change of detail in the French texts which has a bearing on this matter. In Prichard's text, the searchers resolved to adopt a Word if they failed 'to find the Word in him, or about him [HA]'. *In the French versions the searchers, nine masters, did not look for a 'Word' because (as the texts imply) they already knew it. They only resolved to change the Word out of fear that the assassins had extorted it from him.* The word that was adopted in place of Jehova was yet another 'Marrow' word, in a slightly different spelling, and it meant 'the flesh falls from the bones'.

Le Parfait Maçon was another French exposure of 1744, designed, almost certainly, to mislead the non-Masonic public who might have acquired more reliable information from some of the better publications of that class. It was a farrago of rubbish, but the book also contained a chapter on the *Ecossais* [Scots] Masons, from which the following extracts are drawn:

> Those called *Ecossais Masons* claim that they form the fourth grade. . . . Instead of weeping over the ruins of the Temple of Solomon, as their brethren do, the *Ecossais* are concerned with rebuilding it.

The writer goes on to describe how Zerubabel chose the *Ecossais* from the most expert craftsmen; they were awarded higher pay and entrusted with particular words and a sign; these are described and they are quite worthless.

There are eight questions in the Catechism, all trivial, but one of the answers speaks of

> . . . the order given by Nehemiah to all the workmen at the time of the rebuilding of the Temple, to have swords always at their sides, & their bucklers near at hand during work, for use in case of attack by their enemies. . . . (*EFE*, pp 197–79).

Here, in *Le Parfait Maçon*, we have one of the Royal Arch themes linked specifically with the 'fourth degree' of *Ecossais* [Scots] Masons.

Le Sceau Rompu, also published in 1745, has a question in its catechism relating to the adoption of the MMs Word:

Q. How was the Word recovered?
A. The Masters [engaged in the search] agreed together out of fear that the Master's word had been revealed, that the first sign . . . & the first word that would be uttered, should serve in future for Masters. (*EFE*, p 225.)

The final questions in the MM's catechism deal with the interment of Adoniram [Hiram]

Q. What was done with the body of our very worthy Master Adoniram?
A. Solomon as a reward for his zeal & his talents had him interred in the Sanctuary of the Temple.
Q. What did he order to be placed on his Tomb?
A. A gold Medal, in triangular form, on which was engraved the word JEOVA [sic]. Which is the name of God in Hebrew.

The same text in its opening chapter 'A General Impression of Masonry' dates the beginnings of Masonry back to the 'Crusader Princes' who

gave their Assemblies the name 'Lodges', in memory of the various encampments which the Israelites set up in the desert, & to recall the way in which they rebuilt their second Temple (which they did with Trowel in one hand, & Sword in the other) . . .

This may be a reference to one of the themes of the Royal Arch and the Chevalier Michael Ramsay had used almost identical words in his famous Oration in 1737. It may be noted that the *Sceau* catechism contains the earliest mention, in a Masonic context, of the 'Ineffable Name' on a triangular gold medal.

L'Ordre des Francs-Maçons Trahi. The anonymous author-compiler of this work was a shameless plagiarist and he reproduced the 'Summary of the History of Hiram, Adoniram or Adoram' almost word for word from *Le Catéchisme* with a few minor improvements. His final paragraph under this heading describes sundry variations in working and one of these items runs:

. . . Finally, there are some who hold that it was Solomon who ordained the changing of the Master's Word, while others believe that the Masters made the change without consulting him. . . . (*EFE*, pp 258–59).

The Floor-drawing for a Master's Lodge is now vastly improved, but Jehova is still the central theme, and the author adds a note that this 'former Word . . . is never used in the ceremony'. Later, he insists that even the new substituted word is very rarely used:

. . . they avoid, as far as possible, the utterance of this Word, which is regarded to some extent as sacred. The only times they use it are, at the Reception of a Master . . . & when they examine a Brother Visitor who has entered the Lodge in the character of a Master. (*EFE*, p 267).

La Désolation des Entrepreneurs Modernes . . ., 1747, was the second (and greatly enlarged) edition of *Le Catéchisme* described above. Its 'Story of Adoram' follows very closely the wording of the earlier version but the story ends with an additional sentence which is extremely interesting:

. . . They completed the exhumation of the deceased [and] recounted their adventure to Solomon, who, to honour the memory of Adoniram, caused him to be buried with great ceremony in the Temple of the true God, & had put on his Tomb *a golden Medal in the shape of a triangle upon which was engraved JEHOVAH.*

This is the second mention of a triangular gold plate, or medal, bearing the Ineffable Name.

One further item in *La Desolation* deserves mention. Travenol, the author, rejected the theory that Freemasonry was founded by the Crusaders, intending to rebuild the Temple at Jerusalem. He believed 'in accordance with the prophecy of Jesus Christ that the Temple was destroyed for all time', arguing that the Crusaders were following the example of Julian the Apostate, who had attempted the rebuilding in the fourth century AD, and that had failed too.

He also added a lengthy quotation giving an account of that event, which was the source of the vault legend in the Royal Arch. The details are extremely interesting, though not relevant in our present study on the 'Relationship between the Craft and the RA'. The quotation is reproduced in full, however, together with Samuel Lee's version from his *Orbis Miraculum.*

Le Maçon Démasqué, 1751, is the last of the French texts with

Footnote from *La Désolation des Entrepreneurs Modernes . . .*, 1747.
(From *E.F.E.*, p. 332.)

Julian, called the Apostate, because he abandoned the Christian Religion, having formed a plan to rebuild the Temple of Jerusalem, to refute the prophecy of Daniel, & that of J.C. [Jesus Christ], collected the most excellent Workmen from all parts, & gave the superintendence of this great Work to Alypius, his best friend. While working on the foundations, a stone from the first row became dislodged & uncovered the opening to a cavern hewn in the rock. A Workman was lowered, attached to a cord; & when he was in the Cavern, he felt water half-way up his legs. He explored with his hands in all directions, & upon a column which rose just above the water, he found a Book wrapped in a very fine linen. He took it & gave the signal to be drawn up. All who saw the Book were surprised that it had not been spoilt. But the astonishment was even greater, particularly among the Pagans & Jews, when having opened it, they read, first of all, in large Letters, the words, *In the beginning was the Word, & the Word was with God*: & the rest, because this was the complete Gospel of St. John. Later, terrible balls of flame coming from the foundations, made the place inaccessible, having several times scorched the Workmen: so, as this element [fire] continually repulsed them, the enterprise was abandoned. These are the words of Ammian Marcellin.[1] a Pagan Historian of that period, who was as much an enemy of Christians, as an admirer of Julian. *Hist. Eccl. de M. Fleury*. Book 4 Cap. 15.

[1] He lived *c.*330–390 A.D.

Extract from *Orbis Miraculum*, 1659, p. 370.

. . . When the foundations were a laying, as I have said, there was a stone among the rest, to which the bottom of the foundation was fastned, that slipt from its place, and discovered the mouth of a cave therein that had been cut in the rock. Now when they could not see to the bottom by reason of its depth; the Overseers of the building being desirous to have certain knowledge of the [sic] they tied a long rope to one of the Labourers, and let him down: He being come to the bottom, found water in it, that took him up to the mid-ancles, and searching every part of that hollow place, he found it to be four square, as far as he could conjecture by feeling. Then returning toward the mouth of it, he hit upon a certain little pillar, not much higher then the water, and lighting with his hand upon it, found a book lying there wrapped up in a piece of thin and clean linnen. Having taken it into his hands, he signified by the rope that they should draw him up. When he was pulled up, he shews the book, which struck them with admiration, especialy seeming so fresh and untoucht as it did, being found in so dark and obscure a hole. The Book being unfolded, did amaze not onely the Jews, but the Grecians also, holding forth even at the beginning of it in great Letters (*In the beginning was the Word, and the Word was with God, and the Word was God.*) To speak plainly, that Scripture did manifestly contain the whole Gospel, which the Divine tongue of the Virgin Disciple had declared. This, together with the other miracles, which at that time were proclaimed from Heaven, did demonstrate, that not any word of our Lord should fall to the ground, which had foretold the utter desolation both of City and Temple.

For the truth of this story, I am not bound to undertake: yet this I may safely say, that the main substance thereof concerning the miraculous fire, causing the work to cease is true, being attested by grave and sober Authors that lived not far from the times wherein it was acted.

---

which we are presently concerned, although its contents are in general accord with the best of its predecessors, it is not a slavish copy of any of them. Indeed, its whole style is that of a new writer taking a fresh view of the details and procedures.

In the discovery of the corpse of Adoniram, we read:

As this word was the first they spoke, they seized upon it eagerly for the word of a Master, & it was substituted in place of JEHOVA which had been in use until then. . . . upon his tombstone was engraved the former word, surmounted by two crossed branches of acacia. . . . (*EFE*, p 455).

Later, the Orator explains details of the Floor-Drawing [or Tracing Board]:

> You notice a Hebrew name whose significance should be known to you, it was formerly reserved for the Masters of the ancient Lodge, but ignorance of what occurred at the tragic end of Adoniram prevented the brethren from preserving it after his death, & they preferred to bury it with him, rather than expose themselves to the risk of using a word that was known to fellows, & perhaps to the Profane. These initials [M.B.] placed on the head of the Tomb indicate to you that which your Worthy Masters have adopted, your ears have heard it, & my tongue fears to profane it by repeating it. (*EFE*, p 456).

The best of the French exposures have been quoted here, and they show that the sacred Name (which had appeared in uncertain context in *c*1724–25 in English ritual texts) had become 'the former Word of a Master' in the French third degree, and it appeared regularly in their catechisms and 'Floor-drawings', always described as the 'former Word of a Master'.

In 1760, when the new system of English rituals began, the Ineffable Name *had completely disappeared from English Craft usage*, and in 1760–65 there is good evidence that the Name with the 'triangular plate' had become an important feature of the Royal Arch.

THREE DISTINCT KNOCKS, 1760, AND LATER

A new stream of English exposures began to appear in 1760, starting with *Three Distinct Knocks*, which claimed to represent Antients' practice. The English Craft ceremonies had expanded very considerably by this time in every way, ie in catechism, procedure, legend, etc, and there are clear traces of English practices which exhibit French influence – though it would be difficult to say who was copying whom.

Hiram's three assassins are now named and it is in *Three Distinct Knocks* that we find the first version *in the ritual* of the legend which says that those 'secrets were known to but three in the world' and that without the consent and cooperation of the other two, etc, etc. I quote from 'The Master's Part', only those passages that may be relevant to our present study:

So *Hiram* came to the East Door, and *Jubela* demanded the Master's Word: He told him he did not receive it in such a Manner; but he must wait, and Time and a little Patience would bring him to it, for *it was not in his Power to deliver it alone, except Three together*, viz. *Solomon*, King of *Israel; Hiram*, King of *Tyre*; and *Hiram Abiff*. . . . (op. cit., pp 57–58).

At a later stage in this version of the legend King Solomon ordered

. . . those 12 Crafts to raise their Master *Hiram*, in order that he might be interred in the *Sanctum Sanctorum*. And *Solomon* told them, that if they could not find a Key-word in him, or about him, it was lost; *for there were but Three in the World that knew it, and it never can be deliver'd without we Three are together*; but now One is dead, therefore it is lost. But for the future, the first occasion'd Sign and Word that is spoke at his raising, shall be his ever after . . . (ibid p 61).

In 1762, *J & B* representing the ritual of the Moderns, repeated these statements almost word for word, and so too with later texts. It is quite certain that in the English third degree of the 1760s, it was already established that the secret (which Hiram Abif had died to protect) was a secret known only to three, who could only communicate it in the presence and with the participation of all three.

But the whole idea of a threefold sharing of the secret was an invention. There had never been a time in the two or three-degree system when the secrets had been shared or communicated in this way. In all surviving versions of the Hiramic legend, a substitute Word had been adopted in place of the 'lost Word', and the ceremony was complete in itself. None of those early versions gives the faintest hint of another degree or ceremony which would reveal the secrets that were 'lost'.

In effect, the Royal Arch had borrowed, or transferred, or invented materials that would provide for a sequel or completion degree to follow on after the Hiramic legend, and the extracts from *Three Distinct Knocks* etc, quoted here, show that the Craft ritual had been 'tailored' to confirm this.

ACCRETIONS AND CHANGES

In the course of collecting the documentary evidence that could demonstrate the relationship between the Craft third degree and the Royal Arch, we have, within the period 1696 to *c*1760, compiled what is virtually a history of the third degree in England. We have examined the elements in the two-degree system from which it arose; we have noticed the two streams (at least) of Craft-lore which may have laid the pattern for the Hiramic legend. We have examined the earliest printed version of that legend, forming the basis of 'The Master's Part' in a trigradal system, and we have seen how widely Prichard's version was accepted in France (and western Europe) where it was expanded and developed, both in the details of the legend and in the actual performance of the ceremony. It should be emphasised, moreover, that when dealing with the printed esposures, ie documents of dubious origin, the extent to which they are accepted by other and later writers is often the best guide as to the reliance that may be placed on them.

Throughout all this material there is never a hint that *the completion* of the legend (or degree) is still to come at a later stage. The 'lost Word' is lost, or incommunicable, or better still, known and set apart; but the legend and ceremony are complete in themselves, with the adoption of the substitute word as the finale to the story and there is never the hint of a missing 'Part 2' or 'sequel' or 'completion'.

Unfortunately there is no comparable collection of documents for the study of the evolution of the Royal Arch, On the evidence that is available it would be impossible to prove the existence of the ceremony before c1740. There are no *early* printed Royal Arch exposures or rituals. The earliest Royal Arch *ritual* materials that exist today consist of a collection of manuscript texts which, in expert opinion, belong to the 1780s and later. (See 'English Royal Arch MS. Rituals c1780–c1830' by Bro J. M. Hamill, *AQC* 85).

It would not be practicable here to discuss the contents of the Royal Arch ceremony as revealed in the late eighteenth century documents, nor is that necessary, because we are primarily concerned with only two points:

(a) The evidence that bears on its relationship with the third degree;
(b) the accuracy of the statement that it is the *completion* of the third degree.

As to relationship with the third degree, or with the Craft ritual in general, there are two topics on which there is a close and demonstrable link. The first of these is the Ineffable Name.

THE INEFFABLE NAME

The *Oxford English Dictionary* gives two sets of definitions for the word 'ineffable' that are applicable in a Masonic context:

1. That cannot be expressed or described in language; too great for words; transcending expression; unspeakable, inexpressible.
2. That must not be uttered; not to be disclosed or made known (obsolete).

The Name is the Tetragrammaton, the word of four Hebrew letters, Yod, Hé, Vav, Hé, usually rendered Y H W H or J H V H and it is pronounced (by those who are permitted to do so) as Yahweh or Jehovah.

Even within the brief range of definitions quoted above, 'the Name' has enormous implications since it is supposed to express, within itself, those attributes of God which are beyond verbal expression, too great for words. For all whose faith is bound up in the VSL (Old and New Testaments) 'The Name' always had the mysterious quality of representing an idea of the Deity beyond human powers of description. For the Jews, however, 'the Name' is ineffable in a still wider sense because it is forbidden to be uttered – even in prayer – except by the Priests in course of the Priestly Benediction. For all others of the Ancient Faith, when the 'Name' appears in the Prayer Book, or in Holy Writ, a substitute word is used and the Ineffable Name is read as Adonai (= The Lord).

The Sacred Name had certainly appeared in two of our early ritual texts in 1725 and c1725, and at that time it had apparently never been used as a 'Word' or a 'Password'. If it had been so used, we would almost certainly have found it in one or other of the remaining pre-1725 texts that have survived. This suggests that these two documents represent only a purely local version.

In the 1740s we find the Name again in a whole series of French rituals, as 'the former Word of a Master', but *if it was the 'former Word'*, there are no surviving rituals to show whether or how it was communicated. Nor is there any explanation of its total removal from the Craft degrees and its transfer into the Royal Arch, where it came under the direct control of the Three Principals. There can be no doubt, however, that the Ineffable Name was one of the links between the earlier Craft degrees and the Royal Arch.

THE SECRET SHARED BY THREE

This is the second close link between Craft ritual and the Royal Arch. The details have been given in our examination of the *Graham MS* 1726, and later texts of the 1760s. Although those texts discuss the 'sharing' as though it was actual practice, *there is positively no evidence in any of our Craft documents of any secrets actually being shared in the manner suggested.* That practice first came into use in the Royal Arch.

THE QUESTIONS

Nothing that has been said here is intended to deny or decry the status and value of the Royal Arch and its teachings. There are some who will aver that it is the highest and best of our degrees, and that would always be a matter of opinion. But here, our only concern is whether or not the Royal Arch is historically a part of the original 'family' of two degrees, which became three, in or around 1725–30. If not, to try to determine the precise relationship. For the reader's convenience, the questions that were raised at the beginning of this paper are posed again, with the answers.

A. If the RA is the completion of the third degree, are we to understand that the third degree in its present form is incomplete? If so, was it complete in say 1730, before the RA had come into existence?

Ans: The RA is not the completion of the third degree. The earliest third degree, *Masonry Dissected*, 1730, was complete in itself. The later French versions in the 1740s added 'floor-work' and other details, and they too were complete. *All of them accepted the 'substituted word' as the end of the story,* without any hint of a further degree that would reveal the missing word.

The third degree deals with Solomon's Temple, with events and people of approx. 1000 BC The return of the Israelites from Babylon was c538 BC ie about 460 years later. The attempted rebuilding of the Temple under the Emperor Julian (which gave rise to the vault legend) was about 820 years later still, in c360 AD. On these details, there is no basis for arguing that the RA is the completion of the third degree; it is a totally separate story, artificially linked to the third degree by the addition of a few words in the Hiramic legend.

B. Is it possible that there was a kind of embryo of the RA story embodied in the third degree from the very beginning?

Ans: When the RA came into existence in *c*1740, the compilers of their ritual adopted the Ineffable Name, which may have been in use in some Craft workings, though that is not certain. They also adopted the 'Secret shared by three' which had first appeared in the *Graham MS*, 1726; but there is no evidence that any such three-fold practice was ever used in the Craft. To claim that these two items form a 'kind of embryo' of the Royal Arch would be a misleading exaggeration.

C. Did the third degree always contain those elements of 'loss and substitution' which the RA claims to restore to us in its recovery theme? Does 'lost' in this instance really mean lost?

Ans: In our three earliest Scottish texts, 1696–*c*1714, there was no legend and no details of loss and substitution. The word was given on the FPOF in a whisper, but those three texts do not mention the word. Several later two-degree texts (still without legend) do mention the word, always what we might call a 'substitute word'. This suggests that the substitute word *may have been used from the beginning*, ie that was the original word.

From 1730 onwards all our complete texts contain the Hiramic legend and they have the 'loss and substitution' theme. From 1760 onwards they all say that the secret was known only to three, etc. The French texts suggest that the lost word may have been the Ineffable Name. If that was true, there seems to be no doubt that *it was taken out of Craft usage*, perhaps because of the sanctity attached to it. I suggest *it was not lost but set apart*, later *to be embodied in the Royal Arch with strict rules governing its use*. The 'three participants' theme was the source of the well-known passage '. . . without the consent and cooperation of the other two . . .'. Then the Royal Arch, with three entirely different characters, provided the means by which the so-called lost secret (which was never really lost) could be retrieved and given its peculiar place in that ceremony.

D. What is the meaning of the word 'completed' in this particular case? Does it imply that a missing section or fragment of the third degree is supplied by the Royal Arch, or is the latter a separate story, or a sequel, which simply takes up where the third degree left off?

Ans: The answer to question A, above, shows that the Royal Arch deals with events some 460 years after the building of Solomon's Temple. Those events are in no way related to the third degree or the Hiramic legend. All the principal characters are different and the whole story is played against the background of the vault legend, which can be dated about 820 years later still.

The RA cannot be correctly described as the completion of the third degree. Nor is it a sequel, which means the continuation or resumption of a story. I believe the Royal Arch is an extension of the spiritual teachings of the third degree, designed for the Brethren who enjoy their Masonry and are eager to explore further.

Finally, I am convinced that the Royal Arch was an addition to the Craft ceremonies which was specially designed to provide a separate grade for men who had occupied the Chair of a Craft Lodge. This view is widely accepted as the original purpose of the Royal Arch and we find supporting evidence for this in Ireland, in 1744, (vide D'Assigny) and in numerous English minutes concerned with the 'Passing the Chair' ceremony. When the compilers of the RA were shaping a ceremony that would carry the Installed Master (or Past Master) into a wider Masonic sphere, they based their work primarily on the 'vault and discovery legend' which had formed a well known theme of ecclesiastical history in the writings of the early Fathers of the Christian Church. Only a few modifications were needed. The 'little pillar' in the vault (or cave) became an altar. The Gospel of St John, which was 'discovered' in the original (Christian) vault legend, was altered to Genesis I, vv 1–3, and the Ineffable Name, which had no place in that legend, was added, to become one of the major themes in the Royal Arch ceremony.

14

THE OBLIGATION AND ITS PLACE IN THE RITUAL

DURING THE 600 years or so of recorded Masonic history in Britain our Craft ceremonies have grown from their original nucleus, first to two degrees and then to three. They have been expanded and rearranged, embellished, revised and standardised. Yet, despite all the changes that have taken place in the character of the Craft, its objects and its practices, one element has remained throughout as the very crux of the ceremonies – the Obligation. Indeed, the first hint we have in the Craft of something even remotely resembling a ceremony is a reference to the oath or Obligation.

Our study of the Masonic ritual begins, of necessity, with the appearance in 1696, of a whole series of documents, generally described as catechisms or exposures, many of high importance, and some that are only good in parts, but all of them interesting. For the study of the Obligation, however, we are more fortunate, because we have a remarkable collection of *MS Constitutions* or Old Charges from c1390 onwards. They were the oldest rule-books of the mason trade and most of them give details of the brief Obligations in use during the early years of Craft organisation in England, Obligations which were the direct ancestors of the far more elaborate versions in use today.

The *Regius MS* c1390 is the oldest surviving version of the Old Charges and the first that mentions the oath as the essential element in a mason's admission ceremony. But it does not give the actual words of the oath:

> A good true oath he must there swear
> To his master and fellows that be there
> He must be steadfast and true also
> To all these laws, where'er he go
> And to his liege lord the King
> To be true to him above everything.

And all these points, herein before,
To all of them thou must be sworn,
And all shall swear the same oath
Of the masons, be they willing, be they loath,
To all these points . . .

(In modern English).

The oath, of course, related to the 'Charges' or regulations, ie the fifteen 'Articles' and fifteen 'Points' listed in detail in the *Regius MS*. The Articles generally referred to trade matters; the Points were mainly concerned with the prospective mason, as a guide to his duties and responsibilities. The *Cooke MS, c*1410, contained a similar but shorter code, with no mention of an oath, simply a note that

. . . new men that were never charged before
[shall] be charged in this manner . . .

The earliest document that describes how the oath was administered is the *Grand Lodge No 1 MS*, 1583 our third oldest version. It contains an instruction which appears in most of the later versions, usually in Latin, sometimes in English. It begins, *Tunc unus ex Senioribus* . . ., and is given here in English translation:

Then one of the Elders shall hold the book and he or they [that are to be admitted] shall place their hand on the book and the following charges shall be read.

Precise words vary in later texts (and spelling is dreadful) but this is their general tenor, a simple description of the candidate's posture, hand on Book, while the Charges were read, followed by the oath. If we may judge by the unanimity of so many texts on this point, there is little doubt that the admission ceremony was as brief as the words imply. *The Grand Lodge No 1 MS* also gives the actual words of the oath:

These Charges that wee haue nowe rehearsed vnto you all and all others that belong to masons yee shall keepe so healpe you god and your hallydome, And by this booke in yor hande unto yor power.

Amen   So be it

The Obligations in the Old Charges gradually become longer, not because they give any new information, but because of the comprehensive precautions to ensure secrecy, and occasionally we find a phrase that has somehow survived in our modern ritual:

These charges that you have Received you shall well and truly keepe, not discloseing the Secrecy of our Lodge to man, woman, nor child, Stick nor stone, thing moueable or immoueable: so God you helpe and his holy Doome, Amen.

*(Buchanan MS, c*1670)

Or a fuller version:

These Charges wch wee now rehearse to you, and all other the Charges, Secrets and Mysteries belonging to Free-Masonry, you shall faithfully and truely keep together with the Councel of this Lodge or Chamber. You shall not for any Gift, Bribe or Reward, favour or affection, directly or Indirectly, for any Cause whatsoever divulge or disclose to either Father or Mother, Sister or Brother, Wife, Child, friend, Relation or Stranger or any other prson whatsoever. So help you God your Holy doom and the Contents of this Book

(Harris No 1 MS, 2nd half 17th cent.)

The early versions of the Old Charges indicate only a single admission ceremony and they never say whether it was for the apprentice, fellow, or master. That is a problem. Available evidence suggests, very strongly, that in the days of only 'one degree' it must have been for the fellow of craft, ie the fully trained mason. During two centuries up to the mid-1500s there are ample legal decisions showing that an apprentice was the chattel of his master. He was not really free during the years of his indentures. He belonged to his master, who was responsible for his board, lodging and instruction, and under those conditions he cannot have had any status in the lodge.

In 1563 the Statute of Labourers began to recognise the status of apprentices and, around that time, we would expect to find records of their admission into lodges as 'entered-apprentice'. Unfortunately, there are no early lodge records in England that would confirm this, but we have ample records in Scotland. First, the *Schaw Statutes*, a magnificent code of regulations issued on 28 December 1598 by William Schaw, Master of Works to the Crown of Scotland and Warden-General of the Mason Craft. They were addressed to the Lodge of Edinburgh, but 'to be observed by all master masons within this realm'. Among the twenty-two regulations there were rules for the 'booking' of apprentices at the beginning of their indentures, and for their admission into the Lodge as 'entered-apprentice'. There were also rules governing their admission as 'fallow in craft'. Later Edinburgh minutes show that apprentices were usually admitted 'entered-apprentice' after they had served the first three years of their indentures. They generally became fellow-craft some two or three years after the end of their indentures, working during those extra years 'for meat and fee', ie food and wages.

In addition, from 1598 onwards, we have the minutes of two Scottish Lodges (Aitchison's Haven, and Edinburgh) proving the two-degree system in use; but we still have no information on the contents of the ceremonies beyond the 'posture' and the Obligations described in the Old Charges.

Then, in c1670, we find a valuable piece of English evidence, a new form of the masons's Obligation in the handwriting of Randle Holme III, member of a famous family of Chester Freemasons. It was found on a scrap of paper in a volume of MSS, containing the *Harleian MS, No 2054*, a version of the Old Charges also written by him. It runs:

> There is seu^{r}all words & signes of a free Mason to be revailed to y^u wch as y^u will answ: before God at the Great & terrible day of Judgm^t y^u keep Secret & not to revaile the same to any in the heares of any pson but to the M^{rs} & fellows of the said Society of free Masons so helpe me God   xc

This was the first mention of secret 'words & signes' plural, implying more than one degree, but it also indicates that the ceremonies were beginning to take on something of their modern shape, ie, an Obligation followed by the communication of secret modes of recognition. But there are still no details of the ritual or 'secrets' of those days.

In 1904 an interesting two-degree manuscript ritual was discovered and named the *Chetwode Crawley MS*, in honour of a distinguished Irish historian. Its true importance was not realised because of over-cautious students had dated it c1720, a date which greatly diminished its value; it is now dated c1700. In 1930, a sister-text dated 1696 was discovered in the Old Register House, Edinburgh. It is now entitled *The Edinburgh Register House MS*, and the date, 1696, is confirmed by the experts. Finally, a third version was discovered in 1954, now known as the *Kevan MS, c1714*.

All three texts describe the same two ceremonies, but they were not copied from each other; they differ in arrangement, spelling and in certain details, and the *Kevan* has several faults. Their trustworthiness, however, has been validated by the 'Haughfoot fragment' (See *AQC* 63, pp 259–60) and jointly they confirm that this was the ritual practised in the south of Scotland in 1696, and probably during the preceding hundred years. They were obviously compiled as aide-mémoires, and their description of the ceremonies is important in our present study because they reveal material expansions of the Obligation and our earliest information on the penalties.

The EA candidate was put 'upon his knees and after a great many ceremonies to frighten him' he took up the Bible . . . laying his right hand on it'. He was exhorted to secrecy under threat of 'damnation and murder' and after he had 'promised secrecie' he repeated the oath:

> By god himself and you shall answer to god when you shall stand nakd before him, at the great day, you shall not reveal any pairt of what you shall hear or see at this time whither by word nor write nor put it in wryte at any time nor draw it with the point of a sword, or any other instrument upon the snow or sand nor shall you speak of it but with an entered mason, so help you god
>
> (*The Edinburgh Register House MS*, 1696)

After the oath, he was taken out of the lodge by the 'youngest mason' acting as a kind of Deacon. Outside, he was taught the sign, postures and 'words of his entrie', a kind of greeting to the Brethren which was followed by a promise of loyal service to the master and the lodge, under a penalty comprising 'tongue . . . chin . . . throat . . . and flood-mark (all embodied in the 'sign' which was repeated several times.)

The 'entrusting' is not described in any of these three texts, but they all contain Biblical notes indicating that the EA degree was based on two pillars. The ceremony was followed by a catechism of fifteen Q & A which must have been answered for the candidate, because he had not had time to learn the answers.

The second degree 'for master-mason or fellow-craft' was very brief. There was no horseplay. The candidate, on his knees, repeated the 'oath anew' and was taken out of the lodge by the 'youngest master'. Outside, he learned the 'master-sign', posture and words of entry. He returned to the lodge, recited the words of entry, and, in a posture described as the 'fyve . . . points of fellowship' he received a whispered word. Note, these Scottish texts do not describe the

master-sign, nor do they give the 'word'. A few test questions relating
to rank, and that was all.

The *Sloane MS. c*1700, is the next in our series of ritual documents,
now in the British Library. It is headed 'A Narrative of the
Freemasons Word and Signes' and contains a fantastic collection of
signs, grips, phrases and odd tricks by which to recognise a mason. It
contains a catechism including several Q and A that had appeared in
the Scottish texts, and a curious posture reminiscent of the Points of
Fellowship. It also gives the earliest known version of the word
belonging to that posture, but it does not describe a whole ceremony,
and it seems to be a collection of ill-recorded fragments. The
Obligation does not mention a penalty though there is one in the
catechism. The oath runs:

> The mason word and everything therein contained you shall keep secrett
> you shall never put it in writing directly or Indirectly you shall keep all that
> we or your attenders shall bid you keep secret from Man, Woman or Child
> Stock or Stone and never reveal it but to a brother or in a Lodge of
> Freemasons and truly observe the Charges in ye Constitucion all this you
> promise and swere faithfully to keep and observe without any manner of
> Equivocation or mentall Resarvation directly or Indirectly so help you god
> and by the Contents of this book.
> So he kisses the book &c.

The catechism, Q.3 runs:

> Q. which is the first signe or token
>   shew me the first and I will shew you the second
> A. the first is heal and Conceal or Conceal and keep secrett by no less
>   paine than cutting my tongue from my throat

*The Dumfries No 4 MS, c*1710 is our next text, in chronological
order. It begins as a fairly late version of the Old Charges, including
many of the compiler's own 'improvements' and it has a simple oath
of secrecy, without penatly:

> The Charges wᶜ now w[e] Rehearse to you wt all othe[r] Charges & secrets
> otherways belonging to free masons or any that enter their interest for
> curiositie together wt the counsels of this holy ludge chamber or hall you
> shal not for any gift bribe or Reward favouer or affection directly or
> [in]directly nor for any cause Qtsoever devulge disclose ye same to ether

father or mother sister or brother or children or stranger or any person Qtsoever so help you God.

Later, and after the Charges (at a point where a normal version would finish) the compiler has added a mass of new material, including *inter alia*, a ritual catechism of some forty Q & A, a salutation, another block of 'Questions Concerning the Temple' displaying his religious zeal, and much that is irrelevant here. The ritual catechism contains several items that imply *penalties that were not in the Obligation*, but presumably formed part of the ritual that followed.

Q. whay a rop[e] about your neck
A. to hang me If I should Betr[a]y may trust . . .
Q. what punishment is inflicted on these y^t reveals ye secret
A. y^r heart is to be taken out alive y^r head to be cut of & y^r bodys to be buried in ye sea mark & not in any place Q^r christians are buried.

The Trinity College, Dublin MS, 1711, is a catechism of only eleven Q and A followed by signs etc for EA, FC, and MM. It has neither Obligation nor penalty, but the text is headed 'Under no less a penalty'.

A Mason's Examination, 1723, was the first printed exposure, published in *The Flying Post or Postmaster*, 11–13 April 1723. It begins with several paragraphs in praise of the 'Ancient Fraternity' and rails at 'the mean Wretches' who aim 'to bring this Worshipful Society into Contempt. . .'. In a confused description of the ceremony, '*he swears to reveal no Secrets . . . on Pain of having his Throat cut*, and having a double Portion of Hell and Damnation hereafter'. The full text of the Obligation is not given, but there is another reference to the penalty in the catechism:

Q. What is the first Point of your Entrance?
A. Hear and conceal, on Pain of having my Throat cut, or Tongue pull'd out.

These extracts perhaps imply that *the penalties were actually recited in the Obligation itself.*

THE INTRODUCTION OF PENALTIES
The documents under discussion are all interesting, especially when we recognise words and phrases that have survived in our ritual to

this day. But here we are only concerned with the Obligations, and with the appearance and development of the penalties. There are two points of special interest:

1. In the earlier forms of the Obligations in the Old Charges there was a steadily growing emphasis on secrecy, but no hint of penalties.

2. When the penalties began to appear in the late 1600s and early 1700s, we do not find them in the Obligations, but in the ritual procedures following the oath (as we see in the 'Edinburgh Group' of texts, and in several later versions).

By this time (ie the 1720s), more than 300 years since the beginning of mason trade organisation in England, there is no doubt that the mason lodges contained a fair proportion of non-operative members. Evidence is scanty, and it would be very difficult to determine whether the appearance of the penalties *in the Obligations* was a purely natural development, or whether they were introduced as special precautions because of the changing membership.

The Grand Mystery Of Free-Masons Discover'd, 1724 was also a printed exposure, with a Preface deriding the Craft. There is no attempt to describe a ceremony and its forty-five Q and A contain a number of new questions which suggest a new or separate stream of ritual. The very brief oath is without penalty, and the only mention of penalty in this text is in the answer to a 'Point of Entrance' question, where both Q & A are almost word for word identical with that quoted under the *Mason's Examination*, above. I give the oath here only because it is the first version that contains a promise to 'help and assist any Brother as far as your Ability will allow':

The Free-Mason's Oath.

You must serve God according to the best of your Knowledge and Institution, and be a true Leige Man to the King, and help and assist any Brother as far as your Ability will allow: By the Contents of the Sacred Writ you will perform this Oath. So help you God.

*The Institution of Free Masons, c*1725, is a manuscript version of *The Grand Mystery . . . Discover'd*, not an exact copy, but in the points under discussion they are virtually identical, including the 'help and assist any Brother . . .'

The Whole Institutions of Free-Masons Opened 1725, a broadsheet printed in Dublin, has neither Obligation nor penalty. One Q and A simply says:

What were you Sworn to – For to Heal and Conceal

It contains interesting notes on the words that accompanied the Points of Fellowship, and on 'the primitive word . . . and Johova . . . the answer to it', but these are outside our present study.

The *Graham MS*, 1726, still without Obligation or penalty, is nevertheless one of the most important documents of those early days. It begins as a catechism of some twenty-seven Q & A many of them with religious interpretation in the answers. This leads into a whole collection of legends, mainly about Biblical characters, (eg Noah and Bezaleel) and a note on Solomon's Temple.

The Grand Mystery Laid Open, 1726, is a catchpenny broadsheet, without Obligation or penalty. Bro Poole described it as a 'freak, with nonsensical names for anything and everything'. For me, its only item of interest is its collection of six Points of Fellowship, the sixth being 'face to face'. Only one other text cited six Points, ie the *Mason's Examination*, 1723, and there the sixth was 'tongue to tongue'.

A Mason's Confession, (?) 1727, was first published in the *Scots Magazine* for March 1755–56, under a letter explaining that the piece was a confession by a repentant mason denouncing the oath as 'profane and abominable' and the secrets as 'superstitious ceremonies, lyes, and idle nonsense'. The text contains a brief narrative description of the preparation of the candidate and of the initiation ceremony, incomplete, with only a hint of a second degree. There is a catechism of some thirty-five Q & A, about half of them on traditional lines; the remainder are a strange collection, possibly operative, or perhaps a purely local Scottish working. The Obligation runs:

As I shall answer before God at the great day, and this company, I shall heal and conceal, or not divulge or make known the secrets of the mason-word, (Here one is taken bound, not to write them on paper, parchment, timber, stone, sand, snow, etc.) under the pain of having my tongue taken out from beneath my chowks, and my heart out from beneath my left oxter, and my body buried within the sea mark, where it ebbs and flows twice in the twenty-four hours.

Note, triple penalties for the first time embodied in the Obligation, but this particular text was not published until 1755–56, so that it was not known to the compilers of two important versions in 1730.

The Mystery of Free-Masonry was published in the *Daily Journal*, London, on 15 August 1730. It also appeared in printed broadsides under various titles before and after that date. The text is prefaced by a letter from a 'Constant Reader' who submits it for publication as the work of a dead Brother, who had compiled it as an aide-mémoire. Clearly, the sender has no high opinion of the Society or its members, but he offers to buy 200 copies of the *Journal* if they will print the piece.

The text consists of some twenty-six traditional Q & A with a brief description of the initiation ceremony from the 'first Door' to the end of the Obligation. There is no description of a second or third degree, and a Note at the end of the catechism suggests that few masons in those days were worried about taking the senior degree:

> Note. There is not one Mason in an Hundred that will be at the Expence to pass the Master's Part, except it be for Interest.

The Obligation is reproduced below.

From this time onwards the details of the Obligation and of the posture in which it is taken become much more explicit. During the next thirty years there is still only a single Obligation, regularly containing the multiple penalties, though their details are rarely identical.

At the Quarterly Communication on 28 August 1730, within two weeks after its appearance in the *Daily Journal*, Dr Desaguliers, Past Grand Master, commented on this exposure, and recommended measures that 'would prevent any false Brethren being admitted into regular Lodges . . .' but there is no record of his proposals or of any action taken upon them.

Two months later, in the same *Daily Journal*, Samuel Prichard advertised his *Masonry Dissected*, a thirty-two page pamphlet, price sixpence, the first exposure that claimed to give an 'Impartial Account . . . [of] the whole Three Degrees of Masonry'. It became an instant best-seller. There were three Prichard editions, one pirated version and two newspaper editions all within fourteen days. His Obligation in the EA degree was even better than its predecessor in

The Mystery of Freemasonry. They are reproduced here side-by-side:

The Mystery of Freemasonry 1730	Prichard's *Masonry Dissected*, 1730
[The Posture]	[The Posture]
". . . a Square was laid on the Ground, in which they made me kneel bare-knee'd, and giving a Compass into my Right-Hand, I set the Point to my Left-Breast, and my Left-Arm hanging down . . .'	'. . . With my bare-bended Knee and Body within the Square, the Compass extended to my naked Left Breast, my naked Right Hand on the Holy Bible . . .'
[The Oath]	[The Oath]
'I Solemnly protest and swear, in the Presence of Almighty God, and this Society, that I will not, by Word of Mouth or Signs, discover any Secrets which shall be communicated to me this Night, or at any time hereafter:	'I Hereby solemnly Vow and Swear in the Presence of Almighty God and this Right Worshipful Assembly, that I will Hail and Conceal, and never Reveal the Secrets or Secresy of Masons or Masonry, that shall be Revealed unto me; unless to a True and Lawful Brother, after due Examination, or in a Just and Worshipful Lodge of Brothers and Fellows well met.
That I will not write, carve, engrave, or cause to be written, carved, or engraven the same, either upon Paper, Copper, Brass, Wood, or Stone, or any Moveable or Immoveable, or any other way discover the same, to any but a Brother or Fellow Craft.	I furthermore Promise and Vow, that I will not Write them, Print them, Mark them, Carve them or Engrave them, or cause them to be Written, Printed, Marked, Carved or Engraved on Wood or Stone, so as the Visible Character or Impression of a Letter may appear, whereby it may be unlawfully obtain'd.
under no less Penalty than having my Heart pluck'd thro' the Pap of my Left-Breast, my Tongue by the Roots from the Roof of my Mouth, my Body to be burnt, and my Ashes to be scatter'd abroad in the Wind, whereby I may be lost to the Remembrance of a Brother.'	All this under no less Penalty than to have my Throat cut, my Tongue taken from the Roof of my Mouth, my Heart pluck'd from under my Left Breast, them to be buried in the Sands of the Sea, the Length of a Cable-rope from Shore, where the Tide ebbs and flows twice in 24 Hours, my Body to be burnt to Ashes, my Ashes to be scatter'd upon the Face of the Earth, so that there shall be no more Remembrance of me among Masons.' So help me God.'

Again three sets of penalties in a single Obligation, and Prichard in his interesting and valuable catechism of three degrees including the earliest version of a Hiramic legend, still made no mention of an Obligation for the FC or MM.

In 1946, an unknown manuscript catechism, of the EA degree only, was brought to the attention of Bro Douglas Knoop and his colleagues, who published it in that year as the *Wilkinson MS*, c1727. It gave rise to several problems. The watermark of the paper on which it had been written was one which might be dated at any time from 1746 to 1813, and the handwriting might have been even earlier, say 1700 to 1800. On a close study of the whole text, spelling, etc, they dated it as the copy of a ritual working that was in use between 1724 and 1730, ie c1727. The catechism, however, whether written as an aide-mémoire or as an antiquary's copy of an early document, was substantially shorter than Prichard's EA degree, and that also applies to the *Wilkinson* Obligation, reproduced here:

The Wilkinson MS

[22] Q. Can you Repeat it
A. I can
[23] Q. Repeat it
A. I do hereby Solemnly Promise & declare in the Presence of Almighty God, that I will heal & Conceal all the Secretts or Secrecy of a Mason or Masonry that has been heretofore, shall be now, or at any time hereafter, Revealed to me that I will not Speak or Declare them to any Saving a Brother or fellow after due Examination that I will not write them, work them, mark them, Point them or Engrave them: or Cause them to be wrote* Written Marked, Pointed or Engraved on anything moveable or Immoveable
Under no less Penalty than having my Throat Cut, my tongue tore from the Roof of my Mouth, my heart Plucked from under my Left breast & buryed in the Sands of the Sea, a Cables Length from the Land where the tide Ebbs & flows twice in 24 hours, my body to be burned to Ashes, and the Ashes Scattered over the face of the whole Earth that there may be no Remembrance of me—
So help me God, *Kissing the bible*

The existence of these three versions of the EA Obligation, all so closely related, though not copied from each other, implies that Prichard's form of the Obligation must have been in fairly widespread use at that time. This supports the general reliability of his text, and may explain the success of *Masonry Dissected*, which certainly helped to standardise English ritual throughout the next thirty years. In the 1730s there are records of a number of 'Masters' Lodges, more-or-

---

* The word 'wrote' is struck out.

less loosely attached to regularly constituted Lodges, but meeting usually on Sundays, only for conferring the third degree, useful evidence of its growing popularity. Prichard was so successful that during the thirty year gap (1730–60) we have no ritual evidence of any new developments in England, and to see what was happening we have to go to France.

We, the English, had planted Freemasonry in France in c1725, and from 1737 onwards we have a stream of French exposures, several of them quite important in the history of our English ritual. Prichard's *Masonry Dissected* first appeared in a French version as *La Réception Mysterieuse*, in 1738. (The book contained ten chapters, the last nine of them dealing with matters of European history.) Only the first chapter deals with Masonry, and the author-translator added several pages of his own notes at the beginning and end of Prichard's text. The third degree created problems, and may be taken as the compiler's impressions of what Prichard had written; but the main elements were preserved. Here I give only the EA Obligation (translated back into English). None of the early French texts contain Obligations for the FC or MM.

> I promise & swear in the presence of Almighty God, before this Right Worshipful Assembly, that I will be silent & will conceal the mysterious secrets of the Masons, or of the Society of Masons, which they will wish to give me; never will I disclose them, unless it be to a true & lawful Brother & member [*membre*]. Furthermore, I promise & vow that I will not make them known unlawfully, neither by means of writing, nor by printing, nor by drawing, nor by sculpture, either in wood or in stone, by copying any intelligible character or any recognizable alphabet. All this under the fearful punishment [*chatiment restrictoire*] that my tongue be torn from my mouth, & my heart from my left breast, my head cut off & all these pieces thrown into the Sea, where the tide ebbs & flows twice every twenty-four hours, a short distance from the Shore, to be buried there & submerged under the sand of the Sea, after the manner of Mariners[p]; my body reduced to ashes, which shall be thrown to the wind so that there shall remain no memory of a traitor among Masons.

In the later French texts, 1744, 1745, 1747, 1751, the floorwork and procedure of the third degree was given in detail, showing many novelties, and now greatly enlarged and improved, though still based on Prichard's version. *There was still only one Obligation* (for the EA) with penalties as before, but the original 'not Write them, Print them, Mark them, Carve them or Engrave them' was regularly abbreviated.

In 1760 we have the first of a whole new stream of English exposures which, in the absence of any officially approved forms, are our only source of information on further ritual developments. That was *Three Distinct knocks*, a pamphlet of 72 pages, which claimed to give the ritual of 'Antient Free-Masonry', ie the Grand Lodge of England Under the Old Institutions (the Antients), founded in 1751. The work opens with a dedication to the 'Irish Masters of No 1' who dealt with the preliminaries to the foundation of the Antients, and became the Grand Committee in 1751. A substantial part of the dedication is a spiteful diatribe against the Masters, Quarterage charges, monies for 'charitable purposes' that are misused etc. There are several other critical passages in the book.

The text is mainly in the form of catechism, with useful narrative descriptions of the floor-work, so that we get a much better picture of the actual ceremonies. In short, the work covers all three degrees, the third being the fullest version that had appeared up to this time, much of it being entirely new, and each degree now has its own Obligation and penalty. There is also a section headed 'The Charge given to the Officers of a Lodge' which is really a description of The Installation of the Master, with the Obligation which is also taken by the Wardens and Secretary.

We reproduce all three degree Obligations, only to show how they were in the earliest versions available to us, and to facilitate comparison with the forms in general use nowadays.

THREE DISTINCT KNOCKS, 1760

The EA Obligation.

> *Maf.* Stand up and begin.
> *Anf.*   I. W—— V——,
> Of my own free Will and Accord, and in the Prefence of Almighty God, and this right worfhipful Lodge, dedicated to St *John*, do hereby and hereon moft folemnly and fincerely fwear, that I will always hail, conceal, and never will reveal any of the fecret Myfteries of Free Mafonry, that fhall be deliver'd to me now, or any Time hereafter, except it be to a true and lawful Brother, or in a juft and lawful Lodge of Brothers and Fellows, him or them whom I fhall find to be fuch, after juft Trial and due Examination.
> I furthermore do fwear, that I will not write it, print it, cut it, paint it or ftint it, mark it, ftain it, or engrave it, or caufe fo to be done, upon any Thing moveable or immoveable, under

the Canopy of Heaven, whereby it may become legible or intelligible, or the leaft Appearance of the Character of a Letter, whereby the fecret Art may be unlawfully obtain'd. All this I fwear, with a ftrong and fteady Refolution to perform the fame, without any Hefitation, mental Refervation, or Self-evafion of Mind in me whatfoever, under no lefs Penalty than to have my Throat cut acrofs, my Tongue torn out by the Root, and that to be buried in the Sands of the Sea, at Low-Water Mark, a Cable's Length from the Shore, where the Tide ebbs and flows twice in Twenty-four Hours; fo help me God, and keep me ftedfaft, in this my enter'd Apprentices Obligation.

[He kiffes the Book.]

The FC Obligation:

Maf. Stand up and begin.
Anf. I W—— V——.
Of my own Will and Accord, and in the Prefence of Almighty God and this right worfhipful Lodge, dedicated to St *John*, do hereby, and hereon, moft folemnly and fincerely fwear, that I will always hail, conceal, and never will reveal that Part of a Fellow-Craft to an enter'd Apprentice, or either of them, except it be in a true and lawful Lodge of Crafts, him or them, whom I fhall find to be fuch after juft Trial and due examination.

I furthermore do fwear, that I will anfwer all Signs and Summonfes fent to me from a Lodge of Crafts, within the Length of my Cable-Tow.

I alfo fwear that I will not wrong a Brother, or fee him wrong'd, but give him timely Notice of all approaching Dangers whatfoever, as far as my Knowledge leads me. I will alfo ferve a Brother as far as lies in my Power, without being detrimental to myfelf or Family; and I will keep all my Brother's Secrets as my own, that fhall be delivered to me as fuch, Murder and Treafon only excepted.

And that at my own free Will, all this I fwear with a firm and fteady Refolution to perform the fame, without any Equivocation or Hefitation in me whatfoever, under no lefs Penalty than to have my Heart torn from under my naked Left-breaft, and given to the Vultures of the Air as a Prey: So help me God, and keep me ftedfaft in this my Craft's Obligation.

[He kiffes the Book.]

The MM Obligation:

Maf. Stand up and begin, Brother.
Anf. I. W—— V——,
Of my own free Will and Accord, and in the Prefence of Almighty God, and this right worfhipful Lodge, dedicated to St *John*, do hereby and hereon moft folemnly and fincerely fwear, that I will always hail, conceal, and never will reveal, that Part of a Mafter Mafon to a Fellow-Craft, no more than that of a Fellow-Craft to an enter'd Apprentice, or any of them to the reft of the World; except it be to a true and lawful Lodge of Mafters, him, or them, whom I fhall find to be fuch, after juft Trial and due Examination.

I furthermore do fwear, that I will anfwer all Signs and Summonfes, fent to me from a Lodge of Mafters, with the Length of my Cable-tow.

I alfo will keep all my Brothers Secrets as my own, that is deliver'd to me as fuch, Murder and Treafon excepted, and that at my own free Will: I will not wrong a Brother or fee him wrong'd, but give him timely Notice of all approaching Dangers, as far as my Knowledge leads me.

I alfo will ferve a Brother as far as lies in my Power, without being detrimental to myfelf or Family.

And I furthermore do promife, that I will not have any carnal Converfation with a Brother's Wife, Sifter or Daughter, and that I will never difcover what is done in the Lodge, but that I will be agreeable to all Laws whatfoever. All this I fwear, with a firm and fteady Refolution to perform the fame, without any Hefitation in me whatfoever, under no lefs Penalty than to have my Body fever'd in two, the one Part carried to the South, and the other to the North; my Bowels burnt to Afhes in the South, and the Afhes to be fcatter'd before the Four Winds, that fuch a vile Wretch as I fhould be remember'd no more amongft any Manner of Men, (particularly Mafons) fo help me God, and keep me ftedfaft in this my Mafter's Obligation.

[*He kiffes the Book.*]

In 1762, two years after the first appearance of *Three Distinct Knocks*, *J. & B.* was published, claiming (by implication) to describe the ritual of the premier Grand Lodge. During the 1730s that body, the 'Moderns', had authorised certain changes in the modes of recognition in the first and second degrees. Those changes were accepted by the majority of the Moderns' lodges and they appeared in *J. & B.*, but there were several that continued to use the original forms. Indeed, the three Obligations remained almost identical in both workings, their main difference being that *J. & B.* removed from the third degree the candidate's promise that he would 'not have carnal Conversation with a Brother's Wife, Sister or Daughter'.

Thus we have carried our study of the Masonic Obligations from their first appearance as a simple oath of secrecy through all the stages of development up to the point where there were separate Obligations for each degree, each with its own penalties. So far as we may trust *Three Distinct Knocks* and *J. & B.* as repesenting the practice of the rival Grand Lodges in the 1760s, there was no great difference in the form of their Obligations.

But there was no ritual control from headquarters. The lodges practised the ritual they had inherited, or had learned from neighbouring lodges, or had adopted from the exposures that were readily available. In effect, there was no uniformity, and variations persisted in different localities.

The first real attempt to achieve uniformity was made by the premier Grand Lodge in April 1809 when it resolved that it was no longer necessary to preserve the ritual changes that it had authorised 'in or about 1739'. Six months later, in October 1809, a Moderns' Warrant was issued creating the Lodge of Promulgation 'for the purpose of ascertaining and promulgating the Ancient Land Marks of the Society and instructing the Craft in all such matters and forms . . .'. At its first meeting, with the help of several Antient Masons, they began to study the principal differences between the Antients' and Moderns' practices, with a view to an ultimate union. Negotiations between the rival bodies continued, not without difficulties from the Antients, but the union was finally achieved on 27 December 1813.

The nature of the changes that were made in the Obligations can best be judged by comparing the texts of the 1760s with the forms in use today. One further 'permissive change' was made officially by the United Grand Lodge in 1964; that was a minor verbal alteration in all three Obligations, important because it clarified the real implication of the modern penalties.

The 1760s were the period when the degrees were beginning to acquire their speculative polish. The ceremonial and procedural changes that have developed since those days, together with those that were made and largely embodied in the ritual at the union, can only be appreciated after a study of the catechisms and exposures from 1696 up to the late 1700s. That is a fascinating and rewarding exercise.

15

THE EVOLUTION OF THE INSTALLATION CEREMONY AND RITUAL

IN THE WHOLE recorded history of Masonry in England, going back more than 600 years, there is no trace at all of even the most elementary ceremony of Installation until after the formation of the first Grand Lodge in 1717. The rare English minutes that have survived from the pre-Grand Lodge era contain no evidence on the subject. The old Scottish Lodge minutes, from c1600 onwards, provide ample records of the election of the principal officer (by whatever name, ie Deacon, Warden, preces, or Master) but never a word to indicate that the election was followed by any kind of ceremony of Induction or Installation into the Chair.

Dr Anderson published his first *Book of Constitutions*, in 1723. The Regulations, 'Compiled first by Mr George Payne, *Anno* 1720, when he was Grand Master', had been digested in 1723 'into this new Method, with several proper Explications, for the Use of the Lodges in and about *London* and *Westminster*'. They contained, *inter alia*, the earliest rules relating to the formation of a new Lodge, which could not be done without first obtaining 'the Grand Master's Warrant', and without which the regular Lodges were 'not to countenance them, nor own them as *fair Brethren*'. (Reg. VIII).

The book included a two-page section describing 'The Manner of constituting a New Lodge, as practis'd by his Grace the Duke of Wharton', Grand Master in 1722–23. It appeared at a time when the newly-formed Grand Lodge was trying to establish itself as the governing body of the Craft, eager to bring the existing Lodges under its wing and to ensure that new Lodges were encouraged to mark their allegiance by an official ceremony of 'constitution', a procedure that was unknown until that time.

WHARTON'S INSTALLATION CEREMONY

Wharton's 'Manner of Constituting . . .' laid down the procedure to be followed after all the preliminaries had been fulfilled, and it also contained the earliest description of the Installation of the Master *of a new Lodge*. The full text of this historic document is readily accessible to students, and, to avoid unnecessary repetition, the whole procedure is summarised below, quoting the original words where they are of special significance:

(1)   The Grand Master asks his Deputy if he has examined the 'Candidate *Master*' and if he finds him 'well skill'd . . . and duly instructed in our *Mysteries Etc . . .*'

(2)   After an affirmative answer, the Candidate ('being yet among the *Fellow-Craft*') is presented to the Grand Master, as a '*worthy* Brother . . . *of good Morals and great Skill . . .*'

(3)   The Grand Master, placing 'the *Candidate* on his left Hand' asks and obtains 'the unanimous Consent of all the Brethren' and constitutes them into a new lodge, 'with some Expressions that are . . . not proper to be written'.

(4)   The Deputy Grand Master rehearses 'the *Charges* of a *Master*' [which are not printed, and are still unknown at this date] and the Grand Master asks '*Do you submit to these Charges, as Masters have done in all Ages?*' The Candidate signifies his submission.

(5)   The Grand Master installs him 'by certain significant Ceremonies and ancient Usages' [which are not described].

(6)   The Members, 'bowing all together', return thanks to the Grand Master, and 'do their *Homage* to their *new Master*, and signify their Promise of Subjection and Obedience to him by the usual *Congratulation*.

(7)   The Deputy Grand Master and other non-Members congratulate the new Master.

(8)   The Worshipful Master chooses his Wardens. [The remaining business is not relevant to our study of Installation procedure].

The text contains several notes which confirm that there were only two degrees in practice at that time, 1723, but there is no mention of the Lodge having been opened into a particular degree. It may be assumed, perhaps, that all present were 'among the Fellow-Craft', or

'Masters and Fellow-Craft' as Anderson had described them in Regulation (13) of this same *Book of Constitutions*. There is no trace of an Obligation being taken by the Master-designate, nor any hint of a sign, grip, or word being conferred in the Installation at this period. Two items are noteworthy:

(3)   'Expressions . . . not proper to be written'.
(5)   Installation, 'by certain significant Ceremonies and ancient Usages'.

Allowing that the Grand Lodge itself was only six years old; that nobody was excluded or even separated from the work in progress; that no Obligation is mentioned; that the ritual was still in its early formative stage and the third degree still unknown, it is difficult to accept that the ceremony had any esoteric content, or that the 'Expressions . . . and ancient Usages' were anything more than mere flowers of language, typical of Anderson's style, and perhaps of Wharton's too.

The Installation of Masters of Lodges did not become instantly popular. In those early days, when there was no other guidance on the subject, Wharton's ceremony seems to have been treated as belonging only to the constitution of a new Lodge, and surviving minutes show that the Lodges generally ignored it. Masters were elected 'and took the Chair accordingly', as recorded in the minutes of the Old King's Arms Lodge (now No 28) on 6 May 1735. A typical minute of the period may be quoted from the records of the Lodge at the Blue Posts, Old Bond Street (now the Lodge of Felicity No 58): 'This was Election Night and Bro Wright was elected Master Bro White Senr Warden Bro Wise Junr. Warden and Bro Kitchin Secr. and paid there two shillings each for the Honr done them.' [Not a word about Installation].

'Fees of Honour' were not unusual and fines for non-acceptance of office were quite normal. Many Lodges elected their Master twice yearly, but in the Lodges under the premier Grand Lodge, it is almost impossible in the first half of the eighteenth century, to find any minutes that could be taken to imply *a ceremony of Installation*.

THREE DISTINCT KNOCKS, 1760

The earliest description of an Installation ceremony, unconnected with the constitution of a new Lodge, appeared nearly forty years after Wharton's text, in *Three Distinct Knocks*, 1760. It is headed *The Charge given to the Officers of a Lodge*, and begins: 'And first of the Master belonging to the Chair; which they call installing a Master for the Chair.' It contains none of the preliminaries, but the Lodge is apparently in the third degree; there is no mention of election, presentation, reading of the Charges of a Master, or any of the routine procedures which may have been fairly well established at this date. The text seems to confine itself, deliberately, only to the esoteric portion of the ceremony. The new incumbent 'kneels down in the South, upon both Knees; and the late Master gives him the following Obligation, before he resigns the Chair'.

The new Master solemnly swears that he 'will not deliver the Word and Gripe belonging to the Chair . . . except to a Master in the Chair, or past Master . . . after just Trial and due Examination'. He will act as Master and 'fill the Chair every Lodge Night'. He will not wrong the Lodge, nor 'reign arbitrarily', but 'will do all things for the good of Masonry in general' and 'keep good Orders' as far as lies in his Power. All this, under the EA, FC, and MM penalties of those days. Then, still kneeling, he is invested with the 'Master's Jewel', raised from his kneeling posture by the 'Master's Gripe' [ie MM grip]; a Word is whispered in his ear, and the Installing Master 'slips his Hand from the Master's Gripe to his Elbow' and presumably he installs the new Master in the Chair, but that point is not mentioned.

There is no mention of post-Installation procedures, eg the appointment of Officers, Addresses, etc. The next paragraph, still apparently part of the Installation details, is headed *The Master's Clap*. It describes 'the grand Sign of a Master Mason', which was a rowdy Salutation, 'holding both Hands above your Head and striking upon your Apron, and both Feet going at the same Time ready to shake the Floor down'. This seems to have been given by MM's to the newly-installed Master and the context suggests that the Lodge was still in the third degree.

Three Distinct Knocks represented Antients' working, probably imported into England by Irish Brethren; but *J. & B.*, a Moderns' exposure, reproduced it almost word for word, in 1762, though it is doubtful if many of their Lodges were using the Installation ceremony. The importance of these twin texts, in so far as we dare to trust them, is that they show that in the earliest description of the *esoteric* portion of the Installation ceremony, both Antients and

Moderns were using the same procedure. Indeed, there is valuable evidence to show that they did. When John Pennell compiled the first Irish *Book of Constitutions* in 1730, he reprinted Wharton's 'Manner of Constituting a New Lodge' word for word (though he omitted to mention Wharton's name, or the *Book of Constituions*, from which he had copied it).

Laurence Dermott, who later became Grand Secretary of the Antients, had been installed Master of a Dublin Lodge (No 26; on 24 June 1746, before he arrived in England. Ten years later, in 1756, he published *Ahiman Rezon*, the first *Book of Constitutions* of the Antients Grand Lodge, in which he also reprinted Wharton's 'Manner of Constituting . . .' practically word for word, the differences being so slight that they do not in any way affect the synopsis previously given.

The implication is that *Dermott himself must have been installed*, in Ireland, *by a ceremony which was to all intents and purposes identical with the English forms.*

The Antients, in their early years, were somewhat negligent about Installation and this is confirmed by their Grand Lodge minutes:

St John's Day, June 1755
The Grand Secretary [Dermott] was order'd to examine the Officers of particular lodges as to their Abilities in Instaling their successors Upon which Examination it was thought Necessary to Order the said Secretary to attend the Instalation of several Lodges, which the GS promised to perform.

A year later:

June 24th 1756
The Grand Secy. was Order'd to Examine several Masters in the Ceremony of Installing their Successors. and declared that *many of them were incapable of performance* [My italics. H.C.] Order'd that the Grand Secretary shall attend such deficient lodges and having obtain'd the consent of Members of the said Lodges he shall solemnly Install and invest the several Officers according to the Antient Custom of the Craft.

PRESTON'S INSTALLATION CEREMONY

The next stage in the evolution of the Installation ceremony appeared in William Preston's *Illustrations of Masonry*, 1775, in which he outlined the ceremonies of Constitution, Consecration and Installation, under three separate headings. The latter still embodied virtually the whole of Wharton's procedures, but to avoid any misapprehension he added a footnote: 'The same ceremony and charges attend every succeeding installation'. Preston also included the *first full text of the Charges of a Master*, almost identical with those in use today. They had only been mentioned in Wharton's version of 1723. In Preston's ceremony, after hearing them recited, the Master Elect promised submission, and then he was 'bound to his trust' (which may imply that he took an Obligation relating to his duties as Master, rather like the Master Elect's Obligation taken in the second degree nowadays). He was next invested 'with the badge of his office' by the Grand Master and presented with the Warrant, the VSL, *B of C*, tools, jewels, and the 'insignia of his different officers'. He was conducted to the left of the Grand Master, who received homage, after which the new Master received 'the usual congratulations in the different degrees of Masonry'. The remainder of this section dealt with the appointment and investiture of the Officers – Wardens, Treasurer, Secretary, Stewards and Tyler, with the various Addresses, which, though quite short, were already very similar to those in use today. (Deacons were not mentioned in the list of Officers.)

Throughout this 1775 version of Preston's Installation, there is no note of the Master being 'Chaired', or that any secrets were communicated to him; nor is there any hint of an esoteric Obligation (ie, one that contained secrets such as a penalty or Pen. Sn.).

There are useful indications of the adoption of esoteric Installation practices in the records of the Lodge at the Queen's Arms, later the Lodge of Antiquity, No 1 on the Moderns' Roll. Their elections, half-yearly, were recorded regularly, without any mention of Installation, until 8 January 1753, when the minutes record: 'According to the Minutes of Last Lodge Night Br. Moses *was placed in the Chair, as Master of this Lodge*, Bro^r. Burgh, Senr. Warden, B^r. Humphreys, Junr. Warden . . .'. The words in italics are open to wide interpretation, but they do imply, at the very least, some kind of induction ceremony, but still apparently without secrets.

AN ADJACENT ROOM

'Hitherto [ie up to 1792] the ceremony of Installation had been conducted in the Lodge Room. Now and henceforward the Installed Masters withdrew with the Master Elect to another room. The Minutes are not clear, but this practice would appear to have been continued until 1812, or perhaps later. It is not until 1822 that we find it stated that all the Brethren below the rank of Installed Masters retired.' (Firebrace, *Records of the Lodge of Antiquity No 2*, Vol 2, p 120n.)

The separate room, and a ceremony conducted in the presence of Installed Masters only, is the first clear evidence of an esoteric installation within a Board of Installed Masters, though that name had not yet made its appearance. The 'adjacent room' becomes a regular feature of Preston's *Illustrations*, from 1801 onwards, but he gives very little detail of what took place in there. The preliminaries began with the Lodge apparently in the third degree. The Master Elect was presented to the Installing Master, with a brief list of his qualifications, '. . . of good morals, of great skill, true and trusty, and a lover of the whole fraternity. . .'. The Secretary was ordered to read the Ancient Charges and the Regulations, and the Master Elect promised 'to submit to . . . and support [them] as Masters have done in all ages. The new Master is then conducted to an adjacent room, where he is regularly installed, and bound to his trust in antient form, by his predecessor in office, in the presence of three installed Masters'.

This is the whole of Preston's data on what we would call the Inner Working, and there is no hint of any opening or closing for that portion of the Installation ceremony. The remainder of the proceedings are summarised here, from the 1801 edition:

'On his return to the Lodge, the new Master . . . is invested with the badge of his office.'

[The presentations are made with suitable Charges to each, as already mentioned. Preston 'moralised' each item in very familiar language, in a long collection of footnotes.]

'He is chaired amidst acclamations'.
'He returns acknowledgements to the Grand Master [or Installing Master] and the acting Officers, in order.'
'The members . . . advance in procession, pay due homage . . . and signify their subjection and obedience by the usual salutations in the Degrees.'

[This implies that the salutations are well known, but there are no details as to what they were, or how many were given. It also means that the Lodge is closed after each salutation in the third and second degrees, and that the rest of the ceremony is conducted in the first.]

> 'The S.W. is invested with the "ensign" of office, the J.W. with the "badge" of office with a summary of their duties to each; followed by an Address to them jointly.'
> 'The Treasurer is invested.'
> 'The Secretary is appointed, with an account of his duties.'
> 'The Deacons are invested. The "columns" [nowadays the emblems of the Wardens] are entrusted to the Deacons as "badges" of their office.'
> 'Stewards are invested with a brief Charge.'
> 'The Tyler is appointed with a short Charge.'
> 'The W.M. addresses the Lodge; "Brethren, such is the nature of our constitution . . . and unite in the great design of communicating happiness." '

[An early version of our third Address.] Preston's ceremony in an 'adjacent room' in which the new Master was 'regularly installed', must have been a ceremony with secrets, but he gave no details in his *Illustrations*.

We may pause here to survey the situation at this stage. The Ceremony just described was very new, and in no sense official. We shall soon see that the majority of Moderns' Lodges were still without any kind of Installation; their Grand Lodge had made no law on the subject. The Antients were certainly practising Installation, but we have no details and it is doubtful if their ceremony was as far advanced as Preston's version of 1801. There was no standardisation, and we still have no information about the 'Inner Working'.

INSTALLATIONS IN THE LODGE OF PROMULGATION
The next stage in our study is a minute of the Lodge of Promulgation, dated 19 October 1810. This was the Lodge, created by the Prince Regent, Grand Master of the Moderns' Grand Lodge, to pave the way for the union of the rival Grand Lodges: 'Resolved, that it appears to this Lodge, that the ceremony of Installation of Masters of Lodges, is one of the two [true?] Land Marks of the Craft, and ought to be observed.' Here is evidence, if evidence were needed, to show how far the Moderns had lapsed in their neglect of the Installation ceremony, which had been zealously fostered among the Antients by their Grand Secretary, Laurence Dermott, who was already an

installed Master of a Lodge, before he come to London. The resolution, which implied the re-introduction or revival of the Installation ceremony as a 'Land Mark', was one of the major steps by the Moderns towards the standardisation of their procedures, in readiness for the anticipated union. But this was not all. James Earnshaw, Master of the Lodge of Promulgation (and of another Lodge) *had never been installed*, and that had to be rectified. A further minute on the same day resolved: '. . . that it be referred to those members of this Lodge who are Installed Masters, to install the RWM of this Lodge, and under his direction take such measures as may appear necessary for Installing Masters of the Lodge'.

It was arranged that the Installations would take place on 16 November 1810, and the record must be unique:

> 'November 16th [1810]. The proceedings in open Lodge preparatory to the Ceremony of Installation having been conducted in due form, Bro^s John Bayford, Grand Treasurer, Thomas Carr, Charles Valentine, and Charles Bonnor, being themselves Installed Masters, retired to an adjoining chamber, formed a Board of Installed Masters, according to the Ancient Constitution of the Order, and forthwith Installed Bro. James Earnshaw, the R.W.M. of this Lodge and of the Saint Alban's Lodge No. 22. They then proceeded to Install Bro. James Deans, S.W., R.W.M., of the Jerusalem Lodge No. 263, and Bro. W. H. White, J.W., R.W.M. of the Lodge of Emulation No. 12.'

There are several points of high interest in this minute. The WM, SW, and JW, all Masters of other Lodges, were that night installed *for the first time*. Three of the four Brethren who were privileged to conduct the ceremonies and who had formed the 'Board of Installed Masters', were members of the Lodge of Antiquity, which had been using the 'adjoining chamber' for the principal part of the Installation ceremony since 1792. It must also be noted that the 'Board' was 'formed'; there is no hint of formal Opening or Closing.

The Installations on 16 November 1810 were the start of a whole series of meetings for the Installation of Masters of Moderns' Lodges, ceremonies which were conferred only to regularise their status as Masters. The Lodge of Promulgation was primarily concerned with the three Craft degrees. It was not teaching the Installation ceremony, only conferring it, and its labours ended in March 1811. Its post-union successor, the Lodge of Reconciliation, 1813–16, was composed of representatives of both Antients and Moderns, but it was charged only with the duty of demonstrating the approved forms of the Craft degrees. In effect, no official attempt was made during the life of those two Lodges, to revise or standardise the Installation procedures.

In April 1813, eight months before the Union, the Duke of Sussex, as Deputy Grand Master of the Moderns, considering the widespread neglect of the Installation ceremony among the Moderns' Lodges, and that many of their Masters had never been properly installed, so that there were few Past Masters competent to assist in the ceremony, granted a one-year Warrant to a body of eminent Grand Officers and Masters of Lodges, forming them into a Lodge of Installed Masters

'. . . for the purpose of giving Instructions in the Mysteries and Ceremony of Installation and . . . Authority to instal such Brethren as now are or have been or hereafter may be Masters of Regular Lodges, and also any Past Grand Wardens and Provincial Grand Masters who may not yet have received the Benefit of Installation . . .' (*AQC* 84, pp 44–5).

The Warrant stated that these 'Instructions' were to be confined to Lodges in the London area only; there was no provision for similar instruction to be given in the Provinces.

Surprisingly, this Lodge of Installed Masters appears to have been stillborn; there is no shred of evidence that it ever met or acted upon the instructions embodied in its Warrant. It would seem that the birth was premature, because nobody had taken steps to ascertain the form of the Ceremony that was going to be approved by the Antients and adopted by the United Grand Lodge, when that would come into existence. It was not until 1827 that this much-needed instruction was undertaken by another 'Lodge or Board of Installed Masters'.

DEVELOPMENTS SHOWN IN THE *TURK MS*, 1816

Nevertheless, there had been some useful unofficial developments in the Installation procedures during the preceding years, and this is shown by a deciphered copy of the *Turk MS*, of which the original, in cypher, is dated 1816. It is the only complete contemporary version of Preston's Third Lecture, and Section IX of this text deals with the Installation of that period. In the following summary (extracted from the complete text of 'Preston's Third Lecture of Free Masonry', which was collated and published by the late Bro P. R. James in *AQC* vol 85) I have listed only those items of procedure that had not

appeared before 1816, or those that confirm items that were not
clearly described in earlier documents. (The italics throughout this
summary are mine H.C.)

(1) [The M.Elect is presented; Ancient Charges and general
Regulations are read to him and he expresses submission.] A
later note indicates that this occurs in the second degree.

(2) The M.Elect enters into the following 'engagement', covering
his duties as Master and promising 'adherence to the constitutions . . . bye-laws; to preserve and keep in good condition . . .
the books . . . charters . . . furniture, jewels . . . apparatus &
property' etc, and to hand over in good condition etc. *This was a
document to be signed and sealed by the M.Elect in Open Lodge,
prior to Installation.*

(3) [All MM's and PM's adjourn to the Installation room.] The
Lodge is opened in the third degree in the Installation room.

(4) All MM's are ordered to withdraw.

(5) 'The Board of installed masters *is formed.*'

(6) The M.Elect is presented to the Board of Installed Masters, to
receive 'the benefit of installation . . .'.

(7) The Installing Master addresses the M.Elect. 'From time
immemorial . . .' followed by the qualifications 'of good
repute, true & trusty, & in high estimation . . .' and he is asked
to declare whether he 'can accept the trust on these conditions'.

(8) He assents and 'kneels on both knees, with *two installed masters
joining hands, & forming the arch over him*'.

(9) All the brethren kneel.

(10) An invocation is made; '*Almighty father . . . vouchsafe thine aid
. . . sanctify him by thy grace . . . & consecrate our mansion to
the honour of thy name – Amen*'.

(11) The Oath of Office is administered. This is *a clear combination
of the two Obligations taken nowadays by the M.Elect in the
second degree and later in the Inner working.* The first part of
this Ob, contains all the themes of our present-day Ob for the
M.Elect. In the second part, he promises that he 'will never
reveal the secret word & grip of a master in the chair, . . . & not
to him or them unless it be in the presence of three installed
masters'. All this '*under no less a penalty than what has been
before specified in the three established degrees of the order.* So
help me . . .'.

(12) The Installing Master raises him 'up by the right hand *with the grip & word of the master in the chair*', with the words 'In the name of the most high God under whose banner & auspices we act . . . & I pray God to preserve you in his holy keeping, & enable you to execute the duties of your office with fidelity'.

(13) The new Master is then 'chaired & saluted' [no details].

(14) 'The board of installed masters *is adjourned*'.

(15) MM's re-admitted and Lodge closed in third degree.

(16) The brethren return to the Lodge where the rest of the ceremony is completed.

It may be helpful, at this point, to add a few observations on some of the items in Preston's 'Third Lecture' Installation (numbered here only for ease of reference; they are not numbered in the original):

Items 1 and 2. There is no hint, in this preliminary stage, of the M.Elect being obligated in the second degree.

Item 2. The M.Elect's 'engagement . . . signed in open Lodge'. This was the practice in the Lodge of Antiquity from 1788 onwards. (Firebrace, *Records of the L. of Antiquity*, Vol 2, p 79).

Items 5 and 14. The Board of Installed Masters is 'formed', and at the end of the Inner Working, it is 'adjourned'. *There is no evidence of the formal Opening and Closing of the Board of Installed Masters including secret words and signs*, which made its appearance in various parts of England (and more rarely in London) at a later date.

Items 9 and 10. This is the earliest version of Installation procedure that contains *an opening Prayer*. It is specifically related to the new Master and is almost word for word as we have it today.

Item 11. The two parts of Preston's combined Obligation are clearly defined, and they are in fact a much expanded and polished version of the Ob in *Three Distinct Knocks*, 1760, and *J. & B.*, 1762 (summarised earlier in this paper). The second part of Preston's version relates specifically to 'the secret word & grip of a master in the chair', and it carries the same penalties as in the two exposures; an unexpected confirmation! *Apparently the Pen Sn of an Installed Master was still unknown in 1816.*

It is perhaps necessary to take note of one item of ritual and procedure that is conspicuously absent. I refer to the story of Solomon's inspection of the completed Temple and Adoniram's respectful greeting, which gave rise to a 'calling' Sn, the G and W,

and one of our 'Salutations'. In effect, Preston recorded the G and W
of an Installed Master, but omitted the story that gave the supposed
source for those items and for the Sn of 'Humility'.

Preston's 'Third Lecture' deals, very inadequately, with the
procedures following the Inner Working: they had appeared in many
editions of the *Illustrations* and must have been widely known by this
time. But this would not apply to the Inner Working *in its advanced
form*, as given in the 'Third Lecture'. *That material had never been
printed*; indeed, only five manuscript versions have survived and only
one of those – the *Turk MS* – is complete.

It is not easy to assess the importance of Preston's writings on the
Inner Working, and the obvious question arises as to whether or how
far he had invented the work of the Board of Installed Masters, as he
had produced it in his 'Third Lecture', or whether he had simply
collected and arranged materials that were already in practice. The
frequent references, from 1792 onwards, to the work conducted in
'an adjacent room', or in 'the installation room', indicate that certain
esoteric elements must have been in existence and that Preston – as
was usual with him in all his Masonic writings – was responsible
mainly for their arrangement, interpretation and embellishment. The
more polished and elaborate ceremony, depicted in the *Turk MS*,
may have been familiar to a few of Preston's friends and followers
within his own immediate circle; but to the fraternity at large, the
procedures in that form must have been virtually unknown. The
'Land Mark' resolution of the Lodge of Promulgation on 19 October
1810 and the numerous Installations that followed, show that many
London Lodges had never practised the Installation ceremony.
Others, especially in the Provinces, were following inherited practices, right or wrong, simply because they had never heard of any
other forms.

DIVERSITIES OF PRACTICE:
THE 1827 BOARD OF INSTALLED MASTERS

In the circumstances, it is not surprising to find that substantial
diversities of practice had arisen, sufficient indeed to attract the
notice of the Grand Master. The *Grand Lodge Proceedings* for 6 June
1827 announced:

> 'The MW Grand Master stated that finding there was much diversity in the
> Ceremonial of the Installation of Masters of Lodges, and feeling it to be

most desirable that uniformity should exist, His Royal Highness had deemed it expedient to issue a Warrant to certain intelligent Brothers, directing them, after due and careful examination and consideration, to hold meetings for the purpose of promulgating and giving instructions in this important Ceremony that conformity might be produced, and also at such meetings to instal any Masters of Lodges who had been duly elected to office . . .'

The Warrant, dated 6 February 1827, was to run for 'Twelve Calendar Months, and no longer'. It is an important document, but not very well known, and its principal contents are reproduced here, because they enlarge on the information contained in the *GL Proceedings* quoted above:

'WHEREAS it hath been represented to us that, *from the want of immediate source for information and instruction*, there exists some diversity of practice in the Installation of Masters of Lodges; and feeling how important it is that all Rites and Ceremonies in the Craft should be conducted with uniformity and correctness; and with a view, therefore, to produce such uniformity, We have thought it proper to appoint, and do accordingly nominate and appoint our trusty and well-beloved Brothers . . . [ten names in all, including the G. Sec, G. Registrar, and the Masters of seven senior Lodges] to make known to all who may be entitled to participate in such knowledge *the Rites and Ceremonies of Installation as the same have already been approved by us, upon the Report of a Special Committee appointed for that purpose*: And in order the more effectually to carry this our intention into execution and operation, We do constitute the before-named Brethren into a Lodge or Board of Installed Masters, authorising and requiring them to hold meetings for the purpose of communicating Instructions in such Rites and Ceremonies, giving Notice thereof to the Masters of our several Lodges, enjoining their attendance . . . We empower the said Lodge, or Board of Installed Masters, when duly assembled, *to instal into office all such Masters of Lodges as may not heretofore have been regularly installed*, and who shall require the same: And We do declare that this our Warrant shall continue in force for the space of Twelve Calendar Months, and no longer.
Given at London, the Sixth Day of February, A.L. 5827, A.D. 1827,
DUNDAS, DGM.

Several points in the Warrant shown here in italics are of special interest, notably, 'the want of . . . information and instruction'. Next, 'the Rites and Ceremonies of Installation as the same have *already been approved by us*, upon the Report of a Special

Committee . . .'. This 'Lodge or Board of Installed Masters' was only required to give instruction in the Ceremony that had been revised, or arranged, by a Special Committee, *and already 'approved' by the Grand Master.* Apparently nobody outside the Special Committee had had any say in the matter.

The Grand Lodge Proceedings had said that it would be the duty of the 'intelligent Brothers' to install any Masters of Lodges who had been duly elected. The Warrant authorised them 'to instal into office all such Masters of Lodges as may not heretofore have been regularly installed'. This is a clear admission that many Masters had been installed with inadequate or irregular procedure, or had never been installed at all. Little wonder that the Grand Master had taken action.

The Grand Lodge issued a Circular on 10 December 1827, *to the Masters of Lodges in the London area*, announcing the constitution of the 'Lodge or Board of Installed Masters' authorised to hold 'Public Meetings' for the purposes set forth in the Warrant, a copy of which was included in the Circular. Three 'Public Meetings' were to be held on 17, 22 and 28 December 1827, at which the attendance of the (London) Masters and Past Masters was required.

It is surprising that this very necessary instruction was to be demonstrated at only three London meetings, and only for the benefit of London Masters and PM's. It may be that the Provincial Grand Masters were expected to make special arrangements for instruction in their own Provinces, but that is not known. There were approximately one hundred Lodges in the London area at that time, and some 400 in the Provinces. Attendance records for the three 'Public Meetings' (quoted by Henry Sadler in his *Notes on the Ceremony of Installation*) show that seventy-four Brethren were present at the first, thirty-three at the second, and twenty-one at the third, together representing some sixty Lodges in all; so that only two-thirds of the London Lodges obtained instruction, while the Provinces got none at all.

It will be useful, at this stage, to try to ascertain which items of procedure the 'Special Committee' found it necessary to revise. The preliminary business *before* the 'Inner Working' had been expanded and elaborated by Preston, who gave full details of the Charges of a Master, etc, so that we have a reasonably good account of established procedures, except that there may be some doubt as to whether those preliminaries (originally conducted in the second degree of the two-degree system) had been re-arranged in any way after the trigradal system was established.

As to the procedures that followed the 'Inner Working' (except in matters of esoteric detail, which will be discussed later) it is evident that they were already fairly well standardised, in the numerous editions of Preston's *Illustrations*. We know that the Brethren *in procession . . . in the three degrees* paid 'homage' and 'saluted'; but we lack details as to the number and kind of salutes that were given in each degree. We have lists of all the items that were presented to the WM, but we have no firm details as to how those items were distributed between the three degrees; and we also have brief forms of the Addresses. It seems reasonably certain, therefore, that for those Lodges that were eager to work to an established standard, the broad general forms were readily available.

In effect, the main work of the 'Special Committee' must have been directed towards the stabilisation of the 'Inner Working'. Here, we meet with difficulties, because we cannot be sure what kind of esoteric ceremony the Lodges may have been working. At worst, in those Lodges that had no ceremony at all, the Master was elected and took the Chair. Many Lodges must have been using the esoteric Installation described in *Three Distinct Knocks*, or *J. & B.* (as previously outlined). Brethren familiar with our modern usages will not need to be told how inadequate those exposures were.

At best, there would have been a few Lodges, probably all in London, that were using an elaborate 'Inner Working', including a Board of Installed Masters, as described in Preston's 'Third Lecture', which is the only respectable account of the proceedings *inside* the Installation room available to us *before 1827*. Those advanced procedures can only have been known to a fairly limited and select number of Lodges and Brethren; but allowing that the members of the 'Special Committee' had been specially chosen for their task, it may be safe to assume that they were reasonably well acquainted with that Lecture, and that they may well have used it as the best available framework upon which their revisions and recommendations were to be based.

MINUTES OF THE 'LODGE OR BOARD' – 24 FEBRUARY 1827

The Report of the Special Committee, to which the Grand Master had given his approval before the Warrant was issued, does not exist. The wording of the Warrant implies that it would have been a fully detailed survey of the whole of the Rites and Ceremonies pertaining to the Installation; no such document has survived. There is a file of papers in the Grand Lodge Library relating to the 'Lodge or Board of Installed Masters' which contains copies of the Warrant, the Circular to Masters of the London Lodges, attendance records of the three 'Public Meetings' and other related documents; but only one paper remains that deals with the actual work of the 'Lodge or Board'. It is a single sheet, folded to form four foolscap pages, of which the last two are blank.

Page one is a record of what was probably the first working meeting after the Board was warranted and it is the only one that gives some idea of the procedures approved by the Special Committee. It is written largely in abbreviations and there are seven interlinear insertions, probably made after a careful check. In the following transcript they are shown in their proper places and distinguished by italics. There are also three lines of irrelevant material in mid-page which were obviously entered in the wrong place and crossed out by the scribe. They are omitted from the transcript. At the foot of the page there is a note headed 'Qy' [ie Query] and I have placed asterisks in the body of the text to mark the places where that line probably belongs:

[Page 1]   Installed Masters, 24th Feb: 1827
                                Present
                             Bro Meyrick

White   Cant
Bott [erased]   Taylor
Clere   Moore
Smith   Broadfoot
Percivall
                          In □ of 2°

Presentation – Address – Qualifications – Antient Charges & regulations – 1st p^t. of Ob: – F.C. retire – □   op: in 3^d Deg: – M.M. retire –
In Board of Inst: M. – Prayer *according to the religious observance of the parties* – 2^d pt. ob: Entrust *** raise*** – Invest & place in Ch: — then deliver Hir: as Emblem of Power – New Master then places Jewel on Past Master***

[Three irrelevant lines of text crossed out]

Call in M.M. who go round & Sal: by Pen: Sin: then the Past Master proclaims the New M. after which all Sal: by 5. – *three prncl:* [?] *lights* & Tools presented and Cl:

Fellow Crafts called in, go round *alone* Sal: by Sn: second Procl: then *the whole* Sal: 5 – Br: ha: ba: Tools presented – Cl:

EA called in, go round Sal: by Pen: Sin: 3 procl: Sal: by 3 Pen: Sin: & ha: on Ba: –

The PM delivers Wart: Book of Const: & By Laws *Minute Books and Tools – Charge* He then calls upon the officers whom he had appointed to surrender their Jewels of office that the New Master may make his own Selection – The new officers then appointed & invested *pledged* & saluted by 3 –

Qy – Past Masters Grip – Sn: & Sal: of M of A & S.

* * * * * * * *

[Page 2 contains minutes (or attendance records) of three further meetings, held on 3 and 31 March and 27 April, and the dates fixed for five more, 5, 15, and 29 May and 2 and 11 June.]

[Page 2]

Installed Masters 3ᵈ March 1827

Bro Meyrick	Percival
White	Cant
Bott	Moore
Cleere	Broadfoot
Smith	

Broʳ Broadfoot acted as Master.
Bott as SW.
Cleere as JW.
Went thro the Ceremony of Installation as agreed Bro Smith acting as ME.

Private meetg. Friday 27 April [1827] ½ past 7
Saturday   5 ⎫
Thursday 15 ⎬ May at 7
Board to meet 31 March at 7

Saturday 31 March [1827]

Meyrick	Taylor
White	Moore
Bott	Broadfoot
Percival	
Cant	

Friday 27 April [1827]

The respective officers should be pledged previous to investiture*

Meyrick
Percival
Smith
Cant
Taylor

The Board to meet May 29 at 7 o'Clock P.M. for rehearsal
General meetings on Saturday June 2ⁿᵈ & 11 Monday at 7 o'Clock

The Lodges to receive the Summonses at least one month previous & Bro White is requested to procure the extension of the Warrant that it may be inserted in the general summonses.

[G.L. Library: Hist. Corresp. File, 12 B 14]

We may now return to the minutes of 24 February 1827, which are invaluable in relation to the procedures for the three degrees *after the Inner Working*. Most of those procedures were well known before 1827; but the 'Lodge or Board of Installed Masters' arranged them in a fixed form, much as we have them today.

The few lines devoted to the procedures within the Board of Installed Masters, even if we include the 'Query line' at the foot of the page, are not so helpful, and one could wish that the scribe had been more generous. The abbreviations do indeed provide an outline sketch of that part of the ceremony, but much of the detail is missing. It does, nevertheless, furnish confirmation of several items that may previously have been in doubt. This is particularly noticeable when we compare these brief notes with the Inner Working details in Preston's 'Third Lecture'. Several of the preliminaries in Preston's 1816 'Board of I.M's' are shown in the 1827 text *in the second degree*. His long 'combined Obligation' is now divided: its first part, which deals with the Master's duties, is put back into the second degree; the second part, which related to the secrets of the Chair, remains in the Inner Working.

The 'Query line' poses several problems. Obviously it represents two (or perhaps three) separate items:

* This is the only item of Installation procedure in all the eight meetings recorded on this page. In our modern working it would be rather puzzling, but there is a note in the *Henderson Notebooks*, c1835, indicating that the officers – at their investiture – were required to pledge that they would faithfully discharge their duties, the pledge being signified by the EA Sn, in token of assent.
♣ It will be noticed that this minute reverses the sequence of procedure shown in the penultimate line of the minutes of 24 February [Page 1].

(a) The Past Masters Grip.
(b) The Sn: & Sal: of M. of A. & S.

but where precisely do they belong? The Grip undoubtedly belongs with the instruction 'raise', and the query on this point probably refers only to the manner of giving it. The stages in the ceremony are indicated very clearly up to the word 'Entrust'; but entrust with what? The text shows that the new Master was still kneeling at that stage. He might, perhaps, have been entrusted with the Word and Pen Sn of an IM, but it is not certain that the Pen Sn existed at that date.

The 'Sn & Sal of a M of A & S' is somewhat ambiguous. Nowadays we might read it simply as a salutation; no Sn has been mentioned in the body of the text and the salutation would probably be given immediately after the 'chairing'. It is possible, however, that the note refers to a salutation to be given by the whole assembly at the end of the proceedings. For all these reasons the asterisks have been inserted in the body of the text, to show where the various parts of the 'Query line' may probably belong.

The 'Query line' gives rise to another interesting point. It was written on 24 February 1827, eighteen days after the date of the Warrant, which stated that the 'Rites and Ceremonies' had already been approved by the Grand Master. Yet here, on an essential part of the Inner Working, there was a query. In the minutes of 27 April (shown on page 2 of the text) there is record of yet another item of procedure that had not been settled until that date.

If the procedures had indeed been approved before 6 February, why did the 'Board' hold nine meetings for rehearsal, queries, and modifications during the following five months? And why was there a delay of ten months (February to December 1827) before the 'Board' started on its three Instruction-cum-Installation meetings? It seems obvious that the Special Committee can only have given the Grand Master a very rough draft of the proposed work, which they later proceeded to arrange in proper form. This implies that *we cannot accept the detailed minutes of 24 February 1827 as a final statement of the recommended procedures, and that applies especially to the Inner Working.*

Several important items have been omitted, deliberately perhaps, because changes were being made and the precise details were not yet settled. The 'Query line' would seem to support this view:

1. There is no mention of the procedure for forming, declaring, or constituting a Board of Installed Masters, and no hint of a formal Opening or Closing for the Board.
2. There is no mention of a word belonging to the Master in the Chair, or whether and when it should be given.
3. The Obligation probably contained a penalty clause, but no details are given; nor is there any mention of a Pen Sn of an IM.
4. There is no mention of Solomon's inspection of the Temple, and of the Adoniram incidents which gave rise to *several* esoteric items in the Inner work.
5. The salutation to be given by the whole assembly is prescribed for each of the three degrees, but is apparently omitted from the Inner Working.

It is reasonably certain that all of these items were settled to the Grand Master's satisfaction before the 'Lodge or Board of Installed Masters' had completed their three demonstrations in 1827. The absence of a written record of all their decisions may be due to the loss of minutes that had been carelessly scribbled on loose sheets, like those of 24 February 1827; but it may also be that they were never written, because esoteric matters were involved.

LATER EVIDENCE

If we are to reconstruct the ceremony which they promulgated, including the five points listed above, we can only do so from reliable evidence in documents that were compiled during the next ten years or so.

One of the most valuable documents for our purpose is the so-called *Henderson Notebook*, a manuscript volume of some 350 pages, mainly written by John Henderson, who was Deputy Master of the Lodge of Antiquity, No 2, in 1832, and President of the Board of General Purposes of the United Grand Lodge in 1836–37. The book contains his decipherment of Preston's Third Lecture, from the *Turk MS*, together with the Lectures of the Three Degrees and a large collection of notes on various ritual matters, including the Craft Installation ceremony. There is evidence to show that these materials were compiled *c*1830–35, only a few years after the 1827 'Board' had completed its duties.

In 1838, ten years after the 'Board' had finished its work, George

Claret published his ritual, *The Ceremonies of Initiation, Passing* . . . etc, a detailed ritual for all three degrees and the Installation ceremony. It was a perfectly respectable publication, its esoteric and procedural matters being indicated by dots . . ., or by initial letters with dots, eg L . . . F . . ., or R . . . F . . ., etc. Claret was an enthusiastic Masonic ritualist. He had attended six of the demonstration meetings of the Lodge of Reconciliation and had served as candidate at several of them. His ritual achieved a well-deserved success; it was reprinted and there were several improved and enlarged editions. In short, Claret's ritual may be described as the first example (if not the direct ancestor) of the printed rituals that we use today. So far as our present study is concerned, his Installation Ceremony is doubly valuable, because it must have reflected the finished work of the 'Lodge or Board of Installed Masters'.

In trying to gauge the trustworthiness of Claret's work, or of any other documents that describe Masonic ritual and ceremonial procedures (whether they are of reputable origin, or exposures published for profit or spite) there is one final test that is applicable to all of them; that is the degree of acceptance that they achieved within the actual practice of the Craft. Of Caret's status in this respect, there can be no doubt at all. Using Henderson and Claret as guide and check, we return to the five points.

1. Preston, in the *Turk MS*, had said 'The Board of installed masters is formed', and at the end of the Inner Work, 'The board of installed masters is adjourned'. There was no formal Opening or Closing. We have a valuable piece of evidence to confirm this, in the *Henderson Notebook*. After the Lodge has been opened in the third degree, he says:

[The Installing Master] . . . requests 2 P.M's to take the Wardens' chairs & then declares (*totidem verbis*) the B[n]. present to be a board of installed Ms.

The closing of the Board is also by 'declaration', '*totidem verbis*'. The Latin phrase, which means 'in as many words', may well be treated as something more than a mere confirmation that the B of IM was opened and closed by a simple 'declaration'. It also implies that if Henderson had ever heard of any such procedure he had firmly rejected it. This argument may apply equally to Preston's 'formed' and 'adjourned', because it is reasonably certain that if he had known of (or approved) the formal Opening and Closing of the B of IM he would certainly have included them in his work. For final confirmation on this point, we have Claret, 1838: 'The Instg Master gives one knock, and declares the Board of Installed Masters open'. At the end of the Inner Working, the IM 'gives one knock, and declares the board of Installed Masters closed'.

Our present study is concerned only with the evolution of the Installation ceremony as practised in the vast majority of Lodges under English Constitution. Within that 'common form' there are numerous variations of a trifling nature, which do not affect the contents, and it is fair to say that, with a few rare exceptions, the ceremonies, despite variations, are virtually identical. After the Lodge has been opened in all three degrees, MM's retire, and the B of IM is 'constituted' (in the presence of at least three Installed Masters) by a simple 'declaration'; there is no Opening or Closing ceremony.

There is, however, a so-called 'Extended working' of the B of IM in use in a number of Provinces and a few London Lodges, which consists of lengthy Opening and Closing ceremonies, which precede and follow the 'common form'. There is a password to the Opening, and the ceremonies contain, *inter alia*, several Sns, T's, and Working Tools. In Lodges that practise the 'Extended' form, the Installing Master is nowadays required to make a preliminary announcement that the Sns, T's, and W's, are not necessarily known to Installed Masters and are not essential to the Installation of a Master; after this, all present pledge themselves not to reveal, etc, except to an Installed Master.

It would be beyond the scope of this essay to discuss the many problems that relate to the rise of the 'Extended working', its contents and the recurring question of its regularity, which came to a head in 1926 when *the Grand Lodge ruled that its use would be permitted*, subject to the announcement outlined above. I will only add here, after a careful study of the relevant documents, that there is useful evidence that some such ceremony did exist in 1827, but that the Grand Master's 'Lodge or Board of Installed Masters' either knew nothing about it, or decided not to adopt it. My own view, based on Henderson's very emphatic note, *totidem verbis* (quoted above), is that the 'Extended Working', in one or more of its several forms, was known to the 'Board' in 1827, and was firmly rejected by them.

2. The missing 'word' of an Installed Master was, almost certainly, omitted for reasons of caution. We find it, in somewhat debased form, in two catechisms of the 1720s, but neither of them allocates it to a particular degree or grade, so that we cannot be sure how it was used. It reappears, grossly debased, in texts of the 1760s, where it is allocated to the Master, and there seems to be no doubt that the omission of the 'word' from the minutes of 1827 was deliberate.

3. The Pen Sn of an IM, is another missing item, and the inevitable question arises, 'Was it omitted for reasons of caution?'. We must remember that Preston's Obligation in the Inner Working of his Third Lecture, 1816, had said: '. . . under no less a penalty than what has been before specified in the three established degrees of the order'. Clearly, Preston knew nothing of a Penal Sn for the Installed Master, and there is not trace of that Sn in any documents before 1827. Yet *Henderson's Notebook*, *c*1835, and Claret's 'Ceremony of Installing . . .', 1838, both contain adequate indications of a Pen Sn, that had never been previously recorded.

It is impossible to believe that two writers so closely concerned with instruction in the ritual of their day would have dared to invent that Sn, or to describe one that was different from the routine prescribed by the 1827 'Board'. *On the firmly-based assumption that the 'Board's' minute of 24 February 1827 was not a final version*, there seems to be good reason to argue that the Pen Sn of an IM, was introduced by the 'Board' some time between February and December 1827.

4. Solomon's inspection of the Temple. There is no trace of this story in any text before 1827; but the 'Query line' in the February 1827 minute contains a reference to the 'Sn. & Sal: of M. of A. & S.' and that Sn. & Sal. is actually a part of the story. *Henderson's Notebook* contains both Sn. and Sal., but with only a bare hint of the story in which they originated. Claret gives the whole story (including the Queen of Sheba, etc), and both Sn. and Sal. are described in footnotes which have been deliberately obliterated in the print, apparently for reasons of caution. Taking all the evidence into account. I am inclined to believe that the 'Board' queried and considered both the Sign and Salutation, *as two separate items*, and

adopted them together with the story of Solomon's inspection of the Temple, which explained their origins.

5. Here we are concerned only with the 'multiple Salutation or Greeting given nowadays by the whole assembly, at the end of the Inner Working. Preston, in the Third Lecture, 1816, said that the new WM 'is chaired and saluted' but he did not describe the Salutation and it is not clear whether it was given by the Installing Master alone, or by the whole assembly. The 'Query line' implies that the subject was considered by the 'Board', but both Henderson and Claret seem to describe a single Salutation, given or only demonstrated by the Installing Master. I am inclined to believe that our 'multiple' Salutations are a more modern innovation.

So we have traced the rise of the Craft Installation ceremony, from its first appearance in print in 1723, through the early stages of its gradual adoption, and the later stages of its embellishment and expansion, up to the point when it was standardised by command of the Most Worshipful Grand Master of the United Grand Lodge, and promulgated, with his full approval, in 1827. We have also been able to identify – with some reasonable degree of accuracy – those items of procedure which were inadequately described, or totally omitted, from the only official document that survives as a record of the work of the special 'Lodge or Board of Installed Masters'.

There can be no doubt that the Grand Master's objective in 1827 was standardisation, *but the results were promulgated only to Lodges in the London area* and there was no provision at all for similar instruction in the Provinces. In the circumstances, the degree of uniformity that has been achieved, especially in the actual words of the Installation ritual, is really quite remarkable. The Queen of Sheba has disappeared from most modern workings; indeed, one wonders how she ever managed to come in! In the vast majority of English Lodges, the only real variations that have survived are purely procedural. They appear mainly in the Sns and Salutations, where the Lodges have tended to adopt practices which do not conform with those outlined in the minutes of 1827. This gives rise to constantly recurring questions as to which Signs and Salutations ought to be given in the Inner Working, and how many?

Other peculiarities have crept in, either because of inadequate promulgation, or in pursuit of long-established local custom, and a few of them deserve mention. Unfortunately it is not possible to discuss them in detail, and I can only indicate where they are to be found. For example, there are several different versions of the 'Extended Working' of the Board of Installed Masters, with the full Opening and Closing ceremonies. There are also substantial variations in the manner in which the G of an IM is given, and in the way in which the G is used when placing the new WM in the Chair. I have actually witnessed at least four different versions of the Sn of Humility, one of which would require the agility of a contortionist! Apart from this last item, the variations do not matter at all; indeed, they help to make the ceremony more interesting, especially when visiting.

Installation is, above all, the highest honour a Lodge can confer, involving duties and responsibilities of deep significance for the happy recipient, and the ceremony is always interesting and beautiful so long as it is conducted with due dignity and decorum.

APPENDIX

Facsimile pages from

SAMUEL PRICHARD'S MASONRY DISSECTED
1730

(Only the pages showing the degree
ceremonies are reproduced here. For
a full transcription of the complete
text refer to *Early Masonic Catechisms*
2nd edn. 1963)

MASONRY
DISSECTED:

BEING

A Univerſal and Genuine

DESCRIPTION

OF

All its BRANCHES from the Ori_
ginal to this Preſent Time.

As it is deliver'd in the

Conſtituted Regular Lodges

Both in CITY and COUNTRY,

According to the

Several Degrees of ADMISSION.

Giving an Impartial ACCOUNT of their Regular Proceeding in Initiating their New Members
in the whole Three Degrees of MASONRY.

VIZ.

I. ENTER'D 'PREN- ⎫ II. FELLOW CRAFT.
TICE,   ⎭ III. MASTER.

To which is added,

The Author's VINDICATION of himſelf.

By SAMUEL PRICHARD, *late Member of a*
CONSTITUTED LODGE.

LONDON:

Printed for J. WILFORD, at the *Three Flower-d. Luces* behind
the *Chapter houſe* near St. Paul's. 1730. (Price 6*d*)

Enter'd 'Prentice's DEGREE.

[1]   Q. FROM whence came you?
     A. From the Holy Lodge of St. *John's.*

[2]   Q. What Recommendations brought you from thence ?
     A. The Recommendations which I brought from the Right Worshipful Brothers and Fellows of the Right Worshipful and Holy Lodge of St. *John's,* from whence I came, and Greet you thrice heartily well.

[3]   Q. What do you come here to do ?
     A. Not to do my own proper Will,
     But to subdue my Passion still ;
     The Rules of Masonry in hand to take,
     And daily Progress therein make.

[4]   Q. Are you a Mason ?
     A. I am so taken and Accepted to be amongst Brothers and Fellows.

[5]   Q. How shall I know that you are a Mason?
     A. By Signs and Tokens and perfect Points of my Entrance.

[6]   Q. What are Signs ?
     A. All Squares, Angles and Perpendiculars.

[7]   Q. What are Tokens ?
     A. Certain Regular and Brotherly Gripes.

            B   Exam.

[8] Exam. Give me the Points of your Entrance.

Refp. Give me the firft, and I'll give you the fecond.

[9] Exam. I Hail it.

Refp. I Conceal it.

[10] Exam. What do you Conceal ?

Refp. All Secrets and Secrefy of Mafons and Mafonry, unlefs to a True and Lawful Brother after due Examination, or in a juft and worfhipful Lodge of Brothers and Fellows well met.

[11] Q. Where was you made a Mafon ?

A. In a Juft and Perfect Lodge.

[12] Q. What makes a Juft and Perfect Lodge ?

A. Seven or more.

[13] Q. What do they confift on?

A. One Mafter, two Wardens, two Fellow-Crafts and two Enter'd 'Prentices.

[14] Q. What makes a Lodge ?

A. Five.

[15] Q. What do they confift of ?

A. One Mafter, two Wardens, one Fellow-Craft, one Enter'd 'Prentice.

[16] Q. Who brought you to the Lodge ?

A. An Enter'd 'Prentice.

[17] Q. How did he bring you?

A. Neither naked nor cloathed, bare-foot nor fhod, deprived of all Metal and in a right moving Pofture.

[18] Q. How got you Admittance ?

A. By three great Knocks.

[19] Q. Who receiv'd you ?

A. A

A. A Junior Warden.

[20] Q. How did he dispose of you?

A. He carried me up to the North-East Part of the Lodge, and brought me back again to the West and deliver'd me to the Senior Warden.

[21] Q. What did the Senior Warden do with you?

A. He presented me, and shew'd me how to walk up (by three Steps) to the Master.

[22] Q. What did the Master do with you?

A. He made me a Mason.

[23] Q. How did he make you a Mason?

A. With my bare-bended Knee and Body within the Square, the Compass extended to my naked Left Breast, my naked Right Hand on the Holy Bible; there I took the Obligation (or Oath) of a Mason.

[24] Q. Can you repeat that Obligation.

A. I'll do my Endeavour. (*Which is as follows.*)

I Hereby solemnly Vow and Swear in the Presence of Almighty God and this Right Worshipful Assembly, that I will Hail and Conceal, and never Reveal the Secrets or Secresy of Masons or Masonry, that shall be Revealed unto me; unless to a True and Lawful Brother, after due Examination, or in a Just and Worshipful Lodge of Brothers and Fellows well met.

I furthermore Promise and Vow, that I will not Write them, Print them, Mark them, Carve them or Engrave them, or cause them to be Written, Printed, Marked, Carved or Engraved on Wood or Stone, fo as the Vifible Character or Impreffion of a Letter may appear, whereby it may be unlaw-fully obtain'd.

All this under no lefs Penalty than to have my Throat cut, my Tongue taken from the Roof of my Mouth, my Heart pluck'd from under my Left Breaft, them to be buried in the Sands of the Sea, the Length of a Cable-rope from Shore, where the Tide ebbs and flows twice in 24 Hours, my Body to be burnt to Afhes, my Afhes to be fcatter'd upon the Face of the Earth, fo that there fhall be no more Remembrance of me among Mafons.

So help me God.

[25] Q. What Form is the Lodge?
A. A long Square.

[26] Q. How long?
A. From Eaft to Weft.

[27] Q. How broad?
A. From North to South.

[28] Q. How high?
A. Inches, Feet and Yards innumerable, as high as the Heavens.

[29] Q. How deep?
A. To the Centre of the Earth.

[30] Q. Where does the Lodge ftand?
A. Upon Holy Ground, or the higheft Hill or loweft Vale, or in the Vale of *Jehofaphat*, or any other fecret Place.

[31] Q. How is it fituated?
A. Due Eaft and Weft.

Q. Why

[32]   Q. Why fo ?

A. Becaufe all Churches and Chappels are or ought to be fo.

[33]   Q. What fupports a Lodge ?

A. Three great Pillars.

[34]   Q. What are they called ?

A. Wifdom, Strength and Beauty.

[35]   Q. Why fo ?

A. Wifdom to contrive, Strength to fupport, and Beauty to adorn.

[36]   Q. What Covering have you to the Lodge ?

A. A clouded Canopy of divers Colours (or the Clouds.)

[37]   Q. Have you any Furniture in your Lodge?

A. Yes.

[38]   Q. What is it?

A. *Mofaick* Pavement, Blazing Star and Indented Tarfel.

[39]   Q. What are they ?

A. *Mofaick* Pavement, the Ground Floor of the Lodge, Blazing Star the Centre, and Indented Tarfel the Border round about it.

[40]   Q. What is the other Furniture of a Lodge?

A. Bible, Compafs and Square.

[41]   Q. Who do they properly belong to?

A. Bible to God, Compafs to the Mafter, and Square to the Fellow-Craft.

[42]   Q. Have you any Jewels in the Lodge ?

A. Yes.

[43]   Q. How many ?

A. Six. Three Moveable, and three Immoveable.

Q. What

[44] Q. What are the Moveable Jewels ?

A. Square, Level and Plumb-Rule.

[45] Q. What are their Ufes.

A. Square to lay down True and Right Lines, Level to try all Horizontals, and the Plumb-Rule to try all Uprights.

[46] Q. What are the Immoveable Jewels?

A. Trafel Board, Rough Afhler, and Broach'd Thurnel.

[47] Q. What are their Ufes?

A. Trafel Board for the Mafter to draw his Defigns upon, Rough Afhler for the Feilow-Craft to try their Jewels upon, and the Broach'd Thurnel for the Enter'd 'Prentice to learn to work upon.

[48] Q. Have you any Lights in your Lodge?

A. Yes, Three.

[49] Q. What do they reprefent ?

A. Sun, Moon and Mafter-Mafon.

> N.B. *Thefe Lights are three large Candles placed on high Candlefticks.*

[50] Q. Why fo ?

A. Sun to rule the Day, Moon the Night, and Mafter-Mafon his Lodge.

[51] Q. Have you any fix'd Lights in your Lodge?

A. Yes.

[52] Q. How many ?

A. Three.

> N.B. *Thefe fix'd Lights are Three Win-dows, fuppos'd (tho' vainly) to be in eve-ry Room where a Lodge is held, but more properly*

properly *the four Cardinal Points accord-ing to the antique Rules of Maſonry.*

[53] Q. How are they ſituated ?

A. Eaſt, South and Weſt.

[54] Q. What are their Uſes ?

A. To light the Men to, at and from their Work.

[55] Q. Why are there no Lights in the North ?

A. Becauſe the Sun darts no Rays from thence.

[56] Q. Where ſtands your Maſter ?

A. In the Eaſt.

[57] Q. Why ſo ?

A. As the Sun riſes in the Eaſt and opens the Day, ſo the Maſter ſtands in the Eaſt [*with his Right Hand upon his Left Breaſt being a Sign, and the Square about his Neck*] to open the Lodge and to ſet his Men at Work.

[58] Q. Where ſtands your Wardens ?

A. In the Weſt.

[59] Q. What's their Buſineſs ?

A. As the Sun ſets in the Weſt to cloſe the Day, ſo the Wardens ſtand in the Weſt [*with their Right Hands upon their Left Breaſts being a Sign, and the Level and Plumb-Rule about their Necks*] to cloſe the Lodge and diſmiſs the Men from Labour, paying their Wages.

[60] Q. Where ſtands the Senior Enter'd 'Prentice ?

A. In the South.

Q. What

[61]   Q. What is his Bufinefs ?

A. To hear and receive Inftructions and welcome ftrange Brothers.

[62]   Q. Where ftands the Junior Enter'd 'Prentice ?

A. In the North.

[63]   Q. What is his Bufinefs ?

A. To keep off all Cowans and Eves-droppers.

[64]   Q. If a Cowan (or Liftner) is catch'd, how is he to be punifhed ?

A. To be plac'd under the Eves of the Houfes (in rainy Weather) till the Water runs in at his Shoulders and out at his Shoos.

[65]   Q. What are the Secrets of a Mafon ?

A. Signs, Tokens and many Words.

[66]   Q. Where do you keep thofe Secrets ?

A. Under my Left Breaft.

[67]   Q. Have you any Key to thofe Secrets ?

A. Yes.

[68]   Q. Where do you keep it ?

A. In a Bone Bone Box that neither opens nor fhuts but with Ivory Keys.

[69]   Q. Does it hang or does it lie ?

A. It hangs.

[70]   Q. What does it hang by ?

A. A Tow-Line 9 Inches or a Span.

[71]   Q What Metal is it of ?

A. No manner of Metal at all; but a Tongue of good Report is as good behind a Brother's Back as before his Face.

N. B.

*The Key is the Tongue, the Bone Bone Box
the Teeth, the Tow-Line the Roof of the
Mouth.*

[72]   Q. How many Principles are there in Mafonry ?
A. Four.

[73]   Q. What are they ?
A. Point, Line, Superficies and Solid.

[74]   Q. Explain them.
A. Point the Centre *(round which the Mafter
cannot err)* Line Length without Breadth, Superficies Length and Breadth, Solid comprehends the
whole.

[75]   Q. How many Principle-Signs ?
A. Four.

[76]   Q. What are they ?
A. Gututral, Pectoral, Manual and Pedeftal.

[77]   Q. Explain them.
A. Guttural the Throat, Pectoral the Breaft,
Manual the Hand, Pedeftal the Feet.

[78]   Q. What do you learn by being a Gentleman-
Mafon.
A. Secrefy, Morality and Goodfellowfhip.

[79]   Q. What do you learn by being an Operative
Mafon ?
A. Hue, Square, Mould-ftone, lay a Level and
raife a Perpendicular.

[80]   Q. Have you feen your Mafter to-day?
A. Yes.

C   Q. How

[81]   Q. How was he Cloathed?

A. In a Yellow Jacket and Blue Pair of Bree-
ches.

    N.B. *The Yellow Jacket is the Compaffes,*
    and the Blue Breeches the Steel Points.

[82]   Q. How long do you ferve your Mafter?

A. From Monday Morning to Saturday Night·

[83]   Q. How do you ferve him ?

A. With Chalk, Charcoal and Earthen Pan.

[84]   Q. What do they denote ?

A. Freedom, Fervency and Zeal.

[85]   Ex. Give me the Enter'd 'Prentice's Sign.

Refp. Extending the Four Fingers of the Right
Hand and drawing of them crofs his Throat,
is the Sign, and demands a Token.

    N.B. *A Token is by joining the Ball of the*
    Thumb of the Right Hand upon the firft
    Knuckle of the Fore-finger of the Brother's
    Right Hand that demands a Word.

[86]   Q. Give me the Word.

A. I'll letter it with You.

[87]   Exam. BOAZ. [N.B. *The Exam. fays* B,
Refp. O, *Exam.* A, *Refp.* Z, i. e. Boaz.] Give
me another.

Refp. JACHIN. [N.B. Boaz *and* Jachin
were two Pillars in Solomon's *Porch.* 1 Kings,
chap. vii. ver. 21.]

[88]   Q. How old are you?

A. Under Seven. [*Denoting he has not pafs'd*
Mafter.]

                    Q. What's

[89]   **Q.** What's the Day for ?
          A. To See in.

[90]   **Q.** What's the Night for ?
          A. To Hear.

[91]   **Q.** How blows the Wind?
          A. Due Eaft and Weft.

[92]   **Q.** What's a Clock ?
          A. High Twelve.

The End of the Enter'd 'Prentice's Part.

C 2   *Fellow*

Fellow-Craft's DEGREE.

[93] Q. ARE you a Fellow-Craft?
A. I am.

[94] Q. Why was you made a Fellow-Craft?
A. For the fake of the Letter G.

[95] Q. What does that G denote?
A. Geometry, or the fifth Science.

[96] Q. Did you ever travel?
A. Yes, Eaft and Weft.

[97] Q. Did you ever work?
A. Yes, in the Building of the Temple.

[98] Q. Where did you receive your Wages?
A. In the middle Chamber.

[99] Q. How came you to the middle Chamber?
A. Through the Porch.

[100] Q. When you came through the Porch, what did you fee?
A Two great Pillars.

[101] Q. What are they called?
A. J. B. *i. e. Jachim* and *Boaz.*

[102] Q. How high are they?
A. Eighteen Cubits.

[103] Q. How much in Circumference?
A. Twelve Cubits.

Vide 1 *Kings,* *Chap.* 7.

Q. What

| 104 | Q. What were they adorn'd with? ⎤
| | A. Two Chapiters. ⎟
| 105 | Q. How high were the Chapiters? ⎟ *Vide* 1 *Kings*,
| | A. Five Cubits. ⎬ *Chap.* 7.
| 106 | Q. What were they adorn'd with? ⎟
| | A. Net-Work and Pomegranates. ⎦

[107] Q. How came you to the middle **Chamber** ?
A. By a winding Pair of Stairs.

[108] Q. How many ?
A. Seven or more.

[109] Q. Why Seven or more ?
A. Becauſe Seven or more makes a Juſt and Perfeᴄt Lodge.

[110] Q. When you came to the Door of the middle Chamber, who did you ſee ?
A. A Warden.

[111] Q. What did he demand of you ?
A. Three Things.

[112] Q. What were they ?
A. Sign, Token, and a Word.

N.B. *The Sign is placing the Right Hand on the Left Breaſt, the Token is by joining your Right Hand to the Perſon that demands it, and ſqueezing him with the Ball of your Thumb on the firſt Knuckle of the middle Finger, and the Word is* Jachin.

[113] Q. How high was the Door of the middle Chamber?
A. So high that a Cowan could not reach to ſtick a Pin in.

Q. When

[114]   Q. When you came into the middle, what did you fee ?

A. The Refemblance of the Letter G.

[115]   Q. Who doth that G denote?

A. One that's greater than you.

[116]   Q. Who's greater than I, that am a Free and Accepted Mafon, the Mafter of a Lodge.

A. The Grand Architect and Contriver of the Univerfe, or He that was taken up to the top of the Pinnacle of the Holy Temple.

[117]   Q. Can you repeat the Letter G?

A. I'll do my Endeavour.

The Repeating of the Letter G.

Refp. In the midft of *Solomon*'s Temple there
        ftands a G,
        A Letter fair for all to read and fee,
        But few there be that underftands
        What means that Letter G.

[118]   Ex. My Friend, if you pretend to be
        Of this Fraternity,
        You can forthwith and rightly tell
        What means that Letter G.

Refp. By Sciences are brought to Light
        Bodies of various Kinds,
        Which do appear to perfect Sight ;
        But none but Males fhall know my Mind.

[119]   Ex. The Right fhall.

Refp. If Worfhipful.

                                Ex. Both

[120]   Ex. Both Right and Worshipful I am,
　　　　　　To Hail you I have Command,
　　　　　　That you do forthwith let me know,
　　　　　　As I you may understand.
　　　　Resp. By Letters Four and Science Five
　　　　　　This G aright doth stand,
　　　　　　In a due Art and Proportion,
　　　　　　You have your Answer, Friend.
　　　　　　　　N.B. *Four Letters are* Boaz.
　　　　　　　　　Fifth Science Geometry.

[121]   Ex. My Friend, you answer well,
　　　　　　If Right and Free Principles you discover,
　　　　　　I'll change your Name from Friend,
　　　　　　And henceforth call you Brother.
　　　　Resp. The Sciences are well compos'd
　　　　　　Of noble Structure's Verse,
　　　　　　A Point, a Line, and an Outside ;
　　　　　　But a Solid is the last.

[122]   Ex. God's good Greeting be to this our happy Meeting.
　　　　Resp. And all the Right Worshipful Brothers and Fellows.

[123]   Ex. Of the Right Worshipful and Holy Lodge of St. *John*'s.
　　　　Resp. From whence I came.

[124]   Ex. Greet you, greet you, greet you thrice, heartily well, craving your Name.

[125]   Resp. *Timothy Ridicule.*
　　　　Exam. Welcome, Brother, by the Grace of God.

　　　　　　　　　　　　　　　　　　N.B.

N. B. *The Reafon why they Denominate themfelves of the Holy Lodge of St.* John's, *is, becaufe he was the Fore-runner of our Saviour, and laid the firft Parallel Line to the Gofpel (others do affert, that our Saviour himfelf was accepted a Free-Mafon whilft he was in the Flefh) but how ridiculous and prophane it feems, I leave to judicious Readers to confider.*

The End of the Fellow-Craft Part.

_____

The

The Master's DEGREE.

| 126 | Q. ARE you a Master-Mason?

A. I am ; try me, prove me, disprove me if you can.

| 127 | Q. Where was you pass'd Master?

A. In a Perfect Lodge of Masters.

[128] Q What makes a Perfect Lodge of Masters?

A. Three.

[129] Q. How came you to be pass'd Master?

A. By the Help of God, the Square and my own Industry.

[130] Q. How was you pass'd Master?

A. From the Square to the Compass.

[131] Ex. An Enter'd 'Prentice I presume you have been.

R. *Jachin* and *Boaz* I have seen ;
A Master-Mason I was made most rare,
With Diamond, Ashler and the Square.

[132] Ex. If a Master-Mason you would be,
You must rightly understand the Rule of Three.
And * M. B. shall make you free: * Machbenah
And what you want in Masonry,
Shall in this Lodge be shewn to thee.

D   R. Good

R. Good Maſonry I underſtand ;
The Keys of all Lodges are all at my
Command.

[133] Ex. You're an heroick Fellow ; from whence
came you ?

R. From the Eaſt.

[134] Ex. Where are you a going ?

R. To the Weſt.

[135] Ex. What are you a going to do there ?

R. To ſeek for that which was loſt and is now
found.

[136] R. What was that which was loſt and is now found?

R. The Maſter-Maſon's Word.

[137] Ex. How was it loſt ?

R. By Three Great Knocks, or the Death of
our Maſter *Hiram.*

[138] Ex. How came he by his Death ?

R. In the Building of *Solomon*'s Temple he was
Maſter-Maſon, and at high 12 at Noon, when the
Men was gone to refreſh themſelves, as was his uſual
Cuſtom, he came to ſurvey the Works, and when
he was enter'd into the Temple, there were Three
Ruffians, ſuppos'd to be Three Fellow-Crafts,
planted themſelves at the Three Entrances of the
Temple, and when he came out, one demanded
the Maſter's Word of him, and he reply'd he did
not receive it in ſuch a manner, but Time and
a little Patience would bring him to it : He, not
ſatisfied with that Anſwer, gave him a Blow,
which made him reel; he went to the other
Gate, where being accoſted in the ſame manner,
and

and making the ſame Reply, he received a greater Blow, and at the third his *Quietus.*

[139]　Ex. What did the Ruffians kill him with ?

R. A Setting Maul, Setting Tool and Setting Beadle.

[140]　Ex. How did they diſpoſe of him ?

R. Carried him out at the Weſt Door of the Temple, and hid him under ſome Rubbiſh till High 12 again.

[141]　Ex. What Time was that ?

R. High 12 at Night, whilſt the Men were at Reſt.

[142]　Ex. How did they diſpoſe of him afterwards ?

R. They carried him up to the Brow of the Hill, where they made a decent Grave and buried him.

[143]　Ex. When was he miſs'd ?

R. The ſame Day.

[144]　Ex. When was he found ?

R. Fifteen Days afterwards.

[145]　Ex. Who found him ?

R. Fifteen Loving Brothers, by Order of King *Solomon,* went out of the Weſt Door of the Temple, and divided themſelves from Right to Left within Call of each other ; and they agreed that if they did not find the Word in him or about him, the firſt Word ſhould be the Maſter's Word ; one of the Brothers being more weary than the reſt, ſat down to reſt himſelf, and taking hold of a Shrub, which came eaſily up, and perceiving the Ground to have been broken, he Hail'd his

Brethren,

Brethren, and purſuing their Search found him decently buried in a handſome Grave 6 Foot Eaſt, 6 Weſt, and 6 Foot perpendicular, and his Covering was green Moſs and Turf, which ſurprized them ; whereupon they replied, *Muſcus Domus Dei Gratia,* which, according to Maſonry, is, *Thanks be to God, our Maſter has got a Moſſy Houſe :* So they cover'd him cloſely, and as a farther Ornament placed a Sprig of *Caſſia* at the Head of his Grave, and went and acquainted King *Solomon.*

[146]   Ex. What did King *Solomon* ſay to all this?

R. He order'd him to be taken up and decently buried, and that 15 Fellow-Crafts with white Gloves and Aprons ſhould attend his Funeral [*which ought amongſt Maſons to be perform'd to this Day.*]

[147]   Ex. How was *Hiram* rais'd?

R. As all other Maſons are, when they receive the Maſter's Word.

[148]   Ex. How is that?

R. By the Five Points of Fellowſhip.

[149]   Ex. What are they ?

Hand to Hand [1], Foot to Foot [2], Cheek to Check [3], Knee to Knee [4], and Hand in Back [5].

N. B. *When Hiram was taken up, they took him by the Fore-fingers, and the Skin came off, which is called the Slip ; the ſpreading the Right Hand and placing the middle Finger to the Wriſt, claſping the Fore-finger and the Fourth to the Sides*

of

of the Wrist ; is called the Gripe, and the Sign is placing the Thumb of the Right Hand to the Left Breast, extending the Fingers.

[150]   Ex. What's a Master-Mason nam'd.

R. *Cassia* is my Name, and from a Just and Perfect Lodge I came.

[151]   Ex. Where was *Hiram* inter'd ?

R. In the *Sanctum Sanctorum.*

[152]   Ex. How was he brought in ?

R. At the West-Door of the Temple.

[153]   Q. What are the Master-Jewels ?

A. The Porch, Dormer and Square Pavement.

[154]   Q. Explain them.

A. The Porch the Entring into the *Sanctum Sanctorum,* the Dormer the Windows or Lights within, the Square Pavement the Ground Flooring.

[155]   Ex. Give me the Master's Word.

R. Whispers him in the Ear, and supported by the Five Points of Fellowship before-mentioned, says *Machbenah,* which signifies *The Builder is smitten.*

N.B. *If any Working Masons are at Work, and you have a desire to distinguish Accepted Masons from the rest, take a Piece of Stone, and ask him what it smells of, he immediately replies, neither Brass, Iron, nor Steel, but of a Mason ; then by asking him, how old he is, he replies above Seven, which denotes he has pass'd Master.*

The End of the Master's Part.